THE WEALTH OF KNOWLEDGE

Intellectual Capital and the Twenty-First Century Organization

THOMAS A. STEWART

CURRENCY

New York   London   Toronto   Sydney   Auckland

A CURRENCY BOOK
PUBLISHED BY DOUBLEDAY
a division of Random House, Inc.

The Wealth of Knowledge was originally published in hardcover
by Currency in December 2001.

CURRENCY is a trademark of Random House, Inc.,
and DOUBLEDAY is a registered trademark
of Random House, Inc.

Book design by Tina Thompson

The Library of Congress has cataloged the hardcover edition of this book as follows:

Stewart, Thomas A., 1948–
The wealth of knowledge : intellectual capital and the twenty-first century
organization / Thomas A. Stewart. — 1st ed.
p. cm.
Includes bibliographical references and index.
1. Intellectual capital. 2. Human capital. 3. Knowledge workers.
4. Knowledge management. I. Title.
HD53 .S743 2001
658.4'038—dc21
2001047535

ISBN 0-385-50072-6

A different version of Chapter 12 appeared in
Human Resource Development in a Knowledge-Based Economy,
© 2001 by the Emirates Center for Strategic Studies and Research.

1   3   5   7   9   10   8   6   4   2

To the usual suspects:
Baruch, Carla, Dan, Dave, Elizabeth, Gordon,
Hiro, Hubert, Joe, Jiro, John, Karl-Erik, Larry, Leif,
Nigel, Nikos, Tom, Verna, Victoria . . .

CONTENTS

SO NEAR ...

Every idea is an incitement.

OLIVER WENDELL HOLMES, JR.

In the last two decades, three big ideas have fundamentally changed how organizations run. The first was Total Quality Management. Pioneered by W. Edwards Deming and Joseph M. Juran in the 1950s and 1960s, quality swept into Japan—transforming that nation from postwar joke to industrial juggernaut. It's difficult to remember how badly beleaguered American business was a quarter century ago. "We exported God knows how many millions of jobs, our trade balance was shattered," recalled Juran, ninety-three when I talked to him: "We were forced to undertake a counterrevolution." The concepts of Total Quality Management rolled back to the the West in the late 1970s. Using its principles, companies such as Xerox and Motorola rebuilt themselves from the ground up, in the process showing American business how to turn back the competitive surge that threatened to swamp it.

The second big idea was reengineering. Conceived by the academically minded Thomas Davenport and popularized by the evangelizing, best-selling author Michael Hammer, reengineering used the emerging power of information technology as a sledgehammer with which to demolish old bureaucracies and paper-pushing management systems. At its virtuous best, reengineering helped executives and managers improve the processes that snake through organizations—that is, to see organizations as pipelines of horizontal processes rather than as towering arrays of vertical departments. At its virulent worst, reengineering decimated workforces and destroyed the social coherence and intellectual integrity of organizations. In 1992, I stood with one prominent reengineering consultant outside his office in Cambridge, Massachusetts, while he tugged cigarette smoke into his lungs. There, away from the hearing walls, he said: "I know how to put 30 percent of Americans out of a job, and I'm terrified of the consequences." That didn't happen, of course—the capitalist devil finds work for idle hands—but in its heyday reengineering's power and the fear it engendered helped fuel at least two populist political rockets, the presidential candidacies of Ross Perot and Pat Buchanan.

The third big idea is intellectual capital, and it is the idea provoking the richest and deepest discussions in business and economics today. At its core is the simple observation that organizations' tangible assets—cash, land and buildings, plant and equipment, and other balance-sheet items—are substantially less valuable than the intangible assets not carried on their books. Among these are "hard" intangibles like patents and copyrights, information-age assets such as databases and software, and—most important of all—"soft" assets such as skills, capabilities, expertise, cultures, loyalties, and so on. These are knowledge assets—intellectual capital—and they determine success or failure.

Intellectual capital and knowledge management have become the hottest topics in business. Five years ago I used AltaVista to search the World Wide Web for the phrase "intellectual capital." It appeared twenty times; the seventh item on the list stated, "Rome is the intellectual capital of Italy." Today AltaVista finds hundreds of thousands of occurrences of "intellectual capital" or "knowledge management." Intellectual capital has drawn the attention of executives around the world. America's most admired company, General Electric, has incorporated it into its values: "Prize global intellectual capital and the people that provide it; build diverse teams to maximize it." On the *Dilbert* Web site, "intellectual capital" is on the list of business buzzwords used in the "random mission statement generator" (http://www.dilbert.com/comics/dilbert/career/html/questions).

Ideas are valuable. Today we talk about a new economy, but we've known that ideas count as long as mankind has known anything. Today we talk about a knowledge-based Information Age—but the Industrial Age was knowledge-based, too. The schoolbook history of the Industrial Revolution is a history of ideas—steam engines, looms, cotton gins, railroads and radios, telephones—the inventions of people like Watt and Cartwright, Whitney and Westinghouse, Bell and Bessemer. Ironically, the value of ideas isn't taught in traditional, neoclassical economics. Innovation is treated as a mysterious, outside factor.

Just as we know that technology ideas matter, we know that management ideas matter—and we've known this forever, too. In the winter of 1999 I was chatting with a leading executive who previously had worked at H. J. Heinz. It was a truism at Heinz, he said, that you could always find one food processing line that produced 400 bottles of ketchup a minute while an identical line produced 350, and the difference was always management, never machinery. Well, duh. As I wrote in *Intellectual Capital,* in 1758 a Swede named J. Westerman traveled to Holland and England to find out why the Dutch made better ceramics and the English better ships. He found that they used the same machinery as the Swedes—but that the management systems of the Dutch and British were superior. Indeed, corresponding to the technology ideas of the Industrial Revolution are a set of equally important management innovations: the division of labor, interchangeable parts, the assembly line, and at the beginning of the last century, Scientific Management (the work of Frederick Taylor and his disciples), the capstone of factory-system management theory. These ideas created wealth as surely as harnessing steam did. Management also has no place in traditional economics—economists simply leave it out, as if all management is the same and counts for nothing.

Now, as we harness the power of the microchip, we are seeing new revolutions in both machinery and management—revolutions that change what companies are and what they do, with effects that are and will be as profound as those of the ideas that accompanied industrialism. Knowledge has always mattered, but today it is more than part of the story of prosperity. It is the mother lode.

The companies that master the knowledge agenda are the companies that will triumph in the twenty-first century. Because (as we shall see) knowledge has become the most important factor of production and knowledge assets the most powerful producers of wealth, the leaders and organizations that take command of their knowledge will occupy competition's high ground.

I hear, sometimes, that this knowledge stuff is fine and dandy in Silicon Valley, but nowhere else. This is the view that the new economy is only about the Internet—cynically, the view is that it was all a lot of hype to drive Nasdaq stock prices to the giddy, effervescent, irrational heights they attained as the century turned.

No.

First, those of us who were first looking into the value of intellectual capital began our work when what little bit of Internet existed was 100 percent noncommercial by law and by belligerently enforced custom. The new economy was never about the irrational exuberance of the boom in Internet stocks, though some of its boosters and bashers linked the two. Nor is it about the Web and high tech—though, again, the Internet bubble, which will go down in history among the best (i.e., worst) of all market bubbles, clothed itself in new-economy rhetoric.

Second, and more important, knowledge matters to low-tech companies as well as nonprofit organizations and to government agencies as much as it does to high-tech outfits. It also matters vitally in developing economies, a subject I discuss in the Afterword. Even in Silicon Valley, most employees will never encounter anything that's on the cutting edge of science. They will, instead, spend their workdays as most of us do: trying to get a little better, be paid a little more, rise a little in the ranks, do the best they can with the best they can get. Legendary GE ex-chairman Jack Welch says: "An idea is not necessarily a biotech idea. That's the wrong view of what an idea is. An idea is an error-free billing system. An idea is taking a process that used to require six days to do and getting it done in one day. We get 6 percent and 7 percent productivity increases routinely now, mostly because of ideas like that. Everyone can contribute. Every single person."

Most of this book is about showing how that statement can be turned into action, and action into income. My first book, *Intellectual Capital: The New Wealth of Organizations,* published in 1997, argued the case that knowledge had become the most important factor of production in the modern economy—our most vital raw material, asset, and output. The first book also set forth a way to analyze organizational brainpower—a taxonomy, if you will, that described the baskets in which knowledge assets can be found. That scheme has become the accepted standard in the field. And the first book showed how companies were beginning to apply the principles of intellectual capital and knowledge management to improve performance.

It's now possible—and it's now necessary—to take the argument considerably further, both in theory and, especially, in practice. The explosion of interest in the subject has done two things simultaneously: First, it has resulted in a remarkable, marvelous body of new ideas, new evidence, new cases; second, it has resulted in a huge amount of work that is in some way misguided—partly right, wholly stupid, or disingenuously greedy, an attempt to cash in on a trend. It's time to gather the grain and torch the chaff, and in so doing set forth practical means to put into practice these important and exciting ideas.

Part I of this book aims to describe how it is that knowledge matters so much to economies and companies. The idea that a new, knowledge-based economy has come into being was accepted almost too easily, I think—that is, without stopping to examine the evidence for it. The unfortunate result of glib acceptance: Too often, companies lurched into knowledge management, e-commerce, and other Information Age management ideas before they had business reasons for their actions. The knowledge economy is, first and foremost, an economy. It's about money. You need to know where the money is—how knowledge is bought, made, and sold—if you want to have a successful business. Part I does that; it describes what knowledge assets are and how they have become such valuable sources of wealth, and in this context shows how e-business and knowledge management can be done right and wrong.

Part II of *The Wealth of Knowledge* presents a practical, prescriptive, four-step process for managing knowledge assets. This process is the agenda for the twenty-first-century corporation. It defines the knowledge battleground on which a company competes, shows how to identify the knowledge assets that control an industry, describes how to develop strategies to invest in intellectual capital and compete with it, and offers ways to create millions upon millions of dollars' worth of additional value by managing knowledge more efficiently.

Part III extends the theory of intellectual capital, because the knowledge economy tests many assumptions on which we have based business life for more than a century. Why do companies exist in the first place? How should they be organized? How should investors be rewarded—and who *are* the investors? How should people be compensated for their work? As we'll see, in an internetworked, global economy, knowledge assets become even more important: They become, in fact, the *only* connection that holds a company together. We also will plunge into the thick of the nettlesome, controversial, and (as always in business) vital topic of measurement. My first book described some ways in which companies might measure intellectual capital. There has been a lot of progress since 1997. Most important, the case against conventional accounting has become—it seems to most observers—open and shut: It's incontrovertibly true that present financial and management accounting does not give investors, directors, the public, or management the information they need to make informed decisions. It is time, once and for all, to drive a stake through the heart of traditional accounting, which is draining the life from business.

The term "intellectual capital" seems to have been employed first in 1958, when two financial analysts, describing the stock-market valuations of several small, science-based companies (Hewlett-Packard, its annual sales then $28 million, was one of them), concluded, "The intellectual capital of such companies is perhaps their single most important element" and noted that their high stock valuations might be termed an "intellectual premium." The idea lay dormant for a quarter of a century. In the 1980s, Walter Wriston, the former chairman of Citicorp, the largest American bank, noted that his bank and other corporations possessed valuable intellectual capital that accountants (and bank regulators) did not measure.

Ideas whose time has come bloom everywhere at once. About this time, Karl-Erik Sveiby, a Swede, intrigued by the anomalous stock-market behavior of knowledge-intensive companies, began an investigation that produced the first analysis of the nature of intellectual capital. Sveiby and his colleagues and *Affarsvarlden,* Sweden's oldest business magazine, noticed that the magazine's proprietary model for valuing initial public offerings broke down for high-tech companies. Sveiby concluded that these companies possessed assets that were not described in financial documents or included in the magazine's model. With a like-minded group of associates, he convened the Konrad Group (so called because November 12, the day of its first meeting in 1987, is Konrad's name day in Sweden) to puzzle out what these assets might be. In *Den Osynliga Balansräkningen Ledarskap* (The Invisible Balance Sheet), 1989, Sveiby and the group laid the foundation stone for much of what has come after, by coming up with a taxonomy for intellectual capital. Knowledge assets, they proposed, could be found in three places: the competencies of a company's people, its internal structure (patents, models, computer and administrative systems), and its external structure (brands, reputation, relationships with customers and suppliers). Sveiby's model of intellectual capital stands, with some tinkering by others. The pieces are now usually called human capital, structural (or organizational) capital, and customer (or relationship) capital, and they're discussed in Chapter 1 and at length in *Intellectual Capital*.

Shortly thereafter, Leif Edvinsson, an executive at the Swedish financial services company Skandia, persuaded his management to appoint him "director, intellectual capital"; Skandia became the business world's most conspicuous laboratory for intellectual capital studies. In Japan, meanwhile, Ikujiro Nonaka and Hirotaka Takeuchi were developing the idea that one of the primary activities of companies—and a principal means by which they create wealth—is to create knowledge. In the United States, artificial-intelligence specialists were learning how to turn human expertise into software, and reengineering consultants were discovering that it was possible to improve companies' speed and performance by managing the flows of information and knowledge that run through them. In 1991, I wrote a major article on intellectual capital for *Fortune*. It was, I believe, the first time the mainstream business press had paid the subject any attention. I wrote it without turning up Sveiby (who had published) or Nonaka (who had not), barely touched on artificial intelligence, and didn't see that intellectual capital could have any connection with reengineering.

Ignorant of each other, we all knew the same thing: Knowledge had become such an important factor of production that a company that didn't manage it wasn't minding its business. We also knew that almost all companies operated in the dark with respect to knowledge. Knowledge assets determine success or failure, but you will search in vain to find them in a company's books. There is no tested body of knowledge about how to identify, acquire, and exploit intellectual capital. Instead it usually fends for itself—undefined, unaudited, unreported, almost certainly underused.

It's time, finally, to put that to an end. We have come a long way toward understanding how to turn knowledge into intellectual capital, and how to use intellectual capital to increase the prosperity of our companies and countries, and add to the richness of our lives. Hurry up, please: It's time.

ACKNOWLEDGMENTS

One of the joys of my job at *Fortune* and *Business 2.0* is that it both allows and compels me to set out to talk to smart and interesting people. The number of people whose ideas and observations have contributed to my thinking and this book is so long that I can only apologize to the dozens I am sure I have left off this list. Thank you, all: Dan Agan, Verna Allee, Debra Amidon, Charles Armstrong, Bernie Avishai, George Bailey, Jim Bair, Açar and Zuhal Baltas, Margareta Barchan, Laurie Bassi, Anjana Bhattacharee, Jim Baughman, Warren Bennis, Lucinda Berlew, Margaret Blair, Jan Bliechfeldt, Greg Bolcer, Nick Bontis, Piet Boot, Mark Bothwell, Jerry Bowles, Keith Bradley, John Seely Brown, Bob Buckman, Peter Cappelli, Ram Charan, Don Cohen, Richard Collin, Beth Comstock, Bill Conaty, Andree Conrad, Andrea Costa,

Flavia Cymbalista, Bill Dauphinais, Thomas Davenport, Tom Davenport, Stan Davis, Ross Dawson, Steve Denning, Lance Devlin, Joaquim Doering, Peter Drucker, Paul Duguid, Keith Ferrazzi, Dave Fondiller, Gloria Gery, Jack Grayson, Kent Greenes, Feng Gu, Brian Hackett, Stephen Haeckel, Gary Hamel, Charles Handy, Phil Harris, Tom Housel, Bob Howell, Bipin Junnarker, Ira Kay, Steve Kerr, Julia (L&T) Kirby, Kenneth Kline, Peter Kontes, Stan Kwiecen, Elizabeth Lank, Ed Lawler, Larry Leson, Baruch Lev, Michael Lissack, Chris Locke, Greta Lydecker, Britton Mancuso, Brook Manville, Renee Mauborgne, Andrew Mayo, Mark Mazzie, Christopher Meyer, Andy Michuda, Riel Miller, Scot Murray, Roald Nomme, Jiro Nonaka, Carla O'Dell, Jan-Erick Olsen, Sharon Oriel, Nigel Oxbrow, Bindy Pease, Lew Perelman, Gail Pesyna, Sally Peterson, Gordon Petrash, Jeff Pfeffer, Larry Prusak, John Rapp, Paul Saffo, Stephanie Schilling, Richard Schroate, Regina Schuman, Klaus Schwab, Patricia Seeman, Bill Seidman, Adrian Slywotzky, Claude Smadja, David Smith, Dave Snowden, Danny Stern, Pat Sullivan, Karl-Erik Sveiby, Hiro Takeuchi, Don Tapscott, David Teece, Phin Tjhai, Jill Totenberg, Dave Ulrich, Georg von Krogh, Victoria Ward, Jack Welch, Holly Welling, Etienne Wenger, Jack Whalen, Dar Wolford, and Kara Yokley.

I'm particularly grateful to Frances Brennan, a dear friend and a painter of great wit and talent, for permission to reproduce her painting *Measured Bubble* on the jacket of this book. Fanny died in July 2001. She was my mother-in-law's best friend, my wife's friend literally from the day she was born, and mine almost from the minute I met Amanda—and I've been a fan of her extraordinary miniature paintings from the first moment I saw them. There was no more gracious, delightful, or beautiful woman.

Despite having made a wisecrack about editors in the text, I do want to thank those who have edited me so wisely in this book and in my pieces for *Fortune* and *Business 2.0*. Roger Scholl of Doubleday is a superb professional; not only am I lucky to have him on my side, but you are, too, because this book is better for his ministrations. It's also better for the backing of Steve Rubin, one of the rare publishers who understands how to coax responsiveness from those often-balky organizations. In the UK, Nick Brealey has been an exemplar of both editorial acumen and publishing alacrity. Someone once said (I heard it attributed to Mark Twain, but what isn't attributed to him?) that publishers, like the weather, exist to give people something about which they can all agree to complain; if weather is the metaphor, Nick is a day in June. Once again, I owe my perfect agent, Kris Dahl of ICM, thanks for her encouragement, her support, and her ability gracefully to *encourager les autres* at key moments. At *Fortune,* the deft hands of Brian Dumaine, Beth Fenner, Shelley Neumeier, Rick Tetzeli, or Vera Titunik have improved everything I've written, which includes a number of passages that have found their way into this book. They always challenged and sharpened my thinking. Peter Petre has given valuable advice, as has David Kirkpatrick. Last time I got to thank John Huey, then *Fortune*'s managing editor and now editorial director of Time, Inc., for his continued backing for this endeavor and all the other ways in which I have explored the field of intellectual capital; this time I get to redouble those thanks. I owe an extra full measure of gratitude to him, Rik Kirkland (now *Fortune*'s managing editor), and Ned Desmond (managing editor of *Business 2.0*) for their continued support of my work and for making it possible for me and it to reach an even larger audience. At *Business 2.0,* Jim Aley, Amy Johns, and Josh Macht have given me another forum—and more good advice—and earned my thanks also. As before, my special appreciation goes to Geoffrey Colvin, not just for his brilliance but for his forbearance on the innumerable occasions when I've come into his office to float yet another trial balloon or simply to force him to listen to a line I thought clever.

In *Intellectual Capital* I wrote that knowledge assets are of two kinds—semipermanent bodies of knowledge, which is to say expertise, and tools that augment that body of knowledge. I would like to pay special tribute to one of each. First, I am deeply grateful to the New York Public Library, whose collections I used, whose facilities I worked in for three months, and whose librarians and staff (particularly Wayne Furman, who takes care of the Frederick Lewis Allen Room) aided me almost daily. Carved into a wall on the stairway that leads to the library's main reading room from the second floor, where I worked, are these words by Nobel Prize–winning novelist Toni Morrison: "Access to knowledge is the superb, the supreme act of truly great civilizations." What a superb, supreme, civilized place is the New York Public Library!

With me every day was a terrific tool and durable friend, my little Apple Powerbook. There aren't many six-year-old laptops with two books under their belts, and I couldn't have written either of mine without this one, as dear and real as a skin horse. It's long in the tooth now and seems a little slower than it once was; sometimes it gets tired and abruptly decides to take a break. I've had to replace the keyboard and the hard drive; a panel on the back is held on with tape. When this project is done, it will be time to turn this machine out to pasture. (I've got my eye on a slim, fast-talking titanium blonde.) We've logged a lot of miles, typed a lot of words, and played a lot of solitaire. I can say only thank you.

I've dedicated this book to a remarkable group of people, picking a few names from a large list. Many times in this book I refer to "communities of practice," groups of people who gather around a subject, a common interest or passion. They bounce ideas off one another, they compete, they assist, they kibitz and share. I couldn't have written this book without the community of people interested in intellectual capital. Much have we traveled in the realms of intangible gold, and many goodly states and kingdoms and airports and conference rooms seen. They are—we are—friends and colleagues. I offer you this book deeply grateful for your intellectual companionship and help, and humbly (sorta humbly) hoping that it partially pays you back in kind.

My deepest appreciation is, of course, reserved for my family: my wife Amanda Vaill and my children Pamela and Patrick. Once again I have the privilege of thanking them for their companionship and love. Writing, speaking, and reporting about intellectual capital have consumed an enormous amount of time, and their presence has never failed to replenish my energy and my spirits. I'm particularly grateful for Amanda's canny editorial eye and unfailingly wise advice on publishing matters. I said it before and do so again: You three are my only wealth.

PART I

THE THEORY OF A KNOWLEDGE BUSINESS

We are not here to sell a parcel of boilers and vats, but the
potentiality of growing rich beyond the dreams of avarice.

SAMUEL JOHNSON

CHAPTER 1

THE PILLARS OF THE KNOWLEDGE ECONOMY

We are confronted with insurmountable opportunities.

WALT KELLY

Consider a key. Dig into your pocket or purse, pull out your key ring, and examine one of the keys—car key, house key, office, mailbox, trunk-in-the-basement key. I'm looking at the key to the door of my office, a piece of silverish metal about two and a quarter inches long; the name of the manufacturer, Corbin, is stamped on the end where my fingers grip it. A key is a physical object. It has size, mass, specific gravity. It can be dropped, lost, bent, hung on a hook.

A key contains information as well as molecules. The serrations along the top of the business end of the key—if you traced them onto a sheet of graph paper, they would resemble the electrocardiogram of a man with not long to live—are a code. They instruct one lock, and only one lock, to open; the lock has a matching set of cuts and ridges that order it to yield to one key, and only one key.

Keys used to be heavier and less intricate than the one in your hand. (You can put it away now.) That is, they were more massive and less knowledge-intensive; my father-in-law owns a large, rusty, old iron key, about eight inches long, that he uses as a doorstop. The oldest known key is a big wooden bar from which pins stick up like the bristles of a sparse brush. The pins match holes on a wooden bolt that secured a door in the ancient Assyrian city of Nineveh some 4,000 years ago. The fancy, gorgeous locks and keys of the Middle Ages and Renaissance were more show than security; their ingenious metalwork elegantly obscured the fact that picking them was child's play. That changed in the late eighteenth century, when an Englishman, Joseph Bramah, revolutionized locksmithing by manufacturing devices of unprecedented intricacy—that is, by increasing their information intensity. More than half a century passed before anyone managed to pick a Bramah lock.

If you're traveling as you read this, you might have in your pocket a little plastic card that is also a key, the key to your hotel room. The code, the instructions—the knowledge content—of this key reside in the magnetic stripe on one side. When you checked in, the clerk at the front desk stuck the card into a small device and typed in a code matching one that had been set for the lock in the door of your room. You can't see the code; if you compare two card keys, you can't tell if they are for the same or different locks. These keys can also hold a lot more information. They can tell time; if you ask for a late checkout, you might need to present your key to have an extra hour or two added to its clock—alternatively, the clerk might reset the clock in the lock on the door. Similar keys can carry money: The MetroCard in my wallet, which unlocks the turnstiles of New York City's subway, contains $13.50 as I write this, I believe, but no one can tell how much value is stored in it just by looking, any more than you can see the code on a hotel-room key. Before MetroCards, I filled my pocket with subway tokens; I could feel their weight and hear their jingle. If I put more money in my MetroCard, I notice nothing.

In mechanical keys, the physical object and the information are one and the same. The code is literally cut into the metal, visibly and inseparably. If you skip town with a metal hotel-room key in your pocket and the lock is not changed, you could return and unlock the door. That's not so with card keys. Signs outside aluminum smelters warn visitors to remove their credit cards and hotel keys: The magnetic field created by the electricity that pulses through these factories will wipe the cards clean. The hotel-room card will no longer open the door after you check out: The lock will have been changed—physically it will be untouched, but its information component will be new.

Keys are a metaphor that helps to describe how the so-called new economy—the Information Age, the knowledge economy—differs from the old one. Fundamentally, the twenty-first-century economy is one of ever-increasing information intensity. Like keys, the economy is packed with more and more knowledge—data, interpretation, ideas. As with keys, it's the knowledge itself that is valuable—value resides in the code in the magnetic strip, not the plastic. And this valuable knowledge exists independently of whatever physical carrier it's in at the moment: key, Web site, Palm Pilot.

The Information Age isn't just a slogan but a fact; the knowledge-based economy is, indeed, a new economy, with new rules, requiring new ways of doing business. The case for the existence of a new economy has been made and proven beyond the doubt of all but an unreasoning few; I don't propose to remake it here.

The knowledge economy stands on three pillars. The first: Knowledge has become what we buy, sell, and do. It is the most important factor of production. The second pillar is a mate, a corollary to the first: Knowledge assets—that is, intellectual capital—have become more important to companies than financial and physical assets. The third pillar is this: To prosper in this new economy and exploit these newly vital assets, we need new vocabularies, new management techniques, new technologies, and new strategies. On these three pillars rest all the new economy's laws and its profits.

KNOWLEDGE IS WHAT WE BUY, SELL, AND DO

You awaken in the morning when the clock radio turns on, giving you the news and your morning's share of $73 billion in annual advertising spending. Your toothpaste, the product of millions of dollars of research and development and further billions of marketing expenditure, is, on a cost basis, more than 50 percent knowledge. The newspaper on your doorstep, if it is this morning's *New York Times,* contains about 150,000 words, about as many as a fat book. The microwave oven in which you heat your coffee contains a microprocessor.

Drink your coffee, eat something, get dressed. The car you are about to enter, which uses more computing power than it took to put a man on the moon, is an infotainment pod. Automobile companies are stuffing as much intelligence into their machines as they can. Cars now know how much fuel you have and calculate how far you can drive before sputtering to an ignominious halt. They know where you are, and can give you directions and a map to where you want to go. The information-infused car, with voice-activated Internet access, real-time traffic information, and the ability to diagnose breakdowns and notify emergency services automatically in case of accident, will offer a new income stream to automakers and their suppliers. Stuffing cars with smarts, says Ford's CEO, Jacques Nasser, "is about shifting competitive advantage from hard assets to intangible assets."

Knowledge and information* are embedded in every product we use,

---

* It has become traditional in books about knowledge and knowledge management to spend several pages defining knowledge and distinguishing it from data, information, and sometimes wisdom. I feel no need to inflict any such rumination on you, dear reader; dictionaries and common usage are good enough. But it is—I have always maintained—important to make a distinction between data and information, on the one hand, and knowledge, on the other.

Data and information are smaller than knowledge and, if it exists, wisdom. They are also different in kind. In computerese, eight bits equal one byte. But eight—or zubleteen zillion—bits of information do not equal a byte of knowledge. Knowledge is not a sum but a summation, a relation. Data and information plug into knowledge: They are tiles in a mosaic, but they are not its design. Bits of data and information—facts, factoids—can be startling or telling or important, but they're not like knowledge.

Knowledge involves expertise. Achieving it involves time. It endures longer than information—sometimes forever. To be knowledgeable, to know a subject, is something different from and greater than knowing a fact or possessing a lot of information about something.

It is impossible, however, to make a clear distinction between information and knowledge that works for a very large group. This is because one man's data can be another man's knowledge, and vice versa, depending on context. Your deep expertise in accounting, metallurgy, or literature may be an interesting tidbit to the person you sit next to at dinner tonight. Therefore what's information and what's knowledge depends on context.

If this were a study of epistemology or information theory, we might want more precise definitions, but it's not and we don't.

more and more. Your telephone stores dozens of phone numbers, remembers the last one you dialed, records messages from people who called when you were out, and reveals the phone numbers of people who called and did not leave a message. Today's jetliner contains, in addition to sophisticated computers and communication systems in the cockpit, more than a thousand microprocessor chips. What used to be an almost entirely physical experience—the transport of your molecules from here to there in the company of a stewardess whose own molecules were attractively arranged, and with passably edible food—has become e-mail and news and movies and phone calls and computer games and cuisine that resembles nothing found in nature. Airlines' spending on in-flight entertainment and communications septupled from 1992 to 2000 and now totals about $2.25 billion a year.

If I return to the office after a few days away, the stack in my in-box is noticeably shorter than it was when I returned from trips five years ago—and the amount of weightless e-mail is much greater. (Approximately 610 billion e-mails are sent per year, of which at least a third are cc'd to me.) In supply chains, information replaces inventory. Inventories held by manufacturers of durable goods—about $300 billion on average—would be $115 billion greater if they needed to carry as much stock as they did in 1988. Manufacturing companies are creating "virtual assembly lines"—electronic models of the real thing—so as to test factory layout before a real one is built. Their value was described by Ford Motor Company engineer Mark Phillips: "It means we can eliminate a whole phase of building prototypes in the metal, as well as design a production line which we know is going to work before we start building it"—a substitution of knowledge artifacts for physical objects that is worth some $200 million a year.

Elsewhere knowledge makes physical objects lighter. A sleek Nokia 8860 mobile phone not only knows things unimaginable to your grandmother's rotary phone, but, at 4.2 ounces, weighs a fraction as much. Buildings, like phones, are lighter and smarter. Compare a stony, cathedral-like H. H. Richardson building from the nineteenth century to the airy, cathedral-like new airports in Denver or Hong Kong or Oslo. These buildings weigh less per cubic meter—they have more science in them and less stone. The architects who design them have all kinds of specialized expertise that architects a century ago didn't need. (Whether they have Richardson's aesthetic sense is another question.) The buildings are stuffed with intelligent systems for heating, security, and the like, and threaded through with fiber optics and telecommunications cables.

And, of course, we buy and sell knowledge itself. We produce an extraordinary amount of the stuff—annual worldwide production of new information is somewhere between 700 and 2,400 terabytes, each terabyte being the equivalent of a million ordinary books. Sure, a lot of it is garbage, but there's no reason to think the ratio of wheat to chaff is any worse (or any better, for that matter) than it ever was. Much of this production is never sold: For example, only a fifth of the information produced on paper can be found in books, newspapers, and periodicals; the rest is office documents. Indeed, while the production of information (including film, photographs, Web pages, and music) is growing at about 50 percent a year, household consumption remains roughly constant at about 3,400 hours a year—there are only so many hours, after all.

These numbers, astounding as they are, describe only documents, photographs, X rays, films, broadcasts, and other artifacts; they do not include information and knowledge bought in the form of services from lawyers, psychologists, tax accountants, physicians, or consultants; nor do they include knowledge bought (via tuition or taxes) from schools and universities.

In 1999, knowledge was America's most valuable export—the country took in $37 billion in licensing fees and royalties, vs. $29 billion for aircraft. "The most important basis for creating value in the economy [is] the process of creating value from information, throughout and across the economy," said Robert J. Shapiro, undersecretary of commerce for economic affairs in the Clinton administration. Perhaps the most telling and relevant evidence for this statement is found in corporate charts of account. Look at the sales side first. One of the most dramatic changes at General Electric during the tenure of CEO Jack Welch was the company's realization that it could sell services as well as products—not just financial services, via GE Capital, but knowledge-intensive service for products, such as repairs for aircraft engines and installation for magnetic resonance imaging machines. Says Welch: "As recently as 1995, when this initiative was launched, GE derived $8 billion a year in revenues from product services. In 2000, this number will be $17 billion." Product service revenues grew 18 percent annually, vs. 11 percent for GE as a whole. The other side—spending—shows the same pattern. Corporate capital spending—

for all equipment, from trucks to desk chairs, from buildings to laptops, from machine tools to Learjets—totaled $870 billion in 1997. Nearly half of that—$407 billion—was spent on information technology and software. Add $144 billion of corporate spending on research and development and some $55 billion for training, and you have a "knowledge capital budget" that's 20 percent greater than the budget for all other capital items combined. In 1999, Genentech, the biotech company, spent $367 million on R&D, almost four times its spending for capital equipment ($95 million). Pharmaceutical maker Pfizer invested $2.8 billion in R&D vs. $1.6 billion for property, plant, and equipment. Even for old-economy stalwarts, knowledge expenditures are extraordinarily high; in 2000, Procter and Gamble spent $1.9 billion to acquire knowledge via research and development and $3.7 billion to disseminate knowledge via advertising, while paying $3 billion for property, plant, and equipment. Finally, we can gain some sense of how much knowledge people buy and sell by the amount of it that's stolen. The cost to U.S. corporations of misappropriated intellectual property—purloined secrets, infringed patents, and the like—is estimated at $250 billion a year.

Add it all up—apples, oranges, pomegranates, and banana skins—and you come to the inescapable conclusion that more and more of what we buy and sell is knowledge. Alan Greenspan, chairman of the Federal Reserve Board, has estimated that the U.S. GDP, if it could be gathered together and weighed, would tip the scales at about the same amount today as it did a hundred years ago. But its real value, adjusted for inflation, is more than twenty times what it was. The difference does not come from atoms and molecules—it comes from intangibles. But the difference—in health, in wealth, in living standards—is tangible indeed.

Knowledge is what we do. Unsurprisingly, all this buying and selling of knowledge means more and more people spend their working day elbow-deep in the stuff. Ideas, knowledge, and information have always mattered, but today they define our working life, and this is unprecedented.

In 1867, Ralph Waldo Emerson wrote, "Things are in the saddle / And ride mankind." In the knowledge era, brains bestride things. The same three phenomena we saw with respect to buying and selling knowledge show up in working with knowledge: Knowledge is instilled in physical work, making it "smarter"; knowledge work substitutes for physical work; and more and more people are what might be called pure knowledge workers.

Every job, it seems, has more knowledge in it than it did. On North Sea oil rigs, mechanics, who have a dirty, greasy, cold, dangerous job, work twelve-hour shifts. In that period, they hold a wrench in their hand for just two hours. The rest of their time is spent checking manuals, making sure the rigs have the right permits, preparing such permits, testing and measuring, and so on—knowledge work. Construction sites today are in constant communication with architects, contractors, and management via laptop and handheld computer and mobile phone. Blueprint revisions, which once had to be printed and delivered, are instantly posted on Web sites; truck drivers, using Global Positioning System satellites, can schedule deliveries more accurately. The tools are smarter: Carpenters' levels are digital, as are surveyors' instruments, for instance. While construction crews still hammer and rivet, while surveyors still measure and inspectors still inspect, the work, like the tools, is more knowledge-intensive. Says Robert R. Prescott, president of the New York State Association of Professional Land Surveyors: "The profession has gone from being extremely labor intensive to being able to focus more precisely on the analysis of the measurements being taken."

As the knowledge economy grows, knowledge work substitutes for physical labor. Documents once carried by messengers now arrive by e-mail or fax; many who still deliver packages, employees of Federal Express or DHL or UPS, for example, carry handheld computers as well. Routine work is being automated out of existence. In factories, repetitive physical labor becomes the province of machines, and assembly-line workers become, instead of Chaplinesque robots, managers of automatons. The work product of a designer used to be a model; now it's a computer file.

A business's highest-cost processes (R&D and management) are knowledge processes, and its highest-paid people are knowledge workers. So rapidly has the demand for technical talent grown—outstripping the ability of schools to deliver it—that businesspeople speak of a "war for talent." The squeeze is worst—demand is greatest—for jobs in information technology, professional specialty workers, and top management: the most knowledge-intensive jobs. When the economy cooled in 2001, this group suffered least; manufacturing and transportation workers, lower in the knowledge-intensity scale, were more expendable.

New jobs are knowledge jobs. To get a sense of the rise of the knowledge worker, Canadian economist Nuala Beck classified industries according to their percentage of knowledge workers, which she defined as "professionals, senior management and technical, engineering and scientific staff; in other words, the people in the organization who are paid to 'think.'" The "high-knowledge" sector, where at least 40 percent of the staff are knowledge workers (such industries as consulting, computers, pharmaceuticals, and telecommunications), created a net increase of more than 560,000 Canadian jobs between 1984 and 1994. The moderate-knowledge (insurance, logging, pipelines) and low-knowledge companies (steel, pulp and paper) produced just 153,000 and 199,000 jobs, respectively. There's no reason to think the percentages would be significantly different in any developed economy.

Some of this was boom, and booms go bust. But the ratio of brain work to back work has jumped up, forever. According to the U.S. Commerce Department, "By 2006 almost half the U.S. workforce will be employed by industries that are either major producers or intensive users of information technology products and services." New jobs are knowledge jobs—and so are old jobs. I think, therefore I earn.

THE TRIUMPH OF KNOWLEDGE ASSETS

Conventional assets—financial and physical capital—have not disappeared and will not; but given how important knowledge has become, as a product and in processes that add value to work, it's inevitable that knowledge would come to be a more and more important asset for organizations—their *most* important asset.

What is intellectual capital? Simply put, knowledge assets are talent, skills, know-how, know-what, and relationships—and machines and networks that embody them—that can be used to create wealth. The accounting profession, which needs to prepare the books in which companies list their assets and liabilities, has a lot of rules that determine whether something qualifies as an asset or not. The rules are important for that purpose, but not for our purpose. For us, *an asset is something that transforms raw material into something more valuable*. It's a magician's black box: Inputs get put in—a few handkerchiefs, say. The asset does something. And out come outputs worth more than the inputs—rabbits, maybe.

In the old economy, if you took all the value added by a company and traced it back to the asset that produced it, you'd have to credit a fair amount to the physical side of things. This printing press, this rolling mill, this chemical plant, this warehouse—those made the rabbits, those created the value. Indeed, as we'll see later, the physical assets explained why the company existed in the first place.

That's just not true anymore.

It's inaccurate to describe a company in physical terms. Overall, U.S. companies need 20 percent less physical capital to produce a dollar's worth of sales than they did twenty-five years ago; according to Lowell L. Bryan, a partner at the McKinsey consulting firm, "This means that U.S. companies are using about $530 billion less financial capital than they would have used otherwise." You can open the annual report of a company, almost any company, turn to the financial statements at the back, and read about the physical assets: You will find little or nothing that explains the rabbits. The relevant assets just aren't there.

All kinds of companies have almost no physical assets at all. Advertising agencies, professional firms, consulting and computer services companies, and the like make use of a lot of IT, but otherwise their assets consist of desks, chairs, and conference tables. I grew up in Chicago. Sometimes, when I was young, my family drove along the southern tip of Lake Michigan. Out the car's window we saw the smokestacks of Gary, Indiana, which belonged to the great steel mills there—giant, belching things. The "factory" where Yahoo! produces and controls all the stuff that goes into the financial services portion of its Web site consists of three nondescript servers in a basement, with a sign on them saying "Do Not Touch." Even where physical assets are essential, value comes from something else. Semiconductor fabs costs tens of billions of dollars to build; but Intel's far more valuable assets are the ones that go into designing the microprocessors made in them.

Intellectual capital is knowledge that transforms raw materials and makes them more valuable. The raw materials might be physical—knowledge of the formula for Coca-Cola is an intellectual asset that transforms a few cents' worth of sugar, water, carbon dioxide, and flavorings into something for which you pay a dollar or more. Sometimes the raw material might be intangible, like information—a lawyer, for example, takes the facts of the case (raw material), distorts them by using his knowledge of the law (an intellectual asset), to produce an opinion or a legal brief (an output that is of higher value than the facts of the case by themselves).

THE INTELLECTUAL CAPITAL MODEL

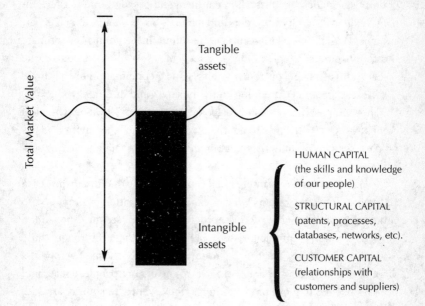

The idea is simple—but important, for if you remember that capital assets transform raw materials, making them more valuable, you begin to understand what intellectual capital is and how it works.

It has become standard to say that a company's intellectual capital is the sum of its human capital (talent), structural capital (intellectual property, methodologies, software, documents, and other knowledge artifacts), and customer capital (client relationships).* Every company has all three, but some emphasize one more than the others: A three-star restaurant succeeds chiefly because of the human capital of its chef; a franchiser like Burger King relies on the structural capital of its recipes and processes; a local diner thrives thanks to customer capital—the waitress who calls you "Hon" and knows you like your coffee with milk, no sugar.

A chemical company might have, as a knowledge asset, the ability to concoct custom chemical compounds that precisely match its customers'

---

*All this is described in detail in *Intellectual Capital: The New Wealth of Organizations* (New York: Doubleday, 1997), Chapters 4–9. No need to repeat it here.

needs. That asset might be people-based, residing in the tacit knowledge of dozens of skilled chemists; it might be media-based, found in the company's extensive library of patents and manuals, or its databases and expert systems; it might be relationship-based, found in the company's intimate ties to customers, suppliers, universities, etc. Most likely, of course, the asset—skill at making custom chemicals—is a combination of the three, in different amounts depending on the business and its strategy.

The point is this: If you are looking to explain why one chemical company does better than another, you will find the answer in its human, structural, and customer capital, not in its boilers, vats, retorts, and alembics.

Two characteristics of intellectual capital give it extraordinary power to add value. First, just as knowledge can displace matter in products, so companies that use knowledge assets deftly can eliminate the expense and burden of carrying physical assets, or maximize their return on those assets. And assets are, or can be, a burden. Says Nicholas Negroponte, director of the Media Laboratory at MIT: "The energy, people, spaces and vehicles needed to move physical things from country to country are suddenly a liability in an age of weightless, sizeless, colorless bits which move at the speed of light."

Thus company after company finds ways to reduce its dependence on hard assets. Citigroup, the financial services goliath formed by the 1998 combination of Citicorp and Travelers, wants to have 1 billion customers by 2010, ten times more than when the companies merged. It can't be done—or it can't be done sanely—using physical assets: It would require building some 250,000 branches. But it can by done by means of intellectual capital—creating software (structural capital) for Web sites, automatic teller machines, Palm Pilots, smart cards, and mobile phones, so that Citigroup customers can bank without being near a bank. Airlines own less than a quarter of the airplanes they fly; the others are leased, as are their engines—in some cases, engines are leased by the hour. Rajat Gupta, the head of the McKinsey consulting firm, has prophesied that within a decade at least one airline will exist that owns next to nothing in the way of physical assets, and relies instead on a virtual balance sheet of intangibles: a brand, a reservation system, landing rights, and a database. In 1997, Sara Lee Corp. decided to outsource most of its manufacturing activities, explaining, "The operating model for today's exemplary companies no longer needs to include significant manufacturing assets" if it has powerful intangible assets, such as brands. The biggest U.S. owner of leases for oil and gas wells on the continental shelf of the Gulf of Mexico is El Paso Energy. Primarily a pipeline company, El Paso got into the production business in 1999, when it bought Sonat, Inc., a little-known Alabama outfit, which had a year earlier acquired the even less-known Zilkha Energy in Houston. Leases were about the only assets Zilkha owned at the time; the company, which had only sixty employees, a bunch of powerful computers, and smart seismological software, contracted out all its production—more gigs than rigs, you might say. The knowledge-intensive, asset-light model, when its new parent adopted it after the merger, saved Sonat $200 million a year in capital spending.

General Electric has taken the idea—substitute knowledge assets for expensive physical assets—and created a management tool that allows it to steadily drive down its reliance on physical assets and increase its intellectual capital, while monitoring results on a regular basis. Under John F. Welch, GE became obsessed with monitoring and improving its productivity—that is, the efficiency with which it produces goods and services. GE measures productivity the right way. It doesn't just measure output per unit of labor; that's a down-and-(very)-dirty measurement that would, for example, show a productivity increase if a company fired a worker and replaced her with a machine, even if it cost more to operate the machine than to pay the worker. Instead, GE measures "total factor productivity"—output per unit of all inputs, whether labor, materials, or capital. Using detailed figures from its Six Sigma quality program, GE can go further into those numbers than ever before: The company tracks how much of a productivity gain came from new equipment (that is, spending money) vs. from new ideas (that is, from thinking). When its European lighting business first started gathering these data, the vast majority of its productivity gains came from buying new gear. Now, more than half come from thinking. A big source of improvement: using process improvements to increase output from old plants, thereby avoiding new capital spending. Says Mike Zafirovski, former head of the GE lighting business and now president of Motorola's personal communications division: "The rule of thumb for capacity additions used to be that the European lighting business needed a dollar of investment to get a dollar of capacity. Now we need $12\frac{1}{2}$ cents." Companywide, GE executives monitor the ratio of plant-and-equipment spending to depreciation. It fell from 1.5 in 1996 to 1.2 in 1998; the goal is to get below 0.8. The idea, said Welch, is to find "hidden factories" built of brainpower.

Cemex, the Mexican company that's the world's third-largest maker of cement and its most profitable in terms of operations, demonstrates another way in which intellectual assets ratchet up the efficiency with which physical assets are used. Making cement is inherently asset-intensive. It's also, traditionally, inefficient in terms of asset utilization, chiefly because demand, however orderly it might seem to be over the span of a month, is almost completely unpredictable in the short run; a construction site that on Monday called for several truckloads of cement to be delivered Tuesday might—and frequently does—cancel and reinstate the order several times because of unforeseeable problems.

Cemex now delivers—over Mexican roads and fighting Mexico City traffic—within twenty minutes of its promised time. The secret is a technique called Dynamic Synchronization of Operations (DSO), developed during the 1990s. DSO is a new asset that lies between Cemex's physical plant and its customers. It is primarily intellectual capital—it's composed of a thin skin of physical material (a few computers) that holds a rich trove of human, structural, and customer capital. Every Cemex truck now has a computer terminal, linked to navigational satellites and to dispatchers in Guadalajara, Mexico City, and Monterrey. Thanks to the connection, and to some sophisticated mathematical models rather like those the airlines use to maximize revenue, trucks can now operate just in time—the nearest truck summoned to the nearest plant to pick up cement and deliver it precisely when the customer calls for it. So much more efficient is the system that Cemex needs one-third fewer trucks—physical assets replaced by an intellectual one. Consultant Adrian Slywotzky calls it "a brilliantly integrated layer of information technology—a bits factory designed to complement and support the atoms factory."

Cement making is a very local business—it needs to be made fresh and delivered quickly, and no one's about to try to transport cement by air. Thus Cemex has limited ability to leverage value of its physical assets; economies of scale work only up to a point, which is about a 100-kilometer radius from the plant. The DSO, however, can be leveraged almost infinitely. The enormous leverage explains why Cemex enjoys remarkably high success from acquisitions, in lands as far from Mexico as Indonesia, Egypt, Spain, and the Philippines. Cement is a commodity. Cemex charges a premium price for it. The premium—the added value—comes entirely from that unique layer of intellectual capital. It also explains why Cemex produces cash flows 50 percent above those of its major competitors.

Leverage, then, is a second reason intellectual assets have become more important than any other kind. Says Baruch Lev, professor of accounting at New York University: "The ability to leverage physical and financial assets is limited and getting more so. The ability to leverage knowledge capital is unlimited and getting less so. An airplane can fly on just one route. A reservation system is limited only by the number of people in the world." To be sure, some knowledge assets are very specialized—you don't see many job swaps between cardiac surgeons and software debuggers—but whole hunks of intellectual capital are so fungible they might as well be money.

At the same time, investment in intellectual capital almost invariably provokes further, complementary investments, producing a self-feeding circle of investment and value creation. For every $1 companies invest in computers, they invest another $9 in other intangibles, such as management, research and development, software, and training. Five years ago, when the idea of a "new economy" was controversial, economists puzzled over the seeming failure of investment in information technology to produce gains in productivity. Those doubts are—or should be—laid to rest now. Since 1994, U.S. productivity (probably underestimated) has grown at a 2.8 percent annual clip, double the average growth rate of the previous two decades. More than half that increase is attributable to information technology, including software—though IT capital stock is just 1 percent of all capital stock. Ubiquitous, ever-cheaper, ever-more-powerful information technology has unleashed a torrent of economic good. Why so powerful? First, information is a factor of production in every industry, from farming to pharmaceuticals. Improve the efficiency with which information is used, and the innovation can be applied everywhere. Network externalities also turbocharge the effects of gains in the use of knowledge. In addition, the skills demanded of knowledge workers require investments in human capital—so the workforce is becoming more skilled, and is able to apply its skills in unplanned-for ways. Cemex, for example, is using its satellite system to provide government-certified high-school educations to all of its hourly workers—an investment in human capital that will further increase the returns from its information system. Finally, as we shall see, to take advantage of information technology and to become a true knowledge company requires new organizational forms—that is, to get the most out of new technology and intangible assets, companies often have to rethink their business model and their organizational design, producing "a round of organizational innovation." Thus technical innovation feeds into social innovation, which feeds into more technical innovation, increasing the value of knowledge assets in a virtuous spiral.

Ultimately, intellectual assets have become more important than any other because only by means of knowledge can companies differentiate their work from their competitors'. Other sources of competitive advantage are rapidly drying up: geography (weakened by electronic commerce and reduced tariffs and lower barriers to foreign direct investment), regulation (which once insulated enormous sectors—transportation, communications, power, and financial services), and vertical integration (less valuable because more and more companies are finding it cheaper to buy on the open market what they once made themselves). You don't need physical assets to gain entry into a business. The specific asset—the differentiating asset—is not the machinery. It's the software and the wetware—the stuff between your ears. It's the knowledge, stupid.

WE NEED NEW MANAGEMENT TECHNIQUES AND NEW STRATEGIES

According to Peter Drucker, all—all—the productivity gains of the twentieth century can be explained by the work Frederick Taylor put in motion at the century's beginning, when he and other proponents of Scientific Management set about increasing the efficiency of physical labor. The thesis of this book derives from the simple fact that even an oil rig mechanic spends most of his time doing knowledge work, and, says Drucker, "Work on the productivity of the knowledge worker has barely begun."

All the major structures of companies—their legal underpinnings, their systems of governance, their management disciplines, their accounting—are based on a model of the corporation that has become irrelevant. There are next to no rules of thumb, no advice, no tried-and-true consulting methods, no academic work on how to make the oil-rig worker more productive during the five-sixths of his time he is not holding a wrench. Knowledge workers are on their own—getting a word of advice here and there from a colleague or a boss, or from self-help books about how to be better organized.

Earlier we looked at theft of intellectual property as one way to measure the economic importance of knowledge. Similarly, we can look at taxation—which some loonies consider theft—as an indication of how little attention we pay to the real sources of wealth. Knowledge assets fly under the tax man's radar, just as they do the manager's. Take property taxes, for decades a primary tool for generating tax revenue from business. Microsoft owns a big campus, but the value of its real estate is nothing compared to the value of its un-real estate. King County, Washington, assesses Microsoft's property at $1.05 billion, about 0.2 percent of the market value of the company as a whole, which is about $500 billion. Microsoft's property tax bill? About $14 million. Neighboring Boeing has a market cap of about $40 billion, less than one-tenth that of Microsoft, and a real-property assessment of $5.5 billion. If you buy a dollar's worth of Boeing stock, you get 14 cents of real property in King County. Boeing pays about $70 million in property taxes each year. According to Ray Scheppach, executive director of the National Governors Association: "The basic problem is that our tax systems were set up for the manufacturing economy of the 1950s, not a high-tech service-oriented economy." In all likelihood, also, the earnings of engineers who work for Microsoft are taxed less than those of engineers working at Boeing. This is because a high percentage of the software company's compensation comes in the form of stock options. Unlike wages, from which taxes are withheld when a paycheck is cut, the value of stock options is not taxed until they are exercised.

You don't have to sympathize with tax collectors to recognize that their problem is yours. Economies work and businesses thrive when resources are allocated efficiently—when markets, managers, directors, and investors know what their most valuable assets are and how to put them to their most productive use. We understand how to deploy financial and physical assets. Now intellectual capital is our most important asset— and in this new economic environment, we are as naive as newborns. We know it exists and know it is valuable; we are like eunuchs in a harem, thinking what marvelous things we could accomplish if only we had the tools. Describing what they are and how to use them is the purpose of this book.

CHAPTER 2

WHAT COMPANIES DO
AND WHY THEY EXIST

Imaginary gardens with real toads in them.

MARIANNE MOORE

I n the woods of western Connecticut, in Roxbury, stand the ruins of an
old steelmaking crucible. It's an oven, essentially—a stone structure
some ten meters square topped by a chimney, not a lot bigger than the
kitchen ovens of European palaces. The mill is downhill from a long-
since-played-out iron mine. Back when, mules dragged sledfuls of ore
down from the mine to the crucible; it was converted into steel with charcoal made from the surrounding forest; a railway spur took it to market.
The railway is long disused, too. The woods, lacerated to make charcoal,
have grown back. For safety's sake a grate covers the mine entrance; up
from the shaft comes a damp, frigid draft.

It didn't take a lot of capital or a big organization to make steel in the
New England woods. It took know-how, but nothing esoteric: More or less

the same steelmaking techniques were used in early New England as were used hundreds of years earlier. Before the age of big machines, steel could be a cottage industry. Not surprisingly, these little companies usually sprang up next to sources of iron. All that changed in the nineteenth century, with Henry Bessemer's invention of a process for making steel that was more efficient, more productive—and much more capital intensive. With the Bessemer process, and later the open hearth, steelmaking became the province of big companies. It couldn't be done without them. It also couldn't be done without more heat than charcoal could sensibly provide, so it became more important to locate steel mills near coal deposits (to make coke) than near iron.

You can make the case—and prove it, if you allow a few exceptions*—that the corporation as we know it came into being to solve the problem of organizing production using complex, efficient, and big machines like Bessemer's converters. A blacksmith could build his own forge, and buy himself an anvil and hammer; a Bessemer converter was, however, beyond the means of a man of ordinary wealth. Investors pooled their money to acquire something none of them could afford on his own; they named a board of directors to represent their interests, which, in turn, hired people with special expertise, either in management or in technology, to tend their investment and make and sell the goods. All of this has become enshrined in corporate law and custom, based on "an underlying assumption that 'the firm' is basically a bundle of assets that belongs to shareholders but is managed for them by hired managers."

Is the assumption still right? Why do people work for companies? Why does *this* group of people gather under *this* corporate umbrella to perform *this* set of activities? Why are they employees rather than freelancers—or why are some of them employees, some freelancers, and still others employees of another company, laboring on our premises? Why does the company's boundary fall *here* rather than over *there*? Why do companies exist?

Says Gerhard Schulmeyer, the CEO of North American operations for Siemens, the giant electronics company: "You only exist as an institution

---

* Mostly companies engaging in long-distance trade, such as the Dutch East Indies Company and the East India Company, whose far-flung, capital-intensive operations required a corporate form of organization. They were the first big companies, but are not the begetters of the modern industrial company.

because people come in to work because they can do their wo
cheaply than on their own. If they leave, you cease to exist." In that s.
ment is the short version of the theory of the firm: Companies—all orga
nizations, for that matter—exist because people come to work for them;
and the people come because the company creates conditions under
which they can work more effectively than they could on their own.
Where there is no advantage, the company will die or be sold and dis-
mantled. The company makes an edge by attracting, acquiring, and
assembling resources—assets—that extend its people's reach. These
resources, and the activities that take place using them, enable me to do
my job better—faster, cheaper, for more money—than I could alone.

The law and economic theory say that a company is a bundle of assets.
Information Age fact says it is really a beehive of ideas. That change has
profound implications for how companies are set up and run, and how they
compete. The opportunity to assemble and exploit physical assets used to
define competitive advantage and explained why companies came into
being. They sprouted where they could take advantage of physical attributes of the land: Corning, Inc., located in rural upstate New York, far from
a big supply of labor and far from its markets, but close to the natural
resources needed to make glass; great merchants set up shop in New York
City because it was at the intersection of two great trading routes—the
American heartland (via the Hudson River, Erie Canal, and Great Lakes)
and the Atlantic Ocean. Alternatively, companies aggregated and managed
man-made assets: At the dawn of the twentieth century, J. P. Morgan led a
great industrial consolidation (of steel companies, railways, and electrical
manufacturers) essentially to redraw the boundaries between companies to
maximize the return on the plant and equipment they owned.

No longer do physical assets explain what a company is or where its
borders fall. Globalization makes it increasingly unlikely that any one
company can control the supply of any natural resource or basic product.
Pure-knowledge companies (such as professional services firms, publishing companies, and financial companies, not to mention Internet companies) may need little in the way of physical assets beyond computers and
desks. Those companies account for a growing share of employment and
production.

Granted, a chemical company needs access to state-of-the-art refineries and factories—but if you were looking to get an edge in the industry,

you wouldn't look to vats and pipes. For the last two decades, chemical companies have tried to compete by working their hard assets harder. Trouble is, that's a me-too strategy: Everybody cuts costs, then everybody cuts prices, then everybody cuts profits. There's still money in this work-the-assets strategy, but it's the money of consolidation, the profit that comes to people who slice themselves the biggest piece of pie, not the profit from baking a bigger one. As far as creating new wealth is concerned, work-the-assets has come to the end of its useful life. Dow Chemical managed to cut capital spending 44 percent in five years—but in the end, Dow's CEO told *Fortune*, "Customers' power just keeps increasing." According to an analysis by consultants at McKinsey: "Essentially, the chemicals industry lacks 'shapers': companies that have generated new profits by transforming the way they do business." Squeeze a lemon long enough and you're left with its rind and a sour taste.

Forward-thinking companies in the industry have figured that the future of competition in chemicals is ideas. In its 1999 annual report, DuPont promised to add value through "knowledge-intensive products and businesses," emphasizing its customer capital: entering e-commerce alliances and creating a "Knowledge Intensity University." Dow Chemical became the industry pioneer in uncovering and selling the hidden value in its unexploited or underexploited patents, creating a significant new source of revenue—$125 million annually, quintuple what it earned before—in just eighteen months. Buckman Laboratories, a specialty chemical maker based in Memphis, Tennessee, has emphasized knowledge sharing within the company. Note how the locus of competition shifts from manufacturing and selling chemicals to something else: to market making for DuPont, to the lab and the legal department for Dow, and to speed and responsiveness for Buckman.

New chemical-industry businesses—online marketplaces, among others—are forming that separate the marketplace from the producer company. Another market maker, Boston-based yet2.com, has created an online agora for intellectual property; DuPont, Dow, BASF, Ciba, Mitsui Chemical, Sumitomo Chemical, and others use yet2.com to buy and sell rights to patents and processes. There's even a business managing "chemical condos"—large chemical plants that make product for more than one company. Every year chemical companies perform some $1.4 trillion worth of transactions, almost all of which used to be handled by whole-salers and sales reps for chemical companies; some piece of it will now be handled by new outfits whose only assets will be servers, customers, and reputation.

What's true of chemicals is true of industry after industry. Finance is a good example. Innovation in financial services has come from separating assets into, essentially, two components: a traditional asset component and a derivative *information* component. These days, everything is securitized: mortgages, credit card debt, loans, leases—even David Bowie's song royalties.

The best companies in every industry have begun the process of identifying themselves with their ideas more than with their assets. Just-retired John F. Welch, Jr., has explained the theory of the firm, GE-style, by explaining his former job description. He did four things: He allocated resources, which is to say budgets; he managed leadership development; he pushed the occasional companywide initiative; and he energized the sharing of best practices. (It's a company joke that within minutes of Welch's leaving a site, the phone started ringing as other businesses asked, "What's this thing you're doing that Jack told us about?") Three of the four, and a lot of the budgeting, have to do with intellectual capital. Lines of business come and go, Welch has said; they are at GE, but they are not GE. Learning, sharing, and the institutions that foster them are what hold GE together. In the opinion of Merrill Lynch analyst Jeanne Terrile, General Electric—a big, industrial company if ever there was one—should not be thought of as an assemblage of businesses in the old sense; rather, it is "a repository of information and expertise that can be leveraged over a huge installed base."

Knowledge is a company's *raison d'être*. There can't be competitive advantage from unskilled work, because anyone can do it; nor can you gain an edge by means of a machine you can buy off the shelf, because anyone can buy it. Advantage, if it's not just momentary, comes from something proprietary—or at least hard to duplicate: a particular kind of knowledge, in the case of a company like Microsoft, or a unique combination of knowledge assets and physical assets, in the case of GE. The other sources of competitive advantage—access to capital, materials, markets, equipment—have largely been competed away. Says David Teece, dean of the Haas School of Business at the University of California at Berkeley: "The essence of the firm in the new economy is its ability to create, transfer, assemble, integrate, protect and exploit knowledge assets."

LOOK, HANDS—NO MA

But why do you need a corporation to do this? Riel Miller, an economist at the Organization for Economic Cooperation and Development, says: "The necessity of adding knowledge at every step in the value chain is beginning to call into question the familiar notion of the firm as an organizational unit." Why build Microsoft, when you can make an open-source operating system like Linux on the Net? Indeed, given the primacy of knowledge, there are many reasons corporations are a less-good solution to the problem of working effectively than they were. The quickest way to increase the production and flow of knowledge in most companies: Vaporize headquarters. There's less *tsuris* sharing knowledge in a small group than in a large organization. It's also easier to generate new ideas: A competitive community of thousands of freethinking small-to-midsized Silicon Valley computer companies ran rings around the independent, hierarchical, midsized-to-big computer companies on Route 128 in Boston.

One way to see why companies exist is to look at the forces that try to tear them apart. They are very strong. First, whole continents on the business map have been opened to intensified competition, due mostly to deregulation and globalization. Utilities, telecommunications, financial services, and airlines, three substantially deregulated industries, together employ nearly 18 million people, almost 14 percent of the U.S. civilian labor force. Globalization has changed safe harbors into teeming free ports. Second, information technology has slashed transaction costs for buying materials, components, services, and labor from sources outside the company, and simultaneously wiped out hundreds of thousands of clerical sinecures. Technological change in the nineteenth century tended to increase the capital intensity of businesses—as the Bessemer process did, for example. This had the effect of raising entry barriers; it favored big companies, which could recoup their investment from a big base of customers. The new technologies of the late twentieth and early twenty-first centuries have the opposite effect—reducing capital intensity (as we saw in Chapter 1), lowering entry barriers, and shrinking the advantages that accrue to mere size. Third, the art of management itself has become a centrifugal force, as companies use benchmarking, for example, to discover that they could be more efficient if they outsourced their shipping or accounts payable departments. Peter Cappelli, a professor at the Wharton School of the University of Pennsylvania, observes: "One consequence of . . . increasing competition . . . is that companies must work harder to find markets where they can enjoy some protection, no doubt temporary, from the grinding pressure of competitors."

The sum: More reasons to quit, more reasons to be fired, more reasons to set up on one's own, and more different kinds of work that can feasibly be done outside the structure of a corporation.

BLESSED BE THE TIES THAT BIND

Remember what Gerhard Schulmeyer said: Companies exist only if people are willing to show up. Well, they do. People yearn to work for companies—and we should examine why. Even the most gung-ho players in the new economy, if they had their druthers, would rather have one employer than hop-skip-and-jump from one knowledge-worker gig to another. By a two-to-one ratio, according to a survey taken for *Wired* magazine and Merrill Lynch, "superconnected" people—who regularly exchange e-mail and use a laptop, cell phone, beeper, and home computer—would rather stick with one employer for twenty years than have five jobs for four years each, even if the money and responsibilities were the same. The share of the American workforce that is self-employed dropped nearly 10 percent from 1994 through 1999.

What, then, ties us to the company? A good answer in the 1950s, says Brent Snow, an organizational development consultant, would have emphasized the safety and resources big groups offer small individuals: "It's a good company; I have an opportunity to move up; I have a future here." On the cusp of the new century, Snow asked employees at Oracle why they work there. The response? "They all start talking about the challenges, the chance to do interesting work on the cutting edge."

Learning is a clause of the "new contract" that people eagerly sign. Listen, for example, to a trio of thirtysomethings at PricewaterhouseCoopers:

John Waterman: "I'm here because I keep learning. Whenever I start to get a little bored, a new project comes along with opportunities for learning."

Tracy Amabile: "The people and the learning are what's primary. I've been provided a lot of opportunities, lots of challenging work in different industries."

Ed Germain: "I've had a lot of training, a lot of project opportunities. For me stagnation would lead to restlessness."

Leaders at another Big Six (or Five, or Four) consulting firm talk about "knowledge handcuffs." At a time when these fast-growing firms offered big bonuses to poach the others' talent, they found people stayed because they feel bound to the knowledge of their firm—the networks, electronic and (chiefly) human, of experts and expertise upon which they rely. A study conducted by Aon Consulting found that the single most effective way to strengthen employees' loyalty is to increase their opportunities for growth.

A second powerful force ties Man to Organization: The company gives you a field on which to strut your stuff. Paradoxically, that is, you depend on the organization to provide the arena in which to be independent. Says executive search consultant David Witte: "Freedom and responsibility are the very best golden handcuffs there are." The freedom of which Witte speaks is not the same as—is dramatically at odds with—the atomistic "You, Inc." idea that we are each of us on our own in a market for talent. To rely on market mechanisms to allocate talent is to admit being unable to do it yourself, says Howard Stevenson, a professor at Harvard Business School: "Markets result when organizations fail, not the other way around."

Tribal loyalty—along with learning and independence—is the third great rope tying people to the organization. A tribe is not the organization as a whole (unless it is small), but rather teams, communities of practice, and other groups within the company or one's occupation.

Tribalism explains an otherwise baffling phenomenon: If the employment "contract" has shifted from paternal and permanent to individualistic and transactional, why have we become obsessively concerned with interpersonal relationships at the office? Why do we care about "fit" and culture? Why not just snarl at one another eight hours a day and be done with it?

Brian Hall, CEO of Values Technology in Santa Cruz, California, documented a shift in people's emotional expectations from work. From the 1950s on, a "task first" relationship to the company—"tell me what the job is, and let's get on with it"—dominated employee attitudes. Emotions and personal life were checked at the door. In the past few years, a "relationship-first" set of values has challenged the task orientation, and Hall believes it will become dominant: Employees want to share attitudes and beliefs as well as workspace, want to establish the relationship (with one another and with the company) before buckling down to the task.

That's not touchy-feely. When the task changes abruptly and often, people need to cling to something that has continuity. As Stevenson points out, "We have to know each other, know how we work together, so that when a crisis comes we don't have to spend a long time coordinating." At Hewlett-Packard, for example, tasks change constantly; more than 50 percent of the company's orders derive from products that did not exist two years ago. The cast doesn't change nearly as quickly as the show. HP's employee attrition rate is usually half the average in the labor markets where it operates; in the 1990s attrition actually fell by a third. "I get benchmarked on this frequently," says Sally Dudley, a manager of human resources and a twenty-four-year HP veteran. "We don't do anything special. We're 'among the leaders' on pay. Our total compensation package is fairly traditional for a large company." HP's magic lies in the primacy of relationships over tasks. Says Dudley: "I've done fourteen different jobs here. Those who have spent most of their careers at HP—and most of us have—don't identify with doing the same thing."

WHY COMPANIES EXIST

In the knowledge economy, I've suggested, the tasks of management can be summarized in the acronym DNA: Define, Nurture, Allocate. But—forgive me for overworking the metaphor—what proteins make up this corporate genome?

To provide purpose. Companies don't plan the way they used to, nor should they; the old strategic planning departments disappeared in the 1980s, when change began to happen too quickly and too abruptly for them. In place of planning, we have purposing,* and it's an important unifying activity of corporations. People often say "things have fallen apart" when a company loses its sense of direction, and the image is accurate. When a company lacks purpose, people leave. Projects end half finished. Energy becomes entropy. Purpose is energizing, and energy attracts people; they will subordinate their individual agendas to the group's. The most quarrelsome egomaniacs in the world—nuclear physicists—worked as a team in the Manhattan Project. Government funds gave them facilities no physicist had ever had before, but purpose made them a company.

The boundaries of the company, then, are partly set by the extent to which its employees share the same purpose. Hewlett-Packard and Agilent Technologies split in 2000 not just because one business was growing faster than the other but because they were no longer trying to do the same thing. Certainly it's not possible for different parts of companies to work at cross-purposes to each other, which, surprisingly, it once was. In the 1970s, a friend of mine worked for a conglomerate whose companies were required to buy from each other whenever possible, to keep the money in the family. The companies were also told to increase revenues and margins every year—even if it meant jacking up prices to their captive sibling customers. It was stupid then, though a sophist might have argued that the synergies outweighed the costs; it's inconceivable now.

To be a magnet for intellectual capital—that is, to provide a place, a culturing medium, and a culture, a community of people to work with and go to. You choose 3M for the intellectual climate (certainly not for the meteorological one). You work for Microsoft because the presence of other bright code writers stimulates and challenges you, gives you help when you need it, provides easy access to experts, allows you to work faster and better than you could in a garret. (For the purpose of this argument, let's ignore the value of hitchhiking on monopoly rents.) The existence of a talented community is, in turn, a magnet for customers. Add a few techies to link your laptops in a LAN, and *voilà*: The company has gathered human, structural, and customer capital.

Economists speak of the need for "complementary assets." My effectiveness as a journalist is enhanced by complementary expertise in pho-

---

* Yes, it does sound like jargon, but "to purpose" is a perfectly good verb; Shakespeare used it.

tography, illustration, design, and printing, not to mention commercial talents like advertising sales. I need these assets, don't have them myself, and might not know how to buy them intelligently. Why should I? The company assembles them for me, lowering the cost I would pay to get them myself.

To host conversations and house tacit knowledge. Markets are conversations, as stated in the first line of *The Cluetrain Manifesto,* a maddening must-read document* by Rick Levine, Christopher Locke, Doc Searls, and David Weinberger. *The Cluetrain Manifesto* describes how the World Wide Web—inherently informal, infinitely interlinked—changed markets by allowing customers to talk to one another and to talk back to sellers. It continues: "What's happening to markets is also happening among employees. A metaphysical construct called 'The Company' is the only thing standing between the two." When the conversation goes badly, Locke et al. say, "the cause of failure can be traced to obsolete notions of command and control."

The very nature of knowledge work destroys control. First, it's collaborative. From our school days we have the image of learning being a solitary activity—alone late at night in the library. That was wrong then and is wrong now. Archimedes was alone in his bath, presumably, when he figured out how to measure the purity of the gold in King Hiero II's crown and shouted, "Eureka!" But learning is usually social. We all know that we learned more from our classmates than from our classes. Moreover, knowledge-intensive products and services are too complicated for even a Leonardo da Vinci to produce alone; they require teamwork among specialists. "When I designed my first chip in 1984, I did it all myself," recalls Bharat Sastri, CEO of Hellobrain.com, an intellectual property exchange on the Web. "The last chip I designed involved the work of sixty-five highly specialized people."

Second, knowledge work is customized. As computing power increases and its cost drops, anything that can be done the same way twice can and will be automated. To create unique, high-value work, we need to do custom work—a deal or a doodad just for you. The same goes for management. Management used to be about ensuring continuity. The idea was

---

*If you haven't, and since you must: www.cluetrain.com.

to make business as predictable as the weather in Yuma, Arizona. Now continuity is the work of machines; management is about change.

Third, knowledge work processes are nonlinear. An assembly line moves only in one direction. Not so knowledge work. It moves by iteration and reiteration—first draft and revision and rerevision and so on. Software is released in a "beta" version so that users can discover its bugs. Web sites are constantly revised. Compared to a physical space like a shopping mall or a city, "Web sites are much cheaper to tune and can be re-launched daily with little incremental expense. Iteration is part of the design process." Manufacturing companies have even discovered the knowledge-creation value of stopping assembly lines. In 1983, General Motors and Toyota formed a joint venture, New United Motor Manufacturing, Inc. (NUMMI), to produce a small Chevrolet in a California assembly plant previously operated by GM. They operated it according to the Toyota Production System. The first time Paul O'Neill, now Secretary of Commerce but then CEO of Alcoa and a member of GM's board of directors, visited the plant, he was aghast to see how often workers stopped the lines—he thought it must be evidence of a bad plant. In fact, stopping the line is the process by which workers continuously improve it: Whenever there's a problem, or whenever they have an idea for an improvement, the line's stopped, the problem's fixed or the new idea's discussed, and work resumes.

Collaboration, customization, constant correction—these activities occur in a special kind of place, and one of the roles of a company is to provide it. Ikujiro Nonaka, coauthor of *The Knowledge-Creating Company* and professor at Hitotsubashi University in Japan and UC Berkeley in the United States, coined the term *"Ba"* to describe such a place. *Ba* is a mental space rather than a physical one; it is shared context, which allows people to work together, knowing that they're—pick your cliché—on the same page, singing from the same song sheet.

Ba is not humbug. Without it, knowledge work can't be coordinated or managed. Says Schulmeyer: "An institution can build a knowledge pool in areas of interest and keep transaction costs lower than they would be without the institution." That's a big deal—transaction costs, he estimates, are as much as 70 percent of the total labor cost for knowledge workers. In particular, *Ba* is important for storing and sharing tacit knowledge. Tacit knowledge is, as the name says, silent: It's all that stuff you know that you can't quite put into words: routines, instincts, feel, experience, know-how. We'll talk about it at length in Chapter 7. Almost always, a significant portion of a company's advantage resides in its tacit knowledge. Explicit knowledge, after all, can be documented in some way—that's the definition of the stuff—which means it can be copied. Explicit knowledge can be kept anywhere—in a cabinet, a library, on a videocassette, in a manual, on a Web site. Tacit knowledge resides in heads, relationships, customs, cultures. When a company houses it, that's worth something.

To offer a warranty. The company's brand and reputation are umbrellas under which I shelter. The company vouches for me to suppliers and customers. Because I write for *Fortune,* people return my phone calls; they might not if I freelanced or worked for a scandal sheet. An investment banker once told me why he stayed with his company rather than set up a boutique of his own. His revealing reason: "I'm not famous enough yet." Similarly, the company warrants colleagues to one another: The engineer in the next cubicle is, just like you, working at Hughes Space & Communications, so you can presume she is talented and trustworthy.

The warranty function works in both directions: The reputations of employees affect the reputation of the company, too. Hiring hotshots can give a company credibility, and losing them can cost it. Usually, though, it's the company that vouches for the person. That's worth something too.

To perform financial and administrative services. A company limits our liability, annualizes our income, tides us over during unproductive patches, collects money owed by our customers, borrows on our behalf, buys airplane tickets and copier toner in bulk at a discount. The amount of time freelancers spend buying postage, chasing overdue checks, and organizing stuff for the accountant is greater than the amount of time they had spent, back in corporate life, dealing with HR, payroll, and other departments. It's a law of nature: Administrivial effluvia runs somewhere between knee- and hip-deep. Fobbing it off on someone else is worth something, too.

Purpose, intellectual capital, conversation and knowledge storage, warranty, services: Each of these is a reason you and I might cede to a company a bit of mastery of our fates, captaincy of our souls. In this list we can begin to see what a knowledge-based company is, and discern an agenda for managing it.

CHAPTER 3

THE E-CORPORATION

More than any other time in history, mankind faces a crossroad: One path leads to despair and hopelessness, and the other to total extinction. Let us pray we have the wisdom to choose correctly.

WOODY ALLEN

The Web changes everything," they—whoever they are—say. Whatever has been will be no more. The former things are passed away, and it will make all things new. Everyone is at risk. Among the most endangered, many observers agreed, was the business that, till software, probably created more millionaires than any other: automobile dealerships. Early in 2000, Greg Lapidus, an analyst at Goldman Sachs, predicted "extinction" for dealerships and "the end of plaid jackets and green pants!" In December 1999, Michael Jackson, CEO of AutoNation, America's largest online direct seller of motor vehicles, predicted that his company would sell $1.5 billion worth of cars via the Internet in 2000. "Dealers are sitting ducks," wrote two consultants from the Boston Consulting Group.

Some duck. AutoNation is actually an amalgam of more than 400 dealers, put together by Blockbuster-builder Wayne Huizinga. AutoNation's
Internet customers search on the Web, but actually buy at company dealerships, where the salesman who takes them around the lot might indeed
wear a plaid jacket. The clothes worn by the much-feared online disinter-
mediators, on the other hand, seem to have been the emperor's hand-me-
downs. It turns out that nothing-but-Net is no way to sell cars when, for
example, 40 percent of new-car sales involve a used-car trade-in.

Clearly the Web doesn't change everything.

By the middle of 2001, dot-com *schadenfreude* had become as tiresome
and unenlightening as e-business *braggadocio* was two years earlier. But
it's a mistake to confuse dot-coms with e-commerce, and understanding
e-commerce is vital to understanding how to master intellectual capital.
Information technology, especially the Web, amplifies and alters the
trends we've been discussing—the rise of knowledge as an economic
good, the importance of knowledge assets, the centrality of human capital.
These long antedate the Web, yet the Web fits the trends of the knowledge
economy so well, one might even say that they called it into being. The
problems and opportunities of twenty-first-century business, that is, are
functions of the importance of knowledge in the economy, not of the technology available to manage and exploit it. E-commerce changes relations
with customers, suppliers, and employees; but the changes it causes are
without exception consequences of the knowledge economy, not causes.
It's possible—all too possible, as hundreds of entrepreneurs have discovered—to get e-commerce right and go broke because you got intellectual
capital wrong.

The cataclysms that in 2000–2001 washed away so many Internet
companies and eroded the market value of so many others don't change
the size of the opportunity. In 1999, *Purchasing* magazine reported that 38
percent of buyers use the Web for at least a portion of their transactions.
In 2000, businesses buying from each other channeled some $336 billion
through the Internet, according to Jupiter Media Metrix, a research group.
By 2005, the same group estimates, Internet business-to-business sales
will total $6.3 trillion—42 percent of the total. Forrester Research esti-
mates the global business-to-business electronic market will be worth $7
trillion by 2004. Even if both estimates are too high by half, "B2B" means

"big to bigger." Same goes for "B2C," the big-to-colossal business-to-consumer market, which Forrester says will be worth $184 billion a year by 2004. That's just 7 percent of total retail sales, but (a) 7 percent is a lot, especially since retail margins are small, and (b) it's highly concentrated. E-commerce sales of groceries probably won't amount to a hill of beans, but a seismic-shifting 25 percent of music will be sold online, as will 13 percent of flowers, two out of five computers, half the software, 12 percent of leisure travel, and 11 percent of apparel—that's one out of every nine items in your closet.

In September 1999, the Cutter Consortium, a research group focusing on information technology issues, released a survey that showed that 65 percent of companies had no e-commerce strategy—a remarkable number considering that the survey was conducted entirely over the Internet, half the respondents said they advertised on the Net, and 38 percent used it to deliver some sort of product. The obvious conclusion, which perhaps we didn't need a survey to learn: A substantial number of companies have been doing business online without the foggiest idea of what they're up to.

Never in history has there been a technology that so suits the storage, sharing, and exploitation of knowledge. Headstrong enthusiasm and headlong confusion were entirely appropriate first responses to the opportunities electronic commerce presents. Now it's time to think.

FOUR LESSONS

There are two basic dogmas about e-commerce, both wrong. The brave-new-world school holds that e-commerce upends almost every old rule of business; the been-there-done-that crowd says that the Internet, like the railroad and the telephone, is yet another improved and faster channel of distribution to which business must adapt.

Rather than pick one of their deities to worship, I'd like to propose a small pantheon of digital divinities. None is omnipotent, but each has its realm, and learning about them is the first step toward learning how e-commerce and intellectual capital affect each other:

• *Management matters.* "Is management dead?" I heard that question at a gathering that included some of the most eminent names in the field—Warren Bennis, Peter Drucker, Tom Peters, Charles Handy, Harold Leavitt. In that crowd, it was like a fart in church.

And about time.

The man who asked it, Steve Kerr, was then the chief learning officer of GE, which meant he ran the greatest management training ground on the planet. He was right to ask. The fact was, for the last two years of the twentieth century, anyone with no mortgage and half a brain ("bounded rationality," economists call it) would have been a fool to worry about management. Why run a business diligently when you can make a couple of zillion dollars by folding copies of your business plan into paper airplanes and flipping them onto the lawns of Palo Alto venture capitalists? Why bother to build management processes that work when Microsoft or Cisco Systems will buy you out and provide you with their processes? No wonder management consulting firms had a hard time recruiting MBAs. The labor market was rewarding entrepreneurship, not management, just as the stock market rewarded brainstorms, not flood control. Even running a failed company looked good on your résumé.

That moment ended when dot.com stocks started swooning like Victorian maidens shown a French postcard, and that sinking spell reveals something. Says Gary Hamel, the strategy savant who heads the Strategos consulting firm in Silicon Valley: "Every one of these will-o'-the-wisp Internet companies is learning that—you know what?—scale and operational excellence and global infrastructure are important."

The Web creates extraordinary opportunities to scale a business. Indeed, to some extent it creates scale willy-nilly: Once you have a Web site, you have a global presence whether or not you have a global footprint. Customer expectations rise accordingly. But scale is never painless—a fact many e-business people and their kibitzers, including one of my kids' parents, underestimated. The first lesson of e-commerce is that scale and execution matter more, not less. This isn't a question of the right mix of "bricks and clicks," though that is one part of the answer; it's about delivering on promises to customers. Jack Welch put it this way: "The key to success is to be customer-centric, because customers will see everything. Nothing will be hidden in paperwork. Where is the inventory? Where is that part? Where is that solution? They will see it all. . . . Execution is very important. . . . Every error you make is transparent on the Web."

There's big money in e-commerce, but the biggest right now might be in applying its technologies inside companies—to rules, procedures, and accounting methods. You can get at it by designing your operations from the outside in, from the customer's point of view: In the jargon du jour, figure out what the front end should look like, and then use technology to arrange the back end in such a way that you never muck up the customer's experience—and at the same time build a highly efficient operation, which chiefly means managing the internal flow of information so that it is rapid, reliable, and cheap.

That means designing from the point of view of knowledge—in particular, the answers to the questions "What do I need to know to serve my customer?" and "What does my customer want to know?" Customers' questions are never about your back end, whether it's a server or a warehouse. The firm exists to deploy intellectual assets that create the value customers desire. It coordinates physical processes (manufacturing, delivery), which it might or might not own, only to serve customers. Says Ian Angell, professor at the London Business School: "The information system is the virtual enterprise. There is nothing else. You are what you claim to be. You are what you can deliver."

The Internet hates boundaries and restrictions of any kind. "Information wants to be free," says one of the first of the Net's proverbs; "The Internet treats censorship as damage, and routes around it" is another. Ignore execution, and customers will route around you.

• *Distribution is more than a cost.* Traditional distributors do three value-adding things. They collect information (names of buyers and sellers, product specifications, knowledge of supply and demand); they shoulder some quality and credit risk for both buyer and seller; and they aggregate inventory, ensuring prompt delivery. (The words a shopper least wants to hear: "We have to order that from the factory.") Online, Dell Computer does all three value-adders but vaporizes the distributor. It uses the Web to aggregate information, instantaneous electronic payment to mitigate credit risk, and build-to-order manufacturing to ensure availability. Typically a Dell customer's computer is assembled to his specifications, loaded with the software he requests, and ready to ship within two hours of receipt of the order—faster than many companies can get finished goods out of a warehouse.

The Dell Business Model sets a benchmark for e-commerce. It's pretty clear that any distributor/dealer is dead if his only claims on a share of the money in the value chain are a window in front and a warehouse out back. With the Web, I can get a window in your den. Obvious conclusion: There will be fewer distributors.

The Net won't kill off all intermediaries, however. Unintermediated Internet is an unnavigable intercontinental flea market, as unwieldy and inefficient as unintermediated inventory. But e-commerce commoditizes a lot of what middlemen were paid for. They need to compete with scale or with knowledge, via such services as logistics, installation, and repair. E-commerce also makes it possible to reduce inventories overall. As that happens, the money tied up in materials, storage, and financing slips its ropes. Up for grabs in the supply chain, says James Duffy, CEO of Benchmarking Partners, a Cambridge, Massachusetts, consulting firm: $1 trillion a year, give or take a few billion. Meanwhile, suppliers have to decide whether to cut themselves loose from dinosaur distributors that don't add value (and perhaps find themselves estranged from customers), or work with them to add value (and run the risk that they will get clobbered by some quick mover, such as Dell, that bypasses the old channel entirely). What's true of middlemen is also true of proprietary distribution. Sales forces, branches, a chain, and delivery fleets that were once the source of a company's advantage can become liabilities if they fail to add knowledge as well as deliver the goods.

Remember what business is about—finding, serving, and keeping profitable customers. Offline distribution channels are like concrete-lined irrigation ditches, where water flows along prescribed lines, whereas the Web is a flat, rich, mysterious Okeefenokee of every-which-way communication, an infinitely branching fractal. If you're too far down the clickstream, any one of a zillion other opportunities may distract me. The Web is so fluid that control over channels is likely to be fleeting—or very expensive.

How do you move up the clickstream? The answer—rather, the way you learn the answers—is to improve your ability to learn about and with customers. Customer learning—how you learn about them, and they learn about you, and how you learn together about your shared enterprise—is one of the key knowledge processes in business. Mastering it is, we will see in Chapter 9, the sine qua non of success in the knowledge economy, online or off.

• *Broadcasting declines in importance, and service increases.* MTV and your radio play music; Napster and Morpheus let you find it yourself. Bankers keep bankers' hours; ATMs serve you at your convenience. Early in the still-young history of e-business, there was a lot of talk about "push" vs. "pull" technology: The daily newspaper is "pushed" at us (under the door, into the box); on the Web (we were told) we would "pull" the news when we wanted it.

Something subtler and more far-reaching happened instead. The mass market, a twentieth-century invention, separated advertising and marketing from sales, fulfillment, and service. The Web rejoins them, because the Internet is fundamentally interactive. People using it want to do something.

The rising power of customers is a basic tenet of the knowledge economy, as I wrote in 1997: "When information is power, power flows downstream toward the customer." Technology has something to do with causing this phenomenon and everything to do with amplifying it. Essentially, the Web alters the balance of power between buyer and seller, usually in the direction of the buyer. The consumer holds the mouse, not you. It's easier to find alternative suppliers, easier to comparison-shop. Says Robert Wayland, a Concord, Massachusetts, consultant and coauthor of *The Customer Connection:* "The basic process by which customers learn about companies and vice versa is the same, except that customers can search a lot faster and more cheaply, so their exit costs are dropping." If you want to woo me by dropping your price, be my guest. The right response, says Wayland, "should be to pay more attention to the substantive pieces of the relationship." That means sellers should shift their focus from announcing or broadcasting information to servicing, which engages a customer by delivering valuable knowledge. The money is in services. In the last forty years, U.S. consumer prices for services have octupled, rising more than twice as fast as prices for consumer durables, which rose by 3.3 times. In the last ten years, services prices have risen three times faster than durables. Prices for labor confirm the trend, with goods producers' compensation rising at a 2.6 percent annual rate vs. 4 percent for service producers. Why do you think Jack Welch and IBM's Lou Gerstner pushed their companies into services?

• *Those who live by cost cutting will die by its sword.* By March 2000, less than six years after Netscape was incorporated, more than 750 networked marketplaces had come into being. By summer, the shakeout was well along as euphoria over how easy it is to create an online marketplace gave way to despair at how hard it was to make one work. Given the former, the latter should have been obvious. In business, nothing easy can be richly rewarding, one reason making omelettes is in many ways a preferable occupation.

Many electronic marketplaces came into being inspired by just one proposition: cutting the cost of procurement. An early form of e-commerce, electronic data interchange, allowed a buyer and a seller to set up a proprietary link, using leased telephone lines, over which they could transmit orders and payment, eliminating a small fortune in paperwork costs. Setting up EDI is expensive, however; moving transaction processing to the Internet makes similar economies available to small businesses—potentially saving up to 65 percent of the administrative cost of purchasing and record keeping. In industry after industry—autos, steel, chemicals, "B2B exchanges" came into being, some sponsored by participating companies, others by new outfits like Ariba, Commerce One, and the Internet Capital Group. Some operated auctions; some created and managed, essentially, electronic catalogues. Lots that had been done by hand, by hard selling, and by schmoozing now was automated, impersonal, fast. And more is to come. New software standards, the most notable of which is XML, Extensible Markup Language, may bring an unprecedented degree of automation, and hence cost saving, to procurement. XML, which allows almost anything salable to be tagged with a unique identifier, could produce a "next-generation Web . . . in which suppliers and manufacturers can let their computers find, buy, and sell goods and services robotically."

Which is well, good, and wonderful; but the medium of exchange is not itself a profit center. Mints make money, not profits. XML was created by the not-for-profit World Wide Web Consortium; another eleemosynary, the Organization for the Advancement of Structured Information Standards, OASIS, helps create and register industry-specific XML "tags." This is not to say marketplaces are worthless; but whether the agora is in ancient Athens, on New York's Union Square, or in cyberspace, it's probably supported by taxpayers or small user fees. With the rarest of exceptions (where a monopolist owns a standard and hasn't yet been caught, for example), the network is not the business.

Nor is cutting prices a strategy; indeed, the greatest danger of a price war might be winning it. That is dot-com pricing mistake number two: Electronic commerce can, no doubt about it, produce a more "frictionless" economy, but one man's friction is another man's profit. Efficiency is always good—it allows capital, including intellectual capital, to be deployed more effectively for a higher return. But efficiency is not the same as price. Auctions run by FreeMarkets, Inc.—actually, reverse auctions, in which a buyer puts a contract out for bid and sellers compete against each other to see who will do the job for the least money—have allowed blue-chip buyers like United Technologies and Raytheon to save, on average, 15 percent of their costs for purchased parts, but at a cost of another sort. To make online auctions work, FreeMarkets' CEO Glen Meakem found, he had to bid apples against apples. He therefore required that competing suppliers

> offer not only to deliver the same part but also to do it on the same schedule, with the same payment terms, inventory arrangements, and everything else. That way each package is practically the same; plastic refrigerator shelves and automobile bumpers become almost as much a commodity as bushels of wheat. All that remains is to find the lowest price, and the best way to do that is through an auction.

E-commerce has increased the range of transactions performed this way. This is one reason that a lot of e-commerce has been conducted without profit. The winner of such auctions is likely to be the guy who is stuck with excess capacity, for whom it's cheaper to sell for no margin than it is to shut down the factory for a week.* The buyer saves, but that's a decidedly mixed blessing: By turning components into commodities, he

---

* Similarly, the winner of conventional auctions, where the direction of the bidding is up, always ends up with an overpriced asset when he buys a one-of-a-kind item, assuming the existence of the auction was known to all potential buyers. That is, by paying the highest price, the winner has set a value higher than anyone else will pay. If the item goes back on the market, its price will be lower, assuming nothing else has changed. (See James Surowiecki, "The Agony of Victory and the Thrill of Defeat," *The New Yorker,* January 8, 2001, p. 31.)

narrows the range of ways in which he can achieve competitive advantage. Reducing options is always a grave strategic decision, which should be made on the basis of value, of which price is just one element. Two things sell on the basis of price alone: commodities and junk. There's a place for each, but it's not Nob Hill. The market maker finds his vigorish reduced by the very process he helped to create. That's one reason stock prices for online market makers melted; FreeMarkets, for example, $341 a share at the end of 1999, sank below $10 in April 2001.

It is a principle of electronic commerce that information is ever cheaper, but knowledge is ever more valuable. If you are in the business of shuffling, selling, or arbitraging information, you are like the man who built his house upon the sand: Its foundation is forever being sucked away by the tide. Knowledge is a rock. Uniqueness, particularly unique knowledge, is where a business wins or loses. Successful electronic marketplaces demonstrate this. Go to buy a computer from Dell, and the company's "configurator" will help you select software and peripherals, and warn you about incompatibilities. Cisco Systems does the same for its online customers. Buyers and renters of GE aircraft engines get access to data that allow them to compare their service and maintenance records with the average of their competitors—and offers from GE to sell their advice about how to improve. Yes, Dell, Cisco, and GE save money by moving transactions to the Net, but they don't make money by commoditizing the selling process: Each of these companies uses e-commerce to add knowledge, for which they get paid. In the mid-1990s, when I was visiting GE Lighting in Cleveland, the public-relations person told me about improvements that had cut manufacturing costs by an impressively large percentage. I mused that those savings might find their way to consumers. His response, spoken in a tone of mock-serious rebuke: "Cutting prices is not a core competence of the General Electric Corporation." I'll never forget it. Dot-coms did.

WINNING ONLINE I: ADDING KNOWLEDGE

Over the portal to Hell, through which Virgil led Dante, were the words *Lasciate onge speranza, voi ch' entrate,* "Abandon all hope, ye that enter here." The warning might better have been placed on the business plans of companies that hoped to make a killing on the Web. The lessons learned (so far) in e-commerce are significant not just because e-commerce itself is a big deal, but because this is not just a nerd's land rush: They are applicable almost everywhere in the knowledge economy.

Big forces are at work. First: A number of dislocations have jarred loose traditional connections between consumers and suppliers. The opening of cyberspace is one. "Customers, new to purchasing online, are receptive to forming new relationships," writes Jeff Bezos, CEO of Amazon.com, just as college freshmen stray from high-school sweethearts to whom, under the August moon, they pledged eternal fealty. Add deregulation: In telecommunications, for example, where once there was just one doorway—in the United States, Ma Bell—now there are enough for the set of a Feydeau farce; the battle for wireless telephone subscribers is so intense that companies showed themselves willing to pay ludicrous prices for licenses to pieces of the electromagnetic spectrum. In financial services, combine deregulation (both intra- and international) with high-speed, cheap data processing and a tax-subsidized explosion of investment in mutual funds; the result is that banks, brokerages, insurance companies, or amalgams of the three each hope to be the center of your newly complex financial life. So old relationships are up for grabs, and new technologies make it possible, in theory at least, for a company to become a clearinghouse for your life as a consumer.

Second, there's all kinds of evidence that consumers want to simplify their lives—and what simpler simplification than to turn big pieces of it over to a trusted guide? Hence the dreams of a Yahoo!, an AOL, a CNET, a Lycos to become your "portal." Buyers are more sophisticated than ever, but they are also overwhelmed by the choices sophistication spawns. Says Bob Frisch, a partner at Accenture: "Five years ago in most American towns a cup of coffee was a cup of coffee, and your options were cream or sugar. If my dad heard the guy ahead of him in line order a doppio latte skinny with arabica beans, it'd be, like, what the hell?" Today if you want call waiting with antilock brakes, free checking, a 56K internal modem, and extra cheese—someone's got it. According to the Yankelovich Monitor survey of consumer attitudes in 1996, fully 73 percent of Americans said "life is too complicated," up from 58 percent in 1985. In a fashion victim's *cri de coeur*, Edina Monsoon, the protagonist of the British sitcom *Absolutely Fabulous*, wailed: "I don't want more choice; I just want better things."

Third, we're pressed for time, with more of us working than ever, and working harder. While supermarket shelves glitter with a dozen varieties of premium olive oil, the Food Marketing Institute says the average length of time a shopper spends pushing a cart is down from forty-two to twenty-eight minutes in the last ten years. As a result, Frisch argues: "Brands have taken on an additional function. They have become a way to navigate through an increasingly complex array of choices, not just a mark of quality." On the loose, confused, and rushed, buyers are ready for a "place" that organizes their world.

Internet portals are the newest coil in a skein of similar schemes to capture customers, to, in effect, own them. You can go a long way back.

Among the most successful and long-lived portals in business history were the great fairs held in the Champagne area of France in the twelfth and thirteenth centuries. For about two hundred years they were *the* places to do business in Europe. All the continent's goods—silks and oils of the south, furs and grains of the north—came here to be sold and bought. These were wholesale markets, not retail—but they were the Comdex of medieval B2B; everyone who was anyone had to come. The fairs—there were six—lasted two months each, and the secret of their dominance was what happened in the second month, when the selling of goods died down and was replaced by a settling of accounts. According to Fernand Braudel, the great historian of early capitalism: "The orginality of the Champagne fairs lay less however in the super-abundance of goods on sale than in the money market and the precocious workings of credit on display there." Financiers and bankers, mostly Italian, set up tables and exchanged currencies, bought and sold short-term credit instruments, even did a little arbitrage. Double-entry bookkeeping hadn't been invented yet, but just about every other financial instrument known today had been. The fairs eventually declined, partly because technological improvements opened new land and sea trading routes, but their central role in finance persisted long after they ceased to be the center of trade in goods. That suggests, Braudel says, that the fairs became successful not because they aggregated stuff but because they provided an efficient mechanism for performing transactions and obtaining information and financial leverage.

Anyone can amass cool stuff. What makes a place work isn't the stuff; it's the fact that it's easier and more valuable to do business within than without. Aggregation gets you in the game. To play it well you also need financial services, the two brand functions (quality assurance and navigation through choices), and something more—a reason why this particular collection of services and brands is worth paying for.

Think, for instance, of another hegemon in business history: Sears, Roebuck & Co. General Robert Wood—who masterminded Sears's transition from catalogue merchant to retailer, officially ran the place from 1928 until 1954, and was its unofficial puppeteer even longer—didn't use the word "portal," but that's what he had in mind when he said Sears would be "the purchasing agent for the American people." And it was, dominating retailing as no store had, has, or will: By 1964 Sears was bigger than its five nearest competitors combined.

Wanna-be Web conquistadors might have studied how Sears exploited two new economic worlds: the between-wars migration from farm to city and the postwar diaspora from city to suburb. Like today's technological changes, these jarred people loose from traditional buying habits. Sears won their confidence by vouching for its merchandise—money-back guarantees were a Sears invention—and by making the store and its house brands more important than the identity of the manufacturers of the goods it stocked. Trust, then, was one of Sears's most valuable assets—as it is eBay's, for example. Aspiration was a second. Sears later became so uncool that it's hard to imagine or remember that, for a nation of ex-farmers and laborers, its name once embodied a dreamed-of middle-class lifestyle. (Today Sears touts other brands as a way to jazz up its name.) Sears also offered the crucial financial services. Sears beat Main Street because at Sears you could buy hardware, dinnerware, and underwear, and pay just one bill. It wasn't just Kmart and Wal-Mart that cleaned Sears's clock. Bank of America hurt Sears too. In *The Big Store,* which chronicles Sears's attempt to transform itself in the mid-1980s, Donald Katz writes of "the revenge of the small shops": Little stores, in malls Sears anchored, nibbled away its business. The mall itself became the portal—the way the network is replacing the desktop as the center of value creation in computing. That wouldn't have happened without Visa and MasterCard—payment-and-leverage mechanisms that allowed customers to shop at lots of different stores but pay just one bill. Sears itself recognized the problem: Though in 1972 more than half of American households had a Sears credit card, Sears rolled out the Discover Card in 1985, so that customers could write checks to Sears even if they didn't shop there.

Nothing like Sears has come into being online, though AOL, the Sears of Cyburbia, shows the most stomach for creating self-branded online products and the best instinct for the middle class. None has invented a way to buy things that leverages the consumer's time or money; Amazon comes closest with its patented 1-Click process, but it's a convenience, not a source of leverage.

Winning online, then, is a consequence of assembling the intangibles that make any knowledge-based relationship work: In a fluid, almost friction-free environment, stickiness comes from people, relationships, and systems. Talent and knowledge, in the form of management, personalized service, community, trust, brand, and editing, create winners.

WINNING ONLINE II: CHOKE POINTS

My wife's great-grandfather was a wealthy Montana rancher till he picked a fight with James J. Hill, owner of the Great Northern Railway. Hill retaliated, refusing to let his trains stop for Bard Vaill's cattle, and ruined him. It's the oldest game in town. Wrap your fingers around a jugular vein, then demand a toll from every passing corpuscle.

Free markets, through the law of diminishing returns, destroy profits; the businessperson's job is to stay ahead of the law by setting up shop in a marketplace that (1) is valuable and (2) can be made less than free. These control points—seizable, squeezable veins where money flows—change over time. A once-priceless franchise becomes just another business, less valuable or no longer controllable. For example, in a high-tech service economy, railroads are less important than they were; they also have less control over shippers, who have work-arounds—highways, airways, pipelines, phone lines.

Think of control points: What images come to mind? High ground, perhaps, like the Round Tops at Gettysburg; places of scarcity, like a spot on Iceland's Hofsá River during salmon season, or in the Lincoln Tunnel at rush hour; key intersections, such as the confluence of Regent Street, Shaftesbury Avenue, and Piccadilly in London.

Once upon a time, distributors occupied one of these catbird seats. Amsterdam's warehouses were the foundation of its prosperity in the Dutch golden age of the seventeenth century, when it was the richest city in the world; when goods moved slowly and unreliably, supply held the whip and demand obeyed.

Today, dominance rarely comes to the owner of a stockpile; in fact, it's not usually an issue of goods at all. Power—the ability to command an outsize profit—has migrated into the hands of people who hold valuable knowledge.

The goal is strategic control—defined not as unlimited power but the ability to make more money than your competitors. Says Adrian Slywotzky, the Mercer Management consultant who is the coauthor of *Profit Patterns,* there are ten ways to get control. The most powerful is to own the standard by which an industry operates. That's immensely powerful but very rare; most standards—the use of English, for example—are not private property. Next comes controlling the value chain, followed by "super market share"—in the eternal battle between Coke and Pepsi, the tide surges first toward one, then toward the other, but never toward a third party. After that come superior customer relations and a powerful brand. Sixth most effective as a source of strategic control, Slywotzky says, is a two-year head start over rivals, followed by a one-year lead; least effective are a significant (20 percent) cost advantage, control of commodity parts, and control of commodity distribution.

These don't change online, but an electronic environment affects the means by which companies can attain and defend them. Online, the importance and wealth-creation potential of physical assets is diminished in key ways. Location matters less. Bookstore chains like Borders and Barnes & Noble scrapped to locate stores in prime malls or on the best street corners; Amazon.com was instantly ubiquitous and equally convenient to customers in Manhattan, Manhattan Beach, and Manhattan, Kansas. Control of physical inventory matters less, because e-commerce reduces how much is needed. It's harder to be a monopoly supplier of any raw material when customers can get information instantly from anywhere in the world: You may be the only game in town, but your customers don't have to limit themselves to shopping in town. Obviously, and importantly, touch—which is to say tangibility—still counts. But it's less likely to be the decisive factor in exercising strategic control.

David Pottruck, president and co-CEO of Charles Schwab, described the Internet's effect on his business this way:

I heard Warren Buffet give a speech two days ago. He said: "I reward my managers for building a moat around our castle and then making the moat deeper, wider and filling it with alligators. I look at our company as a castle, the castle of capital. Other people want to take our castle away and take our capital way. And we want this moat around the company."

And somebody said to me, "What do you do?" I said, "Well, we don't have a moat. I keep trying to move the castle. As people get closer to my castle, I've got to move my castle over here. I've got to constantly reinvent how we serve customers better, faster, more value, more service—reinvent what service means."

Electronic commerce tends to reward mobility more than moats, but it's a foolish businessperson who doesn't use both. Whether you're castle or cavalry, however, your best arms come from an intellectual arsenal. Management, which seemed almost irrelevant when money grew on dot-com trees, is more important than ever. In particular, e-commerce rewards deft, agile, cost-conscious management—a strategy by which companies tie up as little capital as possible in plant and inventory and so are free to turn quickly to exploit a new opportunity or meet a new threat. Second, e-commerce allows companies to leverage information and knowledge assets over a wider base. GE leverages management skill and best practices horizontally over many different industries. Similarly, eBay was able to enlarge the market for collectibles exponentially by finding a way to take knowledge that had been highly and stubbornly localized and leverage it globally. Cisco systems leverages its demand information and structural capital vertically, with its suppliers and even their suppliers (we'll discuss that further in Chapter 6).

Third, the very existence of the Web increases the amount of business that has to take place in a store or office or on a golf course. Automated, hands-off transactions are most suited to commodity products or services (and can turn some items into commodities that used not to be)—a double-edged sword, but a powerful one. At the same time, commerce on the Web demands environments that are high in trust, which can be created by means of communities and brands, for example.

Above all, the Web accelerates and exaggerates forces already powerfully at work in economic life. The existence of knowledge as an economic resource in its own right, distilled out of physical goods or created out of the whole cloth of the human spirit, becomes even more evident online. It's more obvious, too, that companies are made of people, not stones and pipes; and the value of conversation, community, and voice increase, paradoxically, with our ability to conduct business remotely.

Companies, then, are becoming knowledge companies: entities that form around knowledge, like pearls around a grain of sand, and whose transactions consist, mostly, of creating, buying, selling, and processing knowledge. But what does that mean? What do knowledge companies do? Someone quipped: "The difference between theory and practice is greater in practice than it is in theory." In the next part of this book, we'll try to change that.

PART II

THE DISCIPLINES OF A KNOWLEDGE BUSINESS

Perhaps the most valuable result of all education is the ability to make yourself do the thing you have to do, when it ought to be done, whether you like it or not; it is the first lesson that ought to be learned; and . . . it is probably the last lesson that he learns thoroughly. . . . The great end of life is not knowledge but action.

THOMAS HUXLEY

CHAPTER 4

AN INTELLECTUAL CAPITAL STRATEGY: THE FOUR-STEP PROCESS

Here a star, and there a star
Some lose their way.

EMILY DICKINSON

Knowledge management was brand-new in 1995. By 1999, a survey by the Conference Board found, 82 percent of companies were pursuing knowledge management, and almost all the laggards said they planned to join the throng. Unfortunately 82 percent of the 82 percent also said they had established no specific goals they hoped to achieve.

Knowledge management isn't the first step toward running a successful business in the knowledge economy; it's the last. Great management of a lousy or nonexistent strategy is a dumb idea, like commanding an airplane that is gaining speed while losing altitude. Similarly, the best possible strategy will do little good against headwinds stronger than the best your plane can do. Executives all too easily confuse an *organization* with a *business.* They are different. An organization is defined from the inside out—by budgets, departments, org charts, and reporting relationships. A business is defined from the outside in—by markets, suppliers, customers, competitors. With knowledge as with anything else, there's no point in managing an organization that has no business to do, or business you haven't defined.

You can reconstruct the conversation, since you've had the same one: "The solution to our problem isn't to work harder. We're working too hard already. We've got to learn to work smarter. . . ." True, but how, exactly, are you supposed to do that come Monday? In this chapter, we will learn how to construct an answer to that question by taking the first, crucial, and too-often-omitted step: We will reveal the process by which companies can create a strategy for competing on the basis of knowledge and intellectual capital.

FINDING FAULTS

"Can you think of any business like this one?" asked serial entrepreneur Halsey Minor (founder of CNET and Snap.com) and John Hagel, formerly of McKinsey's strategy practice. Between them they'd seen more businesses than the editors of *Vogue* have seen legs. But no, we couldn't think of anything quite like this company, 12 Entrepreneuring, which is interesting in and of itself. More important, 12 is beginning to show how companies can establish a knowledge-based strategy.

Minor, together with Eric Greenberg (founder of Scient and Viant), founded 12 in January 2000 to be, they said, "an operating company whose mission is to reinvent business." That immodest statement means this: 12 aims to start or acquire, then operate, businesses that have the potential to change the game in their industries, an ambition fueled by their own money and some from Benchmark Capital (which bankrolled Ariba and eBay), plus $100 million from other sources, including superstar board members Marc Andreessen (Netscape), Pierre Omidyar (eBay), and Ted Waitt (Gateway). The company's name doesn't refer to a number of people, but to its Ozymandian goal, to have ideas that are off the charts—to create businesses that rate a 12 on a 1-to-10 scale. Unlike venture funds or incubators, 12 wants to operate companies, not just fledge them; unlike Berkshire Hathaway or the old Hanson Industries, I2 wants radical, industry-transforming companies, not established franchises.

Unlike traditional conglomerates, I2 is built on leveraging intellectual capital, not financial capital. The I2 team looks for places where a big idea, a hunk of entrepreneurial talent, and a little money can restructure a whole industry. Says Minor: "In the last century, capital was scarce. Now intellectual capital is more valuable, and the economy will organize itself around concentrations of intellectual capital. You can create enormous businesses that way."

John Hagel is I2's chief strategist. Hagel, who in his years at McKinsey wrote two smart books, identified four trends that, like tectonic plates, are deforming and reforming the business landscape and creating opportunites. First are *reverse markets,* where power moves to buyers. This is a well-trodden trend. Chapter 3 showed how, as markets become more transparent, power tends to move into the hands of whoever's paying. Hagel believes that a new kind of company—an "infomediary"—will organize these reverse markets by aggregating consumer knowledge and using it to negotiate with vendors. A related phenomenon, which Hagel doesn't discuss, is the increasing ability of consumers to self-organize and talk or trade among themselves. Before the courts stopped it, Napster, a software application that allowed anyone who wanted a digital version of a song to download a copy from anyone else who had one and was willing to share, created a market that stripped the supplier not only of reward, but even of the knowledge that his product was being traded. That genie won't stay stopped: A highly decentralized, unmanageable economy of freebies and gossip suddenly has global reach.

A second trend, says Hagel, is the *unbundling and rebundling of corporations.* General Motors separated itself from Delphi, the parts maker that was a GM subsidiary; Lucent, which had been AT&T's equipment supplier, was spun off on its own. A whole new industry, contract manufacturing, has sprung up to serve companies that see no need to own the plants that make their products. The trend is biggest in high-tech manufacturing—Cisco Systems never touches three-quarters of what it sells—where companies like Solectron and Flextronics are part of a $75-billion-a-year industry. It's also afoot in other industries; for instance, *The New York Times, The Wall Street Journal,* the *International Herald Tribune,* and the *Financial Times* have become national newspapers in the United States by shipping their pages electronically to printing presses nationwide. Companies have also hived off operating responsibility for such functions as payroll, information systems, even human resources.

Third, *industry boundaries are eroding* and re-forming: AOL buys Time Warner, financial services converge, cable TV companies enter the phone and Internet industries. My mother used to say, to keep her kids from killing each other, "Your rights stop where my nose begins." We usually knew where the line was. In business, likewise, the boundary between one outfit and another used to be as clear as the nose on J. P. Morgan's face. It's a generalization, but not so windy that it does no good, to say that those old borders were marked by assets as we understood them. Your rights—and your wealth—stopped at the plant gate. That's now a barely tenable distinction.

In a fourth trend, *asset arbitrage,* companies liberate underworked assets. These often are knowledge assets that had been walled in by brick and mortar. For instance, the intellectual assets of Fingerhut (skill in direct marketing, fulfillment, e-commerce logistics), underleveraged by its retail home furnishings business, became a new company, Fingerhut Business Services.

These four trends reinforce one another. British Airways, for example, has unbundled parts of its business to focus on managing its route system. Rather than own airplanes, it leases them; rather than own and operate its own repair facilities, it sold the assets and contracts out the work. (Late in 2000 IBM did a similar deal when it sold its Amsterdam repair facility to Solectron.) For British Airways, owning an aircraft-engine repair facility in Wales was a money-losing proposition, so it off-loaded the plant to GE in 1991. For GE, the plant was an asset that could be arbitraged, put to work servicing engines owned by many different airlines—and it's become Rumpelstiltskin, a cash spinner in a business that's more profitable than selling new engines. In the industry as a whole, boundaries between buyers and sellers, operators and manufacturers, have shifted: American Airlines spun out Sabre, its reservation system, but owns part of Travelocity, an online travel agency.

It's on these fault lines that 12 is building. One of the company's core processes is that of investigating new business opportunities, running ideas over various hurdles. When an idea gets a go, it's surrounded with a small start-up management team led by a "business builder," who is its interim CEO. His (or her) primary job is to get the business up and running, rather like a turnaround specialist or a transition manager in an acquisition; he hires a staff and also can call on 12's "entrepreneurial operations team" of advisers in finance, HR, legal, marketing, strategy, and so on. His second responsibility, assuming the first is accomplished, is to work with 12's leadership to find "permanent" management and work out the business's connection to the mother ship. Will it remain at home? Will a portion or all of the equity be spun out to partners or the public?

12's first business, iBuilding, debuted in the autumn of 2000, and aimed to transform a brick-and-mortar business in the most literal sense. iBuilding attempts to make a unified, knowledge-intensive, Web-based business out of the services and functions in office buildings. Finance, procurement, inventory management, maintenance, work orders, resource planning (such as scheduling loading docks and freight elevators for tenant moves)—in most Class-A office buildings, according to Ken Jones, the business builder in charge of iBuilding, these are managed on clipboards or with unintegrated, DOS-based applications.

This is an operating system for real estate, in effect—an unbundling and asset arbitrage play, and a big one. The idea came out of Tishman Speyer, the big New York realty company that manages Rockefeller Center, among other properties. Tishman, sensing this should be a business on its own, found its way to 12 as partner and customer. iBuilding doesn't intend to own or operate real estate. As Jones says, it's "a tech company." As the business grows, Jones hopes its system will be used not only in skyscrapers but to centralize the management of smaller buildings, or to improve operations in service-intensive buildings such as hotels.

12's second business, named Grand Central, is about rebundling. It's aimed at a hot area of Internet commerce: application services providers. ASPs are companies that offer, in effect, outsourced software. Rather than buy or build software for sales force automation or financials, companies can subscribe to an ASP, which hosts and manages the data and the software. (In a sense, ASPs are like contract manufacturers: They assume responsibility for building, maintaining, and upgrading their clients' information-processing factories, the way contract manufacturers handle their customers' molecule-manipulators.) That's a substantial opportunity: Perhaps half of all IT spending is for self-written software.

Web services like ASPs begin to change the whole definition of an enterprise. A business becomes a collection of applications, some of which it owns, some of which are housed outside, on the Net. Starting five years ago, as a big, abiding consequence of the emergence of a global information network, companies began fuzzing up the boundaries between themselves and the outside world. What's "inside" and what's "outside" is no longer clear.

Data centers once were fortresses—impervious, impermeable, incommunicado even from the next department. Outsiders rarely saw your data. Heaven forfend they should touch it. Says Minor, "Before 1995, no one put an application outside the enterprise. Now you run a few inside the firewall, others are hosted by Loudcloud, others belong to suppliers or customers." For that to work, the hosted applications must talk to each other—so that my sales tool, hosted by Salesforce.com, say, ties in with my human resources tool, hosted by Corio—and with in-house applications. That's the opportunity Grand Central's after: It's an attempt to set a standard (XML-based, for those interested in such matters) to send data and messages among any set of ASPs.

It's far too soon to know if 12 will be a 12 or a 6. However well the company does, it's using a powerful insight. 12 examines vertical industries and horizontal value chains with a new eye. The traditional way of looking at value chains is to see who owns what—to follow the physical movement of goods and services from farm to refrigerator, or from mine to showroom. 12 looks at the intellectual value chain: the flow of goods, services, and information through sets of ideas, processes, and intellectual property. 12 sees a business as if it were a suite of software applications.

It's hard to make the shift to break the intellectual assets out on their own. When you do, however, your image of an industry can change, like an Escher drawing, to reveal opportunities: an infrastructure management business in logistics, or a customer-management business, like Amazon.com. Maybe there's an idea factory inside your assembly plant. Says Scott Durchslag, another ex-McKinseyite on the team: "This is about taking the power of people and ideas to the extreme."

FIND THE KNOWLEDGE BUSINESS

There are four steps in the process of developing an intellectual-capital strategy, and 12 Entrepreneuring exemplifies the first one: *Identify and evaluate the role of knowledge in your business—as input, process, and output.* You're looking for answers to the following questions:

- How knowledge-intensive is the business?
- Who gets paid for what knowledge? Who pays? How much?
- Is this a good knowledge business? That is, does whoever owns the knowledge also create the most value?

In more and more cases, the answer to the last question is yes. The chart on page 60 shows how the stock market has rewarded players in the personal-computer industry. (Some companies included in the data, such as Oracle, Motorola, and IBM, do business outside the PC industry; for them Mercer Management Consulting estimated the value of the PC portion of the company.) In the 1990s, the total market capitalization of the industry multiplied fifteen times, enough for almost everybody to get rich. But a disproportionate share pooled in one place—software. (An awful lot of that flowed to one company, Microsoft.) Not surprisingly, the market capitalization story is also the margin story: According to *Value Line,* during the period from 1991 through 1998, Microsoft's operating margin rose from 39.4 percent to 56 percent; Intel's went up from 31.4 percent to 43.2 percent; manufacturer Compaq's fell from 14.2 percent to 6.2 percent. Distributor Ingram Micro, which went public in 1996, saw its operating margin bump along at about 2.5 percent.

Match the market cap and the operating profits up against the knowledge intensity of what these companies sell. Microsoft sells logic—a series of if/then propositions that can be sold in an entirely dematerialized form. Intel's output is the next closest to pure knowledge—not logic itself, but logic chips. Manufacturers like Gateway assemble these (and other, less knowledge-intensive) items and put them in boxes; distributors put the boxes in boxes and ship them. (Of course, Ingram Micro and rivals like Merisel and MicroAge do more than slap labels on cartons and phone UPS—I'll get to that in a moment.) Look at it another way: If you had a scale on which you could weigh a day's work at each of these companies, the tonnage would be inversely proportional to their margins and market value.

The anomaly in this scheme is, of course, Dell Computer. Dell's operating margin rose during the decade; it was 11 percent in 1998. One possible explanation: Since Dell sells directly to customers, maybe it adds a shipper's sliver of profits on top of the meager manufacturing margin. That might account for the margin, but not for the market value. Wall Street screams if a company tries to grow revenues at the expense of margins.

MARKET VALUE: PC INDUSTRY

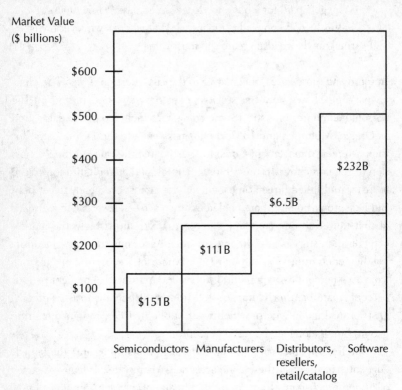

Market Value
($ billions)

$600

$500

$400 $232B

$300 $6.5B

$200 $111B

$100

$151B

Semiconductors Manufacturers Distributors, Software
resellers,
retail/catalog

As of 3/31/98
Source: Mercer Value Growth Database

But Dell, with a market cap of about $115 billion, is worth more than the PC businesses of all its rivals combined, and it also had the highest price-earnings ratio.

Says Adrian Slywotzky of Mercer Management: "On the face of it, Dell is a hyperefficient distributor. Beneath, it's something else." Dell collects a tremendous amount of unique market knowledge. Its famous Web pages are build-your-own sites where buyers can select and customize a computer for personal use, or order one built to their company's specs. Dell knows exactly what every segment of the market wants, with no scrim, no lag—and can see upstream as acutely as it sees downstream. The result, says Slywotzky: "Dell knows more than any other OEM and more than any distributor, because they see the market directly. And they know without guessing."

Dell isn't the first business to become rich and powerful by setting up shop at the intersection of supply and demand. Dell is much like Medco—the pharmaceutical benefits manager that in the late 1980s began aggregating information about the end-user market for prescription drugs. That knowledge became powerful enough to reduce drug makers' margins, and explains why Merck bought Medco in 1993. Cisco Systems, in the networking business, and Charles Schwab, in brokerage, have emulated the strategy. In Schwab's case, for customers who use the Web, the company can see direct, unfiltered, cause-and-effect relationships between research reports and stock or mutual fund sales.

To make money, you have to have something that is both valuable and unique. Though Ingram Micro and its rivals in distribution have long been doing assembly, configuration, and systems-integration work, they haven't been able to do what Dell, Microsoft, and Intel do: use knowledge to produce an advantage—in cost, in responsiveness—that significantly increases their take from the value chain. When Ingram Micro tried to raise prices in 1999, customers crossed the street, the company had to announce earnings shortfalls to Wall Street, and the CEO resigned. In 2001 the entire technology business got clobbered by recession and the PC industry struggled against the additional burden of its product becoming a mature commodity. In that murderous environment, the three knowledge hegemons—Dell, Intel, and Microsoft—suffered far less than rivals Compaq and Gateway, AMD, and Oracle.

You can do this analysis vertically, as we just did, or horizontally, comparing competitors to see who is most rewarded for his knowledge. Looked at from that perspective, there are three 800-pound gorillas in the PC industry: Microsoft, Intel, and Dell each accounts for more than half the value of its piece of the industry—and in each case the secret of its control is an intangible knowledge asset: Microsoft controls a standard, such that all its competitors have to labor to make their software compatible; Intel, which also controls a standard, has a record of being able to innovate faster than its rivals; Dell, in a tough business, outperforms because it owns unique real-time knowledge of supply and demand, and has the ability to exploit it both upstream and downstream to reduce working capital—indeed, Dell, which gets paid by customers before it has to pay its suppliers, has negative working capital, making the company part bank. Yes, both Intel and Dell have major investments in tangible assets, too, but that's not why you wish you'd been among their early investors.

There are other ways to examine whether your business is a good knowledge business. Essentially, you need to compare its current and potential knowledge intensity with its current and potential profitability. Set up a grid like the one below. Pick the measure of profitability you value the most—return on equity, economic value added, return on net assets, EBITDA (earnings before interest, taxes, depreciation, and amortization). There are several possible ways of measuring knowledge intensity. For businesses where innovation is the most vital success factor, you might select research-and-development spending, expressed as a percentage of revenues; that's a useful measure for comparing companies because audited R&D figures are published in annual reports. Related measures of innovativeness include percentage of sales from new products, patents awarded, and patents cited. In businesses whose *raison d'être* is to deliver

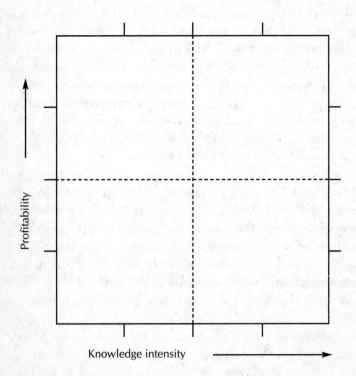

high-quality services, knowledge intensity can be approximated by figuring the percentage of knowledge workers (again, defined by economist Nuala Beck as "professionals, senior management and technical, engineering and scientific staff . . . the people in the organization who are paid to 'think' "); per capita training expenditure is a similar proxy. An excellent if hard-to-get measure of knowledge intensity is to total up all of a company's spending on knowledge: all knowledge bought from outside vendors, from telecommunications equipment to magazine subscriptions, from consulting fees to auditing; all internal knowledge costs, including R&D, training, home-brewed software development and information systems; and all management activities. Again, these costs should be expressed as a percentage of sales. It's difficult, probably impossible, precisely to compare all knowledge spending from one company to another, since companies report general and administrative costs in different ways; but benchmarking databases (such as the PIMS database [see Chapter 14] and studies by the American Productivity & Quality Center),* along with general industry knowledge, should permit a pretty good guess. Last, knowledge intensity can be measured using the tools described in Chapter 14.

You can use this grid in any number of ways. First, you can use it to get a general sense of the knowledge intensity of various businesses. On page 64, for example, courtesy of the Marakon Associates consulting firm, are the thirty companies in the Dow Jones Average as of the end of 2000, with profitability measured by economic value added (return on equity minus the cost of capital) and knowledge intensity measured by market-to-book ratio. Companies like Coca-Cola and Merck, high in the upper right quadrant, show themselves to be both highly knowledge-intensive and highly profitable. These are great knowledge businesses. In Merck's case, the knowledge intensity comes from continuing investment in R&D and marketing; Coke's knowledge intensity is primarily an expression of the company's brand equity. What about AT&T, down on the bottom left—

---

* APQC, based in Houston, is invaluable to companies seeking to improve their management of knowledge. One of its primary services is its International Benchmarking Clearinghouse, which conducts benchmarking studies, whose results it shares with participating member organizations. Visit them at www.apqc.org or write apqcinfo@apqc.org.

PROFITABILITY OF DOW JONES INDUSTRIALS

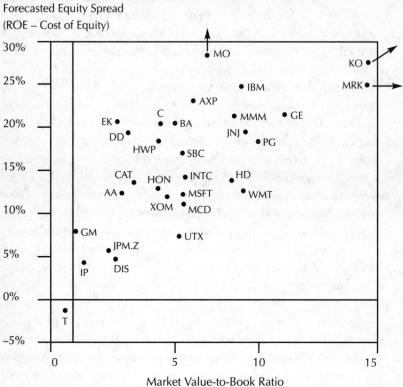

Forecasted Equity Spread
(ROE – Cost of Equity)

AA	Alcoa Inc.	HON	Honeywell International Inc.	MO	Philip Morris Cos Inc.
AXP	American Express			MRK	Merck & Co.
BA	Boeing Co.	HWP	Hewlett-Packard Co.	MSFT	Microsoft Corp.
C	Citigroup Inc.	IBM	International Business Machines Corp.	PG	Procter & Gamble Co.
CAT	Caterpillar Inc.				
DD	E. I. du Pont de Nemours	INTC	Intel Corp.	SBC	SBC Communications Inc.
		IP	International Paper Co.		
DIS	Walt Disney Co.	JNJ	Johnson & Johnson	T	AT&T Corp.
EK	Eastman Kodak Co.	JPM.Z	J. P. Morgan & Co.	UTX	United Technologies Corp.
GE	General Electric Co.	KO	Coca-Cola Co.		
GM	General Motors Corp.	MCD	McDonald's Corp.	WMT	Wal-Mart Stores
		MMM	Minnesota Mining & Mfg. Co.	XOM	ExxonMobil Corp.
HD	Home Depot Inc.				

surely a lot of knowledge is required to design, build, and operate the phone system? The grid isn't saying otherwise; it's saying that the market doesn't put a high value on that knowledge—maybe because it's not worth much, or (more likely) because AT&T hasn't found a way to liberate and exploit its value. In general, as you would expect, the trend line in the grid runs from bottom left to upper right: Greater knowledge intensity is associated with greater profitability.

You can also use this grid to compare one company to its competitors, or one business unit to its siblings. When you do so, remember the bottom-line question: Is this (or can this become) a good knowledge business? You can increase the knowledge intensity of any business by upgrading your network, doubling your training budget, and saying yes to every budget request from the lab. If those steps won't increase profitability, *don't take them*. You're looking for a strategy that invests in intellectual capital to make the business worth *more*.

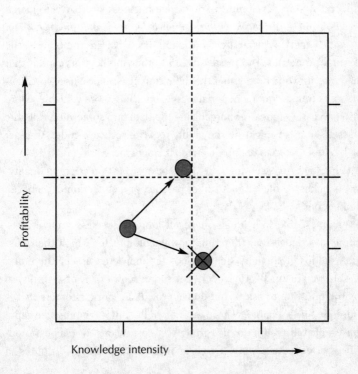

By the same token, if you find that your company or industry ranks low in knowledge intensity, remember—there's a knowledge business buried in that pile of assets somewhere, a revenue stream that flows from intellectual capital rather than some other source. To discover it, you might, if you are a manufacturer, recalculate your costs and margins as if you outsourced all supplies, components, and assembly, reimagining yourself as a design and marketing shop. Or, with McKinsey consultants Jonathan D. Day and James C. Wendler, ask this question: "If our operating margins fell sharply—perhaps as a result of a price war or an irrational competitor's actions—do we have service or information businesses that could remain profitable?" What better way to drive up the stock price and make a bundle for yourself than to give a big, dumb business a radical, profitable restructuring by means of intellectual capital?

FIND THE KNOWLEDGE ASSETS

The second step in developing a knowledge-business strategy is to *match the revenues you've just found with the knowledge assets that produce them*. What is the expertise, what are the capabilities, what are the brands, the intellectual properties, the processes, and other intellectual capital that make money for you? Remember the definition of assets we used in Chapter 1: Assets transform raw materials into something more valuable. Mere data isn't an asset; a means of organizing the data into something valuable is an asset. An asset might be the ability to write software code. An asset might be superior market intelligence. It might be world-class R&D in laser technology. An asset might be a database of best practices, a quality-control checklist, a file cabinet full of patents, or a collection of painfully learned lessons.

Companies, like individuals, have all kinds of useless know-how—including knowledge that they think is valuable but for which their customers wouldn't give a fig. When you look for knowledge assets, therefore, make sure you're uncovering beef, not sacred cows or, worse, bullshit. Here's the question to ask: What do we provide for our customers that is both unique and valuable? These are not skills, but attributes like rapid response, reliability, superior design, lowest cost, widest or deepest product line, better features, etc. Discover these not by listing attributes in some vague way, but by defining them from the outside in—in terms of the expectations and experience of customers. Then check the list: First ask employees to verify (or dispute) the value and uniqueness of the attributes. Do they agree? Is that what they think they're providing? Is that what management rewards them for? Revise the list if you need to, then check it with customers themselves.* Why do they come to you? What aspects of your performance do they find especially valuable, and what can they not find done (or done as well) anywhere else? While you're at it, ask them what they think you overvalue—what you brag about that is nothing special, or that is even inferior. How do your talents and attributes stack up against the competition's?

These attributes are the manifestations of intellectual assets. To find the assets means, again, looking at what produces the rapid response, reliability, superior design that get you business. Identify the assets: Give them names.

Examine, too, the structure of the assets you have thus uncovered. Are they primarily people-based—that is, composed of human capital? Or are they found in documents, intellectual property, and other structural capital, or in relationships with customers and suppliers? (See Chapter 1 of this book and Chapter 5 of *Intellectual Capital* for more on these distinc-

---

*This is the first step in a process of calculating "Company IQ," a measure developed by Bates Gruppen, the Norwegian subsidiary of the advertising company. It is discussed in more detail in Chapter 14. Note that it is possible to map these attributes on a 2 × 2 matrix, with one axis scoring their uniqueness, the other their value. I didn't do it here because I've already inflicted enough 2 × 2s on you, though I rather like this one:

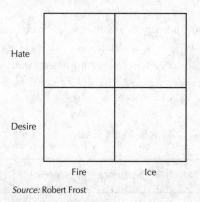

Source: Robert Frost

tions.) Pay particular attention to intellectual assets that are structured differently between one company and its competitors. The McKinsey consulting firm, for example, is human-capital intensive; if you hire McKinsey, a small number of very smart, skillful people will work closely and intimately with your business. Its competitor Accenture, the former Andersen Consulting, has chosen a business model that relies more heavily on structural capital. If you hire Accenture, a larger number of people, led by experienced consultants but including many young, freshly minted MBAs, will work with you; their particular strength will be in adapting previously developed models (including software) to your needs—reuse and customization more than custom service. If the same intellectual asset can take human, structural, or customer form, you may have an opportunity to change your business strategy by changing the way you structure your talents.

In addition to the structure of your intellectual assets, analyze their defensibility and uniqueness. How easy is it for competitors to clone what you so painstakingly nurtured? How mobile are key employees? Can your patent be circumvented? It's standard practice for companies that file a patent to survey the surrounding intellectual-property landscape to see how to defend what they have, and also to see what complementary assets (intellectual or otherwise) they need to develop and exploit their idea. You can perform a similar analysis on every kind of intellectual asset: What complementary assets, physical, financial, or intellectual, does it depend on? Does my talent creating video games put me at the mercy of Sony, or does my ability to operate a hyperefficient airline depend on my acquiring landing rights? What do I have, where are my gaps, and what are the ways to plug them?

Third, analyze your industry to see how value is created and realized. In 1985, Harvard Business School professor Michael Porter described what he called the "value chain." Oversimplified, value-chain analysis tracks inputs and outputs from raw material to end user, showing how value is added at each stage:

A VALUE CHAIN

Logistics in   Production   Logistics out   Marketing   Service

The value chain is such a powerful metaphor that it's easy to forget that it's very much a manufacturing image—indeed, it looks like an assembly line—and ill suits many industries. To apply it to services, particularly to knowledge-intensive services, can involve such Procrustean stretching, lopping, and bending as to distort rather than illuminate what's really happening. A value chain has a beginning, middle, and end. A bank's value proposition is more like a Möbius strip: Depositors in a bank supply the money it lends to borrowers, but they are just as much customers as the borrowers are, just as the borrowers are suppliers of the fees that pay interest to depositors. Companies like these are *value networks* that earn their keep by providing a meeting place for transactions—perhaps facilitating direct connections as do Verizon, FedEx, and Monster.com, or creating pools of capital or risk, like Wells Fargo and AXA, the insurance company. Another set of companies are problem solvers. Law firms, consultancies, hospitals, and laboratories have intake procedures and outcomes, but the activity in between is rarely linear, involving instead back-and-forth collaboration among specialists. These are *value shops*, not value chains: A customer comes in with a problem; there's a workup, a diagnosis, and a plan of action.

These distinctions matter. A value network probably has high fixed costs and low variable costs, and asset utilization is central to its success; a value shop's costs are likely to be the other way around, and its economics depend on the quality of its teams of experts. In a value chain, you usually

A VALUE NETWORK

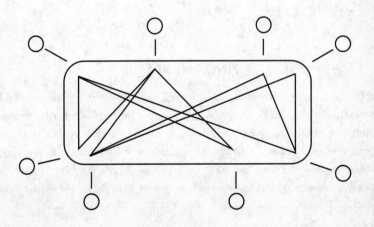

A VALUE SHOP

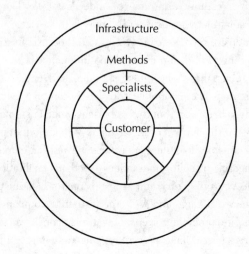

know who is involved: The ball goes from Tinker to Evers to Chance. Not so in a value shop, where today's customer might need a cardiologist and a surgeon, tomorrow's a neurologist and a physical therapist.

Whatever the setup—chain, network, shop—focus on the knowledge and knowledge assets involved. In classic value-chain analysis, there are two parallel tracks—primary activities (shown above in their generic form) and support activities (legal, financial, human resources, etc.) In knowledge-intensive businesses, once-secondary functions might be where vital intellectual assets hide.

FIND THE PLAN

If you've come this far, you have identified the knowledge transactions and revenues in your business—who sells what, who buys what, who profits and how much; you have identified the knowledge assets that produce what's bought and sold, both yours and those belonging to others in your business; and you have looked at the structure of the industry. Next, you need to *develop a strategy for investing in and exploiting your intellectual assets.*

This is not the place for a primer on strategic planning,* but rather for a discussion of the special options knowledge assets present. Any strategy needs a unique value propositon (*something customers want . . .*), a source of control (*that I've got and others can't get . . .*), and a profit model (*with a meter attached*). Knowledge-based strategies need something else. They need to build on the pillars of the knowledge economy: the growing knowledge-intensity of products, services, and jobs; the primacy of intellectual assets over physical ones; and the value of knowledge management. Each suggests an approach to knowledge strategy.

Knowledge-intensity strategies. One family of knowledge strategies exploits the value of knowledge itself by going to market with more knowledge-intensive goods and services. No companies better exemplify the knowledge-intensity strategy than General Electric and IBM, two grand old corporate warhorses that, in the 1990s, transformed themselves into knowledge enterprises and, in the process, lavishly rewarded their shareholders. Not that GE and IBM weren't knowledge-based before. GE established the first U.S. industrial lab to do research in pure science (in Schenectady, New York, in 1900); IBM is the company famous for its one-word motto, *Think*. But in the 1990s, both Jack Welch and Lou Gerstner, the chief executives of GE and IBM, respectively, realized that they needed to increase the knowledge content of what they sold. One of the primary ways they did this was to begin selling product services. Thus GE, in addition to building jet engines for airplanes, invested large amounts of money in the business of repairing and servicing them as well. For airlines, repair and service were costs they wanted to be rid of. For GE, they became a business more profitable than making the engines in the first place—and, notice, one based essentially on the same body of knowledge. IBM similarly increased the size of IBM Consulting and IBM Global Services; in the latter, it began offering contracts on computers made by its competitors as well as its own. It's too facile to describe these changes as just decisions to start selling services. The more valuable insight is that by means of the changes, both companies became more knowledge-intensive. IBM sells network management as well as computers that are nodes

---

* Michael Porter's *Competitive Strategy* and *Competitive Advantage* (New York: The Free Press, 1980 and 1985) are two good ones. *Competing for the Future,* by C. K. Prahalad and Gary Hamel (Boston: Harvard Business School Press, 1994), is another.

on a network. GE not only sells products made according to the demanding quality discipline called Six Sigma; it teaches the discipline itself. By the turn of the century, both manufacturing paragons were getting more revenue for knowledge services than from product sales.

There's more than one knowledge-intensity strategy. As we'll see in Chapter 7, you can decide to increase the knowledge content of what you sell (making smart products) or you can decide to sell the smarts themselves, perhaps in the form of services. In addition, you can choose where the organization's "knowledge factory" ought to be. When Bob Buckman succeeded his father as CEO of Buckman Laboratories, a Memphis-based specialty-chemicals maker, the company's slogan was "Creativity for Our Customers," but all the creating was done in laboratories, with nary a customer in sight. Buckman moved the creativity to the front lines. Today, 40 percent of Buckman Laboratories' employees are out selling and 72 percent are college graduates, vs. 16 percent and 39 percent in 1979. More than a third of sales are from products less than five years old, vs. 14 percent in 1979. Buckman's secret was, essentially, to get chemists out of their labs and onto the road, working with customers at customer sites, and to link them to their colleagues by means of computers.

Asset strategies. The second pillar on which the knowledge economy stands—the fact that knowledge assets have become more important than physical assets—suggests a second family of knowledge-business strategies. One way to exploit knowledge assets is to use them to increase returns on physical or financial wealth; in this way, knowledge becomes a gear that makes hard assets work harder. It's a strategy worth investigating in any business where asset utilization is a big deal, which is one reason oil companies have been among its most assiduous and successful exponents. Faced with declining oil prices during most of the 1990s,* big oil companies pushed desperately to lower their costs. They merged—Exxon and Mobil, British Petroleum and Amoco, Chevron and Texaco—to cut over-

---

* As I write this, early in 2001, oil prices are again high, and energy prices, particularly in California, are wacky. Not for long: Energy, like all commodities, slowly descends in price in real terms.

head (and also to reduce that nasty, price-threatening phenomenon, competition). The best of them also identified, developed, and exploited knowledge assets to operate their gargantuan and costly physical plants more efficiently. Chevron is a case in point. Under the leadership of Greta Lydecker and with the enthusiastic support of CEO Kenneth Derr, Chevron dropped its operating costs in seven years from about $9.4 billion a year to $7.4 billion, a saving Derr credits in considerable measure to the company's ability to use knowledge assets to manage its physical assets more efficiently. For example, a companywide energy-efficiency project collected data from all Chevron facilities to identify the best ways to pinch a kilowatt-hour, then shared the best practices—a knowledge asset— via a community of energy-efficiency experts. That work saved Chevron about $200 million a year. A second effort created the Chevron Project Development and Execution Process, a set of procedures, benchmarks, and lessons learned that improved Chevron's management of major capital projects to the tune of perhaps 15 percent—a billion-dollar saving since 1992.

Almost anyone can gain by using knowledge assets to replace physical assets, whether by reducing working capital (chiefly inventory—see Chapter 5) or finding ways to manage machinery better. The significance of the gain depends on the asset intensity of the business, but the opportunity can be astounding. According to Brookings Institution economist Robert Litan and Alice Rivlin, ex–vice chairman of the Federal Reserve, U.S. truckers stand to gain $75 billion a year by using Internet technology to schedule trucks to run with fuller loads and over the most efficient routes. Today the cost of shipping goods by sea is just a tenth of what it was in the late 1980s. The Pacific Ocean is as wide as ever, but the cost of shipping a VCR across it, once $30, is now about $1.50. Ships are bigger, but not appreciably faster. Fuel's not cheaper. The big saving is in developing information-processing assets that improve the utilization of physical assets and working capital. Highly sophisticated computers run complex mathematical calculations to track containers, plan how they should be loaded and unloaded, and communicate with fleets of trucks and rail cars so that nothing waits on a dock; similarly, customs transactions are handled electronically, with ships cleared through customers often before they arrive at their destination.

A second set of asset-based knowledge strategies involves amassing, using, and trading knowledge assets themselves. One approach: Decide to become an innovation powerhouse—that is, employ a strategy of knowledge-asset creation. That's long been the strategy of Minnesota Mining and Manufacturing, and for the most part has served the company well. Everything at 3M is designed to support its goal of continuously churning out new products and new uses for old products. Though the company appears to be organized conventionally, with business units arrayed in divisions and divisions grouped in sectors, it doesn't operate that way. The real organizational chart of 3M, as one executive described it, is more like an upside-down table. The leaves of the table are some thirty-three technology platforms—knowledge assets from which the company can generate multiple products for multiple markets, such as adhesives, chemical ceramics, fluorochemicals, microreplication, or precision coating. Sticking up from the leaves are hundreds of legs, each a business, some quite small, derived from the technology. An innovation-driven strategy is fundamentally different from one based on harvesting knowledge assets—so much so that it is difficult to run both strategies in the same shop. That's one reason 3M spun out its data storage and imaging businesses to create Imation in 1995.

The basis of another strategy can be the constant reuse of knowledge, as opposed to constant innovation. Reuse underlies the knowledge strategies of two companies we've discussed in this chapters. Chevron sought and found enormous savings by taking knowledge developed in one part of the company—in managing one refinery, say—and reapplying it to another. Accenture's focus is on developing consulting methods, computer code, and other knowledge assets, then selling them again and again to different customers.

Knowledge-asset strategies also comprise decisions about buying, licensing, and selling intellectual property. There are well-developed markets for some intellectual assets, and these represent a powerful way to exploit the value of knowledge. The ten biggest pharmaceutical companies get more than a third of their revenue from products they license from other companies. Keeping knowledge assets in-house isn't always the best way to exploit them. Palm, maker of the Palm Pilot, is betting that its operating system is worth more if it's shared among many manufacturers—Sony and Handspring, for example—than if the company tries to go it alone.

Philips Electronics, the giant Dutch company, turned itself around in the 1990s by means of an intellectual asset strategy. At the beginning of the 1990s, Philips was in trouble: It was slow-moving, slow-growing, barely profitable. Philips had great, innovative technology—the company co-invented the compact disc, for example—but seemed unable to extract much value from its brainpower. (In early 1992, at a time when many U.S. CEOs were being deposed by impatient shareholders, I overheard Philips's chief executive talking about the phenomenon with another CEO. "I'm awfully glad we're not a U.S. company," he said.) Over the next eight years, the company systematically identified technologies it wished to keep and technologies that, it decided, would be more valuable in other hands. Twelve different business units became half a dozen: semiconductors, consumer electronics, lighting, components (such as liquid crystal display monitors), domestic appliances, and medical imaging. Those businesses were chosen partly on the basis of their intrinsic growth potential but also on the company's competitive assessment of its ability to realize the potential. Thus Philips spent more than €4 billion on acquisitions to its semiconductor business, while at the same time unloading a great many other businesses. Among them were well-known brands like Polygram, Bang + Olufsen, and Grundig. Philips also had a little business—its sales were about €25 million a year—in optoelectronics, the relatively young business of sending electrical impulses through fiber-optic wires. In June 1998, Philips traded the business to an unknown little company called JDS Uniphase in exchange for about 20 million shares, 4 percent, of Uniphase's stock. Two years later, that €25 million business had a market value, in Uniphase stock, of €3 billion. Indeed, of the total market capitalization of Philips in 2000, 28 percent came from equity in other companies that Philips acquired by deciding its homegrown knowledge assets could be better exploited by someone else. (JDS Uniphase stock, like that of Corning and other optoelectronics companies, fell sharply when telecom capital spending collapsed in 2001; by then Philips had mostly sold its stake.)

Every knowledge strategy has its risks and potential rewards. Knowledge tends to be expensive to develop and cheap to copy. Therefore, going outside the company to acquire knowledge assets can save money—but also increases the risk that someone else can compete with you. The value of pure-knowledge companies—such as QUALCOMM, which is getting out of the business of manufacturing cellular phones and instead produces just their software, or Rambus, whose microprocessor technology is licensed to Intel, among others—can soar unweighted by the need to build complementary physical assets. They can also plunge like Icarus if the market decides that wax isn't wing enough—as both have. Monsanto took a huge—and, as it turned out, unwise—risk when it split into two companies, one (Monsanto) employing a strategy of innovation in biotechnology, particularly genetically modified agricultural products, the other (Solutia) focusing on best practices in the less innovative chemical business. Philips made a similar set of strategic bets—and in five years more than quintupled the price of its stock.

The point is that knowledge and knowledge assets require the same rigorous thinking as any other part of your business—and every strategic review must include an examination of knowledge assets. That includes a formal knowledge-gap analysis, which should be done once when you are analyzing your assets and again after you have laid out a knowledge strategic plan. Among the questions to ask: What do you need to know to carry out your plans? What do you know already? What do your competitors know? What are your knowledge gaps? How will you fill them—make, buy, or ally? How aggressive should your knowledge strategy be?

MANAGE THE KNOWLEDGE BUSINESS

The fourth step to the knowledge strategy process is to *improve the efficiency of knowledge work and knowledge workers.* A lot of what's touted and deployed as knowledge management comes into play in this stage, and we'll discuss it in detail over the next several chapters. Most companies do a dreadful job of managing knowledge, if they do so at all. That is starting to change. Economic evidence is starting to show that the marriage of computing and communicating is finally improving knowledge-worker productivity in measurable ways. Still, raising productivity in knowledge work requires fundamentally different management questions and approaches. Says management demigod Peter Drucker:

With traditional, manual work, no one ever asked the question, "What is the job?" The job, which was mostly manual work, programmed the worker. In your work and mine, however, nobody programs us. The question with knowledge work is not, "How do we do the job?" The question is, "What should we do?" That's a new question. It has rarely been asked and, even more rarely, answered.

THE FOUR-STEP PROCESS FOR MANAGING INTELLECTUAL CAPITAL

I. *Identify and evaluate the role of knowledge in your business—as input, process, and output.* How knowledge-intensive is the business? Who gets paid for what knowledge? Who pays? How much? Does whoever owns the knowledge also create the most value?

II. *Match the revenues you've just found with the knowledge assets that produce them.* What are the expertise, capabilities, brands, intellectual properties, processes, and other intellectual capital that create value for you? What is the mixture of human-capital, structural-capital, and customer-capital assets?

III. *Develop a strategy for investing in and exploiting your intellectual assets.* What are your value proposition, source of control, and profit model? What strategies exist to increase the knowledge intensity of your business? In what ways can you increase your ability to leverage your intellectual assets? Can you improve results by restructuring intellectual assets (for example, converting human capital into structural capital, or vice versa)?

IV. *Improve the efficiency of knowledge work and knowledge workers.* Bearing in mind that knowlege work does not necessarily follow the linear path that physical labor often does, how can you increase knowledge workers' productivity?

A decade ago, engineers at Bell Laboratories were asked to rate their own productivity. On average, they graded themselves C–, saying they were only 68 percent as productive as they ought to be; at the same time, however, they had no formal way of measuring what their productivity was. Most measured personal productivity by seeing how many items they had crossed off a to-do list; only one out of forty tried to measure his contribution to the company, and nearly half said they received no management feedback about productivity. No wonder knowledge-worker productivity lags.

Drucker's second question follows from the first: "What is the knowledge base required to do the job?" From the answer to these questions comes a third: How should this knowledge base be built, maintained, and managed? "Efficiency-driven knowlege management," as the A. T. Kearney consulting firm calls it, ought to be familiar ground. It's a production problem. Technology plays a major role in the production of knowledge, as it does in managing any production problem. Costs are measurable. Efficiency should be measurable: not in silly numbers, like how many hits a Web site gets—a datum as relevant as woodchuck productivity—but in terms of the productivity of knowledge work and progress toward executing a knowlege strategy. It should be measurable, that is, in profits.

INVESTING IN INTELLECTUAL CAPITAL: WORKING KNOWLEDGE HARDER, SMARTER, AND FASTER

Our England is a garden, and such gardens are not made
By singing:—"Oh, how beautiful!" and sitting in the shade.

RUDYARD KIPLING

The World Bank's field office in Pakistan had a problem. The bank was preparing a loan for highways, but the country's existing roads were breaking down far too fast. The government was considering using a different kind of pavement. The minister of transport wanted an answer immediately: Did the bank know if this stuff was any good? Time was, that question would have come into headquarters in Washington, D.C.; experts would have assembled, perhaps sent a deputation to Pakistan, and then after several weeks solemnly emitted an answer. This time—it was August 1998—the field officer went to the World Bank's Web site and, in a section about transportation, found a bulletin board to which he sent an e-mail describing the problem. Within a day he had a promising reply from Jordan and detailed information about the technology from

Argentina. Within a couple of more days, experts from South Africa and New Zealand put in their two cents, which included the Kiwis' guidelines for getting the best out of the technology.

The officer in Pakistan made his report to the government, but that wasn't the end of it. Says Stephen Denning, who headed the World Bank's knowledge management project: "Now that we have realized that we as an organization know something about a subject we didn't realize we knew anything about, we can incorporate what we have learnt in our knowledge base so that any staff in the organization anywhere at any time can tap into it."

That Web site resulted from the World Bank's conviction that its mission—to help developing nations grow—depended as much on brainpower as on money. "We need to invest in the necessary systems, in Washington and worldwide, that will enhance our ability to gather development information and experience, and share it with our clients," the bank's president, James Wolfensohn, said in 1996. That year the bank asked Denning to create a living map and library of everything it knows about what works and what doesn't in economic development. Just as bank accountants chart cash, loans, and other assets, Denning would chart knowledge assets.

His first job was to define the knowledge relevant to the bank's mission—the first step in the process outlined in the previous chapter. For profit-seeking companies, it's finding what knowledge is bought and sold. Working with an advisory board from the bank's operating divisions, Denning defined some eighty domains of expertise—vocational training, population control, etc.—in fifteen categories such as health, finance, education, and agriculture.

Across each domain, Denning then set out to identify and, if necessary, create knowledge assets, of eight different kinds. The most important was to find the people who live, breathe, and love a subject, the experts, thinkers, knowledge creators, and noodlers—not just bank employees, but kibitzers and clients as well. "Without a community of practice," he reasoned, "it's impossible to build a knowledge base." Second was to create an online presence for the domain, a "place" in the bank's knowledge-management architecture; that's less important than the community, but it's still a *sine qua non*: "We wouldn't be talking about this if the Internet didn't exist," Denning told me.

The network and the Net were the social and technical basics. From them, six other tasks followed: For each domain—there were eventually 114—Denning's team created a help desk, a who-knows-what Yellow Pages, a collection of key sector statistics, records of the bank's previous projects (emphasizing best practices and lessons learned), an electronic bulletin board, and finally provision for outsiders (such as the bank's client countries) to get into the system directly.

Knowledge management at the World Bank is striking for two things— its accomplishments, yes, but also a very successful failure. The bank's knowledge management system didn't try to create a lot of new knowledge; rather, it established a way to discover knowledge that already existed and then organize it so as to make it work harder, smarter, and faster. If knowledge assets matter—and if you're still reading, you agree—they mustn't be indolent. Most knowledge lives the life of Riley, curled up on someone's couch, asleep between sheets in someone's file cabinet, undisturbed on someone's hard drive; or it potters around in its own garden, unknown to and oblivious of a wide world of application. *If Only We Knew What We Know,* sighs the title of a fine book by Carla O'Dell and C. Jackson Grayson; "If only H[ewlett] P[ackard] knew what HP knows," echoed Lew Platt, that company's CEO from 1992 to 1999, his voice one in a Mormon Tabernacle Choir singing the same dirge. And knowing is only part of the problem; a corporate Hamlet, brilliant but unable or unwilling to act on what it knows, might as well know nothing. Our purpose in this chapter is to describe some practical steps companies can take to overcome ignorance and inertia.

CREATING KNOWLEDGE LEADERSHIP

In the last three years of the twentieth century, the title "chief knowledge officer" spread through the corporate world as fast as zebra mussels, those freshwater mollusks from the Caspian Sea that in less than a decade found their obnoxious way into every Great Lakes inlet and bay. By 1997, a fifth of the *Fortune* 500 employed someone who, in role if not always in title, was chief knowledge officer; by the end of the decade, rare was the big company without one.

I was leery of knowledge czars. These days executive suites are filled with chiefs of one thing or another who are notable chiefly for their lack of Indians. CXOs, they're called, and too often X, the unknown, is what good they do. Charles Lucier, the first CKO at the Booz Allen & Hamilton consulting firm, put the question well: "How many change leaders do you need?" Chief knowledge officer, chief information officer, and chief learning officer—are these real jobs, or are they the Larry, Moe, and Curly of the Information Age?

The short answer: They are real jobs—maybe not for the long run, but essential to get knowledge off its duff. There's a large, coherent, and profit-generating set of responsibilities that appropriately belong to one person—that is, it's a job. Unless someone holds the position, it won't get done.

CKOs showed up first in professional service firms, where, they claim, knowledge is the stock-in-trade. Says John Peetz, who held the position at Ernst & Young: "For us knowledge management is critical. It's one of our four core processes—sell work, do work, manage people, and manage knowledge." In his self-written job description, Peetz outlined three responsibilities for a CKO: evangelizing about the value of sharing knowledge; running and backing projects that find, publish, and distribute knowledge around the firm; and managing a staff of about 200 people, mostly in the firm's Center for Business Knowledge in Cleveland, and a firmwide infrastructure of Web sites. That's the right way to parse the job, though E&Y's is an unusually large operation.

None of those pieces is trivial. Take sermonizing. Nowadays, to say knowledge should be shared rather than hoarded is like saying motherhood is good—but that never stopped a willful child. In every organization I've seen, collegiality contends with subverters, wiggle-outers, and a few outright foes. Auditors, lawyers, security officers, personnel staff—everyone wants to keep secrets. Sometimes the secret-keepers have a point: Some forms of knowledge sharing, such as price-fixing, lead to the hoosegow. Some are leaks. A few years ago, signs at Xerox cautioned employees against blabbing confidences in elevators and hallways; yet we know that companies should encourage casual chat in places like hallways, because it's a powerful way to share ideas, according to studies—done by Xerox.

Part of the CKO's job is to nose out the difference between discretion and hoarding and to be a sort of in-house American Civil Liberties Union, arguing for the maximum freedom of speech, because most top staff people—the general counsel, the head of HR, the CFO—have institutional reasons to censor. The destruction of the World Trade Center by terrorists has given terrible new evidence of the importance of all kinds of security. This "culture war," as Peetz calls it, also rages in the business units. Says Erin Spencer, who served as Global Director of Research and Knowledge Management for Andersen Consulting (now Accenture) in the 1990s: "There's always some group that claims that its knowledge is so special that it mustn't be shared." A drug company's product-development teams must be discreet; but new-drug approval goes faster if knowledge is shared. In investment banking, M&A types may say there's no way to swap ideas without revealing clients' confidences. Could be; or could be a power trip. Either way, it takes a top-level guy to balance competing claims.

A second part of the CKO's job thus becomes polishing, packaging, and presenting knowledge—such as best practices—across functions or business units. These tasks range from exemplary small efforts, first stones in the pond, to huge projects that collect whole bodies of knowledge. In between, CKOs set companywide standards of format, access, and technology. Says Laurence Prusak, the head of IBM's Knowledge Management Institute: "There are a couple of competing visions for the CKO role. In one he leads a small group, one to four people, who act as catalysts; in the other, the CKO has heavy responsibility for a lot of databases, a technical infrastructure, and so on." At the World Bank, Denning did a lot of proselytizing and catalyzing, but his team's work product, the bank's knowledge management system, fell into the infrastructure-building category; most consulting firms have substantial, heavily staffed knowledge-management departments. At rabidly centrifugal Johnson & Johnson, by contrast, CKO Michael Bertha views his work as mostly arranging introductions for people with similar interests or problems. In general, the more decentralized a company, the more important the CKO's social-director role and the less meaningful it is to be an encyclopedist.

Jobs like this have a way of fading into the corporate woodwork—and should. In the 1980s, VPs of Quality appeared on organization charts, their names and pictures in annual reports; early in the 1990s came Rulers of Reengineering; now you find Emperors of E-commerce and CKOs. They have in common the need to execute an initiative that affects all lines of business and functional disciplines but isn't naturally part of any one of them and, furthermore, disrupts business as usual. Successful people usually can't spare resources, attention, or their best people to do anything except protect and extend their successes. Like the Ephesian silversmith Demetrius, who railed against the preaching of Paul because his livelihood depended on making gewgaws for the great Temple of Diana, they have cash flows at stake.

To get traction, new management ideas need independent funding and freedom from operational responsibility—and they need clout. ("I can call spirits from the vasty deep," Shakespeare's Owen Glendower boasted, to which smart-aleck Hotspur replied: "Why, so can I, or so can any man, but will they come when you do call for them?" Clout is when you can say, "They will if they know what's good for them.")

I know of no company that has substantially improved the productivity and value of its intellectual capital without a strong chief knowledge officer or a CEO so committed to the process that he might as well have carried the CKO title too. "You have to professionalize the management of knowledge assets," says Elizabeth Lank, who did just that in five years in the CKO role at ICL, Britain's big computer-services company, a subsidiary of Fujitsu of Japan. Leadership always matters.

CREATING KNOWLEDGE ASSETS

One of leadership's first jobs is to help an organization sort out what's worth knowing. As Lank puts it: "Don't manage all your knowledge, but decide what knowledge is critical." Call it a knowledge audit, call it knowledge mapping— by any name, the first step toward making knowledge work harder is to rouse it from its couch and line it up for inspection. "For us at ICL," Lank said, "the most important knowledge was *who knows what where*—the map of the experience and skills we have." When Lank started Project VIK—Valuing ICL Knowledge—she literally made a map. On a big piece of paper she drew ovals that represented ICL's knowledge assets; they numbered about a score by the time she was done, and included such competencies as designing the architecture of systems and developing new sales prospects. This was not a static document. In 1998, for example, ICL formed a strategic alliance with Microsoft. Lank recalls, "Suddenly knowledge of Microsoft technology became a much more important strategic asset, and I added it to my map."

Knowing about its powerful partner was—had to be—a key asset of ICL; but who knew what where? Centuries ago cartographers wrote "Here be monsters" on the edges of their maps. Whatever you think of the Beast of Redmond, that wouldn't do in this case. It turned out that ICL knew a lot about Microsoft, just as the World Bank knew a lot about asphalt, but the knowledge was scattered and self-centered: Purchasers here, programmers there, technicians hither, and consultants yon all knew a great deal about whom to call, whom to ask, how to configure, how to tweak, and how to fix, but never before had their knowledge been put into coherent, searchable, and transmittable form.

There's a major principle here: *Like pearls, knowledge assets form around irritants, such as real business needs.* Keith Todd, ICL's CEO when Project VIK began, griped: "All the knowledge systems were set up to support the chief executive—but it's the guy on the front line who really needs to know who our best technical experts are. Knowledge is most valuable in the presence of the customer." To reverse the systems' polarity, ask Peter Drucker's two questions: "What is the job?" and "What is the knowledge base required to do the job?" That means mapping knowledge assets should be done not by a CKO sitting in headquarters and, like the Kansas school board, deciding whether the kiddies need to learn the truth about evolution, but by a CKO helping business unit managers do their jobs. This is to say, further, *knowledge assets are created by asking customers what they expect you know and can do.* Knowledge asset registers shouldn't be overflowing, Lank advises: A work group or a department probably needs to focus on no more than half a dozen key skills. Those are the ones in which it should invest, the knowledge it should in some sense formalize.

All maps are fictions—two-dimensional simplifications of four-dimensional reality (time being the fourth dimension, and—where knowledge is concerned—often the most important one). To make sure your map relates to real life, connect knowledge assets to business processes and projects. Lank actually drew the connections—lines from her ovals to key processes like "prospecting for work." She also maintained a ledger of major corporate projects (and encouraged business unit heads to do the same) and tracked which projects were likely to employ which bodies of knowledge. She could then work with project leaders to make sure they got what they needed, and also, in the aftermath, added what they'd learned to the body of knowledge.

What goes in the ovals? The World Bank's list is a good one:

A community. If a body of knowledge is vital to your company, it has a community of practice—a group of people who may not be in the same department but who work, play, fiddle, and talk about the topic. The CKO should know who these people are, make a point of acknowledging their group identity, and offer help—financial and technical—so they can get together for a real or virtual beer every once in a while.

A place. If I want to tap into the market-research expertise of XYZ Corp., I ought to be able to go somewhere—online, almost certainly—that purports to be its home. I say "purports" because no space can truly collect and display even an eensy-beensy knowledge asset. But I need to know where to find the iceberg's tip.

A help desk. Every knowledge asset needs a librarian, whose job is two-fold: first, to give the tour to newbies and visitors, so they don't irritate the animals by asking dumb questions; second, to keep the place neat, to make sure out-of-date knowledge is purged from Web sites, and when someone says, "I don't have time to summarize this for the database," to stand over him till he does it.

A Yellow Pages. I'll discuss this in Chapter 8 along with other high-value knowledge projects. A who-knows-what directory is not the same as a community of practice. The latter is a club whose members know each other and value their work and, to varying degrees, their privacy. The former announces for the world to see the fact that Pamela_Ashby@xyzcorphq.com is the expert in contracts, but Patrick_Marquis@xyzcorphq.com is the entertainment law guru.

A primer. A quick introduction to the body of knowledge—frequently asked questions, a little bit about what you guys do here. What's the scope of the business? What do you sell? Who buys it? What goes into it? Part of a primer is a vocabulary. Companies and work groups need to have a shared functional vocabulary.*

Knowledge artifacts. The head and heart of any knowledge management system are the connections it makes among people, but its body consists of recipes, reports, databases, and other knowledge artifacts: documents, Web

---

* More than most people realize, companies risk the confusion that comes when people are "separated by the same language," as Shaw put it. In the waning days of Digital Equipment Corp., an internal consultant there told me about a meeting involving six or eight top executives who were discussing the company's strategy. Most of them had worked together for more than a decade; all of them talked all the time about the "architecture" of computer systems; and each of them had a different idea of what "architecture" meant in DEC's context.

pages, videos, and so on that describe how to make bleach, how to fix a Xerox machine, how to get FDA approval for a new drug. Inevitably, you (the knowledge manager, the people in the community, the users) will spend a lot of time adding and editing artifacts—I'll discuss this in detail in Chapter 7—but don't worry too much about it at first. Connection first, collection second.

A *bulletin board* where people can ask, "Does anybody know?" with a reasonable chance of receiving an answer from someone who actually does know. This may require intervention by the help desk/librarian.

A *doorway,* which is to say some sort of link between the knowledge asset ("Welcome to XYZ Corp.'s Legal Eagles Brief Place") and the rest of the organization. Since there is a difference between inside and outside, you'll have to make judgments about what to let outsiders see. Err on the side of openness.

Knowledge is not a scarce resource. Ignorance is—in the sense of knowing what to ignore, and how to cut through clutter, how to anticipate the direction from which demands on your talents will come. That is why mapping and creating knowledge assets begin with strategy and seek constantly to be validated by the market. Chevron, we saw in Chapter 5, built its knowledge strategy around the value of managing costs. Like Elizabeth Lank at ICL, Chevron's Greta Lydecker produced a paper document, titled "'Best Practices Resources Map." The Lydecker projection emphasized collecting and documenting money-saving processes and techniques. The big question for a service company like ICL, as for the World Bank, is different: "How do we marshal talent and resources to respond quickly to a client's needs?" For them, though it can be marvelous to codify knowledge, it is even more important to create systems and a culture that encourage continuous sharing and reinvention.

CREATING KNOWLEDGE CONNECTIONS

There's a paradox—almost a contradiction—in knowledge work. On the one hand, it is custom work. We talked about that in Part One: Whatever can be repeated can be automated and can become subject to Moore's Law. Its costs plummet; a rival reverse-engineers it; margins drop faster than a male stripper's trousers. Special work, unique work, increases the value of your relationship with your customers and gets you margin.

At the same time, the economics of knowledge reward leverage, and hugely. The economics of information make this so. First, there is no sure correlation between knowledge input and knowledge output. Double your production budget, and you will produce twice as many widgets. Double your R&D budget, and you have no way of knowing if you will double its output. Knowledge production is demand-driven. Furthermore, the cost of producing knowledge is little affected by how many people eventually use it. Usually its cost structure is heavily front-loaded—whether you're producing a new jetliner, a legal brief, software, or anything else. The marginal production cost may be nearly zero—a few clicks of the mouse, a couple of phone calls, a trip to the copying machine. It costs just as much to produce an episode of *The West Wing* if one person watches it as it does if 50 million people do so. Economies of scale matter in every business, but where knowledge is the product, the returns to scale go off the charts. Failure to leverage it, therefore, is stupid.

KNOWLEDGE COSTS ARE FRONT-LOADED
Ratio of sunk cost (cost of first copy) to marginal cost
(cost of subsequent copies)

Book	Automobile	Windows 95	TV broadcast
50,000 : 1	1 million : 1	100 million : 1	∞

So how do you combine customization with leverage? There is no magic answer, but that is a magic question. It is fundamentally the job of the knowledge leader to be asking constantly, *"Who else can use this stuff?"*

Case in point: Outside London, in the green and pleasant Thames Valley village of Marlow, stands the headquarters of Rank Xerox, the 80-percent-owned subsidiary of Xerox. Xerox, for all its faults,* has great expertise in benchmarking and sharing best practices. Benchmarking is a

---

* I've got a million theories about why Xerox's profitability fell off a cliff in 1999–2000. There are several proximate causes—a misbegotten or ineptly executed sales force reorganization, an inability to match HP and other printer makers as the copier and printer markets converged, accounting that might have disguised problems, etc. Underlying all that, something in Xerox's culture seems to shy away from urgent and emphatic action. It second-guesses itself obsessively. That's the bad news. The good news—for others if not always for Xerox—is that Xerox is therefore a fount of terrific ideas that can work better if applied with full-throated zeal.

matter of identifying who's best at something (in your company, in your industry, in the world), not by guesswork or reputation but by the numbers: The Widget division cuts an invoice for fifty-five cents; Gadgets, for forty-five cents; and Doodads, for thirty-five cents; so Doodads is the benchmark. Best-practice sharing means documenting how Doodads does dunning, then plagiarizing.

Like most companies, Xerox usually benchmarked costs. In late 1993, folks in Marlow got the idea of doing it to sales. The project was given to a team sponsored by Lyndon Haddon, a company director who was running operations in Eastern Europe, the Mideast, and Africa. Haddon and his crew set up a simple and remarkably successful program of plug-and-play benchmarking. Team members gathered all kinds of sales data, making country-by-country sales comparisons. It took just a couple of weeks to find eight cases in which one country dramatically outperformed the others. Somehow France sold five times more color copiers than its sister divisions. Switzerland's sales of top-of-the-line DocuPrint machines were ten times greater than those of any other country. One country suffered a 15 percent attrition rate when service contracts came up for renewal, but Austria lost only 4 percent.

Step two: Simply find out how it was done. Don't try to figure out why—just document the process. The team wrote up the eight cases and what the top country did. The book was given to each country's sales and service manager along with data about how his group compared to the benchmarks.

Implementation, of course, is where good ideas run aground, usually on one of three rocks: data denial (it just ain't so), exceptionalism (our market's different), or you-can-lead-a-horse-to-water-but-ism (your suggestions deserve careful study). When a company is decentralized, those rocks are close to the surface. Here denial wouldn't work because the documentation was about results: The Swiss were indisputably selling more DocuPrint machines. Xerox skirted the other two by giving country managers face-savers and choices. Country leaders were ordered to copy their colleagues' methods—but were allowed to pick whichever three or four (of the eight) they thought would work best. One surprising mandate from on high: Don't think, just do. Said Haddon: "They absolutely could not change anything in year one. Don't do the normal and say 'I can do better than that.' No one could be certain why something worked; so if you made a change, you might alter the very thing that was key." In most cases, country managers visited the benchmark country and copied and installed its method in a matter of weeks.

The results were breathtaking. For example, by copying France's practices in selling color copiers—chiefly improving sales training and making sure that color copiers were pushed through dealer channels as well as direct sales—Switzerland increased its unit sales by 328 percent, Holland by 300 percent, and Norway by 152 percent. Overall, Rank Xerox's internal audit group found that the program generated an extra $65 million in sales. That was 1.4 percent of sales. By the end of the second year, the combined incremental sales growth was 3.64 percent.

There are a couple of obvious lessons from this story. First, exceptionalism is the exception. Most production people know this by now, but, Haddon says, "it was a cultural shock for marketing people." Tell them France is better, and they say, "Well, the French are different."* Learning from differences is the point.

The biggest lesson: There's more knowledge lying around your shop than you think, and if you can put it to good use, it represents a lot of easy money. The value of knowledge assets can be multiplied many times, because they can be shared. As management consultant Sid Caesar said, "The guy who invented the first wheel was an idiot. The guy who invented the other three, he was a genius." Sharing knowledge is a core process of any knowledge company. I will discuss it—what works, what doesn't, and why—in the next chapter and in Chapter 11.† The essential observation here is this: *Every valuable piece of knowledge can be put to use by someone else, too.* A factory cannot be in two places at once, but an idea can.

---

* With this sentiment the French, of course, agree.

† It is worth mentioning here, however, the piece of hardware that has been documented to be the most effective means of sharing knowledge. It is called a coffeepot. Coffeepots are cross-functional and nonhierarchical. They encourage informal discussion. Serendipitous things happen around them. They are part of one's daily routine, and, except for wimps who drink decaf, are always stimulating. However, they do not scale well; people on different floors, in different offices, and in different time zones are rarely found around the same coffeepot. Also, some of what is shared around a coffeepot may be unrelated to increasing shareholder value, and what passes for knowledge might not always withstand rigorous analysis. The single greatest opportunity in knowledge management is to develop coffeepots that avoid these problems.

MANAGING IN REAL TIME

A few years ago—not all that long ago, but I'm not sure Jeff Bezos owned a razor—I opened my American Express bill on a Sunday night, about 10 P.M. In the envelope was a statement stuffer that offered a 25 percent discount on Michelin Green Guides. My family and I were planning a trip to France that summer, so I called the 800 number on the flyer. I got the following message: "Our office is now closed. Please call back during regular business hours, blah blah." Angry, I hung up. The next day, after I ordered the books, it dawned on me how remarkable it was that I had been annoyed—to the point of wrath—at being unable to buy a book at 10 P.M. on a Sunday.

Welcome to real time. Business moves faster than ever, and this isn't temporary: The Information Age is structurally fast and inherently volatile. This profoundly affects intellectual capital strategy, as well as all management practice. The reason for speed is simple: The pace of an economy is set by what's most valuable. If that's land, then commerce ambles with the turning of the seasons and slow changes in land tenure and fertility. No matter how fast your ship or fleet your messenger, there was a time to plant and a time to pluck up that which was planted. "We will sell no wine before its time," said advertisements for Paul Masson wines. Industrial goods moved faster, at the speed of clipper ships, then steamships, then railroads and trucks. Companies built large factories at transportation centers like Chicago or Essen; it took time to bring everything together in one place, but it was worth it to maximize manufacturing efficiency, because manufacturing value mattered most. Clarence Birdseye learned how to freeze vegetables; beans and peas became industrial products, shipped from field to factory to urban or suburban dining room, carried by fast, refrigerated trucks. I, who grew up in the Midwest, remember when the only fish in the Jewel was local, canned, or frozen—fish sticks, salmon steaks.

Today knowledge and information carry the greatest value. Information moves at literally the speed of light. Business must learn to move as fast.

A company is a mechanism for concentrating capital to create value. In the industrial era, when value was embodied in what you manufactured, you had to concentrate physical capital: You raised money to build factories, which took lots of money and lots of time—time to raise the money, time to raise the roof on the factory. Now the capital that matters is intellectual capital, and you can concentrate it much more quickly. You don't need to funnel it through a pile of expensive assets. In almost every business—not just in Silicon Valley—you can start a company a lot faster and cheaper than before. When the assets you need are people and ideas, the velocity of the economy increases exponentially and permanently.

Everything else must hurry to keep pace. "Coordinating the flow of data among a company's constituencies—customers, suppliers, internal departments, the sales force—is *the* software problem of the Internet Age," one of my colleagues observed. Factories become smaller, modular, dispersed instead of centralized, so that goods can be assembled quicker, closer to the speed with which information—the order and the specs— moves. Clothing makers, when the whims of fashion blow, can log onto a database run by a company called Fasturn, describe the size, color, and style of what needs making, and get back a list of factories around the world that can make the item. At Fairway uptown, I can buy perch from Lake Victoria in Tanzania, fresh as news. And companies, all companies, begin to have to operate in "real time"—on the fly, without pre-meetings to discuss the meeting where we'll plan what to say in the meeting—a phenomenon that will change management utterly.

"We fly an airplane that can't ever land," says Phillip Harris. West Pointer Harris is the CEO of PJM Interconnection, a little-known company with a big job: managing the electrical grid for the Middle Atlantic states. From a bomb-hardened underground control room in Valley Forge, Pennsylvania, PJM dispatches electricity over 8,000 miles of high-voltage lines, balancing the grid through heat waves, lightning strikes, blizzards, and other events. PJM coordinates 540 generating units (owned by utilities and other power producers) with a capacity of 58,000 megawatts— the third-biggest operation of its kind in the world, after Electricité de France and Tokyo Electric. PJM also conducts the markets in which this power is sold, matching bid-and-ask offers on a monthly, daily, and hourly basis. Those prices swing radically, typically in summer from as low as $5 per megawatt-hour at 3 A.M. to $45 at 3 P.M. Negative prices have been recorded, where a generator pays someone to take its power rather than shut down; and in the Midwest prices have spiked as high as $7,000 per mwh.

PJM Interconnection is a splendid example of business in real time. Operating in real time means more than keeping the cash register open twenty-four hours a day, seven days a week—anyone can do that. Real time means being actively engaged with customers and suppliers—dealing, deciding, learning—at whatever level is necessary, at any time. It means operating according to the here and now of the market, not according to forecast, budget, or plan: building to order, not to stock; making major decisions in the fray, not in the staff meeting; never stopping, even if something goes wrong.

There have always been a few real-time organizations, like air-traffic controllers and big-city police forces. All organizations operate partly in real time—think of pouring molten steel, buying and selling stock, or producing live television. But a whole large business working real time, all the time—that's new, and it's spreading faster than red wine spilled on a white shirt. Says Gerhard Schulmeyer, CEO of U.S. operations for Siemens Corp.: "More and more, companies have to be able to manage in real time or near-real time. Our biggest pitfall is that we go offline and make plans. The customer is online, and he doesn't care about your plan. He wants what he wants now, and is always one click away from your competitor." It's 10 P.M. Do you know where your business is?

Real time is coming because of four trends. First is the rise of truly global corporations—not just companies with globe-girdling branch offices. Global companies make important decisions and serious money around the world, which means around the clock.

Second, "regular business hours" have steadily lengthened. Twenty years ago New Yorkers relied on the corner liquor store to cash checks after 3 P.M. and on Saturdays. On Wednesday afternoons German shops shut like intimidated oysters. Now—I hate to pick on American Express again, which is a wonderful company—a friend e-mailed me on a recent holiday weekend: "Amex just pissed me off. I needed some computers immediately, so I used my Amex Platinum. It didn't get approved because it was outside my normal spending habits. I called them up and yelled at them. They can only approve it when they can confirm I have the funds in my bank. While I was talking to the stupid bitch on the phone I checked my account on the Web and I could see that I have the funds, but Amex can only confirm stuff over the phone and Union Bank is closed until Tuesday. Amex also won't let me talk to anyone in charge until at least Tuesday." Forgive my friend's name-calling and consider the complex transaction involved: a holiday weekend, an out-of-the-ordinary purchase that set off an expert system's warning signal, the need for two companies to share accurate but semiconfidential information to approve a sale for a third company. Yet what was unreasonable about the request? *He* could see his bank balance on the Web.

The third reason for the emergence of real-time business is the Web. It enriches and transforms the 24/7 experience. On the Web I can interact as well as transact. I can slap the racks and comparison-shop; I can give and get feedback; I can be inside your company, not just talking to a salesperson. Fourth and finally, the increasing speed of computers speeds up everything computers are used for, including business processes. Call that the Basic Law of Business Acceleration. Batch-processed work flows online and is done instantly. Compare today's e-mail to yesterday's outbox full of memos, which were collected by the mailroom, sorted, and delivered—a twenty-four-hour process, even if the recipient was next door. It takes less time to get a credit application approved—a process that used to require days or weeks—than to get your shoes shined. Says Richard Schroate, head of Executive Insights, which advises CEOs and chairmen on business and technology strategy: "Companies aren't just choosing to operate in real time. Physics forces them to."

Many functions—purchasing, distribution, working capital management—are already closing in on real time. The whole business is there when it can pass three tests:

First, it produces in response to actual demand. Electricity is an almost mystical example of a "derived demand" product: The power that makes a lightbulb glow literally doesn't exist till you flip the switch, and vanishes when you turn it off. Says PJM's Harris: "There is never any inventory; electricity is instantaneously produced and consumed; you don't buy it to put on a shelf." Now everybody wants to become like electricity. The Dell business model is based on derived demand; your new Dell computer comes into being only after (usually just two hours after) you buy it. Dell has factories with no storerooms: Trucks pull up to a loading dock, are emptied as orders come in, then pull away and are replaced by full ones. Carmakers are moving in this direction. Commercial fishermen have asked PJM for advice on setting up a real-time market so they can sell their product as it's caught, while still at sea. It couldn't be catch-to-order—the International Brotherhood of Fishes is ornery that way—but it's possible to imagine a crew changing course, changing equipment, staying out longer or coming home sooner in response to real-time market signals, rather than operating catch-as-catch-can.

Second, real-time business depends absolutely on absolute reliability. "If we make a mistake, we shut down the East Coast," says Harris, "and if we have a problem, we can't stand down—we have to fix it on the fly." A real-time business requires scads more reliability even than stringent quality controls. There's no inventory buffer: The downside of lean manufacturing, where materials arrive just in time, is increased vulnerability to interruptions—for example, from work stoppages. There's no time buffer, either: Decisions have to be right, because you make them with the customer in the room, not back at the office.

Third, a real-time business connects that way to the outside world, not just intramurally. Says Saj-nicole Joni, CEO of business advisers Cambridge International Group: "This requires audit and feedback structures—financial, customer satisfaction, news about what's happening. If you need twenty-four hours to link and think, you're not real-time." Last, a real-time business treats employees the same way. "There's a real advantage of having people see the value of their work on a daily basis," says Nobel Prize–winning economist Ronald Coase. Knowledge workers rarely do the same thing again and again; they need instant feedback about their performance and their customers' needs.

All of this implies staggering changes to structural capital—particularly in how information systems serve employees—as well as in customer relations and human resources. Here are some of them:

FROM PLAN TO SIGNAL

In the beginning is the plan—that's how most businesses run. We make budgets, forecasts, schedules. We array our work on a value chain in what looks like chronological order: First we buy stuff, then we do stuff, then we sell stuff. Time, in a business like this, is something we manage. Business in real time is completely different, both logically and chronologically. For a real-time business, in the beginning is the signal—out in the market a cricket rubs its legs together, and the company leaps into action. The value chain runs backward: First sell, then make. Stephan Haeckel, a strategist at IBM, describes the difference between managed-time and real-time businesses (which he calls "sense-and-respond organizations") this way: Traditional organizations are run like buses, with routes to follow and schedules to meet; real-time organizations are taxis, which respond to a waving arm or a voice crackling on a two-way radio. Customers expect your attention at their convenience, not yours. When opportunity knocks, it barely gives you time to answer the door. One March day in 2000, I had arrived at the airport in Singapore. I was tired and standing in line to clear immigration. There were about ten lines, each with about twenty people in line. Suddenly an immigration agent came and opened a new line. There was a chance for advantage—quite literally, first-mover advantage—and it was competed away in about four seconds flat. That's what the Information Age is like.

Drop by Onvia.com, which operates an online marketplace out of Seattle, Washington, devoted to the needs of small businesses. Here they can purchase everything from computers and furniture to debt collection and Web-page design. More than 31,500 sellers have registered with Onvia. Put in a request-for-quote for, say, a $2 million property insurance policy, fill in some details about what's to be insured, specify whether you want ten or fifteen bids, and click "submit." Odds are you'll have your quotes within the hour; if it's a Web page you want, you'll have your bids in twenty minutes. If you're not that fast, tough noogies. Says Onvia.com's founder and president, Glenn Ballman: "The marketplace of the future will be like this—minute-to-minute, second-to-second transactions." As we saw in Chapter 3, electronic B2B markets aren't everything their first ardent advocates imagined, but they have absolutely changed the game when buyers and sellers don't know each other already. It's a long way from the Yellow Pages.

This new game has new rules. Here are four:

• *Decisions that once were made internally are now made with and by outsiders—customers or the market as a whole.* Real-time interaction means sharing information and decision making in ways you've never done before. Customers can follow their packages through the FedEx and UPS systems. GE Power Systems goes further: Buyers of its turbines not only help write the specs but can, from their Web browsers, actually watch their machines being built. Customers decided how Onvia.com stocks its virtual shelves. Says Ballman: "Most companies start with a product, and the customer is a by-product. We started with a customer base—accounts with small businesses—and surrounded them with the products and ser-vices they asked for." And why not? Says Chris Locke, coauthor of *The Cluetrain Manifesto*: "In olden days you took your product to the market, and marketing was about trying to identify who to spam. But real-time, emergent markets literally don't exist until some voice, like the Magic Flute, pipes them out of the ether. In real time, the question becomes what it always should have been—not how do we package what we've made, but what should we make?" Once again, Drucker's question: not "How do I do the job?" but "What is the job?"

• *The more choices people get, the more they want.* You can't—mustn't—be all things to all customers. But when buyers get choices, they will start choosing—and sometimes choose something different. Empowered cus-tomers insist on knowing what's going on. PJM used to post the price and demand for electricity (which vary dramatically) every fifteen minutes. Now buyers and sellers want the dope, and get it, every three seconds. Onvia.com tells customers about prices and liquidity in its markets—in the Northwest as I write, public-relations services are scarce, a seller's market—and displays live information on a "Wall of Data" suspended above the room where its employees work. Says Ballman: "Our philosophy is to feed real-time information back to participants: how many requests-for-quote are waiting, whether prices are up or down, how the last seven days compare to the average."

Why open the kimono on information companies usually keep under wraps? There is a cost—information is power, and you're surrendering some—but in return you get higher, more valuable knowledge: You can watch the market from the catbird seat, knowing what's hot and what's not. In a real-time market, exchanging information is as valuable as exchanging cash. That requires unprecedented openness, outside and in. In February 2000, when Ford gave free computers and bargain Internet access to all its employees, CEO Jacques Nasser said one reason was "to make sure our employees—every one of us—is connected to what's going on in the marketplace so that we know where consumers are heading."

• *Time is present time and distance is zero.* Whatever the customer wants, he wants it here now. Says Harris: "Present time is what I have to deliver. Real time is what I have to manage." He means this: A customer might not want your service all the time, but he might want it at any time; therefore you have to be ready all the time. The first principle of running a real-time business is real, radical empowerment—empowerment that puts both intelligence (eyes and ears) and power wherever the organization touches the marketplace.

• *Volatility is baked in; live with it.* None of this is news to Susan M. Smith, vice president of Knowledge-Based Industries at Royal Bank of Canada, the biggest financial services shop in the friendly giant to the north: "We have to learn as we go how to lend based on intellectual and intangible assets in a marketplace where growth and volatility are extraordinary." The old rules were—are—literally written in manuals that tell Royal Bank staff what makes for a creditworthy customer in a given industry. Forget them, Smith tells her staff. They don't fit biotech, where lead times are endless but sales can explode in a matter of weeks. Or software, where one can mass-produce without a plant. Or the borderless world, where a competitor can go anywhere presto or appear from nowhere without warning. Says Smith: "A company in Winnipeg with five employees might make its first sale to Tokyo or Berlin." With few tangible assets, knowledge companies have few flywheels, few drags, and little safety, at least until they grow old and predictable.

On a lakeside near Zurich, a city where Lenin plotted Bolshevist revolution, ur-capitalist Dean LeBaron, former chairman of Batterymarch Financial Management, contemplates the information revolution: "We financial analysts were brought up looking at charts whose x-axis represented time. You'd see trends. Time was a wave. In the new economy, I'm beginning to think time is a quantum. What comes next bears no relationship to what came before." That glorious abstract image becomes earthy as LeBaron explains: "It used to be that information oozed out into the market. Now it's dumped out all at once."

HASTE ELIMINATES WASTE

The paradoxical solution: more speed.

In 1999, Alcoa reduced inventories by more than a quarter of a billion dollars while increasing sales by just under a billion dollars. The company's ratio of inventory to sales jumped from an excellent 1:8 to a terrific 1:10, one reason Alcoa substantially outperformed every other stock in the Dow Jones Industrial Average. "It didn't happen because I told people to cut inventory," says Chief Financial Officer Richard Kelson. Credit goes to the Alcoa Business System, an adaptation of Toyota's production methods that took more than $1.1 billion out of the aluminum maker's cost base. A big piece of it: getting Alcoa, as much as possible, to operate in real time.

By eliminating filters and emptying catchbasins for information and resources and producing to actual demand rather than to forecast, companies can actually reduce volatility. The faster knowledge moves, the faster the quanta shoot out, the more quickly you can adjust. When cycles get shorter, their volatility decreases, the way speed smooths out a bumpy road. Furthermore, says Richard Schroate of Executive Insights: "You can put all your assets to their highest and best use." In particular, you can work knowledge harder and make decisions faster.

Alcoa, already the aluminum industry's low-cost producer, began rolling out its new manufacturing methods in 1998, aiming to cut costs further and improve responsiveness. "We were ill-prepared to meet customers' needs," says executive VP Keith Turnbull, who leads the effort: "We'd ship out of a pile of dead stuff"—inventory—"and if we didn't have what the customer wanted we'd make the pile bigger." When Turnbull goes into one of Alcoa's 228 plants, his first task is to classify every gram of inventory by cause, then attack the cause: Is it safety stock, caused by an unreliable process? A buffer, caused by uneven demand? A store, the result of changeover time—for example, when a rolling mill, which likes to produce from wide to narrow, feeds into a paint line, which likes to work from light to dark? A FIFO queue, to bridge a time gap or some other imbalance between two processes?

Managing in real time helps drive waste out. First, with real-time information, buffer stocks can go way down. Ignorance of what's really happening in the market is the main reason they exist. I need buffers because I don't know demand, and demand varies (which it always does—the only question about any forecast is the degree to which it is inaccurate). Worse, when there's an abrupt change in demand, news of which moves upstream slowly, the result is chaos: wasteful drawdowns and buildups of stock. Second, real-time information helps Alcoa fix plants, eliminating safety stock, which is produced by unreliable processes. Most manufacturing processes are too complex to be foolproof. Also, the more flexible a process, the more ways it can get out of control. Machines get jostled, temperatures change, bugs turn up—all the stochastic* stuff that makes Murphy's the law of the land. Reliability, therefore, can't just be designed in; it has to be worked in, every day. At Alcoa, as at Toyota, any worker who has any problem—a machine out of kilter, a product defect—or who has an idea, pulls a cord summoning a leader, with the aim of handling it then and there. One problem, one cause, one time, at once—that's how the plant gets better, rather than by batching tasks off to engineers to be solved later. Third, inside the plants real demand dictates production as much as possible; that is, a worker in an upstream process responds to real-time, "pull" signals from workers downstream—ideally, workers he can actually see. Visual cues are so important that Alcoa has been taking out enterprise resource planning software and replacing it with traditional kanban cards, the slips of paper Toyota uses to zip requests for parts through its plants. Says Turnbull: "Workers need the authority to buy and sell. Joe says to Marie, 'I need three extrusions by such and such a time'; Marie says yes or no, then she goes upstream and buys what she needs to make the extrusions for Joe."

Fourth, since the idea is to produce to order, not to stock, it's critical to decide where the customer's order enters the plant. For a customized extrusion or forging, the order should enter the plant as far upstream as possible—so the company can respond instantly. That's less important for a standard piece of sheet. This is a key knowledge-management decision, since customization is a key output of knowledge work. To see the difference, compare three burger joints: the 21 Club, Wendy's, and McDonald's.

At 21, your burger's cooked to order; when the waiter tells the chef what you want, the meat is raw. The inventory is, literally, raw material. Your Wendy's burger is precooked, then customized—for me, cheese, pickles, mustard, onion, and usually but not always tomato. You have stocks of in-progress inventory. Lunch at McDonald's is standardized— two all-beef patties, special sauce, lettuce, cheese, pickles, onions, on a sesame-seed bun—and wrapped up before you pull into the parking lot, though you can make special requests. McDonald's carries a stock of finished goods. From a burger-manufacturing standpoint† you'd want

---

* *Stochastic,* meaning conjectural or unpredictable, is business-school jargon for "shit happens."

† I realize this isn't the only standpoint. At 21, you also want your martini.

BURGERS BUILT TO ORDER

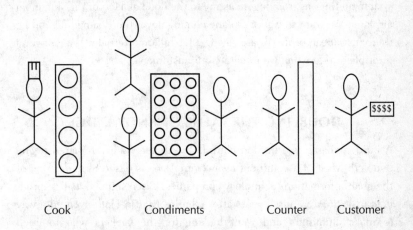

Cook   Condiments   Counter   Customer

the 21 order to enter directly at the kitchen, because the chef needs to know what you want; the cook at Wendy's needs to know aggregate burger demand, nothing more; however, the people at the condiment table need to know your preference, so you'd enter the order there; and at McDonald's, the order should come straight to the counter, because the people there are the ones who need to know what you want. Says Turnbull: "The location of the last store is an absolutely critical decision. You can put it in late in the process, in which case the customer takes it out of stock. You can put it way back in the beginning, or you can have a special order line."

The results of this kind of thinking are showing up all over Alcoa. A wheel factory in Székesfehérvár, Hungary, gets ingot in response to real-time demand; a plant in Sorocaba, Brazil, turns its inventory sixty times a year. A Hernando, Mississippi, extrusion plant, a money-loser when it was acquired in 1998, delivers custom orders in two days (vs. three weeks before) and makes money. In Portland, Australia, producing molten metal to meet real-time demand from the adjacent ingot mill improved asset utilization so much that the plant eliminated ten of twenty-four vacuum crucibles. This—$832 million, toward the $1.1 billion target—took less than eighteen months. Real time flies.

CEO Alain Belda calls inventories "monuments to incompetence"—a hedge against inefficiency, your own or that of your supplier or customer.

"Now we will work with Ford and Boeing and other customers to take our system all the way from ingot casting to the hood of a car or the skin of an airplane. We want to watch a plane coming down the Boeing line and be there just ahead of it. We are saving $1.1 billion internally. We will get a multiple of that when we integrate our customers."

DOUBLING THE VALUE OF KNOWLEDGE

A burden shared is a burden halved; an intellectual asset shared is one doubled. Most of a continent away from Alcoa is Cisco Systems, one of the great information-technology companies. Cisco shipped its first products in 1986, a hundred years after Charles Martin Hall invented a way to make aluminum and went looking for the backers who founded Alcoa. Cisco's management of working capital has been as exemplary as Alcoa's—its ratio of sales to working capital jumped from 3:1 in 1997 to 7:1 in 1999—in part because it, too, makes knowledge work harder and faster, on a real-time basis.

Cisco's real-time management is worth examining not only for its many years of great success but also in light of the company's spectacular troubles in 2001, when it wrote off $2.5 billion worth of inventory and laid off 2,500 employees. In the shocked aftermath of Cisco's write-down, some (including the company) blamed the speed with which IT capital spending up and died. Sales did fall 30 percent in one quarter, an astounding drop. Others preferred to blame the hubris of management and poke fun at its claims to have found a better way to run a business. Certainly CEO John Chambers's blithe comments that the company does better in hard times did little to encourage his employees to be alert for signs of trouble. Few noticed that Cisco's catastrophe was, in large part, the result of its abandoning rules of real-time management that it had pioneered.

Cisco's manufacturing couldn't be more different from Alcoa's—or more like it. Alcoa is asset-intensive; Cisco isn't. Alcoa owns 228 plants; Cisco uses thirty-six, of which it owns but two. One of them is downstairs from the San Jose office of Randy Pond, senior VP for operations. The rest belong to top-flight contract manufacturers like Jabil Circuit, Solectron, and Flextronics. It's "virtual manufacturing," Pond says, made possible by "a suite of tools and processes that lets me manage an extended enterprise that I don't own, as if I do own it."

The key to it, per Pond: "real-time data on a real-time basis so my partners know what goes on in my business every single day." As much as possible, Cisco and partners work with the same stream of information—so it does double duty. Pond calls it a "true consumption tool": Every day Cisco compiles its inventory, forecast, order backlog, and thirteen weeks of data about what parts and subassemblies it consumed each day to make what products; every day its partner compiles data on run time, queue time, lot size, and yield; every night computers combine the two data streams, like the Río Negro and the Río Solimões, into an Amazon of information; every morning the supplier can see what to build that day. Says Pond: "With true demand signals we remove the whipsaws, and a supplier can schedule better."

Cisco works the other end of the process—selling—the same way. Eighty-five percent of Cisco's sales are entered directly from the Net, available instantly in Pond's office or in that of CEO John Chambers. Validation and testing are also online and real time. One tool tests machines as they are built, and won't print a packing label for a machine unless every test has been done and passed. Another tool checks a customer's order as he enters it, to make sure that he hasn't asked for incompatible gear—the high-tech equivalent of ordering queen-sized sheets for a king-sized bed. Except for commodity parts, Cisco's supply chain is entirely visible, as live as bombs over Baghdad.

These tools, plus automated procurement, direct stock replenishment, and shortened cycle time, save about $400 million a year, by Pond's reckoning—Cisco's share of the reduction in working capital. That $400 million doesn't include the saving in capital—all the equipment Cisco doesn't have to carry on its books, and the improved utilization its suppliers get. Says Pond: "If we could cut cycle time more and create a flexible enough supply chain, we wouldn't need forecasts or manufacturing resources planning at all. They just add time."

That's the theory, and when Cisco put it into practice, life was grand. But the principles of real time—responding to real demand, absolute reliability of data, learning to live with volatility—are strict. Believing in them halfway is worse than not following them at all. Cisco made several mistakes. In the summer of 2000, it began to build up its inventories, directly contrary to the ideas of real-time management. The reason was laudable—to shorten the delivery time for complex, hard-to-make products—but the reasoning was fatally flawed. It required the company to forecast demand, and the demand in this case was in large part from fledgling telecom companies that were on what turned out to be the late stages of a capital-spending bender. Worse, Cisco made long-term contracts with suppliers without similar arrangements with sellers. That's a basic management mistake: You can't tie down one end of your business while the other's left to flap in the wind—particularly in a volatile market. When telecom capital spending collapsed, Cisco was surprised (because it was giving too much credence to forecasts) and unable to untie its supply contracts quickly enough. Fully 70 percent of the written-off inventory was for telecom equipment. (California's electricity-market crisis in 2001 exemplified the same mistake. In that case, utilities entered into fixed-price sales agreements while not tying down the price they paid to electricity suppliers. When the latter soared, the former nearly destroyed the utilities.) Cisco knew better, and should have trusted what it knew.

When a knowledge asset can serve a whole supply chain, all its participants can benefit. Honeywell's consumer products group sells Fram auto filters, Autolite spark plugs, Prestone antifreeze—all in all, about seven thousand stock-keeping units, or SKUs. Planning manufacturing schedules once began with customers' forecasts, which were modified by customers' real orders. Big orders got filled first. If there were backlogs—inevitably there were—the company went after the biggest dollar value first. This was optimal from Honeywell's viewpoint—the only viewpoint the company could take, given what it knew. But it was not necessarily the best viewpoint. Says David Berges, president of the group: "The most important thing for our aftermarket customers [that is, auto parts dealers] is to have at least one of every single SKU—a hole on the shelf is bad for them."

Real-time information makes it possible to see and think differently. Today 80 percent of Honeywell's consumer product sales are captured in real time on cash registers at the point of sale. As a result, Honeywell can anticipate when its customers will run out of stock, and adjust accordingly. Result: In one year Honeywell's fill rates—the percentage of a customer's order it can complete by the date the customer wants—rose from a bit over

90 percent to 98 percent. There are fewer holes on customers' shelves, but also about 10 percent less inventory in Honeywell's stockrooms.

FLYING BY WIRE

A balance sheet is a snapshot, a still photograph of a business's assets and liabilities at a moment in time—December 31, usually. A budget, similarly, is a frozen-in-time statement of good intentions for the year, which is thawed out, revised, and refrozen a couple of times as reality changes. While you're running your business by looking at photo albums and eating frozen lima beans, a few companies are getting live action and greens straight from the garden.

Enough metaphor. Here's the point:

The greatest advantage of working knowledge harder and faster is better decision making. Real-time companies decide faster, of course— no small thing—but also differently. "Real-time understanding of production processes and the vagaries of consumer demand, are reducing the degree of uncertainty and, hence, risk," according to Fed chairman Alan Greenspan. The minds of customers are no longer opaque. When companies have live, hot information—not sales-last-week but sales-right-now— they can adjust on the fly. They can also drive decision making deep into the organization without sacrificing management's ability to superintend. Root-level empowerment plus near-to-hand executive guidance is a powerful combination.

Says Alcoa's CFO, Richard Kelson: "The issue isn't the information; it's what you can do with it. The earlier you get information, the easier it is to fix a problem." Alcoa, late in 1998, saw softness in its aerospace markets early enough to shift its production mix from hard to soft alloys and avoided overstock problems that had occurred in similar situations before. In the days when lighting company Tungsram was owned by the Hungarian government, managers waited months for even the most basic information about sales, costs, and inventories. Management and reality became weirdly asynchronous. By the time problems became visible, they were disasters; by the time solutions were proposed, the problems were new. No one could be held responsible for his actions.

With real-time information a company can devolve power radically and let people be responsible. A first-line manager can look at margins and products and know exactly what the effect of his decisions will be. They can act faster—and top management is more comfortable letting them act.

"Now you have all the stuff to run the business on a seamless basis," says Kelson. That, dear reader, is more than a good thing. It's a necessary thing, if for no other reason than the Basic Law of Business Acceleration. One small instance: Think of "dynamic pricing," the euphemism for that fact that fixed price lists are going the way of turntables, sidesaddles, and Marxists, being replaced by auctions and Dutch auctions and haggling, for everything from airline tickets to electricity to, God help us, cans of Coke. How can you possibly run a business with month-old information when prices change as often as RuPaul?

And how can you possibly manage by command-and-control? The only answer to volatility is agility. Yes, certain prudential matters—vision, values, strategic aims—need offline deliberation and mustn't be jostled in the hurly-burly. The systems that feed supply and demand info must be fast and 100 percent reliable. Real-time books are like sashimi: You can slice and dice them, but you can't cook them. To manage in real time means that every decision involves both time and money, so everyone must know the math that relates the two. Everyone must have complete access to the data he needs and understand the company's key knowledge assets: its methodologies, relationships, and people. ("What is the job?" "What is the knowledge base?")

Beyond that, give folks a few algorithms, a compass, and a sack lunch. Paul Hindes, the president of Watcher Technologies, a Datek Online Holdings subsidiary that provides software and support for demanding Wall Street broker-dealers, tells employees there are four rules:

"You can't be an asshole with clients.

"Tell me if my fly is open.

"Be responsive but not dumb.

"It's really, really okay to make mistakes."

That sounds about right.

CHAPTER 6

THE CASE AGAINST
KNOWLEDGE MANAGEMENT

Our primary purpose in this book is to teach you how to cook, so
that you will understand fundamental techniques and gradually
be able to divorce yourself from a dependence on recipes.

SIMONE BECK, LOUISETTE BERTHOLLE,
AND JULIA CHILD

A few months ago, I decided to attack my messy desk at home. I laid
its big drawer on my lap and began searching for things to discard.
Among my discoveries, toward the bottom at the back on the left,
was a manila folder. In it were about two dozen carbon sets. Carbon sets,
used to make copies of a letter, were ubiquitous in the days when office air
vibrated with the clacks and dings of typewriters, the birdsong of a business
rain forest. When I showed these to my children, they had no idea what
they were. Each carbon set consisted of two sheets of 8½" × 11" paper,
joined at the top by an easy-to-tear-off strip. The top sheet was a piece of
single-use carbon paper, flimsy as a negligee; beneath it was an almost
equally diaphanous sheet, often yellow, for the copy. You put one or more
carbon sets behind a sheet of letterhead paper and screwed the package

into your typewriter; when you were done typing, you tore away the strip, tossed out the carbon paper, and kept the copy. Carbon sets were one of the great inventions of what Warren Bennis and Philip Slater called the temporary society: no more smudged fingers from reusable carbon paper; no more illegible copies because you reused it too many times. Near as I can figure, I helped myself to this slim folderful in about 1988, just about the time desktop computers were beginning to make them obsolete.

Carbon sets made possible one of the simplest and best managing ideas I've ever seen, circulating correspondence. At the book publishing company where I saw it, circulating correspondence worked like this. Whenever you wrote a letter—and we wrote a lot of letters—you made two copies, one to file, one to circulate. Every week (or every so often) you took the circulating set, culled any that included confidential dope or made you look more stupid than usual, stuck on a buck slip, and put them into your outbox; generally by the time the folder returned it was time to refill it and send it out again. (An unwritten but religiously obeyed rule said that you never held on to a folder more than a day.) Everybody participated, including the chairman and the president. There were about fifty on staff, about ten of them secretaries or assistants, and some departments sent just one folder, so that altogether I saw perhaps two folders a day, each containing two or three dozen letters. To scan them and send them on took about as much time as drinking half a cup of coffee.

"A whale ship was my Yale College and my Harvard," said Herman Melville's Ishmael; when it came to learning my job, circulating correspondence was mine. I could see how my superiors ran the office, but their letters opened a window into how they conducted business with the world outside; I aped things more experienced colleagues did, and saw how they handled tricky situations; I copied useful addresses into my Rolodex (another antique). I admired the stylishness of several colleagues—one avuncular, one flip, one elegant, one just plain brilliant; my own letters got better partly because I knew they would be read by people whose admiration I sought in return. I saw how other departments worked and got a sense of how to do my job so as to make theirs easier. I picked up industry gossip and kept myself in the company loop. I learned who knew what, which made me better at asking for advice. The precaution of rereading letters before circulating them gave me a chance to notice and learn from some of my own mistakes.

Circulating correspondence was obligatory, easy, fun, cheap, and genuinely useful. As such, it stands in stark contrast to much of what passes for knowledge management.

THE KNOWLEDGE-MANAGEMENT IMPERATIVE

Knowledge is your most important raw material.
Knowledge is your most important source of added value.
Knowledge is your most important output.
If you are not managing knowledge, you are not paying attention
   to business.

That proposition, the knowledge management imperative, undergirds a growing edifice of ideas, techniques, and technologies. International Data Corp., a research group that focuses on technology, estimates that poorly managed knowledge costs the *Fortune* 500 about $12 billion a year. Reasons for the lost money, by IDC's reckoning: "substandard performance, intellectual rework, and a lack of available knowledge management resources." You don't need numbers like IDC's to know the need is there: Just ask yourself how much time you waste searching for information that ought to be at your fingertips, how many times you've looked endlessly for a document only to find it on your neighbor's desk (or toward the bottom at the back on the left of your own desk drawer), how many times a mistake could have been prevented if only someone had known to check with you, how often you've wished you had a secretary as good as the chairman's. Contrariwise, ask yourself how many times you have been frustrated by having to explain who you are and what you want to the latest clueless factotum of a company with which you have done business for years.

The response to the need for knowledge management has been astounding. In *Intellectual Capital* (1997), I wrote, "If the subject of intellectual capital ever spawns a business fad, it will be under the guise of 'knowledge management,' because there's money to be made selling software, systems, and consulting services with the touted goal of allowing every person in an organization to be able to lay his hands on the collected know-how, experience, and wisdom of all his colleagues." I was more right than I dreamed or feared. Knowledge management has become KM, and there are national and international KM conferences, local KM forums, a *Journal of Knowledge Management* and a *Knowledge Management* magazine; a search of the World Wide Web turns up some 544,000 occurrences of the phrase "knowledge management." By IDC's estimate, knowledge management software and services will be a $6 billion industry in 2002. A 1998 survey by the Cranfield School of Management in the U.K. found that European companies spend 3.7 percent of revenues on knowledge management, more than they spend on R&D.

Fads aren't necessarily bad. Sometimes—often—faddists fail; in so doing they perform a service for the rest of us, showing where not to tread, showing us the boundaries of the possible. Sometimes, against all odds or at least against conventional wisdom, they succeed—performing a greater service, showing us possibilities we never imagined, the penicillin in the mold.

But when a business bandwagon gets rolling, sometimes it's unclear for whose benefit the music is playing. Two groups, each under pressure to show its worth, grabbed hold of the idea of knowledge management: human resources and information systems departments. Beleaguered HR, which begged for a "place at the table" with the CEO while showing little in the way of provable business benefit beyond the fact that it was cutting costs by outsourcing itself, saw "organizational learning" as a great way to keep the CFO at bay—at least until someone began wondering what it is, really.* Over in IS, meanwhile, awkward questions were arising about

---

* In 1988, Arie de Geus, head of group planning for Royal Dutch/Shell, published an article in *Harvard Business Review* ("Planning as Learning," March/April 1988) in which he wrote a sentence that became celebrated: "The only competitive advantage the company of the future will have is its managers' ability to learn faster than their competitors." Organizational learning, a subtly mutant offspring of that idea, holds that organizations themselves can learn. It's easy to dismiss the notion by defining it away, saying that knowledge requires a knower, learning a learner, and knowers and learners are people, not organizations—after all, de Geus said that it's *managers'* ability to learn that will matter. And "organizational learning" is a term worth killing: As opaque as the yellow fog in "The Love Song of J. Alfred Prufrock," it is a marvelous way to obscure one's ineffectuality.

Clearly, however, groups have different cultures, ways of reacting to new information, and these amount to epistemologies. The great historian of early capitalism

THE CASE AGAINST KNOWLEDGE MANAGEMENT 111

what all these computers were actually doing for productivity and why every IT project ran late and over budget. Happily, knowledge management came along just as reengineering—the computer-intensive radical redesign of business processes—ran out of steam and hence budget, and has continued strong through at least three additional computer spending sprees (enterprise resources planning, Y2K, and e-commerce). When it comes to finding a reason to keep the budget growing, these guys are *good*.

As far as "owning" the term *knowledge management* is concerned, IS won largely because techies truly do have fabulous new stuff: Developments in information technology in the 1990s fit the needs of knowledge management almost perfectly. Furthermore, where there's a lot to sell there's a lot of marketing money, which helps define agendas. HR plays a leading role in only a fifth of corporate knowledge-management efforts.

Fernand Braudel describes how Asian visitors to early modern Europe marveled at and mocked the way European fashion changed from year to year—now elaborate coiffures, now simple cuts, now fanciful shoes, now practical ones. Yet, Braudel suggests, fashion—stunning, silly, or both—betokened a cultural hunger for innovation: "Can it have been merely by coincidence that the future was to belong to the societies fickle enough to care about changing the colours, materials and shapes of costume, as well as the social order and the map of the world—societies, that is, which were ready to break with their traditions. There is a connection." Similarly, every business journalist worth his expense account knows that some companies are quick to innovate and adapt, while others are breathtaking in their thickheadedness. A whole sub-discipline of consulting, change management, has developed to counter this obtuseness by means of carrots, sticks, and firecrackers strategically placed near one or another corporate buttock. Still, some companies just don't get it—new managers, new consultants, new technologies, new competitive threats, new opportunities come and go, and these outfits plod along. The phrase may be foggy, but there truly are organizational learning styles, and it's not taking personification too far to say that some companies are quicker studies than others.

Culture turns out to be difficult to manage directly. You cannot get results just by saying, "Let's change our culture," any more than you can spread joy by saying, "Don't worry, be happy." You change culture by changing work, then providing ways to help people get the work done—cheerleading, counseling, training, equipment, financial incentives, and so on. An American colonel in Vietnam, deriding a propaganda campaign to "win the hearts and minds" of the Vietnamese people, said, "Get 'em by the balls and their hearts and minds will follow." He spoke undiplomatically and in a bad cause, but he knew his change management.

HR is so marginalized—wrongly, for reasons this chapter will suggest—that in almost half of these efforts it's not even involved in rewards, compensation, and employee retention; only in training does the department play a significant role, and even there more often than not its role is limited at best.

In return for their victory, technologists seem to have promised never to evangelize, even among fellow geeks, without a disclaimer in the form of a PowerPoint slide that warns, "Technology is just an enabler."* It's one hell of an enabler, however: From movable type to html, technology has done more to manage knowledge than all organizational development consultants put together.

Knowledge management is knowing what we know, capturing and organizing it, and using it to produce returns. Nothing in that definition says anything about computers, but modern knowledge management is inconceivable without them, and in some sense they created it. The United States, with its just-do-it culture and aggressive IT sector, has a knowledge-management industry led by sellers of intranet software, data warehouses, online knowledge libraries, decision-support technology, and consulting services. Says David Smith, head of the knowledge-management effort at Unilever, the Anglo/Dutch consumer-products giant: "Probably because the big consultancies are U.S. firms, there's a tendency to look for a prescription. To leverage their staff the consultancies have to break their services into trainable, prescriptive lumps that are repeatable across businesses." In practice, that has meant setting up a suite of applications that usually include the following:

An intranet: On everyone's computer, a way to get to basic company information and access to more specialized knowledge-management tools.

Data warehousing and data mining: In haystacks of data are needles of knowledge. By mining transaction data companies can find patterns of behavior by individual customers, track the efficacy of advertising and other sales promotion, or discover other valuable patterns that could never have been found before.

Decision support: Particularly for employees who deal with customers,

---

*The disclaimer is also necessary so that when a project goes wrong, IS can say, "Hey, technology is just an enabler," and point the finger elsewhere—at HR, for example.

decision-support software brings rules, ratios, and other in/
the desktop. At Cigna Corp., the insurance company, underwri..
decision support built into the software the underwriter uses to process
applications. A nursing home in California wants insurance? The custom-
built software tells you the nearest earthquake fault and how dangerous
it is; it gives guidelines for assessing risk factors like staff training or
sprinkler systems, and so on. The system is kept up-to-date and supple-
mented by new expert analysis, feedback from the claims department, or
insights from the underwriters themselves. Other expert systems assist
technical workers—engineers, for instance—by alerting them to errors in
designs.

Groupware: These are technologies, of which Lotus Notes is the
granddaddy, that allow workers to collaborate (including sharing files and
documents) however far from each other they may be. Napster and
Gnutella, file-sharing technologies that fueled a global crime wave of
music piracy, could make a legitimate contribution if they were adapted
for knowledge management.

Customer relationship management (CRM): Software that integrates all
of a company's information about its customers (sales, marketing, service,
even profitability) so that, in theory, they can create an institutional memory for each account. Close cousins to this are sales force automation tools
that connect sales reps with customer history, price lists, and other information. The Holy Grail of CRM is "one-to-one marketing," by means of
which companies hope to give hundreds or thousands of customers service as personalized as that of a Saville Row tailor.

Online information sources: These range from news wires to a corporate Yellow Pages to internal libraries of best practices and methodologies
(see the discussion of the World Bank in the preceding chapter and of
BP/Amoco in Chapter 8). These are accessible from the intranet, as is the
Internet.

Electronic bulletin boards: Places to ask, "Does anybody know?" and
get answers.

As time marches on and Moore's Law with it, all of this technology gets
swifter, stronger, and subtler. Why, then, is there a persistently nagging
sense that it misses the point? A couple of stories will get us toward the
answers.

"ONLY CONNECT"

Jack Whalen, a sociologist, works at Xerox's Palo Alto Research Center. A few years ago, he was brevetted to the Institute for Research on Learning, a nonprofit group Xerox supported, and spent a couple of years studying how people, computers, and expert-system software interacted in a customer-service call center in Lewisville, Texas, north of Dallas.

The software (in this case, Inference Corp.'s CasePoint) was supposed to help employees tell customers how to fix problems with copiers—paper jams, faded copies, and the like. When the call-center operator typed words spoken by a customer—"jam," for example—the software would search its memory bank of diagnoses and solutions; as the customer continued to speak—"document feeder . . . noise"—the search would narrow, in theory till the right problem and right solution appeared. Xerox was after greater productivity, of course: faster, better answers in less time, costing less money. Trouble was, employees weren't using the new software. Management's diagnosis: They needed an incentive to change. Confident CasePoint would prove to be more productive than what it was replacing, the company held a monthlong contest in which employees earned points (which translated into cash) each time they solved a customer problem, by whatever means. The winner by a country mile was an eight-year veteran named Carlos, with more than 900 points. Carlos wasn't a big favorite among managers—"He's a cowboy," said one—but his victory was no surprise. Carlos really knew his stuff, and everybody, including Carlos, knew it. He almost never used the software.

The runner-up was a shock. Trish had been with the company just four months and had no previous experience with copying equipment. Her six hundred points more than doubled the score of the third-place finisher, and she didn't even have the new software, only an older, less sophisticated system. She had a secret weapon: She sat right across from Carlos. She overheard him when he talked; a single mother, highly motivated, she apprenticed herself to him and persuaded him to show her the innards of copiers during lunch breaks; she asked other colleagues for their tips, too, and built up a personal collection of manuals and handwritten notes about how to fix problems.

The case of Carlos and Trish says a lot about knowledge management. The point isn't to diss the software; CasePoint has many fans and documented triumphs. We English majors relish stories about the limitations of technology—it's just an enabler, after all—but not the least of its virtues is that it scales. Sure, Trish learned better from Carlos than anyone did from CasePoint, but how many people can sit next to him?

Managing knowledge is not a matter of choosing software vs. wetware, classroom vs. hands-on, formal vs. informal, technical vs. social. Knowledge management uses them all—and motivated employees will find unexpected new ways to put knowledge to work. Success depends on recognizing that all these need each other. To see how these interdependencies work, consider the case of PricewaterhouseCoopers.

If I hear one more consultant say, "Knowledge is the only thing we have to sell," I will take up narcolepsy in self-defense, but it's true; a big firm like PwC (with 160,000 partners and employees in 150 countries) has no reason for being if it cannot bring its collective brainpower to bear on clients' problems. When PwC was formed in 1998 (from the merger of Price Waterhouse and Coopers & Lybrand), the firm's top priority was to begin to act as one. Creating and sharing a collective universe of knowledge was vital. Seemingly trivial issues like nomenclature—do we call this process redesign or process reengineering?—had the potential to produce havoc otherwise.

Ellen (Lin) Knapp, PwC's chief knowledge officer, responded with an elegant, powerful intranet. On KnowledgeCurve, consultants and auditors find repositories of best practices, consulting methodologies, new tax and audit insights, links to outside Web sites and news services, online training courses, directories of in-house experts, and more, including links to an extended family of knowledge repositories for the audit and consulting practices, which contain in-depth collections and links in such areas of expertise as the mining industry, risk management, and SAP software. These days all professional firms of any size have something like it: a library, conference center, and Yellow Pages—on steroids and accessible from your laptop.

"Yet," says George Bailey, one of the firm's managing partners, in an echo of Xerox management's trouble with CasePoint, "there's a feeling it's underutilized. Everybody goes there sometimes, but when they're looking for expertise, most people go down the hall." Human beings are screwy that way. When your computer freezes up, looking at the manual comes fourth, after futzing with it yourself, asking a neighbor, and calling a help desk. We're so perverse that the stops on our quest for help are in inverse relation to the reliability of the source.

A bit before the two firms merged, a U.K.-based Price Waterhouse consultant, Jon Z. Bentley, and a few colleagues—a group of "self-selected creatives," Bentley puts it—took it upon themselves to create a network where they could "collaborate so as to be more innovative." They set up a Lotus Notes e-mail list. It has no rules, no moderator, no agenda except the messages people send. Any employee can join the list, which became known as "The Kraken," after someone joked that creativity in PwC was like the mythological sea monster who, in a poem by Tennyson, lies "far far beneath in the abysmal sea" and sleeps "his ancient, dreamless, unin-vaded sleep."

Today about five hundred people are members of the Kraken. Though it's unofficial and ever-so-slightly renegade (a firm with so many accoun-tants is never really renegade), Bailey calls it the premier forum for knowl-edge sharing in PwC. It's still on Notes, though that technology isn't really suitable for a list as large as the Kraken has become. It's difficult to search the archives, and, on a busy day, every member might find as many as fifty Kraken messages with the day's other e-mail: a recipe for infoglut, one might think. Technologically, the Kraken is to KnowledgeCurve what Carlos is to CasePoint.

But it works, and so well that other Kraken-like creatures are spawning in PwC. The question is why. Bentley, Knapp, and Bailey offer a number of hypotheses. First, it's demand-driven. The founders imagined that peo-ple would spark discussion by uploading white papers and the like—that is, they expected that users would pile logs of content in the fireplace and these would generate fire in the form of questions, critiques, and the like. Instead, the spark comes first: 80 percent of Kraken traffic starts with questions: Does anybody know . . . ? Does anybody have . . . ? Has anybody ever done something like . . . ? Sometimes—surprise—a question provokes a four- or five-page response, with real research having been done for no reward other than the satisfaction of having helped. Second, the Kraken gets at tacit and latent knowledge, provoking responses from people who didn't know they had something to contribute until they heard the discussion; similarly, it tolerates fuzzy, badly formed questions better than formal databases, where one often needs a bit of expertise even to begin. Third, it's front-of-mind, right there in the morning mail and cof-

fee—you don't have to make a decision to go there. Fourth, it's full of opinion, held strongly, rightly or wrongly. There's an old saying at Xerox PARC:
"Point of view is worth 80 IQ points."*

In all these ways, the Kraken differs from KnowledgeCurve. The latter
is supply-side; it's full of documents, artifacts, and other explicit knowledge. (People do go: It gets 18 million hits a month, though most are for
downloading HR forms, etc., not for knowledge sharing.) The content in
its repositories aims to be canonical rather than iconoclastic. The Kraken's
a conversation; KnowledgeCurve and its cousins are compendiums.
KnowledgeCurve is about teaching; the Kraken is about learning. You
can't have one without the other. There's an ancient (as these things go)
debate over whether knowledge management happens best by design or
by emergence. Says Knapp: "I find myself coming down dead center in the
middle of the argument."

WHAT KNOWLEDGE MANAGEMENT NEEDS

"Technology is just an enabler" symbolizes part of the problem because it
begs the question "Enabling what?" One flaw in knowledge management is
that it often neglects to ask what knowledge to manage and to what end.
Knowledge-management activities are all over the map: building databases,
measuring intellectual capital, establishing corporate libraries, building
intranets, sharing best practices, installing groupware, leading training programs, leading cultural change, fostering collaboration, creating virtual
organizations—all of these are knowledge management, and every functional and staff leader can lay claim to it. But no one claims the big question:
Why? If you listen to sales pitches for knowledge-management technology,
sooner or later comes the phrase "a few clicks of the mouse," and with it the
line "We can put all we know into the system, so that the knowledge of
everyone is available to anyone, 24/7, with just a few clicks of the mouse."
One technologist, describing his own habits, might have been describing
the knowledge-management dream when he said:

---

*The ability of a strongly held viewpoint to compensate for diminished intellectual
ability explains why problems that seem intractable in the morning become perfectly
solvable over a few beers.

Most of my memory now extends into files or the web somewhere. I know very little about the people/dates/events in my own life without Net access, but then I'm rarely away. Everything is one click, a couple keystrokes and some scrolling removed from short term memory. . . . It's not what you know, it's how fast you can access all the things you don't know. And if you can get that time down to a few seconds, then you effectively know everything.

To know everything is, of course, Temptation's archetype: "Ye shall be as gods . . ."

Defining and selecting. "If you build it, they won't come." That's the other obligatory PowerPoint slide. When knowledge-management sites aren't visited and tools aren't used, it's not because they're badly designed. Neither snow nor rain nor heat nor kludgy interfaces keep people from something they truly need. Nor are they unvisited because they get inadequate publicity. Word of mouth has never been faster or more powerful than it is now, with e-mail for a turbocharger. Knowledge-management resources go unused for one reason only: They're not useful. Either the work isn't connected to the knowledge or the knowledge isn't connected to the work.

Just as managing a business depends on deciding what business you are in—General Motors builds cars, not parking lots, gas stations, or highways—so knowledge management must begin by selecting the knowledge to be managed. It's no good assembling a library full of everything anybody could conceivably want to know about everything (besides, the World Wide Web already did it for you). IBM Global Services's David Snowden points out: "We should be finding out what it is we're going to manage before deciding how we're going to manage it."

Before undertaking any knowledge-management effort, answer four fundamental questions:

What is the work group? The knowledge base *Fortune*'s writers work with is not the same as the one our advertising salespeople need. There is overlap, sure—for reasons of editorial integrity we ignore it—but both groups need to know business trends, know something of the personalities and ambitions of business leaders, and have a feel for the innovations, strategies, and expectations of individual companies, any of which might suggest a story or affect the prospects for an ad. We both need writing and presentation skills, and a certain confidence that allows us to phone strangers and ask for their time or their money. Some of this is information; some is knowledge. In either case, we use the stuff in different contexts, to different ends. Knowing how to present it and how to teach it depends on that context, an important element of which is the work itself—what we're trying to do with what we know. Only within this context can one know what knowledge is relevant.

The first task of knowledge management is therefore to select what one might call a unit of analysis, or a unit of management, and to place primary responsibility for the content of knowledge management there. This is not necessarily a functional unit. Cross-functional project teams, for example, clearly need a "knowledge space" that is shared. Nor is it to say that the center, the CKO, has no role. Some resources everybody needs; if there is no common knowledge, there is no reason to be one company. Also, the look and feel of knowledge-management applications should be fairly standard, so that an engineer who wanders into marketing can find his way around. Certain policies—about privacy and confidentiality, for example—need to be consistent. The ringmaster runs the show, but he doesn't do the clowns' work for them.

What does the group need to know? It is important, as I've suggested, to distinguish between information and knowledge. (See p. 6.) Information tends to be transient, knowledge abiding. Every work group needs information management and information resources, which range from magazine subscriptions to databases. You can find out what people need by asking them, and arrange the fastest, cheapest, most effective way to get it to them.

You find out what knowledge they need by asking their customers, too. Most of us rarely deal with a whole body of knowledge—instead, if you'll forgive the metaphor, we nibble on it a fingertip at a time. Think about those underwriters at Cigna, giving insurance quotes to customers in California. There's a large body of knowledge about seismology and another husky corpus of actuarial expertise, but Cigna's underwriters don't need it. For them, the knowledge-management task is to create a tool that combines actuarial and seismic knowledge quickly, to teach the use of the tool, to develop interviewing and customer-relations skills, and to connect them to experts when special problems arise. The knowledge-management problem for Cigna's actuaries is entirely different.

In the difference lies a principle of knowledge management: *Knowledge should be managed within a context in which value is created*. "Design, development, and deployment of a system to support knowledge management must therefore be carried out with only one organization in mind—yours," not that of the industry or even other divisions of your company, if they create value differently or use different knowledge.

Are you a standardizer or a customizer? Chapter 4 pointed out the strategic choice between innovating and reusing of knowledge. For a company that reuses knowledge, reinventing the wheel is a no-no, and it's good knowledge management to build a virtual storehouse containing the specs for every wheel ever invented. That kind of encyclopedia of corporate know-how is doomed to becoming an expensive failure for a shop where invention is the necessity. Jon Bentley imagined that the Kraken would be filled with volumes of research papers; he was wrong, because the group's members were "creatives" whose purpose was "to be more innovative." They wanted a café, not a library. Their questions are unstructured, their problems may be new; they don't want answers so much as they want to talk to smart people; for innovators, the goal of knowledge management will often be to improve a person's chance of putting together the right team of experts. One of the great dangers of knowledge-management technology is that it can lead you to invest in the systems and infrastructures of knowledge reuse when innovation is your company's value proposition. If nothing else, that's a waste.

By contrast, production strategies (whether customized, mass-customized, or mass-production) where you mostly know what knowledge you need, the tasks are mostly well understood, the processes mostly routine, and the problems mostly familiar, lend themselves to a knowledge-management strategy of codification and automation, librarianship, and stewardship. This will be true most—not all—of the time for companies that are set up as knowledge value chains, as discussed in Chapter 4.

Even in these cases, beware the danger that technology can be an enabler in the same sense that an alcoholic's spouse can be one. John Seely Brown and Paul Duguid warn against what they call "Moore's Law Solutions" to problems:

Moore's Law solutions . . . take it on faith that more power will somehow solve the very problems that they have helped to create. . . . More information, better processing, improved data mining, faster connections, wider bandwidth, stronger cryptography—these are the answers. Instead of thinking hard, we are encouraged simply to "embrace dumb power." More power may be helpful. To the same degree, it is likely to be more problematic, too.

Too often "dumb power" produces a higher-level stalemate, just as automobiles fill however much highway is built and work expands to fill the time allotted to do it. When I first began writing about the knowledge economy and mentioned the problem of information overload, a man in the Midwest wrote me several ardent letters arguing that the problem could be solved if only people did exercises to strengthen their eye muscles, so they could read faster and with less fatigue.

What's the nature of the knowledge? Knowledge, like a woman's jacket, can be constructed or unconstructed, prim or revealing, tailored or loose-fitting. Knowledge management goes wrong when it tries to clothe a body of knowledge in an unbecoming style. Here's the problem, as set forth by Jeffrey Kay, chief technology officer of Engenia Software in Reston, Virginia:

It seems that technology is inversely proportional to the amount of content transferred. Consider the range of technology from face-to-face conversations (lowest technology) to Instant Messaging (highest tech) and the range of content accordingly.

Face-to-face—low tech, highest content, including facial expressions, voice inflections, as well as the words themselves

Telephone—higher tech than F2F, lower content, loses facial expressions

E-mail—higher tech than telephone, lower content yet, loses voice inflections

Instant Messaging—higher tech than e-mail, lowest content yet, loses well-thought-out paragraphs of information (excluding this post, of course :-)). Hopefully we'll figure out how to use this technology to increase the content of our collaboration, not continually reduce it. I don't know if anyone else has coined this law—if not, perhaps someone will be generous enough to name it Kay's Law of Collaboration.

Kay's Law of Collaboration is one journalists understand; because mostly we're going after unstructured knowledge, we "know" face-to-face interviews are "better" than phoners, for example. In general, the simpler the question, the higher the technology. E-mail's fine to check the spelling of your name, but to talk about the future of your business, we should meet.

Kay proposed his law on an e-mail forum, where it sparked debate:

This is all wrong [said Tony Finch, a Unix software developer working for Covalent Technologies] . . . Fidelity or bandwidth or whatever you want to call it is not the same as content. Most F2F interaction is not high-content: written communication is, because it allows you to take the time to make more reasoned arguments with references to sources, etc. Not only that, written communication is more efficient since the writer doesn't have to repeat the same message for different audiences, and the readers can skip the parts that aren't relevant to them; with F2F communication you have to trade the two off against each other.

Kay replied:

Tony—As you might expect, I disagree with your definition of content. Content doesn't have to be written to be "high." Your use of the term "fidelity" is interesting and could likely replace my use of the word "content," but it doesn't really change the point. . . . The point is sociological and could probably be better stated as follows—use of popular collaboration technology is inversely proportional to fidelity of the communications. Stating it that way just doesn't have quite the ring that the original does—technology is inversely proportional to the amount of content transferred. Keep in mind that this isn't a purely scientific maxim—it's an observation about how we live.

Efficiency isn't really the point at all, although I could make a reasonable argument that all this "efficiency" has reduced the amount of content in our conversations. For example, this note is a very efficient way for us to have this conversation—piecemeal, as we have time— but you miss the intensity of which my fingers are hitting the keys on the keyboard (viz., the expression on my face, the volume and intonation of my voice) in making these arguments. For all you know, I could be sitting back, uncaring, making this response or I could be really angry at your assertions. . . . There's no way for you to know this because this part of the content isn't making the transition through the technological medium that we've chosen for this discussion.

Finch and Kay are talking about two different kinds of communication, two different kinds of knowledge. Finch is looking for reliability, authority, and the value associated with efficiency and replicability ("so the writer doesn't have to repeat"). He is looking for reusable knowledge, and what one might call "knowledge transactions"—what a Cigna underwriter wants when he's calculating risk factors for an application for insurance. Kay is looking for collaboration, richness, and the kind of value associated with intimacy and "fidelity." He's looking for ways to improve knowledge creation or discovery, and what one might call "knowledge relationships"—what a Cigna actuary wants when consulting a seismologist about the Palmdale Fault in order to write an algorithm that quantifies the risk.

Information technology better suits information than knowledge. It even tries to change knowledge into information-like objects. When it succeeds, you've got a problem. Says Amrit Tiwana, author of *The Knowledge Management Toolkit*, who teaches in the business school of Georgia State University: "Technology helps collect, store, transfer, and distribute information. Information does not necessarily translate to knowledge, for much knowledge is too tacit and too obliviously ingrained in people's heads to be codified—let alone transferred electronically."

TACIT VS. EXPLICIT KNOWLEDGE

The word *tacit* comes from Latin, meaning "to be silent or secret"—tacit knowledge is knowledge you have but do not express. It's the complement of explicit knowledge. *Explicit,* also from Latin, means "to unfold"—to be open, to arrange, to explain. It almost means "to document." At the end of texts in Latin, medieval scholars used to write "explicit"—it is unfolded, it's an open book. One of those wonderful compound German nouns—*Fingerspitzengefühl,* "a feeling in the fingertips"—is roughly synonymous with tacit knowledge, and highly descriptive of my favorite illustration of the difference between it and explicit knowledge: Imagine yourself standing behind your teenager who needs your help with the computer—it almost doesn't matter what task, so long as it's familiar and just a wee bit complicated. Your tacit knowledge is literally a *Fingerspitzengefühl*; your hand wants to take the mouse to show how the job's done; if you do, you will infuriate your child, who will grab the mouse back. If, on the other hand, you try to explain what your fingertips know ("first, move the cursor up to the toolbar and select that whatever-you-call-it icon, the third, no fourth, from the left . . ."), you will stumble and become tongue-tied; following your semicoherent instructions, your child will accidentally close the document he was working on, and will become infuriated. It is thus the fate of the parent of an adolescent to appear to be either a controlling brute or a total idiot.

Most high-value knowledge work is thick with tacit knowledge. Partly this is because so much explicit knowledge has been automated. Your calculator knows the multiplication tables and Ford's robots know how to affix a windshield wiper assembly, so the work that's left to do is figuring out what equation to set up to solve the problem of how to fix the robot when it starts attaching the wipers to the radiator grille.

Almost all explicit knowledge belongs in the domain of structural capital. Here are documents, databases, intellectual property, manuals, formulae, recipes, procedures, etc.—the stuff Tony Finch was after. (Some contracts with customers and employees might be explicit forms of human and customer capital.) The essential tasks of managing explicit knowledge are the following:

assemble it
validate it
as much as possible, standardize and simplify it
keep it up to date
leverage it
make sure everyone who needs it knows that it exists, where to get it,
    and how to use it
automate and accelerate the processes of retrieving and applying it
add to it
sue any bastard who steals it

None of these is trivial, but none is brain surgery. We know how to do them, provided we intelligently ask, What work group? What knowledge? What business model?

Tacit knowledge is mostly found in human and customer capital, in people and relationships, and not even brain surgery can get at it (though sometimes psychotherapy does). Thus most of the stock of intellectual capital is tacit. So is a great deal of the flow. The value-creating activities of knowledge companies are collaborative, customized, and nonlinear; they are also fast. They call upon unstructured knowledge and often require answers to questions that are unclear or at least new. They employ mysterious and almost inarticulable processes of research, alignment, assessment, support, stimulation, connection, storytelling, and judgment. People are trained in the use of explicit knowledge; they are counseled in the development of tacit knowledge.

Most work involves explicit and tacit knowledge in combination. Most knowledge management, however, limits itself to explicit knowledge; if it doesn't ignore tacit knowledge, it does a lousy job of getting at it. In their book *The Knowledge-Creating Company,* Ikujiro Nonaka and Hirotaka Takeuchi describe a four-stage process by which knowledge grows and is transferred, which they call SECI: socialization, externalization, combination/creation, and internalization. In the SECI process, tacit knowledge becomes explicit as I take what I know and externalize it (by typing these words, for example); then explicit knowledge becomes tacit as it is internalized.

Knowledge is socialized when one person shares it with another in a tacit manner ("watch what I do and see if you can do it"); it's externalized when it's made explicit (typed up into a manual, for instance); and so on around the square. The idea is that knowledge management happens, in significant part, by the process of explication. I can get something from my head into your head by turning it into an artifact (a document, a file, a video, a piece of code) that we can then ship around the Net.

Well, yes—partly. The Web and the intranet are astounding tools for sharing and transferring explicit knowledge; certainly they're the best mankind has ever had for disseminating knowledge quickly and widely. But many kinds of knowledge don't lend themselves to explication. They are "high-touch." Learning a language involves explication and explanation, grammar and vocabulary, and the like. But real language learning involves soaking it in tacitly; no matter how well you do on a *dictée* in class, you won't sound French until you have spent enough time among

THE SECI PROCESS

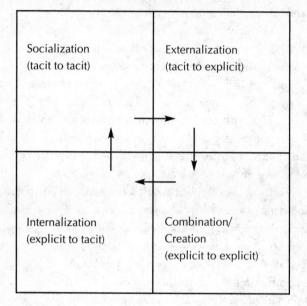

Source: Adapted from Nonaka and Takeuchi, The Knowledge-
Creating Company

Frenchmen. Cooking is another example. When making pastry dough,
temperature and humidity influence how much water you add to the flour.
A recipe gets you close, but at a certain point, French cooks say, *il faut
mettre la main à la pâte,* "you must put your hand in the dough." Technol-
ogy-mediated knowledge management can't do much with tacit knowledge. IBM's David Snowden, the best thinker I've found on the subject,
says quite baldly: "Sharing tacit knowledge . . . cannot be achieved
through an Intellectual Capital Management System," by which he means
all the stuff technology enables.

In 1998, Nippon Roche, the Japanese subsidiary of the global pharmaceutical company, faced a clearly foreseeable drought of new products—a
serious business problem. Till new drugs were approved (a tortuous
process in Japan, as elsewhere), the company desperately needed to
increase sales of existing drugs like Furtulon (an anticancer agent),
Draganon (which stimulates neurological function), and the antibiotic
Rocephin. These had been slowly declining, as is the way with older med-

icines; Furtulon sales, for example, had sagged from ¥29 billion a month in early 1996 to a nadir of about ¥22.8 billion in early 1999.

There were bright lights in this dark sky, however: Nippon Roche had several salespeople—medical representatives, or MRs—who far outperformed the rest. Here was a classic knowledge-management problem: Learn from the best and teach the rest. Selling drugs involves four kinds of knowledge—product knowledge, targeting, getting access, and selling. The best MRs handled each one a little differently. The average salesperson got product and medical knowledge strictly from the manual; the best also acquired hands-on knowledge by watching medical procedures and talking to patients and physicians. The best reps did lots of market research and used many information sources to set clear targets; the average MR used fewer resources and had less clear goals. In terms of selling skills, the best were, like good salespeople everywhere, carefully attuned to what the customer said he wanted and were always trying to close a sale, never just chatting. All of these were examples of explicit knowledge: They can be discovered, analyzed, and to a large extent taught.

The fourth body of knowledge, access, was a black box. Somehow the best MRs managed to get appointments with doctors and hospitals where others found closed doors. According to Nippon Roche's president, Hiroaki Shigeta: "The excellent MR knows everything about timing. He has a knack to get to know doctors based on his own experiences. He comes up to them when his competitors are not around. He knows it. He has a knack and experiences. I did not think that our previous way of training had much impact on this. It was so hard to get an MR to learn this kind of tacit knowledge through TV or communication."

How do you teach a knack? Twenty-four of the company's best salespeople became part of the SST—Super Skills Transfer—program. Brought together to talk, they themselves couldn't explain how they opened doors. Nor could they imagine teaching what they couldn't tell. But they could show. Rather than revise the sales representatives' manual, the group discarded it and prepared a new one, full of stories, diagrams, and metaphors. Then they went on the road, in groups of three, to every sales district in the country. They had no authority, no budget, no staff—just knowledge, and Shigeta's order that they be allowed to spend a month talking to MRs, accompanying them on calls, hanging around in the office, and, after, kibitzing, then moving on to another sales district. To help each other as they toured, the SST teams kept in touch by phone, e-mail, and occasional meetings.

Tacit knowledge transfers the way acne clears up, almost imperceptibly over time till the morning you see a face in the mirror and wonder who that handsome devil is. After SST visits, seven out of ten MRs said it was now easier to visit "difficult big potential key accounts"; six out of ten said they felt more confident about their ability to deal with "difficult doctors." Sales turned around; monthly sales of Furtulon, for example, rose above ¥24 billion by the spring of 2000.

Tacit knowledge is—sometimes—explicable; more often, it's demonstrable. The first and often most difficult task of managing it is to find it. Tacit knowledge doesn't announce itself. It wears no name tag saying, "Hello! My name is Jane! Ask me about market segmentation analysis!" It's very much part of day-to-day work—and that is where it leaves its spoor. Embedded in the e-mail of a company is a rich picture of its employees, customers, and suppliers. Just as circulating correspondence showed me who did what and knew what, e-mail reveals communities of practice and pockets of expertise. Some very interesting software from companies like Tacit Knowledge Systems gets at this information. Basically, it extracts key words from a worker's outgoing e-mail and uses them to build a profile: Jane Doe's outgoing mail would presumably use words like "market analysis" and "segment" and might reveal that her recent projects have had to do with household products and young parents. (The worker gets to edit and control her profile, and the system also includes various privacy safeguards akin to my ability to keep letters out of the circulating correspondence.) If I have a question about laundry detergent and query the system, Jane's name ought to come up. Learning what she knows is another question, but at least I'd have a sense of where to begin.

There's no escaping the eternal tension in management between technologist and humanist, hard and soft, Theory X and Theory Y, Hobbes and Rousseau. The danger is that the tension becomes a struggle from which one side or the other emerges victorious. That's when knowledge management gets into trouble. No one can doubt that managing knowledge is a good thing provided, however, that the same rules that apply to knowledge are the same as those that apply to managing anything else. Chief among these is to manage what matters to the business—to focus out, on markets, customers, and suppliers. Andrew Michuda, the chief executive of Sopheon, which provides knowledge-management software and manages a network of thousands of technical experts and analysts whose services it sells to customers, perfectly describes how knowledge management goes wrong: "KM has hit a wall when it is generically applied. You need the richness of human interaction with the efficiencies of technology, focused on a knowledge-intensive *business* application. Knowledge management is much more effective if it is not a stand-alone button on somebody's PC but is integrated into a key business process."

What do your customers expect you to know? What intellectual materials—facts, bodies of knowledge, technologies, and so on—do you call upon? Are they found in documents or brainpans? Do your customers come to you for new ideas or for flawless execution of the tried and true? How does work actually get done around here? The answers to those questions will reveal the structure and content of your knowledge-management efforts.

"The customer is always right"—in business, that's where all the ladders start. Knowledge management, as it's usually thought of, is a support function. That's not a knock. Every company—whether it is high-tech or low, new-age or old-line—can gain from managing knowledge better, just as it can from superior financial management. We all need support, as the folks at the Bike and Maidenform companies know; but for what? A knowledge strategy should not stop with knowledge management. It should not start there, either. It should begin with a strategy for selling knowledge. We'll look at that next.

CHAPTER 7

A NEW OFFERING:
SELLING KNOWLEDGE PRODUCTS

Once out of nature I shall never take
My bodily form from any natural thing

WILLIAM BUTLER YEATS

Neal Workman knows a bright idea when he has one, and one day in 1985 he had one. Workman had recently started a company grandly named Debt Management Services. It was a collection agency. Workman, who lives in Portland, Maine, figured that lobstermen—small businessmen whose customers were also mostly small businesses, and whose inventory would rot before it could be repossessed—needed help chasing deadbeats. "I could have collected debt for the shoe industry, I suppose," Workman says, "but I really liked driving from Portland to Halifax, talking to the people. I love the ocean, the mystical places along the coast."

That day, however, Workman was in Manhattan, near South Street Seaport, and the owner of a big fish restaurant had just turkey-trotted him out the door. In the window of a ship's chandlery across the street Workman saw a bullhorn—the kind Sunday sailors shout "Ahoy!" through. "You know how loud those things sound indoors?" Workman laughs, recalling how he reentered the busy restaurant with his new bullhorn to inform patrons that the owner had stiffed the honest Mainers who'd caught the fish on their plates. He got his payment and his first glimpse of a big idea: Timely information has economic value.

The company has a new name now—what it is and how it got there is part of the story. It's still small and privately held; Workman says his sales are a bit under $6 million a year, about 22 percent of which is pretax profit. These days collections produce 20 percent of profits—but occupy a 0 percent share of the owner's mind. While fishermen worry about what they catch in their nets, Workman is up late thinking about what he's catching on the World Wide Web. Workman's transition from bullhorns to the invention of a virtual marketplace is the story of a business transformed by the new economy. It shows how knowledge can be not just a tool or an asset, but a product—a product whose economics are delicious.

As Workman tells it, he realized early that the information he collected was more valuable than the bills he collected. Debt collecting is subject to the law of diminishing returns; as he says: "There are only so many bad guys and so many dollars." His first employee—a then-nineteen-year-old whom Workman used to coach in hockey, now Vice President of Sales James Bonnvie—was badgering him to buy a newfangled Macintosh computer, saying: "You've got to save all your collection files; this stuff is too valuable to leave strewn on the floor." Suddenly Workman realized why: "I'm on a collection call in Colorado. I fly out, People Express, $89. I'm looking around, noticing the Seattle Sea Foods calendar on the wall, reading upside down on his desk, looking for past-due bills. I ask to go to the bathroom—always do that, because it's always in the back so you walk through the whole building. And when I'm done, I get in my rental car and immediately write down all the names and numbers I can remember seeing. Because if he ain't paying my client in Hooterville, Maine, he's not paying Miami Crab and he's not paying Seattle Sea Food. The real money is not collecting debt. The real money is: Who else wants to know this guy's not paying?"

Thus was born Workman's first knowledge product: a $1,000-a-year subscription to a fortnightly mailing that told fishermen which customers were slow to pay or wouldn't pay. The pitch: Better to buy an ounce of pre-vention—information—than suffer a pound of cure. Workman told clients: "You don't have to sell 'em to find out they're no good—you can read Neal's little shitlist."

As his Mac began filling with data on deadbeats, Workman stumbled upon a marvelous attribute of knowledge products. Facts, unlike fish, can be on more than one plate at the same time. Their economics, like their physics, permits quantum states; in this case, the same facts that help fishermen avoid bad debt helped Workman collect it. "I could use the knowledge forward or reverse," he says. "I'd bring my list of subscribers when I was on a collection call and say, 'Before you throw me out, these are the people who will be reading about what we decide today.'"

It's a revealing lesson about knowledge: Publishing is better than hoarding, provided, however—and it's a big "however"—that you have a source of added value that you can defend against competition. "There are three kinds of companies," Workman believes. "Some companies hit the wall. Some spend a lot of money and effort trying to get over or around the wall. And some build the wall." With knowledge products—as with any kind—building walls is vital. The product should be valuable but also knockoff-resistant.

The fresh-fish business turned out to be a superb place to learn that speed is a structural attribute of the Information Age. In 1987 Workman began seeing fax machines everywhere he went. His second knowledge product was born: "I said—ah ha!—if we're faster, we're better, because this whole business is based on melting ice cubes. It's fish today, cat food tomorrow." The product: a faxed Flash Report. "I'd call from the airport back to Maine, I'd say, 'Bob didn't pay the eight grand, how many people can we fax this to?'" So successful was the Flash Report that in 1990 Workman renamed his company SeaFax. If knowledge is the added value—and can move at light speed—then he who's firstest gets the mostest. SeaFax's most important measure of quality—posted in the office for all to see—became its win/loss ratio, which measured how often SeaFax was first to its clients with news of a bankruptcy, merger, fire, or other event. When SeaFax was second, Workman exploded.

Knowledge product number three was a credit report; the obvious line extension of the collections business is to publish reports that describe good guys as well as bad guys, with bank and trade references. That brought Workman into direct competition with a Long Island company called Seafood Credit, which had several years' head start—which meant it had a database. Still, says Workman: "I had a big advantage because he was manual, files in his drawer, and I had that stupid Apple Mac. I could save, retrieve, copy, and paste." (Seafood Credit wasn't entirely manual, but it used its computers for more traditional number-crunching.) He sat down with potential customers and asked them how Seafood Credit's reports could be improved, then made a promise: an up-to-the-minute report faxed within forty-eight hours. In August 1999, Seafax bought out its erstwhile rival.

SeaFax's collections business was pouring in rivers of information. With technology and a few phone calls, those streams became a pool, then an ocean, and computers allowed Workman's people to fish in it for almost any kind of knowledge product. Says Workman: "When you have data you can move and manipulate and manage, oh my God, you can sell the same data to everyone on the org chart. You can turn a credit database into a marketing database into a collections database."

Workman had come upon another trait that gives knowledge peculiar, and wonderful, economics: The content is independent of the package. The physical key is not the same as the code it carries. One after another, new knowledge products came out of that insight. For example, as SeaFax grew to thirty-five employees on two floors, the company produced a daily in-house newsletter to make sure everybody knew the day's trade news and gossip. One day a customer saw it and asked: "If you know, why don't I know?" The SeaFax NewsWire quickly became the company's biggest product.

"When you backbone your business as an information business," Workman says, "the opportunities hit you right between the running lights. You can just leverage and leverage and leverage." For instance, people who buy lots of seafood also buy meat and poultry—so meat processors and poultry farmers became a new market for essentially the same credit information. Because the database is live—worked with every day—Workman says it's fresher and more accurate than databases that aren't compiled by people chasing deadbeats. So once a year stop, print up all the names, addresses, and phone numbers, sell ads, call it the SeaFax Red Book, and price it at $179. Do the same for meat and poultry. Take the same information and put it on a CD-ROM. Same content, different package, and this package you can sell for $300, with a manufacturing cost of $1.50. Or keep the package but change the content: Add credit reports to the CD-ROM, build contact-management software into it, publish it quarterly; now someone buying or selling mahi-mahi can find his best business prospects with just a few keystrokes. That product, the Eureka CD-ROM, now outsells the NewsWire.

"I'll tell you what we sell," says Workman. "We sell *whew*. Some guy filed Chapter 11 this morning? *Whew*, I'm not his creditor. That's what we sell. The rest is just delivery tools." The Web is the ultimate—for now—delivery tool. In early 1998, Workman recalls, "I'm giving the tour to our newest employee, our Webmaster. He looks like Howdy Doody—crew cut, his eyes bug out—really smart. We walk by one cubicle; the woman there is putting down the phone, and she says, 'I just verified so-and-so burned down last night.' And I say, 'Okay, Mr. Internet, it's 10:20. Your job is to set us up so that at 10:21 anyone who is selling so-and-so knows he burned down last night.'" Channel SeaFax, up and running that summer, did that: It added to the credit reports (already online) a ticker-tape stream of names. If a subscriber clicks on a name, up pops the news: So-and-so burned down last night.

Ultimately *whew* makes a market work. Following the train of thought that had carried him so far, Workman made a huge bet—huge for a little company—that it could become the market itself. In 1998, with a million-dollar investment, he set up a Web site called Gofish.com. He began piloting one of the very first of what would be called "B2B marketplaces."

Workman's always in a hurry, but rarely in a rush. "We have to build the database," Workman explained in 1998, "and populate the place with buyers and sellers. Till we do that, we won't charge them. Then we will." The following year, he renamed the company Gofish.com and made SeaFax a subsidiary. Not till November 1999 did Workman go live and start charging for access to the Gofish Web site, where buyers (all of them vetted for creditworthiness by SeaFax) post what they want and sellers (all of them vetted for quality by SeaFax) post what they have. If, say, Legal Seafoods wants five hundred pounds of red snapper, the system will automatically deliver the request to sellers known to have snapper, or retrieve information from sellers who have told the system what they have in inventory. Sellers have the reciprocal opportunity to search for buyers. For subscriber-sellers, the credit database is part of the system, so they can avoid bad customers; tit for tat, buyers (like shoppers on eBay) report back on the quality and freshness of what they receive, creating a running tally for each seller. With funding from CMGI, one of the most effervescent of the dot.com bubble stocks, and with additional, more seasoned, financing from GE Capital, Gofish offers the whole panoply of SeaFax knowledge products. It also offers financial services via alliances with GE Capital and CIT Financial Services, who will buy a seller's receivables. Workman's little company now has 110 employees and a European branch office—all built, as Workman never tires of reminding himself and employees, on melting ice.

WHY SELL KNOWLEDGE PRODUCTS?

As with anything in business, the meaning and value of managing intellectual capital can be realized only in the marketplace. Even internal activities must be managed so that they serve markets and customers (real ones, not ersatz "internal customers") as directly as possible. High-impact knowledge management comes from managing knowledge projects that create and improve returns on intellectual capital, supporting knowledge processes that add value to your company's work, and selling knowledge itself. (See chart on page 136.) We'll begin with the third of these: Companies that long ago understood that knowledge is what their customers are *buying* have somehow managed to avoid the obvious corollary: Knowledge is what you're *selling*. Without a strategy for taking knowledge to market, knowledge management is meaningless. Selling knowledge products is one of the major business opportunities of our time.

Knowledge can be sold explicitly—what am I bid for this insight?—or incorporated in a bundle of other goods and services, as a mechanic's skill is when she rummages under the hood of your car. There's much to say for this implicit sale of knowledge (I'll say some of it as we go along), but there is valuable stuff to be learned by first focusing on the explicit—that is, by thinking of knowledge as a product in its own right.

In a television commercial that aired in 2000, ABB, the giant Swedish-Swiss manufacturer of electrical machinery, says of itself: "We build

HIGH-IMPACT KNOWLEDGE MANAGEMENT

Knowledge Products	Knowledge Projects	Knowledge Processes
Embedded (instilled) knowledge (smart products and services)	Knowledge and expertise maps; community building	Knowledge sharing
		Innovation
	Building and mining knowledge bases	Customer learning
Distilling and selling knowledge as a product	Reusing knowledge	Staff development
Selling knowledge consumables	Creating knowledge assets	
Leveraging intellectual property		

Source: Adapted from Dan Holtshouse, Xerox Corp.

knowledge." *Fortune's* advertisements claim that the magazine will "replace what the martinis destroyed." Those are but two of many examples of companies advertising knowledge as a product. "Ride New Ideas," Ford says; wear them, too, says Louis Boston: "Clothing. Accessories. Ideas." Britain's Scotia Bank advises you to "Invest in what you value most—knowledge," and if the market leaves you feeling ill, remember with Eli Lilly that "Knowledge is powerful medicine." Famously, "THINK," and record the result on a ThinkPad, unless you "Think Different" and use a Mac. Behind the slogans is a hard fact: Companies sell knowledge because that's where the money is.

Consider some challenges Hewlett-Packard faces. With sales of $49 billion, chiefly in computing (mostly servers and PCs) and printing and other imaging devices, HP has a business that's substantially subject to Moore's Law. That law, which says that the price of a given level of computing performance drops by half approximately every eighteen months, makes the pursuit of processing speed a dangerous but inescapable game. Lose it and you're stuck selling a product that's half as good (or twice as costly) as your competitor's. Win it and you get to tell your stockholders,

We've got this hot new product; only problem is, it sells for half as much as the product it's replacing. To Moore's Law add open systems, which make it difficult to "lock in" customers; toss in a proliferation of new competitors, shorter and shorter product life cycles, and rising customer expectations as businesses and ordinary folk come to depend on 100 percent reliability from computers. Then put substantial parts of the company in mass-production manufacturing businesses like printers, facing competition from low-wage markets. The margin squeeze is almost unbearable. In the ten years from 1988 to 1998, HP cut its operating expenses from 39 percent of sales to below 24 percent. Cost of goods—the parts in the box—is now over two-thirds of HP's costs. For consumer goods like printers, the cost of goods rose to about 80 percent. Between 1992 and 1998, after Compaq ignited a price war, PC manufacturers' gross margins dropped from about 40 percent to about 15 percent. For HP, pressure on margins is a way of life, and (too often for Wall Street) a grueling one.

How to respond? A few companies—IBM in mainframes, Microsoft and Intel in PCs, Cisco and Sun in networking—manage to hold sufficiently large private domains of knowledge that they have created standards in parts of the market, giving them a wee bit extra because the companies that congregate at their standards have to, in effect, tithe to them. Dell, as we saw in Chapter 4, obtained control of private knowledge about supply and demand—which reduces its costs, enables it to be nimbler, and eliminates inventory (always a good thing, but a grand thing when the value of items in stock depreciate at a Moore's Law clip). Apple, after a nauseating foray into an open sea where it licensed its operating system to be used by others, brought back Steve Jobs and his vision of an alternate universe, smaller but much more elegant than the big wide one. ("I feel like I've jumped off the *Titanic* and landed on a classy little yacht," I read in the first batch of circulating correspondence from a new colleague who'd arrived from a struggling behemoth competitor.) HP, by joining with Intel to codevelop a next-generation microprocessor, made an effort to get on the inside of a standards tent. "It better work," then-CEO Lew Platt told me in 1998: "I bet the company on it." He hadn't, really. HP had other strings to its bow: It could manage costs relentlessly—which it does well, but which gets tougher and tougher as you get better and better. It could, and did, rid itself of slower-growing divisions. It could, and does, innovate like crazy to stay ahead of the plunging cost curve and to create, at least temporarily, places to catch its breath because it has something cool and unique.

Most important, Platt and successor Carly Fiorina, like competitors almost everywhere else in the information-technology business (including IBM and Cisco and, recently, even Microsoft, which sees the value of its hegemony over the desktop slipping), tried to push into selling knowledge. Configuration, systems integration, consulting, service, network design, and management: These knowledge products and services represent a chance to step out of the path of plunging prices. IBM's CEO, Louis Gerstner, announcing superb fourth-quarter-2000 results, found in them affirmation of one of the premises of the company's strategy, to wit: "The marketplace is increasingly driven by services and solutions, not products."

Any knowledge-based company—which is to say, yours—has to get into a knowledge-based growth game, and that means finding a way to put a price tag or a meter on the smarts you sell. In the absence of proprietary knowledge, manufacturing economies of scale are doomed to fight a rearguard defense of profitability. There are only two sources of competitive advantage: differentiation (no one else has it) and cost (no one can produce it for less). Globalization, outsourcing, and a century of Scientific Management have made it harder and harder to achieve either by means of physical assets, materials, and processes. The search for another model drove HP in 2000 to pursue buying the consulting services of PricewaterhouseCoopers—because they can make more money selling knowledge than boxes. That deal having fallen through, HP found itself face-to-face with the problem, knowing where the solution is, but not certain of the best path to it.

One certainty is that hardware leads nowhere. I wrote that sentence in the summer of 2001, a few weeks before HP announced a merger with Compaq—another computer company strong in hardware and struggling to overcome weakness in services. The market reacted furiously, driving both companies' stocks down so much that it is possible the merger will not occur. It's no wonder. Earlier, Merrill Lynch analyst Thomas Kraemer had gone so far as to state, "[In the enterprise computer hardware industry] hardware companies do not exist; there are no hardware companies, and there have never really been any. . . . Hardware is actually leverage, distribution, and a commodity, not an industry. Once a firm's software differentiates it, the company can charge customers high prices for hardware as well as for software. . . . Openness is a sham and . . . being as proprietary as possible is the way to go."

It's simple, really: If knowledge is the value you add, sell it. Every business these days—manufacturers, service companies—claims it sells "solutions." The most successful businesses behave as if they mean what they say.

TWO TYPES OF KNOWLEDGE PRODUCT

It's not simple, of course, or more people would do it. The first complication: thinking through what a "knowledge product" might be. High-brainpower activities produce knowledge products for which people pay a premium price. Many are legal monopolies because they are unique or enjoy intellectual property protection; others are quasi-monopolies because they can be customized or can become an industry standard; others are rare because the personal and organizational abilities they rely on are hard to copy.

There are two basic ways to create knowledge products, says Stan Davis, coauthor of *Blur: The Speed of Change in the Connected Economy.* One comes from asking, "We've got some knowledge—how do we make it into a product?" The other answers the question "We've got a product—how do we add knowledge to it?" In the first case, knowledge is distilled, packaged, and sold; it is, if you'll permit me an ugly phrase, "productized knowledge." In the second, it is instilled and sold—brace yourself for an even uglier phrase—in a "knowledgized product."

(Excuse me while I clean the keyboard.)

Instilled knowledge is everywhere. Obvious examples include computers, cars, copiers—devices suffused with smarts. Says Michael Zack, professor of business at Northeastern University: "These are cases where we put the knowledge into a box and sell it to you and you don't have to know it yourself to get the benefit from it."

There are two key points here: First, the knowledge is buried, so the consumer doesn't need to know it to use the product. That's a tried-and-true knowledge-selling strategy. A driver today does not need to know how to adjust a carburetor or replace a brake lining. But when automobiles were new, they were as unstable as Windows 3.0. "You had to be a mechanic to drive one," says Internet pioneer Carl Malamud, or rich enough to hire someone called a *chauffeur*. The French word's literal meaning is "stoker"—the chauffeur's job was to know how to keep the thing from shutting down. Ease of use, which the scornful call "dumbing down," is productized knowledge.

The second key part of Zack's statement is "benefit." Consider this paradox: (a) The cost of knowledge storage and distribution plunges so fast that these days MIPS should be priced in ringgits rather than dollars; yet (b) total spending on information technology continues to rise, and is now a greater portion of U.S. GDP than the auto industry. And $a + b = conclusion$: People are "knowledgizing" damn near everything, from toilets to toasters. With a number stored in the memory of a mobile phone you can call a smart vending machine and get a Diet Coke, the cost of which will appear on your phone bill, which you can pay online. There's not a tangible item in that transaction, not even the drink, which has no calories and whose value, according to CFO James Chestnut, consists of brand equity and marketing know-how. Before many more Thanksgivings come and go—mark my words—Intelligent Turkeys with embedded microchips will signal when they need basting and shut off the oven when they're done. No doubt you'll be able to customize the signal—a dinner bell for traditionalists, a gobble-gobble for the ghoulish.

The decision to instill knowledge—capability, intelligence—into a product must meet the same commonsense test any feature should meet: Does it add value customers will pay for? And, a bit more recherché, do different market segments have different knowledge needs? Time was, drivers paid extra for automatic transmissions, which freed them from knowing how or when to clutch and shift. Now a subset of drivers pays extra for manual transmissions, which allow them to use their knowledge of the gearbox to save fuel or have more fun behind the wheel.

INSTILLING KNOWLEDGE

Indiana-based Lincoln Re, the reinsurance arm of Lincoln National Corporation, has done an excellent job of thinking through the value proposition of knowledge products. Lincoln Re is one of the largest and best-regarded companies in the health and life reinsurance business. Reinsurers' customers are other insurance companies; when you buy a policy, your insurance company reduces its exposure to risk or balances its portfolio by selling off a portion of the risk (and the income) to a reinsurer, like a bookie laying off a portion of his bets on the Belmont Stakes. Says Arthur W. DeTore, who heads both strategic planning and knowledge management for Lincoln Re: "If reinsurance is purely risk transfer, it's a commodity product. Our goal is to decommoditize reinsurance. So we try to provide a higher knowledge-content solution than our competitors do."*

DeTore looks for "economies of knowledge." The easiest way to understand economies of knowledge is to compare them to two other types of economizing. Economies of *scale* reduce unit costs by means of mass production: Global Amalgamated Widgets can force suppliers to quote a better price for raw materials than the one Upstate Gadgeteering gets, and saves on unit manufacturing cost because it built big, dedicated assembly lines for a single product. Economies of *scope* save money by using the same infrastructure for many kinds of offerings. Because Procter and Gamble already has a sales, marketing, and distribution system for household products, it can deliver a new brand of detergent for less than a company that has to start from scratch. Economies of knowledge, as DeTore defines them, often resemble economies of scope: They "allow customized, intelligent solutions to be delivered more cost effectively by increasing the customization and knowledge content in a service without dramatically increasing the cost"—that is, they spread the cost and multiply the value of expertise, usually via technology or through alliance partners. To find them means matching customer needs against Lincoln Re's expertise—but also making sure that *this* knowledge added to *this* product will increase shareholder value for Lincoln Re, measured by discounted

---

* DeTore and his colleague Mark Clare are coauthors of a book called *Knowledge Assets Professional's Guide to Valuation and Financial Management* (San Diego: Harcourt Professional Publishing, 2000). If you're serious about putting intellectual capital to work, first finish this book. Then—and only then, but definitely then— run, do not walk, and buy Clare and DeTore's. It's dense and in spots difficult, but that's the point. Nowhere else have I seen such specific, rigorous advice on analyzing the costs and benefits of managing and selling knowledge.

cash flow tests. There are six ways to increase cash flow—remember them? Increase revenues or margins, or reduce costs or capital requirements or the cost of capital or taxes. If adding knowledge to a product doesn't accomplish one or the other, it doesn't get done. Says DeTore: "If all we do is hire a bunch of people to produce expertise, we just drive up our costs."

Lincoln Re looks for economies of knowledge by examining its *customers'*—that is, insurance companies'—value chain and asking, "How can we add value by instilling knowledge?" At every link in the chain, it turns out:

Distribution: Ordinary term life insurance is a commodity and can be sold inexpensively, by direct sales rather than through costly sales agents. Specialized term insurance—former smoker, diabetes in the family, perfect driving record, flies her own plane to vacations in malarial swamps, swims ten miles a week, has a spouse, a Harley, a minivan, and a black Labrador named Spot—has the potential to be much more profitable, but it's hard to sell direct and few insurance companies have a big enough database to calculate all the risk factors. A reinsurer, however, sees many times more data than most insurance companies; its actuarial knowledge can be turned into an expert system for customers, allowing them to sell nonstandard term insurance through direct channels. So Lincoln Re built the Lincoln Mortality System and the Lincoln Underwriting System, natural-language expert systems that allow its customers to reduce their distribution costs.

Product development and pricing: The same mortality and underwriting data that help Lincoln's customers to reduce distribution costs also help them to increase margins by pricing insurance more accurately and raise revenues by offering policies in cases that might have seemed too difficult for a small company to analyze on its own. In addition, company actuaries share insights about emerging problems—news that hasn't yet shown up in injury or mortality statistics, for example—through its Knowledge Enhancement and Experience Program.

Underwriting risk: The essence of reinsurance is understanding and bearing risk—and is the only place where traditional reinsurers sell their knowledge to their customers. Lincoln Re has broadened its offering here with LincUP, a knowledge product that offers self-insured customers the ability to calculate their exposure to risk, and thus their own reinsurance needs, by going online to match Lincoln Re's massive actuarial data against the customer's location, workforce demographics, occupational categories, and so on.

Claims administration and ongoing relationships with customers: Health maintenance organizations worry greatly about unusual, highly expensive claims like organ transplants. In addition to reinsuring these risks, Lincoln Re helps reduce them. The company sees dozens of transplant cases a year; a typical HMO might see one or two at most and not know how best to handle them. So Lincoln Re formed an alliance of doctors and hospitals that are leaders in transplant surgery. In exchange for referrals from Lincoln Re, the medical centers offered volume discounts. The insurer also created a case-management product for HMOs by bundling the services of expert case managers into the reinsurance product it sells to HMOs. That commands a higher price.

You get the point, but in case you don't, C. K. Prahalad of the University of Michigan put it this way: "Creating knowledge products will be a source of competitive power."

DISTILLED KNOWLEDGE

Companies teem with intelligence that can be turned into products, but most of the time people inside the company can't see it. Like plankton in the sea, this knowledge is part of their environment, invisible to the naked eye—yet it can feed great whales. Chances are you already produce knowledge products that you don't see because they're bundled with something else or because it simply hasn't occurred to you to sell them. Remember Neal Workman's customer, who saw the company's internal daily news briefing and asked: "If you know, why don't I know?"

Here's the secret: *You find knowledge products not by looking at your own value chain, but by looking at that of your customers,* as Lincoln Re does. General Electric's aircraft engine division distilled a knowledge business out of its "real" business when it converted its expertise in making engines into an engine-servicing business (now more profitable than manufacturing). Now GE is creating a new product line: Having learned how to reduce the amount of time an engine spends inside a GE shop, the company is offering airlines the chance to let GE experts reduce their time taking engines off, getting them to the shop, and putting them back on; "wing-to-wing" service, GE calls it. Nuovo Pignone, an Italian maker of high-power compressors and turbines that GE acquired in 1994, created a $600 million business in two years—that's a 25 percent revenue increase, and with higher margins—by turning its manufacturing knowledge into installation, maintenance, and repair products. GE's competitor in medical systems, Siemens AG, uses knowledge instilled in a product— CAT scan equipment fitted out with modems that dial back to Siemens about the uses to which they are being put and alerting the company to maintenance problems—to expand its service business. Another example: London-based Thomas Miller, the dominant maritime insurance company, which insures cargo ships and freight containers. In the ordinary course of business, Thomas Miller's employees collect and use an enormous amount of information about maritime law and customs rules; they have maps of virtually every harbor in the world, know where natural hazards lie, etc., etc., but not until the 1990s did it occur to anyone in the firm that this valuable knowledge was also salable. Now the *Miller Encyclopedia* has become an important product.

TIE Logistics, a small private company in suburban Boston (sales between $5 million and $10 million a year), offers a good look at this second kind of knowledge product—where knowledge is distilled, packaged, and offered for sale. Says Professor Zack: "This company made the leap from managing freight to managing knowledge." In the late 1980s, Bill Habeck, now TIE Logistics's president, was working at Bay State Shippers (since sold to C. H. Robinson Company); there he developed an information system called Command. It let end users track rail and intermodal shipments—both cars and containers—everywhere in North America, serving up data on location, transit time, causes of delays, volume by customer, maintenance records, and so on. It was so cool for its time that the product is displayed in the permanent Information Age exhibit at the Smithsonian Institution. In 1992, Habeck set up on his own, bringing Command with him—in effect, extracting the knowledge portion of the old Bay State and putting it into a separate business. Now a sister product called REZ-1 allows shippers to reserve rail containers from Conrail, Norfolk Southern, Union Pacific, and several smaller railroads and agencies—all in all, about 15 percent of the continent's rail containers. "We don't sell software in the traditional sense," says Habeck; nor is it really a service. Instead TIE Logistics gathers, checks, and organizes information from carriers and users, then "productizes" it through Command and REZ-1 into a series of offerings: services for tracking shipments, reserving containers, and billing; several tools that allow customers to improve asset utilization, for example by forecasting fleet needs and keeping track of how long cars or containers stand empty; and studies aimed at developing industry best practices, such as analyses of roadblocks. "We have two or three other products in the pipeline," Habeck says, including possibly expanding to cover waterborne freight. Most of this knowledge existed before, but it was, as it were, dissolved in the business of moving things from one place to another. By distilling it, Habeck is able to do several things. First, he can collect and move it faster, because he no longer has to wait for the physical goods. Second, he can sell it more than once—first to the shipper, second to the party whose goods are being shipped, and perhaps to third and fourth parties. He can combine information about one shipment with dope about others and create still more things to sell to still more people. When Judith Martin was at the start of her career as "Miss Manners" her *Washington Post* colleague, humorist Art Buchwald, gave her a piece of advice about how to succeed as a writer. "Never sell anything only once," he told her, explaining that the material he used in his newspaper columns he repackaged and resold in hardcover books, then in paperback, then told and sold again on talk shows and in paid speeches. That's what distilled knowledge is all about.

PSST! WANNA BUY SOME FILTHY KNOWLEDGE?

For too long—and too often still—companies have sold knowledge as if it were smut: hidden under the counter or in the pockets of a trench coat rather than in the open. Just off the Zócalo in the center of Mexico City are government-run arcades where silver- and goldsmiths sell their wares—shop after shop after shop, each brightly lit to show the glistering rings, pins, necklaces, a metallic cornucopia. All of it sold as if it were fruit, too: by weight. Customers, of course, choose one necklace over another because of design—that's what they're buying, but the jewelers are not allowed to charge for it.

The first element of knowledge-product strategy is definitional: Tease out what knowledge and capabilities customers are paying for, then put a price tag on it. Often the knowledge is hidden. A lawyer sells more than knowledge of the law, for example; negotiating ability, relationships with other lawyers, and knowledge of his client's priorities are also valuable. In the heyday of IBM, the company sold smart machines but also sold peace of mind: No head of information systems, the saying went, ever was fired because he bought IBM equipment. Today that attribute helps IBM sell its technology consulting services.

Make a list, a catalogue of knowledge products and potential knowledge products. These include knowledge distilled and sold on its own, and knowledge instilled to make a "smart product." To help people see the possibilities for the latter, consultant Stan Davis likes to ask them to answer this question: "What would a Coke machine like to know?" There's a long list of possible answers, some of which Coke machines already do know. It might want to know its inventory, its location, and the phone number of its distributor, so that if it runs out of Diet Dr Pepper it can ask for replenishment; it might want to know if it is broken and how to inform a repairman; it might want to know whether money is real or counterfeit; it might want to know the phone number of a police station, etc.

Do this with everything you sell. The chair I am sitting in—what might it want to know? The computer you use: Why can't it contain its own diagnostic software to tell you what went wrong? The commercial you produced: Does it want to know who watched it? How much would it cost to find out? How much would it be worth to know?

Next, explore the various ways this knowledge can be packaged and sold. The alert reader—maybe the drowsy one, too—will have noticed that I've been fuzzing up the line between "product" and "service" in this chapter. Ultimately it's not a very meaningful difference, and where knowledge is what's sold it's often an arbitrary one. *The New York Times* I picked up from the doormat this morning is product; the same content offered online is a service. The original version of the chart (on page 147) was made by Mark Clare and Arthur DeTore to classify knowledge assets, but it can also be used to categorize knowledge products. Every "unit" of

SAME KNOWLEDGE, MANY FORMS

Knowledge Type	Content	Structure	Reasoning	Example
Culturally based	Tacit	Tacit	Tacit	Nordstrom
Intellectual property	Explicit	Explicit	Tacit	Patent
Process-based	Explicit	Explicit	Explicit	McDonald's
People-based	Tacit	Tacit	Tacit	Mentoring
Media-based	Explicit	Tacit	Tacit	Guidelines
Electronically indexed	Explicit	Explicit	Tacit	Hypertext
Electronically active	Explicit	Explicit	Explicit	Expert systems

Source: Adapted from Mark Clare and Arthur DeTore, *Knowledge Assets*

knowledge, they figure, has three attributes: content (what it's about), structure (how it's organized), and reasoning (how you get at it—individual thinking, brainstorming, collaborative work, etc.). Thus culturally based knowledge—the way we work around here, the *je ne sais quoi* of the boys in pinstripes that drives New York Yankee haters bonkers—is tacit in content, structure, and reasoning, but the process of selling tickets can be spelled out from start to finish.

You can use this chart in two ways. First, where you have already identified knowledge products, you can map them onto the chart, then look around the chart for other ways to package and sell the same knowledge. Knowledge is fungible, transubstantiable, and transformable. It can be reified—that is, made solid, as the insights of my brain are bound between these covers—or be dematerialized. A valuable offering of Walt Disney's theme parks, for example, is its culturally based knowledge of service and safety; Disney's hiring and training methods are a process-based, explicit version of that knowledge, which Disney sells to other companies in the form of seminars held at its parks. Knowledge can almost always be sold in more than one form. Two weeks before I started writing this chapter, a public relations person tried to interest me in a company that makes a piece of software that was, she assured me, a CEO in a box. She didn't say whether it was cardboard or pine.

Second, you can use the chart to identify knowledge you haven't realized you have. The *Miller Encyclopedia* didn't exist as an in-house knowledge product; it was a bunch of stuff Thomas Miller's people knew, until the company thought to sell its knowledge directly to its customers.

You're creating what consultants call a "choice board"—and with it, the need to make choices. Different modes of selling knowledge carry different risks and opportunities. Their economics are not the same; they require different management processes and skills. (Managing software is nothing like managing people, for example.) There is no one right choice, ever—always in business, your mileage may vary—so you will have to decide your own best route to success. Here are some of the questions:

Risk. Each product strategy carries its own set of risks. When knowledge is people- or culturally based, you have the option of leaving it there, unproductized. That's the choice made by lawyer David Boies, who argued the U.S. government's antitrust case against Microsoft. The only way to buy his knowledge is to hire him; Boies even left the ritzy Cravath, Swaine & Moore law firm to operate on his own. The risk: David Boies gets hit by a bus. Flemish baroque painter Peter Paul Rubens, who taught himself to paint by copying the masterworks of others, productized his knowledge by setting up an enormous workshop where dozens of painters—among them Anthony Van Dyck and Jacob Jordaens, who later became masters in their own right—did much of the work while he supplied direction and finishing touches. The risk: knockoffs. People have bought paintings thinking they are by Rubens, but they turned out to be the work of lesser hands. Today fashion talent is frequently purloined—beneath the arcades around the Piazza del Duomo in Milan you can buy quite good copies of Prada and Gucci, a short walk from the real thing on the via Montenapoleone.

Often productized knowledge can be protected by patent or copyright. The risk: By filing a patent you make explicit what might have been hidden, providing a road map for copyists when the patent expires. You can manufacture smart products—but risk their being reverse-engineered if a competitor takes it apart to see how it works, and puts together something with similar functionality that doesn't impinge on your intellectual property.

On the other hand, to leave the knowledge in someone's head—in the form of know-how rather than a patent—is to run the risk that people who leave the office tonight might show up somewhere else tomorrow, like Robert Noyce and Gordon Moore, who defected from Shockley Transistor Corporation to form Fairchild Semiconductor, then did it again to start Intel, acts of brain-cell meiosis that left both progenitor companies hurting.

Scale: If you have a moderately complicated financial life and hire an accountant to prepare your income tax returns, you will pay several hundred dollars. For about $100 you can take the same W-2, 1099s, and shoe-box full of receipts to H&R Block. For $19.99 you can buy Quicken's TurboTax software and do your own return on your PC, which asks you questions and does your arithmetic. Or you can buy a paperback of J. K. Lasser's *Your Income Tax* for $15.95, in which case you will need to do your own arithmetic. In this instance, four sellers have chosen four different ways to market essentially the same knowledge. Of the group, the personal accountant, though the most expensive, is probably the least wealthy, if we count Block, Quicken, and Lasser as one person. Different knowledge packages have different scale economies, and by selling his knowledge as a personal service, the accountant has implicitly decided that his talents are best marketed one-on-one. (Maybe he doesn't have managerial skill; perhaps he prefers the higher gross margin of private practice.) At Helsinki University of Technology in Finland, Antti Koivula led a project team that developed a consulting methodology for team building. His group was able to charge about $70 an hour in consulting fees. Looking at the numbers, Koivula realized he could make more if he repackaged the knowledge as a software product, which he called Team Coach Plus. That paid him more than $4,000 an hour.

Explicit knowledge is inherently scalable. It's easy and cheap to make a million copies of the engineering specs for a Rolls-Royce, but that might not be the right way to sell the product.

Leverage. Like cash, the same knowledge can be used for many different activities. Unlike cash, knowledge, used once, can be used again and again. In the summer of 2001, while traveling in Italy, I inadvertently used my MasterCard to try to get cash from an ATM, but entered my bank card's personal identification number. I realized my mistake, got the credit card back, and tried again with my bank card—and went on my way. At home a couple of weeks later, I received a letter from the company that issues my MasterCard. We noticed, it said, that you were unsuccessful in an attempt to use the card at an ATM. Have you forgotten your password? Might we tell you about all the exciting ways you can incur 18 percent interest charges by using our card?

The information about my mistake at the ATM was collected by the issuer's anti-theft, anti-fraud department; but someone realized that the same information could be leveraged into a marketing opportunity.

Knowledge can be leveraged in the marketplace as well as internally: packaged one way, it can be repackaged and sold again. One of the most innovative companies in Singapore was called Kent Ridge Digital Labs. KRDL developed a computerized clinical brain atlas. (KRDL and another company have since merged to become the Laboratories for Information Technology, and the brain atlas products have been spun off into a new company, Cerefy.) Neurosurgeons rely on detailed atlases of the brain's structure when planning their intricate operations. KRDL's genius was recognizing that a digital adaptation of printed brain atlases would allow the company to market the same information in many different forms. There's a print version. There are two different electronic versions (on CD-ROM) designed for medical students and teachers. Another is for clinicians. There's a plug-in library of images from the atlas and another library of geometrical models of brain structures. In the works is an atlas suited to the special needs of neuroradiologists. Through a company called BrainOnCall.com, Cerefy is licensing the atlas to leading surgical and medical companies around the world, some of whom may install it in the electronic brains of their imaging and diagnostic equipment. Obviously, the brain atlas is a prime example of the way digital content can be shaped and reshaped in different ways. But that marvelous, valuable fungibility is available whenever you can isolate knowledge. As Judith Martin began the career that brought her fame as etiquette expert "Miss Manners," her friend and *Washington Post* colleague Art Buchwald gave her a piece of advice about how to succeed as a writer: "Never sell anything only once." His jokes and satiric stories, he explained, began life in his newspaper column, which he then collected into books, which then enjoyed second and third lives in book-club and paperback editions, plus translations; and then he told the same stories on the speaking circuit. Nice work if you can get it—and you can get it if you try.

Of every knowledge asset and knowledge product, ask: Can this be leveraged and sold again? It's by no means a sure thing. There's a special grove of cypresses on Boot Hill beneath which are laid the plans of companies that thought their skill in one business would play in another. Conglomerates, those gargantuan corporate heterogenies of the 1960s, were built around a knowledge product—sets of financial controls—put in place across many different businesses. The syllogism went like this: Top financial management is the most important determinant of corporate success; conglomerates can deliver top financial management; ergo conglomerates will be successful corporations. The major premise (and maybe the minor one as well) was wrong. Every company needs good financial management, but in a supporting role for other, more critical intellectual and other assets. Conglomerates trade at a discount to the market.* Likewise Coca-Cola's knowledge of consumers' tastes served it poorly when the company tried to run Columbia Pictures. Fizz ain't buzz.

Explicit vs. implicit pricing: Buckman Laboratories, a midsize chemical company based in Memphis, Tennessee, with 1,300 people in more than seventy countries, takes itself seriously as a knowledge company. Buckman is a major seller to the paper and leather industries. Most of its customers require chemicals formulated especially for their product lines and their plants' idiosyncrasies. Therefore, says Melissie Rumizen, Buckman's longtime chief knowledge officer, "Buckman really sells chemistry, not chemicals." But it usually bills for chemicals—burying the price of the knowledge in the price of the chemicals. Not always, however: Buckman actually operates the "wet-blue" tanning operation for a big agribusiness customer, under a service contract—and in this instance for Buckman chemicals are a cost.

Most of the time knowledge is sold implicitly: When you go to Brooks Brothers and buy a suit, you don't know what portions of the price go to

---

*General Electric, the exception that proves the rule, is a conglomerate that trades at a premium to the market. As we saw in Chapter 2, this is because finance is just one of several knowledge assets that GE leverages across its businesses.

design, tailoring, and fabric; at an auto dealer, the sticker price will be explicit about the cost of the air-conditioning, CD player, and dealer prep, but leaves implicit the cost of finance, training, and design. These are cases of knowledge instilled, often hidden. Mostly it works, but it has dangers, the biggest of which is that your customer might end up undervaluing it, because all he sees is its manifestation in an object or service. Traditional full-service advertising agencies, for example, perform several knowledge functions. They do market research, offer consulting on brand and image and marketing, create advertisements, and plan and execute advertising campaigns. Traditionally they were paid, however, only for ad production and placement; the planning, consulting, and research were implicit in the price. Now those services are becoming unbundled and priced separately. Ditto stock brokerages. Old-line brokerages buried the price of their research in their trading fees. Discounters like Charles Schwab pulled them apart and charged just for execution. Now superdiscounter E*TRADE, realizing that winning a price war has a downside, began offering customers the chance to pay extra to get research reports; Morgan Stanley, which gives full-commission customers "free" access to all its research, now has a limited package of research for sale to its discount-brokerage customers. Unhappily, the analysts, now that they need to sell their services, seem to have lost some of their independence of thought.

Ross Dawson, CEO of an Australian consulting firm with the multiple oxymoronic name Advanced Human Technologies, points out that almost every transaction involves some mixture of three components: products (something you receive, tangible or intangible), black-box services (something done for you), and knowledge transfer (something that enhances your abilities). You can choose to put the price tag on any or all of the three, based on your reading of the competitive map. The moral's this: However you price knowledge—implicitly or explicitly—make it a considered choice, and make sure you know what its costs and value are, because someone's likely to come along and unbundle your business. "In an environment in which services have been unbundled," Dawson observes,

> one of the key issues is distinguishing between the commoditized and differentiated elements of the offering. There will always be an element . . . offered which [is] commoditized, and competitive pricing

strategies must be applied in those cases. However, the differentiated elements of the offering should be priced as much as possible based on the value to the client.

In general, it's good to make the cost of knowledge explicit: If knowledge is what you're really selling, your customers should know what they're really getting. David Smith, chief knowledge officer of Unilever, tells about a company that makes adhesives used to seal the seams and flaps of cardboard packaging. Employees discovered a new manufacturing process that would be twice as advantageous for their customers: It used less glue and increased the speed with which box-making machines could work. The company's dilemma: It charged for glue, not knowledge. Unless the company had a way to make the price of knowledge an explicit part of its business model, its discovery was worse than worthless.

Governance. Sometimes knowledge worth selling is worth more sold by someone else, as we saw in the case of Philips Electronics (see Chapter 4). AT&T's old equipment-manufacturing division was shut out of many lucrative opportunities because phone companies preferred not to buy from a competitor. Spun off as Lucent Technologies, the gear makers did better. Lucent's recent problems don't change the fact that its knowledge was and is more salable from its own house than from Ma Bell's back porch. Early in 2001, Procter & Gamble bet that its marketing know-how was a product worth selling on its own, not just bundled into every box of Tide, tube of Crest, or bottle of Pantene. Rather than set up a marketing division and inviting others to buy its services, P&G created a stand-alone company in a joint venture with Worldwide Magnifi, Inc., a California maker of Web-based marketing technology. Project EMM (for "enterprise marketing management") combines the marketing know-how of former P&G employees, software developed by both partners, and Worldwide Magnifi databases and data storage centers. Says P&G Global Marketing Officer Bob Wehling: "Creating this new company . . . is consistent with P&G's . . . desire to get greater financial value out of core assets like R&D inventions and marketing know-how."

All the issues of product marketing—channel management, line extensions, product life cycles—apply to knowledge products as they do to any other. It's worth singling out two issues unique to knowledge. One has to do with test marketing and market segmentation. The costs of knowledge-intensive products tend to be heavily front-loaded. (See Chapter 5.) You therefore may not be able to afford the old luxury of test marketing to small elite groups, then rolling your product out to the world. You probably need a faster return on your investment; furthermore, knowledge products have relatively short life cycles, not only because of Moore's pesky law but also because the minute your product is in the market, someone's figuring out how to piggyback on all your expensive R&D and design.

This opens two related product strategies. The first one we might call selling "knowledge consumables." It's the old give-away-the-razor-and-sell-the-blades trick: Microsoft makes zillions from selling upgrades. Second, rather than sell to elite markets first, go straight for what Chan Kim and Renée Mauborgne, professors at INSEAD in France, call "the price corridor of the mass." Interestingly, in the knowledge economy it's often possible to reverse the old elite-to-mass-market progression. Time was, a cultural artifact would go from narrow, high-priced, elite release toward broad, mass-market, cheap release. For example, books start out in hardcover, go to mail-order book clubs, then go to paperback. Likewise with drama—shows went from live theater to film to television and videotape.

Now we're seeing the reverse. *The Lion King* started as a movie for about $7.00 a ticket; now you can rent it for $3.50 or be one of a couple of thousand people who see a theatrical version on Broadway, where the top price is about $100. Music CDs sell for $15.95, but the bands make more on tour selling pricey tickets to smaller audiences. Authors like Art Buchwald write books that retail for $25, but he might get as much as $50,000 to tell an audience of two hundred—$250 a head, if you weren't doing the math—some of the stories they could read for much less. Knowledge products used to have to earn their way to the mass market; now they are as likely to have to earn their way to a narrow, elite one.

UNDER MY SKIN

One important way to sell knowledge is to position your company and products in the midst of an attractive knowledge community. One example of this kind of knowledge community is America Online—AOL doesn't so much sell knowledge as provide a mall and a bunch of coffee shops, places to talk. A more interesting example might be Cisco Systems. Cisco sells networking products and services, all of them highly knowledge-intensive offerings. Cisco's strategy is not just to sell products, but to bring its customers into its orbit, its solar system. John Chambers, the CEO, talks about:

> an emerging "Internet ecosystem"—a new business model for Internet-connected businesses to serve Internet-connected customers. The open nature of the Internet encourages complementary business alliances that create a unique set of interwoven dependencies and relationships. Since Internet ecosystems are open, they encourage new members to participate and foster a collaborative relationship among members.

The point: Cisco wants you part of its system, not 3Com's, not Lucent's, not Juniper Networks's. To exercise that gravitational pull, they have to build a knowledge community, a fellowship, and make it pay.

Cisco has done this systematically and in broad daylight. First, they bring their employees into it. Every employee owns stock. They are trained over the Cisco Learning Network, a Web and multimedia environment that's the same worldwide; it allows real-time learning on demand. Some of that knowledge is turned into other teaching tools and products and distributed via something called the Cisco Networking Academy, which works with schools, governments, customers, and community organizations at 2,500 locations in thirty-nine countries. It teaches students how to build and design networks. The carrot: Students can take a Cisco Certified Networking Associate exam, which tells prospective employers that the candidate can handle Cisco equipment. By subsidizing its customers' training programs, Cisco makes it harder for them to leave, because their human capital is linked to Cisco's. Longer term, the academies seed Cisco's future.

There's more. Cisco sells industrial-strength networking gear, but licenses its technology to companies that make networking for small business and home offices. Think "Intel inside"—by licensing, Cisco's technology and brand can be present in the consumer market while Cisco itself keeps most of its own work at the high-end (and high-margin) part of the market. This costs Cisco nothing; to the contrary, licensees pay Cisco for the privilege of increasing the value of its brand. On top of the licensing program, Cisco's Resource Network provides information and tools for small businesses; among other things, the network connects small businesses (which often want to outsource highly technical information processes) with application service providers and other sources of technical support. Like Cisco's licensing program, the resource network helps Cisco reach markets that are smaller than it could otherwise afford to pursue; at the same time, it forms customer capital between Cisco and technical support companies. And—not to leave the big boys out—Cisco created a network of alliances with KPMG, Motorola, and Hewlett-Packard to offer consulting, Web design, network design and integration, and other services. It all adds up to an almost frighteningly comprehensive strategy to sell knowledge so as to link Cisco indissolubly to its customers.

CHAPTER 8

A NEW AGENDA:
MANAGING KNOWLEDGE PROJECTS

"The horror of that moment," the King went on, "I shall never, *never* forget!"

"You will, though," the Queen said, "if you don't make a memorandum of it."

LEWIS CARROLL

One score and two years ago, give or take, I got a lesson in how to be a manager. I led a department in a small, entrepreneurial company. We didn't plan; we improvised. When cash was short, checks came more slowly; when it was really short, they sat in the president's desk drawer till someone begged. We had so little in the way of administrative systems that the burdens of my office took less time than I had spent trying to get my boss's attention in a previous job at a bigger company. There are no Edens without serpents, however, and the owners of the company, who were getting on, decided to sell it. They hired someone from outside to make the books orderly enough for a buyer to fathom. One day there arrived on my desk a form on which I was expected to propose next year's budget. It came with instructions, but I wanted advice, so I called a friend at another company and asked, "How do I do a budget?"

"Just take last year's budget and add ten percent to everything," my friend said.

"We didn't have a budget last year—this is the first budget we've ever had."

"Then remember: The most important line in any budget is 'Other.'"

Management is about continuity and change, predictability and contingency, the plan and "Other." It's an oversimplification—but not false—to say that twentieth-century management mostly concerned itself with predictability. Scientific Management aimed to find and impose the one best way to do a task. Alfred P. Sloan transformed General Motors from a poster child for chaos theory into the very model of a modern corporation by combining decentralized production with uniform planning and financial controls—a *pas de deux* of ego and superego, with id a third wheel. Peter Drucker almost single-handedly turned management from a handful of rules of thumb to a body of knowledge; schools of business administration grew to codify it, shape it, pass it on. W. Edwards Deming, Joseph Juran, and other theoreticians of quality control and Total Quality Management taught that variation is wrong and processes could and should be controlled.

As a young man, guru-to-be Charles Handy worked at Royal Dutch/Shell in a division that made ingredients used by other divisions to make things that eventually sold to customers. Handy's job was to learn his home division's cost, add a percentage to it, and quote that price to the division downstream, which had no choice but to pay it. "Business is easy," he remembers telling himself. Capital was scarce and much of it was tied up in facilities—factories, stores, refineries, warehouses, offices—that had to be safeguarded. As a result, observes Richard M. Zavergiu, a transportation consultant in Canada: "Manual workers as well as highly skilled managers were rooted in physical place." They filled highways and waited for suburban trains so they could show up at that place on time, every time. Mohammed came to the mountain, or the office. Writing midway through the century, Frederick Lewis Allen observed: "We would almost find it appropriate to call our present economic system 'managementism' rather than 'capitalism.'"

Today that seems as outdated as a TV western. What can continuity possibly mean to a Cisco Systems, where revenues grew from $4.1 billion to $18.9 billion in the five years through June 2000, then plunged 30 percent in a matter of months? What's predictable for a company like Hewlett-Packard, where half the orders come for products less than two years old? For an Ericsson, where tying up capital in manufacturing equipment simply slows the company down? In the swiftest of all industries, financial services, products have the life span of weird subatomic particles. Sir Brian Pittman, then chief executive of Lloyds TSB in Britain, said: "If we introduce a new consumer banking product in the morning, we know if it is a success before we go to lunch." Budget *that*.

When advantage is fleeting, so is the chance to exploit it. This demands that people and resources move rapidly inside and among corporations, creating teams where there's no time to set up departments, alliances where there's no time to build capabilities. Today, capital is neither scarce nor shod in concrete. Albuquerque is a mouse click from Zimbabwe. Where the value of knowledge exceeds the value of fixed assets, the worker is worth more than his tools. So the mountain comes to Mohammed: As many as 19 million Americans are telecommuters, working at least part time from home. "Creativity shouldn't get restricted by time or space," says the chief executive of Sybase software, John Chen. "Telecommuting is almost a requirement." Consultant Vincent DiBianca asks executives how long their companies need to get a smallish group of people (a dozen or two) up and running on a new project in a new location—the whole shebang, including getting the funds, picking the people, getting their bosses to sign off, backfilling their old jobs, preparing facilities, running in phones and local-area networks, etc. Answers run the gamut from six months to six weeks. But some companies—Warner Lambert is one—tell him they've got it down to just six days.

PROJECTS: CHANGING ROOMS

This is by way of introducing the subject of managing knowledge projects. Again oversimplifying, but within the limits of seemliness, managers exercise their art in four overlapping domains: people, functions, processes, and projects. Each of those domains—that is, the content of managerial work—has to change to reflect the increased value of knowledge and knowledge assets vis-à-vis materials and tangibles. In the domain of people, for instance, human resources practices that worked efficaciously if cruelly for Roman legions or Nelson's navy are unlikely to attract, motivate, or retain the electronics experts, linguists, and mechanics of the twenty-first century's knowledge-based military. Nor will the century-old Taylorist principles of people management—principles that at the time were a major advance for the dignity of labor—suit the employee-investor of the dawning century. "Why is it that when I buy a pair of hands, I always get a human being as well?" asked Henry Ford—an enlightened employer for his time. What's true of human resources management is equally true of the management of functions, processes, and projects; all must change.

Project management, in particular, becomes more important, one of the core disciplines of a knowledge company. Projects matter more because more change happens. Even a generation ago, the vast majority of managers in the vast majority of companies spent the vast majority of their time managing continuity. They tracked the parts, managed the payroll, kept the line humming, made sure the sales report was accurate and on time. Surprises—even good ones—were suspect. Today, change outranks continuity. Technology, deregulation, and globalization have undammed backwater industries, turning them into free-flowing rivers of competition. The faster the environment changes, the more valuable the ability to adapt. Not only that, continuity requires less and less management, as a few computers replace armies of clerks and middle managers whose job was to give senior management a monthly explanation of any variance from the budget. Continuity is the agenda of machines, and machines are more reliable than ever.* Change is the job of people, and people are as

---

* *This isn't to say that continuity is without value.* There's a great deal to be said for a quiet day at the office, or for dwelling a little on the top of an S curve before leaping off onto the bottom of the next one. The years 2000 and 2001 broke the neck of many a dot-com lemming who might have wished he'd moved more slowly, for example. Continuity is a nontrivial management challenge and its rewards—witness the $2 billion GE claims to have reaped in 1999 alone from its Six Sigma program, which is a companywide attempt to bring every process under control as statisticians define it—are significant. But even where control is the destination, the project (which is to say change) is the train that gets you there.

unruly as always—arguably more so. Change is the domain of projects, and why they are so important. The portfolio of projects is the agenda of the twenty-first-century corporation. In particular, knowledge companies must know how to select, design, and manage *knowledge projects,* which increase the value of knowledge or change the way a company uses it. Collecting best practices is a knowledge project: It gathers previously uncodified data, analyzes it, and turns it into a piece of structural capital. Other kinds of projects include business process redesign, competitive intelligence studies, building a corporate Yellow Pages, holding knowledge fairs. One company's portfolio might not resemble in the slightest another's: "Every organization has a unique collection of knowledge assets and distinct business problems to which those assets must be applied."

All projects share two traits, or should. First, by definition, projects are finite. They are limited as to time—with a start date, a schedule, a deadline (and an extension)—and space, which is called "scope" in project-management jargon. Getting scope right is vital to a project's success; project managers are taught to resist "scope creep," which occurs when people lengthen the list of things a project is supposed to accomplish (without changing the budget or the timetable, of course). Second, projects produce change. A building stands where a green field was. A task formerly done by hand is done by machine.

To these, add two traits particular to knowledge projects. First, they produce two outcomes, or should. Just as "every economic activity produces more information than it consumes" because information, when used, is almost never used up, so every knowledge project ought to produce (1) knowledge within the scope of the project (e.g., now we have a comprehensive directory of all our customers) and (2) knowledge transferrable elsewhere (this directory can serve as a template for other directories, or can be used by the service reps as well as the sales force). It should, therefore, be possible to leverage the results of a successful knowledge project, producing a capital asset. Second, knowledge management almost always begins with a project. If it's done wrong, the end of the project may be knowledge management's end, too. After a six-month, three-continent investigation of intellectual capital and knowledge management, a consortium from seven of the world's top knowledge companies emphasized: "Here is our advice for companies who want to find practical ways of making more money from their knowledge resources: *Define several improvement projects in various areas of the knowledge field."*

Where do they start? Among companies that manage knowledge, the half-dozen most common projects (and the percentage that undertake them) are the following:

Creating an intranet (under way or planned at 72 percent of companies surveyed)—that is, a computer-network-based piece of infrastructure that allows people to post, store, and search through documents, video clips, and the like, and that connects with e-mail and other means of communication.

Creating knowledge repositories and data warehouses (57 percent)— nodes on the network or simply stacks of books and documents in a conference room. Repositories are libraries of stuff people might need: procedures, references, blueprints, templates, and answers to common questions, gathered in one place rather than scattered hither, yon, and beyond anyone's ken. Data warehouses are electronic files—every order, every check—housed in a format that you hope lets you answer questions such as "Are Iowans who buy frozen broccoli less likely to own Volvos than Virginians who have American Express Gold Cards?"

Setting up decision-support tools (53 percent)—like Cigna's Underwriters' Desktop and the case-based reasoning tool provided for Xerox call-center operators (see pp. 114–15), these are usually software that holds a worker's hand as she solves a problem. Mostly the knowledge involved is explicit and practical ("If the customer's washing machine won't start, first have him check that it is plugged in"); more sophisticated software, such as Autonomy, can give suggestions about unstructured knowledge.*

Implementing groupware (44 percent)—another family of software, the patriarch of which is Lotus Notes. Groupware lets people share ideas informally via discussion threads, forums, and e-mail groups. At PricewaterhouseCoopers, the Kraken uses groupware (see p. 116).

Helping knowledge workers network (39 percent)—forming networks

---

* These are neat applications. Basically they watch what you're typing and notice recurring words and synonyms—for example, if I were running one of them it would notice words like *decision-support, Xerox, software,* and *knowledge,* in this paragraph—and feed them to a browser, which searches your hard drive, your intranet, or the whole Web for documents that contain the same words. A small window on the screen tells what documents or Web pages it has found, alerting the user to the existence of material he might want to check out.

among knowledge workers fertilizes collaboration and reduces waste, because it provides a means by which people who are working on similar projects in different parts of an organization can find each other. The least technology-intensive of the common knowledge projects, supporting networking chiefly involves giving executive blessing and sponsorship to these informal groups.

Mapping internal expertise (38 percent)—in a small shop where everybody knows everybody, you can find out at the coffeepot who's an expert in, say, analyzing the financial statements of real-estate investment trusts. In a bigger place, you might want a directory that allows you to look for knowledgeable people by topic, like the Yellow Pages.

It's a decent list—you've seen variations on it in Chapters 6 and 7. One thing's missing, however: In and of themselves, none of these projects will make money. That's not to say they're boondoggles. In fact, each can be useful *in the service of a project that improves performance in a measurable way.* Knowledge projects for knowledge management's sake are a way to spend money without a mechanism to make any. They are carts. Let's check out some horses.

SOW SMALL, REAP BIG: KNOWLEDGE MANAGEMENT'S $700 MILLION MAN

On a wet spring day in 1999, two score American Boy Scouts—members of Troop 184, based in London, the sons of expatriate workers—were on the beaches of Normandy. Pelted by cold rain, they tramped and scrambled from Utah Beach to Omaha Beach, places where, perhaps, a grandfather or great-grandfather had dodged hot metal fifty-five years before. Warm and dry in London a few days later, their scoutmaster, Kent Greenes, said: "We did this five years ago. We want to do it every five years, so we remember. So we have this history burned in our brains."

I was talking to Greenes because he was, as best I could figure, knowledge management's top moneymaker. In 1997, John Browne, CEO of British Petroleum (now BP Amoco), asked him to improve the company's performance by using knowledge more efficiently—sharing best practices, reusing knowledge, accelerating learning, and so on. Greenes assembled a ten-person team, which used that first year to bone up and take a few practice swings, netting $50 million. In 1998 they went to work in earnest, and in one year brought $260 million to the bottom line, plus $400 million more that was probable but not yet booked. They did it by means of knowledge projects—not done at headquarters, but done the same way Greenes led his Scout troop: by getting out into the field and doing real work in real circumstances: "Since we always start our work focusing on some tangible business outcome—for everything we do—it's very clear the impact that our knowledge management work has. This is something I've learned over years of trying to manage big change projects."

A simple premise underlies the work the BP team did: Practice makes improvement, and improvement makes money. Says Greenes: "Every time we drill a well, or do anything, we get better at it without even trying. If

KNOWLEDGE TRANSFER

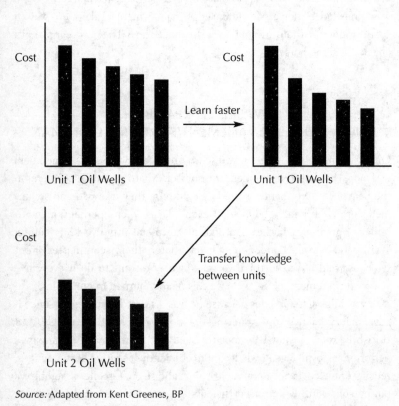

Source: Adapted from Kent Greenes, BP

you try—if you take time to think—you can get better faster. If you can transfer that learning between business units, they can get better in even less time. We estimate that is worth half a billion a year in drilling alone."

Premises and estimates don't go far at BP Amoco, a company of engineers, roustabouts, and finance guys with an ethos shaped by bullshit-intolerant environments like Alaska's North Slope, where Greenes himself ran an oil field in the early 1990s. Flat and decentralized BP Amoco has little use for toffs from headquarters. Business unit heads—there are about ten dozen—sign "performance contracts" for certain financial, environmental, and other results, then are left pretty much on their own. In that culture there was no way for anyone to come up with a project, even a good project that had the chairman's imprimatur, unless it solved a business problem. But performance contracts have the gravity of a personal promise. People will do anything ("even try a new idea," Greenes jokes) rather than fail to deliver—and if someone from headquarters can help do that, they'll listen.

Greenes' first move, therefore, was to prove he could solve problems—that is, show that knowlege management could make money. He did that by seeking an example of someone who, like Molière's unwitting proser M. Jourdain, was a knowledge manager and didn't know it. He found his case in the Schiehallen oil field, where a team drilling a new well spent six months pestering colleagues from other old fields to share tips before going out onto the rig. They got teased for being wimps—but saved so much time on the platform (at $100,000 to $200,000 a day) that they came in a muscular $80 million under budget.

Thus armed, Greenes began knocking on doors, looking for business units that had tough targets, needed help, and weren't afraid to ask for it. Browne told Greenes, "Engineer your pilot projects for success." Looking for people who want to make them work, avoiding cynics or suck-ups. Greenes' rule: He would pay only for his own team's expenses. Everything else had to come from the business unit: "Their own money, and their best people, not just a couple of IT guys."

For 1998, Greenes assembled a portfolio of fifteen projects where knowledge management could make a financial difference. Among them: helping the company enter the Japanese retail market; working with a polyethylene plant in Europe to reduce downtime; doing a "refinery turn-around"—a once-every-few-years scheduled shutdown, maintenance, and refurbishment operation—in Rotterdam. To each he brought a small kit of tools—"real simple stuff"—to assist in capturing old knowledge and bringing in new knowledge.

Lots can happen during the four or so years between refinery turnarounds, for example. People leave, taking experience with them. New technologies come on line. At another refinery, two years ago and ten time zones away, someone invents a faster way to do a job. So Nerefco, the Dutch refinery, got a "peer assist"—a facilitated, two-day meeting where people who had done refinery turnarounds shared their knowledge with the Nerefco team before the project began. The facilitators' job was to keep discussions focused and specific. Explains Greenes: "If you say, 'Tell me everything you know about X,' people resist, not because they don't want to share but because it seems like too big a job. But if you ask in a specific enough way, they're happy to tell you." Nerefco was happy it listened: The tips and ideas the team collected in those two days saved $9 million.

The peer assist is for learning before doing. The "after-action review" (adapted from a U.S. Army practice) is for learning while doing, by taking just fifteen minutes at the end of any identifiable event—a sales call, a valve repair job—to ask four stock-taking questions: What was supposed to happen? What actually happened? Why is there a difference? What can we learn from this and do differently? The secret of after-action reviews is to keep them simple and do them every chance you get, till they become automatic: Like someone who reads the paper every day, you suddenly discover you've learned an enormous amount. "The Retrospect" is a more elaborate facilitated postmortem—learning after doing. In it, project participants get together, talk about what worked well and worked less well, and try to distill what they've learned. Here the facilitator, in addition to keeping the discussion specific, has the additional responsbility of keeping attention on what can be learned, not whom to blame. Retrospects usually produce documents.

Call them microknowledge projects: Peer assists, after-action reviews, and retrospects are local, cheap, and effective. These tools, employed in all the projects in Greenes's portfolio, explain almost all the money they made. I can't think of a better first stab at knowledge management than to train every project manager and every team leader in the use of these tools and to require that they be used. (Call that a metaproject, a project about projects.) This is a project that needs more energy than budget—

Greenes's whole team had just ten people, recall. It will pay steady, small dividends to the people who have to do the work—that is, project and team leaders. And it can quickly make knowledge management part of the ordinary way a company conducts business.*

IF YOU BUILD IT, THEY MIGHT COME: YELLOW PAGES, INFRASTRUCTURE, AND KNOWLEDGE ASSETS

Microprojects, like microorganisms, need a supportive environment, and the BP team had three bigger projects designed to enhance the company's knowledge climate. One was named "Connect": a voluntary intranet-based Yellow Pages to make it easy to find expert help. Within a year of Connect's going online, more than 12,000 employees (out of what were then 100,000) put themselves into the system. The idea of a Yellow Pages is obvious, as I wrote in *Intellectual Capital:* "It should be so easy to construct a corporate Yellow Pages that it's remarkable how few companies have done it." Nearly five years later, their continued scarcity suggests that there are not-so-obvious problems. Indeed, Yellow Pages make sense only under certain conditions.

Having a real business need is the most important. Connect works at BP because the company is decentralized and global—that is, when you need help you're likely to be far away from it, on an oil rig in some place so godforsaken it's not even exotic, and the company has a consistent technical vocabulary—which means that a seeker of help and an adver-

---

*General Electric's celebrated Work-Out is a comparable example of a simple management tool that became part of how a company does business. Work-Outs, begun in 1989, are meetings that can be called by anybody to address any problem, from niggling to humongous, with no boss in the room. When the participants have a plan—kill that stupid form, replace that balky pump—they take it to the boss, who must say yes or no on the spot, no haggling, no waffling. Originally Work-Outs were three-day, attention-getting, facilitated events—"unnatural acts in unnatural places," said Steve Kerr, now GE's chief learning officer—designed to get rid of waste, speed decision-making, and spark empowerment. Now they're part of the fabric of GE life, so common that there's probably one every day in each sizable GE facility, without management's knowing about it till someone pops in saying, "We had a Work-Out and need to talk to you," and so fundamental that GE trademarked the term and in its values statement says, "GE leaders . . . are committed to Work-Out."

tiser of expertise can be reasonably certain that they're meant for each other. "We pinched the BP Amoco Connect system," Elizabeth Lank told me when she worked for computer services company ICL; more than 6,000 of the company's 20,000 employees put themselves in the expertise directory, and, she observed, "it worked best in communities linked to a specific process." That is, Yellow Pages work best where people have a shared context that gives both questioner and asker a common mission and language. People prefer to search for answers in familiar surroundings; before they use an expertise directory, they need to know what they're looking for and to be able to qualify the expertise of the people they find. The same holds for the expert: No one will volunteer to be who-you-gonna-call if most of the callers are nincompoops and noseyparkers.

A good Yellow Pages, nevertheless, can be a valuable knowledge project—if you remember the rule: Knowledge projects must solve someone's business need. How many people really need such a document often enough to justify the effort to produce and maintain it? If the answer to that question is "enough," then someone must already have invested the time to jury-rig an expertise directory and would kill for something that's really good. Start there, then roll it out. Knowledge projects create their greatest value when the knowledge in them is leveraged; but *leverage requires a fulcrum*. The CEO's secretary or the head of the communications department is likely to have a nascent Yellow Pages in his desk drawer. Xerox's late Webmaster Bill McLain created a Webmaster's Knowledge Base from all the queries he received; among its by-products was a database of all the employees who ever helped him answer customer questions—probably the most complete directory of internal expertise in the company. The technology center of Deere & Co., the farm-equipment manufacturer in Moline, Illinois, fielded a lot of calls from sales, service, and manufacturing; to help people who answered the phone when the center's regular receptionist was at lunch or on vacation, a secretary there made a simple list of topics followed by the names of people who were familiar with them. It eventually grew to become "People Who Know," a sophisticated searchable database of in-house and outside experts, run for Deere by Sopheon, a Minneapolis company formerly called Teltech, which maintains a network of more than several thousand academics, recent retirees, and other technical experts, whom it makes available to subscriber companies.

Infrastructure projects. Knowledge management fails when "people need common information but don't need each other." So says Andy Boyd, who has the wonderful title "new ways of working consultant" at Royal Dutch/Shell. Inscribe that in red ink and italics before undertaking any expensive knowledge-management infrastructure project. (If you don't, you'll need the red ink to report the project's results.) Knowledge projects, even expensive ones, succeed when they are about important topics that engage people's passions. For Shell, as for BP, one business problem is that people who need to pick each other's brains—instrumentation engineers, say—may be perched on separate oil rigs worlds apart. To connect them, Shell funded nearly 150 communities of practice, supported by Web sites, editorial help, and facilitation. Each expertise network—which includes e-mail, chat rooms, and a library of best practices produced and warranted by members—costs between $500,000 and $1 million to set up, and gets ongoing editorial and other support from headquarters knowledge-management staff. Multiplied by 150, that's real money, even for a big fella like Shell, so nothing gets funded unless network sponsors put up a business case; for example, engineers in Shell's polypropylenes business have promised that by sharing tips and best practices globally, they can get rid of $16 million of machine downtime. On a $1 million investment, that's really real money.

Shell's project resembles "Virtual Teamwork," the only truly costly knowledge project under Greenes's purview. The Virtual Teamwork infrastructure was set up in the mid-1990s in BPX, the exploration and production arm of British Petroleum, and consisted of technology that was astonishing for the time—desktop video conferencing, multimedia e-mail, scanners, a real-time shared whiteboard, and other goodies that let someone in Venezuela sit at the virtual elbow of a colleague in Alaska. "What made it work," Greenes says, "is that we spent as much money on coaching and training as we did on the technology." The pilot project, with about 150 units, cost $12 million in 1994—with half the money spent not on the gear but on teaching people how to get the most out of it. The first year's quantifiable benefits: about $30 million.

Virtual Teamwork was based on the observation that most of the time it's cheapest and most effective to get help by talkng to an expert, not reading a manual. Face-to-face, live conversation gets at tacit knowledge, and allows questions and answers. ("See the red button? Push it and tell me what happens. . . .") One of its first wins came when a piece of drilling equipment went kaput on a ship in the North Sea; by putting it in front of a camera and connecting live with an expert in Aberdeen, BP was able to get the machine running again in a day, without having to helicopter some-one to the ship or send the part to shore. Virtual Teamwork began before Greenes's group came into being. Greenes's group's contribution was to help expand the project after the pilot, to get the leverage good knowledge projects should have, and to train.

Preserving knowledge assets. There's a special place in heaven for edi-tors. I don't mean my editors, though they have a special place, too; I mean people who, for gain, glory, or the good of the cause, take it upon themselves to dive for, select, and string the pearls of wisdom, or at least knowledge, that form around the irritants and stimuli of working life. Peer assists, after-action reviews, retrospects, bacon-saving conversations with a newfound expert, money-saving fixes over virtual networks: They're all great, and the learning all fades. It's my unprovable theory that group memory is a product, not a sum; that is, if we each remember 80 percent of what happened, our total recall is not 160 percent but 64 percent.

Preserving institutional memory requires "documentation." The word is in quotes because, as we shall see, more is involved than documents. Documentation is an aftermath, however, of doing knowledge projects. Says Shell's Boyd: "Our view is, just get people talking to each other. Then start building things like electronic networks. The worst thing you can do is launch a big, empty knowledge repository."

The next-worst thing might be, however, to create no repository whatso-ever. At BP Amoco, Greenes used what was learned from the team's knowl-edge projects as the material for a project that the knowledge-management team itself led, though it worked with people in line positions: to create what they called "Knowledge Assets." These are folders on the intranet, a score of them. They bear titles like "What does BP Amoco know about restructuring?" ". . . building retail sites in new markets?" ". . . human rights?" ". . . refinery turnarounds?" and so on. The fact that the titles are in question form suggests—as declarative names might not—that the contents are a work in progress and contributions are welcome. Inside each folder are dozens of electronic artifacts: documents, checklists, video clips, and, most important, hypertext links that permit someone to send e-mail to people who have stories to tell. "They are not about giving people answers,"

Greenes emphasizes, "not a bunch of bullet points. The most important part of any Knowledge Asset is the link to the people who were involved."

Perhaps because chief knowledge officers like to show off their repositories, people have a tendency to think of these assets as being something that gets uploaded to a Web page somewhere. That is too limited a view; they can take many forms, and can incorporate tacit as well as explicit knowledge. Some examples follow.

Mostly Explicit

Every year Philips Electronics' components business sells billions of dollars' worth of displays—cathode-ray, liquid-crystal, and projection screens for computers, televisions, and so forth. To support the complex, rapidly changing business, Philips's Knowledge Team, which operates out of headquarters in Eindhoven, the Netherlands, produces a "Display Factbook." Its purpose is to make easily available the best knowledge about display technology, uses, and markets, so as to standardize terminology and methods, save time people spend digging for information, and create a basis on which the company could better manage its portfolios of technologies and products. Not least of its virtues is that it ends arguments over what the facts are. All kinds of stuff go into the factbook: market value, volume, and share numbers, trends, and estimates; costs and analyses of cost drivers; competitive intelligence; R&D road maps; detailed product specifications; information about components and their suppliers. Some of the data are confidential and closely guarded, but most (90 percent) aren't. Published in limited quantity on paper, also live on the Web so that it is always up to date, and thoroughly revised semiannually, the Display Factbook is a document that no one department at Philips would or could have produced on its own, and a classic example of a project that collects, edits, and publishes explicit knowledge.

Explicit and Tacit

Unilever, the world's second-largest consumer-products company (after Philip Morris), ran a different kind of knowledge project, designed to produce many different kinds of knowledge assets, ranging from recipes (literally) to soft assets like research agendas and interpersonal ties. The project began late in 1996, after Unilever combined several food divisions in a new grouping, called "Culinary," a multibillion-dollar-in-sales category of soups, sauces, salad dressings, and other foodstuffs whose brands include Ragú, Calvé, Hellmann's, and Knorr. Over the next couple of years, Unilever's knowledge-management team held a series of knowledge workshops, each of which brought together anywhere from a dozen to two hundred people from the Culinary area. (Most workshops were for small groups.) Their purpose was to "capture what we know and don't know" about some aspect of their global business, many of whose parts came together via acquisitions. There was lots of knowledge to impart and ignorance to disperse. Any cook who has ever shared the kitchen with an in-law can understand one thing Wouter deVries learned conducting some of the workshops: "Every company was making almost the same product in completely different ways with different equipment." Unilever makes sauces for pasta in Italy, rice in China, and potatoes in Holland, and for the most part employees had concentrated more on the particularities of their own products and markets than on the issues common to them all, like how to build manufacturing facilities for sauces. A knowledge workshop about that produced a 50 percent reduction in the time Unilever needs to design, plan, and commission a new plant. From headquarters "knowledge engineers" (I don't make up these terms) helped turn stuff like that into artifacts that they then made sure to share around the world—classic "hard" structural capital. The most valuable assets produced by the workshops, though, say deVries and his colleague Manfred Aben, are soft assets. Some was customer capital, for the knowledge workshops included lots of research into consumer behavior. Foremost, though, the workshops produced human capital in the form of communities of practice; having met, studied, shared, and played, workshop participants went home with names, phone numbers, and a sense of common practice and concern. "In this way, experience and proven practice are shared and applied across the world very rapidly . . . building on trust between the participants."

Mostly Tacit

IBM Global Services captured tacit knowledge in a fascinating project run by David Snowden. The Holy Grail of Global Services is to make deals with major accounts to build, maintain, upgrade, and operate customers' data processing and information networks. These are multiyear contracts

with multinational corporations, and their revenue is measured in multiple millions of dollars. IBM competes for these accounts with Cap Gemini, Compaq, EDS, Hewlett-Packard, and others. Typically the sales effort
goes on for months, sometimes for years; dozens of people might be
involved on both IBM's side and that of its potential customer. A win, if it's
a good contract, makes a year; a loss voids a whole lot of work—and some
deals turn out not to have been worth winning.

Given the complexity of the negotiations, the number of people
involved, and the fact that each deal is different, there can be no recipe
guaranteed to make the soufflé rise every time. Moreover, because the
bidding process is long and the deals multiyear, executives tend to move
on before a client engagement is ended, taking valuable history and experience with them. It would be tremendously valuable, therefore, to know
when a negotiation is on track or in trouble, whether a deal's turning sour
but can be saved, or where to turn to solve problems. To do this, Snowden
reassembled successful and unsuccessful bid teams some time after their
pitch had won or lost, put each team in a room with food and a facilitator,
and asked them to reconstruct the story of the bid, paying particular attention to what went wrong and right, what they felt, what they did about it,
and what 20-20 hindsight told them. The sessions, often raucous and
funny, lasted a full day. As the conversations went on, of course, people
amended and expanded what their colleagues said, creating a *Rashomon*-
like multivoiced narrative that, Snowden says, was nearly as rich as real-
time observation would have been.

Once the story was told, the teams and their facilitators created a "decision-information flow map," an abstracted view of the bidding process as it
actually happened. (This differed, of course, from the officially mandated
process; indeed, every team that won its bid deviated from the official
process at one or more crucial junctures.) At this point the teams were
taught a little intellectual-capital jargon and asked to review their process
map and identify the intellectual assets they called upon at each key decision point—and also the assets they looked for and were unable to find.
Did you consult experts? they were asked. Who were they? Did you need
to use a pricing or risk model or some other formal methodology? What
approval committees were involved, what documents did they require, and
what knowledge did they add? Collating this information, Snowden and his
colleagues made a big, messy wall map of Post-it notes and colored tape,

DECISION-INFORMATION FLOW MAP

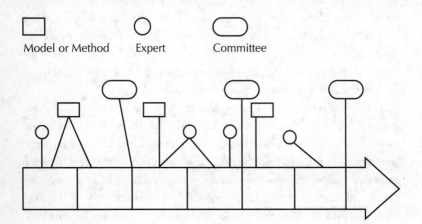

displaying the process and the various explicit and tacit knowledge assets associated with it. The process map was a benefit in itself, since it documented the actual (not the theoretical) bidding process, which had been tacit before. It also created a register of all the models, methods, and other knowledge assets that might be needed along the way, together with comments about their effectiveness. (This generated a to-do list of its own.) The real value, however, was in uncovering registers of tacit knowledge—who knows what, who knows whom, who helps, who hinders. Along with it came a lot of stories about obstacles overcome. This kind of information is almost folkloric, and folklore doesn't lend itself to three-bullet-point PowerPoint slides. One of the significant benefits of the IBM project was that Snowden and his team, like Jacob and Wilhelm Grimm, collected and preserved stories that would otherwise have been lost as the people who witnessed them went on about their lives in the company.

PROJECT PORTFOLIOS AND MANAGING KNOWLEDGE ASSETS

Projects are investments, just as stocks and bonds are, and should be thought of as part of a portfolio, which should be diversified and balanced with respect to risk, market, technology, and so on; success should be judged by the success of the portfolio as a whole. There are many ways to manage portfolios, ranging from complex mathematical tools (most of which "see more visibility in text books and journal articles than in corporate offices") to methods so casual they're the equivalent of buying stocks by throwing a dart at the tables in the newspaper. Financial measures are the most common way to manage portfolios, comparing projects on the basis of calculated net present value or internal rates of return. But they're not the best way, according to a major study of the practices and performance of the new product portfolios of 205 U.S. companies. In fact, they're the worst. The study tracked new-product development projects, but there's no reason to think its conclusions do not apply to any portfolio of projects, whether for new products or IT installations or changing the management practices of a company. Far more successful than a single-minded reliance on financial measures (even the most sophisticated, such as Monte Carlo simulations and real-options pricing) is a multimeasure strategic approach, in which "business strategy decides the split of resources across different categories—for example, by types of projects, markets, or product lines—to create strategic buckets. And strategic considerations dominate the decision to do (or not to do) certain R&D or new product projects." The best-performing companies think portfolio management is very important; have a clear, established, and formal method of evaluating portfolios, with rules everyone knows; and in this process employ more than one way to decide when to back a project and when to back off, ultimately judging a project on the basis of its contribution to a larger strategy.

Businesses are living organisms; documents are dead. Ad Huijser, who heads the research arm of Philips, says knowledge "is not something that can simply be taken out of a database and used whenever it is needed, without any further reference to its owners. . . . In nearly all cases, the knowledge itself has to be qualified by the owner, who can provide the answers to many questions that prospective users may ask. For example: Is it also applicable in my situation? Under what conditions did you obtain that knowledge? Have you applied it on other areas? Is it changing over time?"

Connection, not collection: That's the essence of knowledge management. The purpose of knowledge projects, therefore, is to get knowledge moving, not to freeze it; to distribute it, not to shelve it. Successful projects usually have a mixed purpose, as we've seen; they're set up to solve a problem in the expectation that the solution, or the knowledge the project produces, will also add to the intellectual capital of the organization. By themselves, Cap Gemini Ernst & Young consultants say, "very few contribute to the much touted goal of 'organizational transformation'"—and that's good. Every project should have integrity as a project: It should have a manager who is accountable for profit and loss, and the profit shouldn't be inflated by imagined, hoped-for, or ancillary benefits, even if they're real. Never buy meat on the basis of its potential to make gravy.

"Begin at the beginning . . . go on till you come to the end: then stop"— in Lewis Carroll's quip lies both the power and the weakness of knowledge projects. They're manageable; they're visible; they're discrete. But they can also be discreet, their lessons unlearned except by participants, their impact limited to the people more or less directly involved. Projects by themselves are like chin-ups without aerobics. Says Jac Fitz-Enz, founder of the Saratoga Institute, which is (rare bird) a truly smart group of HR analysts: "When knowledge gained somewhere doesn't move elsewhere, that's not a learning organization; that's just a bunch of projects."

We'll turn next, therefore, to the processes that move stuff.

CHAPTER 9

A NEW DESIGN: SUPPORTING KNOWLEDGE PROCESSES 1: PROCESSES THAT CREATE

Allez voir les productions des autres, mais ne jamais copier que sur nature.[*]

—AUGUSTE RENOIR

The first sentence of the first chapter of the greatest book ever written about business and economics says that nothing has improved productivity more than the division of labor. In an example so famous it's almost a parable, Adam Smith describes how the making of pins "is divided into a number of branches":

One man draws out the wire, another straights it, a third cuts it, a fourth points it, a fifth grinds it at the top for receiving the head; to make the head requires two or three distinct operations; to put it on, is a peculiar

---

[*] Go and see what others have produced, but never copy anything except nature.

business, to whiten the pins is another; it is even a trade by itself to put them into the paper; and the important business of making a pin is, in this manner, divided into about eighteen distinct operations, which, in some manufactories, are all performed by distinct hands, though in others the same man will sometimes perform two or three of them.

Civilization itself grows from the division of labor, Smith suggests—at least, he observes, there's a direct correlation between the development of the one and the extent of the other.

Trouble is, it's not always true. Smith himself recognized that one cannot always get the most value from something by breaking it into sub-somethings. A few pages after describing his pin factory, he points out that when the course of a great river like the Danube is divided among several different nations, each state on the way can obstruct the flow of commerce, mucking up the system. Smith concluded that the value of dividing labor was limited by the size of the market, but we might propose an alternative interpretation: The value of dividing labor must be weighed against the value of combining it.

Even then—even if one could be almost certain of the better course—we could be sure to find people stubbornly following the other one. Why?

The oldest of all manufacturing industries, textiles, offers an excellent example of how rocky is the road from knowledge to action. Apparel factories are labor-intensive, most of the labor is sewing, most of the laborers are seamstresses, and most of work is organized as in Adam Smith's pin factory. Each seamstress performs one operation: One fashions cut fabric into cuffs, another makes sleeves, another sews cuffs to sleeves, another stitches sleeves onto bodices, etc. The system is called the "progressive bundle system" because each morning each seamstress receives a bundle with her day's work, which at the end of her shift progresses down the line to the station of the person whose operation comes next. Given the amount of labor involved, management has long focused on reducing labor costs, using the whole tool kit of scientific management and industrial engineering—automation, time-and-motion studies, new machinery, and human resources practices ranging from the carrot (incentives) to the stick (e.g., the Triangle Shirtwaist Company). In the unending pursuit of cheap labor, much of the industry migrated from New England to North Carolina and Georgia and eventually to the Philippines, Indonesia, and Bangladesh.

As the amount and price of labor decline, other costs become relatively more important, and the progressive bundle system's flaw becomes evident: There's a whole lot of money tied up in those bundles of work in progress. Sewing a pair of trousers involves about forty operations. If each worker gets a bundle with a day's work, and each bundle moves along as scheduled, it might and often does take forty days to make a pair of pants. That's long enough for God to flood the earth. A typical U.S.-made man's suit requires thirty to forty days, but only 105 minutes of sewing; a dress shirt dwells twenty to twenty-five days for eighteen minutes of sewing; a simple T-shirt spends five to eight days in a factory and receives about ninety seconds of work, a ratio of waiting to attention that makes a visit to the doctor look like an efficient use of time.

There is an alternative, called team sewing or modular production: "Instead of breaking sewing and assembly into a long series of small steps, modular production entails grouping tasks, such as the entire assembly of a collar, and assigning that task to members of a 'module,' or a team of workers." In the 1980s some people called this the Toyota Sewing System because it is one of a family of so-called "lean production" systems pioneered in Japan, particularly in the automobile industry. Team sewing works. Overall, it cuts costs about 14 percent, according to one of its advocates, Eileen Appelbaum, an economist at the Economic Policy Institute in Washington, D.C. One big saving is time—that twenty-day shirt is out the door in one—which drops the work-in-progress inventory from weeks to days. Workers, who learn more skills and enjoy more variety in their jobs, evince higher satisfaction, which lowers turnover and its attendant costs. Team sewing requires more sewing machines but needs 25 to 30 percent less space. What worked spectacularly for cars seemed sufficiently worthwhile in the needle trades that in the 1980s the American Apparel Manufacturers Association and the Amalgamated Clothing and Textile Workers Union began touting team sewing as a boon to them both.

Yet as of 1996, team sewing accounted for less than 10 percent of all clothing assembly in the United States, and by 1999 not much more. There are a number of explanations. In some cases, it's not the right answer: If "one size fits all" is not true of socks—as those of us with size-twelve feet can testify—why should it be true of sock manufacturing? In one high-profile case, prematurely hailed as "a landmark in labor relations," modular production at Levi's went wrong, perhaps because it was poorly implemented or (with hindsight, most likely) because at the time Levi's was melting down everywhere, having misread consumer taste and botched its response to the challenge posed by chains like The Gap. Whatever the cause, publicity about Levi's scared some and gave others reason to bear those ills they had rather than fly to others they knew not of. Other companies were so intent on exporting or outsourcing production that they couldn't have cared less about team sewing, which requires more management attention than the bundle system: Why worry about managing the factory or when you're trying to off-load it? Why train workers you plan to lay off? Finally, team sewing really comes into its own when the whole supply chain converts to on-demand, just-in-time systems; the factories, often small shops, wait until their customers demand change.

Inescapable, however, is the sense that the bundle system persists because people can't get the pin factory out of their heads: That is, they can't convert what they know into a new way of working. Needle-trade-press articles about team sewing are of two types: "yes" and "yes, but," with the latter saying, in essence, "It might be good overall, but it won't work here at XYZ Corp." Maybe so. More likely, though, XYZ Corp. is stuck on the old road with no path to the new one: It doesn't have a way to institutionalize new ideas. A frustrated executive at Xerox told me, "You can see a high-performance factory or office, but it just doesn't spread. I don't know why." Jeffrey Pfeffer and Robert I. Sutton, both at Stanford University, have written a fine book about this "knowing-doing gap," which highlights the importance of a culture that prefers action over talk and human-resources policies that motivate by example and values rather than by fear. These are good steps. But where's the path?

WHY KNOWLEDGE PROCESSES MATTER

Knowledge companies need an organizational design that converts insight—knowledge, smarts, invention—into institutional behavior. They need, in other words, knowledge processes. Products embody knowledge and the value of knowledge: They are how it is sold. Projects are the mechanisms by which companies create or invest in intellectual capital, rejigger the way they use knowledge, or experiment: They produce change. Knowledge and intellectual capital fully flower, however, by means of knowledge processes: They institutionalize them. Products die and projects end; processes last.

An asset—intellectual or any other kind—is like a stone gathering moss on the top of a hill. Physicists say the stone contains potential energy; start it rolling downhill, and the potential energy becomes kinetic energy and can do work. The metaphor is by David Norton, the president of the Balanced Scorecard Collaborative, who adds: "How do we realize the potential value? Through value-creating processes. These are the structures that create value from intangibles."

If there is one management lesson that the last dozen years taught above all others, it is the importance of uncovering, managing, and improving business processes, those sequences of handoffs and other events that snake through organizations and connect the work of one function to another. Total Quality Management and reengineering, each in its way, focuses on processes. Many companies even changed their organizational design from vertical—that is, functional—to horizontal—that is, based on processes. Gregory Alan Bolcer, chief technology officer of Endeavors Technology, puts it this way: "Rather than thinking of what group you are with, think of what activities you are performing and how they relate to others in the corporation. Processes, not structures, are the key building blocks for e-businesses"—and for any other kind. That imperative applies, in spades, to knowledge companies. Knowledge, say John Seely Brown and Paul Duguid, "is generated in practice"—that is, by small groups, usually by projects they do—"but implemented through process. . . . Formal organizational processes are generally needed to turn inventions into marketable innovations."

There are a number of "knowledge processes" in business. Research and development is the most familiar, and one of the few that get conscious management attention. Planning is another. These are both knowledge-work processes, as are such others as marketing, customer service, consulting, decision making—managing is itself a knowledge-work process. In addition, a number of processes are components of knowledge management; among them are knowledge creation, documentation, validation, refining, and distribution. Third, every process has a knowledge component, which is often and unfortunately neglected. Does your customer-service process have a means to collect, feed back, and learn from the knowledge it generates? Says Thomas H. Davenport, the Accenture consultant who is one of the founding fathers of reengineering, knowledge-oriented managers should examine every process to make sure it reflects the knowledge imperatives of the business. Do your human-resources processes take knowledge into account, for example? Does employees' knowledge behavior—how well they learn or share, for example—influence their evaluation, compensation, and advancement? Does HR's planning process systematically analyze the company's future knowledge requirements, for example, by asking if the company needs to grow or hire more electrical engineers or more people who speak Turkish?

Each of these processes has something to do with or to knowledge. Some, like R&D, emphasize *creating* knowledge: Something new results. Some are mostly concerned with *discovering* or finding knowledge: Market research, for example, doesn't invent knowledge but instead seeks to find out what consumers think. Some processes chiefly involve *packaging* knowledge; documenting the results of a project or mapping a process are examples. *Applying* knowledge is another sort of activity; call-center operators at Xerox apply what they know, either from experience or from the know-how stored in the software that helps them. The primary activity of another set of processes is *reusing* knowledge; it is vital for tasks as different as benchmarking and object-oriented software development.

To boil it down further, all knowledge processes involve two basic kinds of activities: producing new knowledge (by creating or discovering it) and sharing existing knowledge (by packaging, applying, or reusing it). Producing and sharing, of course, feed on each other—you discover or invent something new, then package it so that I can apply it and find ways for others to use it over and over.

It's an established principle of management that a process ought to have an "owner." Most companies are organized by function—marketing, manufacturing, shipping, marketing, sales, and so on. The major business processes, whose performance significantly affects how well the company does, cross between departments, the way the Danube crosses several national boundaries on its way to the Black Sea. Without an owner responsible for the health of the process as a whole, there's no one to prevent the folks upstream from polluting the water or the people downstream from damming its flow—each department doing what suits its purposes best without regard for the whole. (The jargon-afflicted call this suboptimization.)

From the vast geography of knowledge processes, we'll discuss (in this

KNOWLEDGE PROCESSES

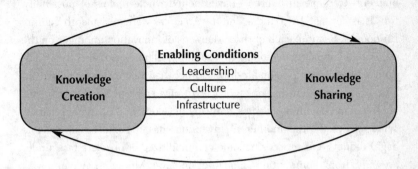

Source: The Performance Group

chapter and the next) three in particular, each a major waterway for knowledge and value. Each, in other words, is a process that CEOs ought to monitor and that, in companies of any size, ought to have an owner who is someone of vice presidential caliber, clout, and rank. Knowledge creation, customer learning, and knowledge sharing all matter lots, and all could be done lots better. Each deserves a book to itself—but for each we can at least discover some of the problems and the principles by which they can be solved.

KNOWLEDGE CREATION

The literature on innovation is considerably longer than my arm. This I know from having stacked and measured a small portion of it, which happened to be on the floor of my office. It can be summarized as follows: Innovation is either a machine or a magic garden. Because it is a machine, companies should design it, oil it, power it up, and manage it. Because it is a garden, companies should create conditions under which it can flourish, stand back and let the magic occur, then harvest it.

Innovation is both, of course. That's a management problem, because the two ways of managing innovation seem contradictory: One's hands-on, the other's hands-off. Look, Ma! What now?

New ideas, products, and services matter more than ever. One reason:

There's lots of room to innovate. Developments in infotech, nanotech, and biotech—to name just three—have opened whole realms of possibility, worlds as new as Africa, India, and the Americas were to sixteenth-century Europeans. Second, each of those domains of innovation impinges on the other. Developments in biology, for example, will make possible the invention of computers based on life-forms rather than silicon. There's plenty of less exotic cross-fertilization, too: Electronics substitute for mechanics, banks compete with brokerages, software developers compete with banks. Third, necessity, the mother of invention, has become an implacable nag. Products and services become commoditized or obsolete fast, under pressure from competition, globalization, and Moore's Law; one way to cope with a leaky bucket is to refill it faster. Fourth, intellectual capital has grown so important that it, rather than ownership of physical assets, explains why companies come into being and why their boundaries fall where they do. (See Chapter 2.) Consequently, "Knowledge creation gets . . . to the very core of what makes a firm a firm. We're saying that firms produce knowledge, that they could produce a heck of a lot more of it, and that knowledge is where their competitive edge comes from." I invent, therefore I am.

You don't need to read that big stack of stuff to increase your company's capacity to innovate. Just follow these five simple steps—a process to create an innovation process, barded with a few ideas about how to manage one. Mostly what follows is about new-product development, but, with a few adjustments, it's equally applicable to any kind of idea generation, such as coming up with new marketing ideas or new ways to manage a company.

1. Build a business case. Any company—even yours—is full of the germs of fabulous ideas. If you doubt this, give a senior executive a shot at a substantial bonus if she can triple the number of proposals made via the good old-fashioned employee-suggestion program. The problem isn't germs; it's germination. By definition, innovating takes time from your day job. People need permission to do it; more than that, they need to know that it's part of their job to do more than their job. Whatever means you use—rules or the lack of rules, hectoring or welcoming—people at all levels of the company need to know that hardheaded business reasons demand innovation, so that they can stand up to the forces (the boss, the deadline, the customer) that want noses applied only to grindstones.

In the late 1990s, Borg-Warner, the automotive components maker, found that it needed to restart its innovation engine. New stuff hadn't been a priority for more than a decade, during which the company rearranged its capital structure and assets—a leveraged buyout in 1987, a return to public listing in 1993, and a narrowing of its product portfolio to focus just on automotive parts and systems. Now Borg-Warner needed to grow; the way CEO John Fielder figured it, Borg-Warner, with 1999 sales of $2.7 billion, had to become a $5 billion company by 2004 to remain a top-tier supplier in the industry, and at least $600 million of that would have to come from new products. Just as lottery sales go up when the jack-pot gets fat, a big, real number, with a deadline, changes behavior: With $600 million at stake, innovation got top billing on agendas at Borg-Warner; it got budgets to hire staff and consultants; it got access to executives.

That's a machine approach to making the business case—setting a goal. 3M, famously, has a magic-garden approach, telling researchers to spend 15 percent of their time working on projects that aren't in the budget— noodling, fiddling, playing around. To goose its innovative ability, profes-sional services firm PricewaterhouseCoopers did something that has elements of each—it made the business case personal. Says George Bailey, one of PwC's managing partners: "We'd give speeches about how important innovation is—'evolve or die' and all that—but there's a difference between talking about it and convincing people about it. People were still measured on billable hours." To change that equation and to reward, celebrate, and encourage innovation, the company sponsored a contest. With the world's largest roster of employees who earn more than $100,000 a year, it wasn't likely they would get people's attention with mouse pads or gift certificates for dinner at the Olive Garden. Instead, in July 1999 the firm announced a prize of $100,000 to be given to each of 150 innovators, who could be indi-viduals or teams. Like the prospect of being hanged in a fortnight, a hun-dred grand concentrates the mind, even the consulting mind, wonderfully. Yet for a firm the size of PwC, $15 million's not too much to pay for even one great idea, and it's chicken feed if it produces a flock of them. Which, of course, it did: By the 1999 deadline, PwC had seven hundred applica-tions from seven hundred individuals and teams. Among them (and among the winners) was FPML, Financial Products Markup Language, a way to stick electronic name tags on financial derivative products (using the XML software protocol), developed by PwC with J. P. Morgan; FPML makes it possible for financial institutions to trade derivatives and other instruments over the Net and has become the industry's e-commerce standard. Another was a process for restructuring worthless real estate assets held by Japanese banks; a third was a certification for lumber products (inspired by "Dolphin Safe Tuna" labels) that marks them as having been harvested according to standards of sustainable forest management. Would these have happened without the contest? Maybe—but not all. The contest sent an electrifying message to the company about the importance of innovation, which (helped by the fact that the contest is being repeated) increased the amount of innovation the firm does and the prestige of the people who do it. Furthermore, by publicizing ideas, the contest speeded their adoption and diffusion. "No one's even asking if we got our money's worth," says Bailey. "We got it many times over."

2. *Take a snapshot.* Working with a small Maryland consulting firm, Business Innovation Consortium, Borg-Warner did a formal assessment of its innovation strengths and weaknesses. BIC does this in two ways: First, it analyzes the histories of successes and failures—that is, listening to stories about innovation successes and failures, and examining them for what they reveal about company attitudes and how things go right or go awry. Storytelling is an important way 3M nourishes its innovative culture. New employees attend a class in risk taking. They come with their supervisors and are taught, among other things, to be willing to defy their supervisors. One story they hear is how the CEO five times tried and failed to kill the project that became the wildly successful Thinsulate. Stories are powerful carriers of cultural messages. Miss Manners wrote that married couples are seated apart at dinner parties because "they tell the same stories, and they tell them differently." 3Mers tell them the same.

Second, BIC asks, in interviews and with surveys, a whole lot of questions. "Generally," says David Sutherland, whose title at BIC is Source of Inspiration, "we find problems when the pieces of the value chain aren't well connected: The marketing organization isn't well connected to R&D, which isn't well connected to product development, etc." Sometimes the disconnect is cultural and shows up in areas such as hiring practices. Says Sutherland: "You're not going to get innovation if you're hiring for fit."

Borg-Warner had two problems. First, says Simon Spencer, an engineer who holds the new title Innovation Champion, "Borg-Warner never

KEY QUESTIONS FOR AN INNOVATION SNAPSHOT

Here are some of the questions the Business Innovation Consortium seeks to answer with an "innovation snapshot" of the strengths and weaknesses of a company's innovation process. The purpose of the questions is partly to rate the company: How innovative a place is it? It is also to describe the company, with no value judgment implied: When do we innovate? How do we do it? No list (especially no abbreviated list, such as this one) will work for every company or industry, of course, but these suggest issues involved in developing knowledge-creation processes.

- Does the company understand its customers, market, competitors, and external environment (regulatory, political, etc.)?
- How does innovation figure in strategy documents (for example, do value and mission statements mention it?), strategic goals (e.g., does the company set targets for sales from new products and services?), and strategic plans (how much is allocated for innovation in capital spending and expense budgets? how many people are assigned to work on new products, services, or other innovations?).
- Does the organization behave consistently with its strategic intentions? (What is the ratio of hat to horse? Is there lots of talk and little budget?)
- Does the company have a structured approached to innovation? Is innovation defined clearly? Is there a process by which ideas become products? Do people know what it is? Are there people who are accountable for innovation? Do they have authority commensurate with their responsibility?
- Where does responsibility for innovation rest (individuals, teams, leadership, etc.)?
- Are there sacred cows, parts of the business where innovation is taboo?
- How well does the company tolerate disagreement, conflict, ambiguity, divergent thinking, and unconventional behavior?
- What are newcomers shown and told about innovation during orientation programs and in their first months on the job?

had a 'process' to deliver innovation. It just happened." Or didn't. Without a process, good ideas, like seeds in the parable, can fall on the road and be taken away by birds, or on rocky soil and never sink roots, or among thorns and be choked. Says Sutherland: "Borg-Warner had ideas, but nowhere to take them."

That's a surprisingly common problem. Ask yourself, about every company you've worked for, what you'd have done if, at home one night, you had an idea for a new product, even a whole new line of business. Would you:

- Tell your spouse and forget about it?
- Tell your boss and let him forget about it?
- Tell your boss and hope she remembered to give you credit?
- Try to find the people most likely to act on the idea but give up in frustration after a few days, and hope to God your boss didn't find out you were sneaking around behind his back?
- With your boss's blessing, tell the people—you'd know who they are—who could help you evaluate and develop the idea?
- Copy your address book, open a password-protected file on your computer, and start phoning venture capitalists?

Borg-Warner's second problem, balkanization, is common, too. Borg-Warner's six business units, each with its own R&D budget, staff, and priorities, were so autonomous that there was little chance for ideas to bounce back and forth among them. That weakened one of the proven stimuli of innovation—the meeting of unlike minds—and was especially debilitating in the automotive industry, where new ideas increasingly involve integrated systems. One of Borg-Warner's early moves, therefore, was to create two company-wide councils—one for sales and marketing and one for technical people—which meet regularly to cross-pollinate.

3. *Throw a party.* There's no point in mapping a sleek, elegant innovation process, laid out on a score of stylish PowerPoint slides, if you've got nothing to process. That's like showing up for your first tennis lesson with a $300 Yonex Ultimum RQ Ti-2000 racquet and a pair of Nike Air Zooms. Instead, as the shoemaker says, just do it.

To get ideas flowing, Borg-Warner planned an innovation summit, a three-day bash in the old Dodge mansion outside Detroit. Good brain-

storming isn't random; it has a topic. In preparation for the innovation summit, the technical and sales and marketing councils studied trends and
selected one that looked rich with opportunity. Over the next several years
the electrical systems in automobiles, currently (forgive the pun) operating
on its twelve-volt battery, will be remade to run on forty-two volts. The reason for the switch is that twelve volts aren't enough to meet all the
demands—from CD players and phones to instant heat—now placed on a
car's electrical system; the new standard was set at forty-two volts because
it's a lot more power, but not enough to create any danger of electrocution.
More power makes many things possible that weren't before.

Seventy people came to the summit, all primed to present and debate
ways to exploit the forty-two volts opportunity; in two days, the summi-
teers came up with 140 power-train-specific ideas, which they discussed
and, eventually, winnowed down to four. The last afternoon, the company's strategy board—the senior leadership, including the CEO, Fielder—
arrived to hear presentations of the top four ideas. The potentates then
retreated in camera, emerging an hour later to endorse one, which they
funded on the spot. (It's a smart pump for coolant and oil that can turn on
or off instantly, on demand; because it runs only when needed, it saves
fuel.)

"An event like this is a tactic," says Spencer. "It creates time and space
and pressure." The result is what Dorothy Leonard, a Harvard Business
School professor who's an expert on innovation, calls "generating creative
options." General Electric's original Work-Out sessions (see p. 167) were
similar to Borg-Warner's innovation summit, applied to the in-house
process of spawning ideas for managing the company. Brainstorming is
just one way to create options. Role playing is another: The CIA and some
corporations have generated creative options by setting up teams of people whose job it is to pretend to be the competition. New blood also ener-
gizes innovation. Most autopsies of failed R&D projects show the same
thing, says Chad Halliday, the CEO of DuPont: "The questions asked by
management were answered well; it was the questions we had no idea
about that killed us." The main reason: Too many old friends, who tend to
be people from inside the company, or among its familiar customers, and
speakers of its native language. "Find new friends," Halliday ordered, and
now every major DuPont R&D project gets a visit from three outsiders—

academics, brainy types from different industries—who spend a few days looking at the research, asking questions, deflating balloons, or suggesting entirely new approaches to problems or applications of ideas. "Creative abrasion," Leonard calls it; if it rubs you the wrong way, purr.

4. *Design a process.* The basic stages of innovation—market sensing, idea generation, focusing, development, prototyping and piloting, rolling out, and measurement—are easy to sketch, tricky to do. Every company has its own strengths, weaknesses, hot buttons, and third rails. Therefore, says Sutherland: "The best way to design a process is by doing it." One of the best things about the Borg-Warner innovation summit was its outcome: a high-profile project that the company's top people had endorsed and funded, because top management is unlikely to let a few snags stop a good idea in which its prestige is invested. That first project is like a first child who heroically machetes his way through the jungle of his parents' rigidities and misconceptions and thereby makes life easier for the siblings who follow behind. At Borg-Warner, the on-demand pump became the prototype for the innovation process. Spencer's position—innovation champion—was created to manage it. That is, he is the process owner. This is a position that he hopes will disappear, but, he says, "there's a need for the next few years for a champion to keep the momentum going." In the summer of 2001, he convened a second innovation summit, focused on technologies to improve fuel economy and reduce emissions, a subject area chosen the January before.

Knowledge work, remember, is nonlinear, moving forward by iteration and reiteration, backtracking and tacking. (See Chapter 2.) Knowledge creation processes are no exception to this principle. There is a "supply chain" for knowledge creation, which on paper goes like this: science base —> market knowledge —> invention —> product development —> process development —> application development —> customer process development —> plant support —> customer support. In real life, knowledge creation no more goes like this than the course of true love runs smooth. Says DuPont (whose R&D supply chain that is):

> While the traditional supply chain for a product is all about the flow of materials, the innovation supply chain is concerned with the flow of knowledge. *The two are not managed in the same way.* The innovation

supply chain isn't linear, although the physical chain is. Innovation is an iterative process. In fact, pieces of the innovation supply chain can be done in parallel. The flow has to be managed—globally, so that knowledge is shared rapidly and appropriately. Speed is the key. . . . The fundamental unit of work will be international teams and affiliations tied into a global effort.

5. *Don't stop.* Since innovation is both a machine and a magic garden, keep oiling the one and fertilizing the other. To improve the machine at Borg-Warner, Spencer is leading efforts to improve the company's biggest innovation weakness, its skill at market sensing. He says: "We've been focused on GM, Ford, and Chrysler and how many widgets they need next year." Now, learning from 3M's "lead user process," Borg-Warner is paying additional attention to avant-garde buyers; it's also studying regulatory bodies for hints about where markets may move, an example of "finding new friends," if that word can be applied to regulators. He's also greasing the machine's wheels by providing information technology—collaboration tools and an intranet for starters—to keep the process manageable as it carries more and more projects.

Magic gardens need support, too. At Borg-Warner, the garden is getting a whole new tech center in Detroit, designed to encourage serendipitous encounters and lucrative lagniappes. "We're building in all we've learned," Spencer says: open communications, easily reconfigurable space, a "fun" atmosphere, walls that will be covered with pictures that celebrate past and current Borg-Warner innovation. It's easy to go wrong thinking that wild new offices and foosball games are all that's needed to jump-start innovation, but it's also temptingly easy to be a derisive Grinch. Maybe you did walk two miles to school in shoes with holes in the sole through snowdrifts higher than a DeSoto's tailfin: That doesn't mean free Coke machines are evil.

The goals of an innovation process are to get more and better ideas and increase the number of them that get put into practice. Most of the time, when people think of innovation's magic garden, they think of it only as a place for idea generation—a sandbox, a skunk works, a special place where the rules of the day job are left behind and the mind is free to roam. But there's a magic garden for idea execution, too. A group of scholars at

Rensselaer Polytechnic Institute, who have been studying radical innovation by established companies, discovered the importance of a "radical innovation hub"—a place—or a community—that provides support for new ideas. Even better in a big company would be several innovation hubs, to guard against the danger that one could turn into a central place to shoot down ideas. 3M, for example, has so many different labs and types of labs that no one is entirely certain how many there are, and there are lots of ways for a researcher whose project is turned down to look for a new sponsor. In their language, 3M executives regularly use environmental and other metaphors that show they think of the place like gardeners rather than machinists.

But machines work, too, and that's the fundamental point: You don't need to decide between managing innovation and inspiring it. Do both. Whenever you think you're getting good at one, do the other.

CUSTOMER LEARNING

In the knowledge economy, information battles inventory, and usually wins. Companies build vast databases of information about customers. They collect it, buy it, mine it, use it, and sell it—so much of it that there are big legal questions about who owns it, substantial political debates about privacy rights, and even the possibility that customers might seize the initiative and offer to let companies have information—for a price. Till customers wrest control or the Feds crack down, though, there's little you can't learn about your customers. Do it right, and you can paint a bull's-eye on every wallet.

What a lousy way to do business.

You don't win this battle by piling up information: In the long run, a data warehouse is just a storage facility. The real high ground on this battlefield is not a heap of information, it's the top of a learning curve. In particular, it's mutual learning: creating a process whereby seller and customer learn with, from, and about each other, and customers learn from other customers. The premise is simple. If only you knew what your customers want, you could sell more to every one of them; and if only your customers knew what you can do, they would buy more from you. A well-developed, two-way customer learning process will make me yours and keep you mine.

The customer-learning process is just about as vital as any process can be. In this Webbed world, companies need knowledge processes that compensate for the value stripped from physical processes; processes that provide a way to get to and keep profitable customers. The knowledge buyers and sellers have of each other is customer capital, and it's worth plenty. An intercontinental study of top manufacturing operations by the A. T. Kearney consulting firm picked five companies for an award for global excellence in operations. In the domain of process improvement, the quintet got 27 percent of their gains from work they did jointly with customers, vs. 6 percent for other companies in the survey. A study of the dynamics of intellectual capital by Nick Bontis of McMaster University* confirms that, showing that customer capital is the single most important influence on revenue per employee and profit per employee. It is the only conduit through which human and structural capital flow before they deliver bottom-line results. Says Bontis: "If you're not absorbing the knowledge from customers and suppliers, you're not doing anything. 'The customer knows best' is more than an old saying."

Customer learning is usually a balkanized process. Every company has lots of channels for getting information to and from customers. Advertising, market research, customer-satisfaction surveys, complaint letters, warranty claims, sales reps' call reports—these have existed ever since God asked Adam why he chose the competition's product over His own, and Adam replied, "I don't know, my wife does the shopping." These streams of information almost never flow together, however. In the 1980s, when Xerox hired quality guru Joseph M. Juran, one of the first things he asked to see was a list of the ten most common reasons its current machines broke down; when he compared it with the causes of field failures for the preceding models, he found that the lists were identical: "They knew these things were failing, and they didn't get rid of them"—because two customer-learning streams (market research and service) never connected. It seems obvious that product developers should learn from complaints about earlier products, but in real life the barriers are immense: Field service reps are far from the laboratories; the cultural distance between service people and engineers can be enormous; *and it's no one's job.*

---

* The study and its methodology are described further in Chapter 13.

The power of customers is growing in every industry, chiefly because they know more than they did, with help from technology. Go to Yahoo!, search "shopping" for this book, and in seconds you can compare price and availability at several different bookstores. Go to Amazon.com and you can see what other readers think of it, and what other books they bought. Consumers still buy automobiles from lots, but about 70 percent of them check the Web, and turn what they learn into negotiating power. Patients talk back to their physicians, quoting medical journals. Sometimes consumers share information formally, banding together to consolidate buying power. Says Robert Wayland, a Concord, Massachusetts, consultant and coauthor of a book called *The Customer Connection:* "The basic process by which customers learn about companies and vice versa is the same, except that customers can search a lot faster and more cheaply, so their exit costs are dropping. The company response should be to pay more attention to the substantive pieces of the relationship."

You can't lick customers, so join them: Enlist their power on your behalf. That means a shift of focus from selling to learning. Customer-relationship management as it's usually practiced doesn't do that, as C. K. Prahalad observes: "Most CRM strategies view customers as outside, static entities; the goal is to obtain a 360-degree view of each customer—hence, the need to automate and integrate various customer interface touchpoints. . . . It's a company-centric view of the customer, with a focus on efficiency gains." CRM is a $4-billion-a-year business, and likely to double in a few years, and for good reason. But it's just one blade of a scissors.

Customer learning cuts with two blades. It allows customers to invest their capital in you. Microsoft, it's estimated, got $500 million worth of technical advice by shipping Beta versions of Windows 2000 to outside software engineers. Cisco Systems, picking up on an idea pioneered by Lotus Development when Notes was new, manages an online service whereby customers help each other solve their problems—thus aiding customer service while giving Cisco access to lots of talent at no cost. Amazon.com's knowledge of buying patterns of its shoppers has improved the company's ability to offer suggestions to them—the jury's still out on the success of the company as a whole, but between 1999 and 2000 the average purchase by an active Amazon customer rose from $108 to $134, and the company says it is making profits on its book, music, and video sales, where it knows customers best. "We know more now," says Jeff Bezos, the CEO.

Most important, consider the fact that value creation itself, more and more, is a collaboration between buyer and seller. In a mass-production economy, things are made, then sold: Customers visit shops or consult price lists and catalogues and pick from what the manufacturer has on his shelf, in any color so long as it's black. Many services—car rental, restaurant dining, moviegoing—follow the same mass-production model: Seller proposes, buyer disposes.

Now, however, buyer and seller work it out together, which makes their relationship entirely different. Says Barry Libert, director of MIT's New Economy Business Lab, "Before companies wanted to own the means of production; now they want to own the means of acquisition—to own the economic transaction." My accountant is only as good as the collaboration I offer him, and your lawyer can't help you if you don't tell her what's going on; we cocreate the knowledge and the value.* Other services—which for years were offered only in a mass-produced way or a great expense—can be personalized. Tivo lets users watch television shows according to a schedule they devise themselves, rather than the one set up by the networks. In the late 1990s, Canadian Pacific Hotels—whose twenty-seven properties include Toronto's Royal York and SkyDome Hotels and that grand old Rocky Mountain pile, the Banff Springs Hotel—decided it wanted to get more, and more loyal, business from frequent individual business travelers—a highly lucrative bunch who are, says marketing VP Brian Richardson, "the most discerning and demanding customers in the history of mankind." Frequent-guest programs were out: Customers said they preferred getting airline mileage. What they wanted was recognition of their individual quirks and preferences. So CP Hotels offered customers a contract: Join our frequent-guest club and tell us what you want—twin vs. king-sized bed, low floor vs. high, etc.—and we'll move heaven and earth to get it for you every single time. It wasn't easy: The skills and systems needed to get fifty Japanese tourists fed, checked out,

---

* There's an excellent discussion of the cocreation of knowledge, and hence value, in the professional services industry in Ross Dawson, *Developing Knowledge-Based Client Relationships: The Future of Professional Services* (Boston: Butterworth-Heinemann, 1999), pp. 171–87.

and onto a bus with their baggage aren't the same ones needed to satisfy a CFO who wants a hypoallergenic pillow, a copy of the *Globe and Mail,* and Mountain Dew in the minibar. Management structures had to change: At each hotel, a champion—a process owner—was appointed and given broad, cross-functional authority to see to it that the staff lived up to the expanded promise the chain had made to its most valuable customers.

Notice what has happened: When one of these people checks into a CP hotel, the service he gets—the thing he buys, what the hotel sells—is something he helped to design. It could not have been created or delivered without a process by which both parties could learn about the other. That's becoming true of products that were once mass-produced, such as personal computers, as well as services. Dell and its customers design and configure computers before they are made: The pattern is sell first, then make. (The change from make-then-sell to sell-then-make has significant implications for accounting and corporate governance, explored in Part Three.) Powerful and inexpensive information technology makes mutual learning and value-creation feasible on a large scale.

A fully developed customer-learning process will have four traits. First, it will emphasize communication over information mining. Without a process of mutual learning—which permits smarter buying and selling—there's little basis for customer loyalty in a low-friction knowledge economy. Second, customer learning needs to be integrated across functions—that is, not just confined to marketing, sales, and service but reaching into new-product development and even HR and finance.

Third, the process should create a kind of relationship capital that is as valuable to the buyer as it is to the seller: Indeed, both sides should be able to quantify the value of the relationship. There are a number of well-tested ways for sellers to measure the value of their customers.* Flipped around, those tools become measurements of the value of customer capital to the buyer: Switching costs (the cost of finding a new seller, the cost of getting him up to speed about your desires and requirements, the cost of learning how to make nice to the accounts-payable people, etc.) are one token of what loyalty to a seller is worth; buy-

---

* See pp. 240–43 of my *Intellectual Capital*; see also Frederick Reichheld's *The Loyalty Effect* (Boston: Harvard Business School Press, 1996), or see someone who helps companies and investment bankers evaluate acquisition targets.

ers who have invested in learning how to use Oracle financial services software are more reluctant to learn PeopleSoft than are buyers who have no established relationship.

Finally, the customer-learning process should be so visible day to day that you can't imagine running the company without it. No company I know of has a customer-learning process in which all four elements are fully developed, but Wal-Mart comes close, and definitely meets the fourth criterion: You can't imagine the company without it. Every Saturday morning in Bentonville, Arkansas, two rivers of customer information come together: detailed, up-to-the-minute sales data, collected from every cash register in every store, crunched and analyzed by store, region, category, product, and every other which way; and rich, up-to-their-elbows reports from managers who spent all week on the road visiting stores—including competitors' stores—asking questions and soaking up impressions. When Jack Welch, CEO of General Electric, sat in on one of those meetings, he was so blown away that he adopted the process. GE, with next to no retail operations, transformed what it saw at Wal-Mart into a technique it calls Quick Market Intelligence (QMI). All top GE managers, regardless of functional specialty, regularly call on at least one customer, then hold regularly scheduled, intense meetings where they, other managers, salespeople, and others pore over data and share anecdotes to get a pulse of the market, devoted to nothing but discussing what customers say and do. In typical GE style, the same setup is replicated in many places and at different scales. Cross-functional new-product development teams, for example, visit customers to discuss and test-drive ideas, and feed what they learn both to R&D and to account managers. The emphasis: increasing the two-way talk with customers.

Health care giant Kaiser Permanente, with 8.6 million members and $15.5 billion in operating revenues, uses the Web to create a customer-learning process. At www.kponline.org, members can read medical encyclopedias, confidentially query a nurse or pharmacist, and participate in open discussions on topics ranging from pregnancy to gerontology. These are moderated forums—Kaiser doctors and psychologists read every posting and often step in to give advice or correct misinformation. One out of nine users reports getting information that saved them from coming in to see a doctor; an identical number learned something that prompted them to come in. Most important, says Lisa Silvestre, who is in charge of the site, the online community is changing how Kaiser and its members learn about each other and about health: "Learning occurred in silos—between doctor and patient in an exam room, or in surveys we sent out. But nothing organized it or brought it in through one gate. This does. We have thousands of letters and postings, a gold mine of information. I won't be surprised if one day an epidemic like AIDS is discovered this way."

"Nothing organized it or brought it in through one gate"—that's the opportunity a customer-learning process can exploit. Closeness is what customer learning is all about, because you can't be close to someone who is not close to you. That's how, in an e-commerce environment, a customer-learning process moves you up the clickstream; how, in any environment, it builds a valuable shared asset composed of comfort, trust, meshed social as well as technical systems. As surely as information trumps inventory, real communication trumps mere information.

CHAPTER 10

A NEW DESIGN: SUPPORTING KNOWLEDGE PROCESSES 2: PROCESSES THAT SHARE

Un artiste original ne peut pas copier. Il n'a donc qu'à copier pour être original.*

JEAN COCTEAU

Can we talk?

Can we ever. Chatterbox humanity never shuts up. Sharing knowledge and ideas is the most natural thing in the world. Do you want to know a secret? How was your day, dear? You won't believe what that idiot said. What did you learn in school today? I saw the most fantastic movie over the weekend. People are instinctively loquacious. That's why you make them sign confidentiality agreements.

Then why is sharing knowledge so hard at work? Why do ideas sit off in one corner of a company, as inert as argon, when they could bubble and

---

* An original artist cannot copy. So if one copies, he is original.

fizz and precipitate gold somewhere else? Frequently at knowledge-management conferences someone wants to know how to get people to contribute to online libraries and databases.

"Knowledge is power," they say, "so how do we keep people from hoarding it?" Or: "How do we incent people to share?"

It's the wrong question, and not just because *incent* isn't a verb. (Nor is *incentivize,* except among yahoos: Try *motivate.*) A bribe is the wrong reason to do the right thing. Carla O'Dell, president of the American Productivity and Quality Center, which maintains a benchmarking clearinghouse for members, observes that "there aren't enough mouse pads, trinkets, and T-shirts in the world" to keep a reasonably large intranet stocked with common knowledge.

Just because sharing is human nature doesn't mean it's simple. The complexities are suggested in this comment by a doctor, who contributed it to an e-mail discussion: "Tell me if I have this right. First we need an audience that is willing to listen. Second we need a speaker who is not only willing to speak the words but knows his audience well enough to know what words to speak, and finally an audience with the capacity to consider the meaning of the words and to act on them. If all this is true, there is a lot more to the so-called power of words than what is being called the power of words."

THE (NOT ALWAYS) OBVIOUS IMPORTANCE OF KNOWLEDGE SHARING

We've already hung a few pelts on the wall to display the monetary value of knowledge shared: the three quarters of a billion dollars produced in one year at BP Amoco; Chevron's $200 million reduction in annual energy expenses; the sales turnaround at Nippon Roche; Buckman Laboratories' gain in sales of new products; and so on. There's lots more: By sharing ideas among thirteen semiconductor fabrication plants, Texas Instruments was able to increase production capacity—essentially for free—by an amount that would have cost $1.5 billion if built. We'll hang a few hundred million more before this chapter is done.

But figures like those don't begin to capture the value of sharing knowledge, which is so great that it's one of just three business processes for which General Electric's CEO Jack Welch took personal responsibility. (The others were allocating resources and developing people.) Says Welch of the empire he is now passing on: "These companies have nothing in common except leadership and best practices," but that's not chopped liver. The ability to share and leverage expertise is why GE works as a global company. In 1988, when GE started benchmarking other companies and sharing best practices internally, people embraced the notion, but with reluctance, as one might embrace a loved one who had come in from a hard run on a hot day. It's obvious to anyone who spends time in GE that hesitation has turned to obsession. Never in business history have so many people talked so much to so many other people. Ideas get shared by means of dozens of councils: regionally based Corporate Executive Councils for the pooh-bahs, a Marketing Council, Technical Council, Sourcing Council, Finance Council, Human Resources Council, Sales Council, Manufacturing Council, Quality Council, and more. Each business operates similar cross-business or cross-functional networks, which meet for a day or two every few months. Probably every professional in the company—tens of thousands of people—sits on at least one cross-business or cross-functional council. At meetings, everybody is expected to bring something—an idea that made a few bucks, a process that's quicker than the old one. Go to these meetings, says Larry Johnston, who runs GE Appliances, "and you see thirty people writing all day long." Knowledge sharing, at its best, is more than a process—it's almost an instinct.

One benefit of knowledge sharing is the ability to participate fully in global business. A company with customers in many countries, or with customers who are themselves global, must offer a uniform standard of service to customers everywhere. The Singapore office of the Baker & McKenzie law firm cannot serve its clients well—whether they are local companies or local branches of international outfits—without quick, effective knowledge-sharing with the firm's Washington headquarters and its other branch offices. It also needs a process whereby tax specialists in Britain or Bangkok can easily collaborate with a client's tax attorney wherever he is. Hewlett-Packard is obliged to girdle the earth with offices to provide round-the-clock technical support to customers anywhere. Each of its three dozen customer-response centers is networked with every other one, so that technicians anywhere in the world have identical, real-time access to and records of a customer's problem; they can easily pass a knotty problem to the best expert wherever she is, or move an especially time-consuming one from an office staffed by its night crew to a place working at full daylight strength. It wouldn't do (and couldn't work) if the various centers could not share technical knowledge, customer knowledge, and ways of approaching problems, which one might call cultural knowledge.

Knowledge sharing is essential in crises—to let the troops know and to bring the best talent from wherever it is to the trouble's epicenter. Executives of Unilever who served in Brazil during the years it suffered from hyperinflation learned an enormous amount about how to cope with currency devaluations and similar tribulations. During the Asian financial crisis that began in 1997, Unilever dispatched a team from Brazil to Asia, then sent them north as the crisis spread to Russia.

Perhaps most important, knowledge sharing builds social capital, trust, morale, and culture. Whatever your business imperative—speed, innovation, frugality, quality, customer focus—knowledge sharing helps it. At HP, the culture is so strong employees say that they can sniff each other out in a roomful of strangers. That makes it easy to change jobs within HP—indeed, about 10 percent of HP's employees move to a new job within the company each year. That helps lower HP's attrition rate to one-third of the industry average. Its recruitment cost is low; training is faster and cheaper than it otherwise would be.

Says Gary Hamel, CEO of the Strategos consulting group:

The pace of economic evolution is a function of the number and quality of interconnections between individuals and the ideas they hold. As connectedness goes up, the ability to combine and recombine ideas accelerates as well. And it's in those juxtapositions of ideas that we find new possibilities. If wealth creation comes from the number and quality of interconnections, we're going to have to create companies that have those connections across them all the time. Microsoft talks about the "digital nervous system." But the digital nervous system is not SAP or your e-mail system. It's the ability to create the kind of whirling dervish–like dance of talent and ideas and capital that you find going on in the Silicon Valley—but inside the company.

Hamel's observation is richly ironic. Why should it be, as he suggests and observation bears out, that knowledge sharing happens so well in Silicon Valley, where competition is keen, and less well within company walls, where collaboration and cooperation should reign? The paucity and tenuousness of knowledge-sharing connections is startling. Korn/Ferry International, the executive recruiting firm, surveyed more than 4,500 managers, scientists, and engineers, plus 500 more corporate leaders, in large companies around the world, 72 percent of whom said that knowledge is not reused across boundaries in their companies. Only 12 percent said that they had access to lessons learned elsewhere in their own businesses.

An annotated look at knowledge sharing at three companies, each of which has had problems as well as successes, gives some of the reasons why and reveals the principles that make knowledge-sharing processes work.

COPYCATS: VERNACULAR KNOWLEDGE SHARING AT XEROX

These are terrible times at Xerox, its stock trading (in September 2001) below $10, its bonds at junk levels, its very survival in doubt. Xerox's problems—a disastrous sales force reorganization, bloated costs, questionable accounting, and a tough market (when troubles come, they come not single spy but in battalions)—were only beginning to emerge in June 2000 when I arrived in Rochester, New York. It was Flag Day nationally, June 14, but "Teamwork Day" at Xerox, the eighteenth occurrence of an event that began when the company, which has major operations in Rochester, pioneered Total Quality Management in America. Quality saved Xerox, then badly beleaguered by Japanese rivals. Now struggling again, the company is betting on sharing knowledge. Says Anne Mulcahy, the president and probable next CEO: "Quality may help a team figure out how to solve a specific problem. But the really big payoff comes when they share that solution with other teams."

So the theme of Teamwork Day 2000 was knowledge sharing. The subtext was anxiety. The context was the Rochester convention center, turned into an intramural expo with 111 booths, balloons, logo-tagged T-shirts, popcorn, and the usual trade-show gimcrack, except that no one was holding a drawing for a Palm Pilot or a Big Bertha. Teams came from purchasing, manufacturing, sales, engineering, corporate, customer service; some had names that were cute ("X-Selleretaires"), some that were opaque ("GFI/LIA Self-Directed Team"), and some that were both ("The A-Maze-ing PSP Team"). All in all, more than four thousand people—exhibitors, managers, visitors from Xerox's nearby office tower or one of its several sites in the Rochester area—traipsed, schmoozed, and ogled.

Among the highlights: behind a man garbed as a wizard, a booth for Xerox's Eureka database. This is the famous (among those who read the work of the company's former chief scientist, John Seely Brown) online collection of fix-it tips prepared by copier repairmen, and it's whiz-bang stuff: Used by fifteen thousand people on a quarter million repair calls a year, the shared knowledge in Eureka saves Xerox some $11 million a year. Eureka now has an important line extension, to collect, share, and reuse solutions to software problems as well as those involving hardware.

Eureka is a great example of what might be called vernacular knowledge sharing—that is, harvesting, organizing, and passing around insights that come from the grassroots of an organization. The Toyota Production System and GE's Work-Out are based on the same amply proved premise: Ordinary workers know things that are tremendously valuable when gathered and shared. The problems with grassroots knowledge are that, like grass itself, it's low to the ground, it's easily mowed down, and usually it spreads by dividing its roots—which means slowly and only to adjacent territory.

Because they're low to the ground, grassroots groups need higher-ups to act as scouts and flacks. In Rochester, there were five teams from different plants that all had been working on safety, ignorant of one another. They might have remained so—busily reinventing each others' wheels—but for the fact that Teamwork Day organizer Mary Bernhard, whose title is "Program Manager, Corporate Quality and Knowledge Sharing," put them all in the same part of the convention-center floor, with other teams that had stuff having to do with the work environment. "We put the teams into 'knowledge zones' so that they would talk to their neighbors," Bernhard explained; work environment was one zone, as were customer relations, products, operations, and so on.

One of the most consistent, important, and ignored pieces of research about knowledge sharing is this: *It won't happen if people are not near each other.* In a landmark study in the 1970s, MIT professor Thomas J. Allen examined how often researchers at seven different laboratories communicated with their colleagues. On random days over periods of three and six months, participants were asked with whom they had communicated that day about technical and scientific matters—that is, questions about the wife and kids didn't count. The interactions were matched against the walking distance between the researchers' desks. Says Allen: "The general shape of the curve is probably not surprising to anyone. . . . It is the actual rate of decay that is surprising." Ten meters between desks—thirty-three feet—is all it takes for communication to become a trickle. Allen reexamined the data to compare behavior when people were in the same work group. Organizational bonds increased the amount of communication—but the startling drop-off after even a short increase in distance was just as pronounced.

THE PROBABILITY THAT TWO PEOPLE WILL COMMUNICATE AS A FUNCTION OF THE DISTANCE SEPARATING THEM

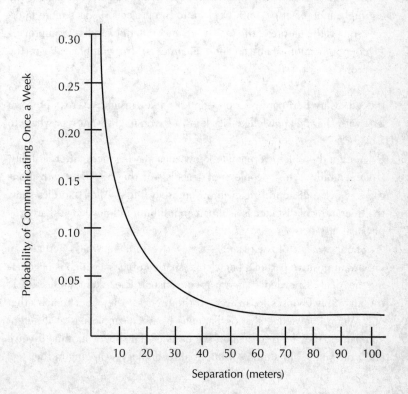

Everything we know about transactions says distance matters in a big way. For example, economists studying international trade have puzzled over "the disproportionately large dampening effect that physical distance appears to have . . . distance appears to matter much beyond what might be explained by transport costs." Have e-mail and the Internet and cheap long-distance phone rates reduced the importance of distance as a factor in knowledge sharing? "Absolutely not," says Laurence Prusak, head of the IBM Knowledge Management Institute. "The research is still valid." Even in a broadband world, propinquity matters.

And sometimes propinquity isn't enough. According to an executive in a communications-industry company in California:

> We had four teams working on process redesign, all on the same floor in the same building and totally unaware of the others working on the same task. . . . To keep management meetings to a modest hour a week we don't share each project with other teams, so nobody caught the duplication of effort until weeks into the projects. What's more interesting is the nature of the topic everyone undertook to fix . . . improving communication about an internal process. To paraphrase Pogo, the problem is still us.

Indeed, Mary Bernhard goes on—and it's a key insight: "Xerox's problem isn't with sharing knowledge—it's knowing who might want it or where to look for it."

A second problem vernacular knowledge sharing faces, after visibility, is vulnerability. Most people aren't rebels—or they're rebels with mortgages. Cock a disapproving eyebrow and they'll fold. Allen's studies show that hierarchical distance is as much an inhibitor of knowledge sharing as physical distance.

Snobbery is a proxy, usually—a negative form of what's actually an important positive part of a knowledge-sharing process, which is negotiating the "deal." Knowledge sharing is consensual. The asker chooses to ask, the answerer chooses to answer. In the process, they check each other out. When knowledge sharing happens between employees at different companies, they tend to deal on the basis of "I'll show you mine if you'll show me yours." In studies of informal technology-swapping in the steel industry, MIT professor Eric von Hippel found that sharing didn't happen—or didn't recur—unless each side felt the other was exchanging something of equal value. A kind of snobbery entered into the decision to share or not: Does this company have stuff as good as ours? Hierarchy is a crude way of doing the same thing: Executives guard their tongues around hourly workers, and vice versa; Ph.D.s share more openly with other Ph.D.s than with less-educated others. This is a problem when signs become more important than substance—when I am so blinded by the glamour of your Armani suit that I cannot see the glow of your good mind, or when hoity-toity academic elitism prevents a tenured professor from footnoting the work of a mere bachelor of arts.

Yet this process of checking people out can actually help knowledge sharing. Bernard Avishai, director of intellectual capital at KPMG, has developed a list of conditions that make knowledge sharing possible. The first is that the asker must have an important task. Looking for help takes effort and carries risks; without a sense of urgency or significance, questions go unasked. He must also have some sort of grounding in whatever he's asking about—enough to know roughly what to ask—and have reason to believe that he's asking someone who will give a good answer. He and the answerer have to have a (mostly) common language and sense of purpose. And he needs to feel that there's no penalty for asking. For her part, the person being asked needs to have experience that allows her to understand the question, must feel it's intelligent or important enough to be worth her valuable time, and must share a language or strategic vision with the asker: I won't tell you where the doubloons are buried unless I have a sense of what you will do with the information. Not least, the answerer needs to be assured that there's no penalty for answering—in other words, that she's not telling a secret or won't get in trouble if her answer differs from the party line.

People navigate among these rocks pretty well in social situations: They meet at a cocktail party, check for wedding rings, ask how they know the host and hostess, find out which part of town they're from and where they went to school. Business adds a level of complication—probably because you can choose the people with whom you socialize but cannot always choose your colleagues, and because the worst your hostess can do is not invite you next time. Royal Dutch/Shell's Andy Boyd found that some Japanese engineers were reluctant to post questions to the company's online bulletin boards, ashamed of disclosing their ignorance in a setting where a superior might see the question; intermediaries posed the questions for them, disguising some details. Remoteness poses another set of challenges, as does technology. The whole process of negotiating the meaning of a question is more difficult online than off—that is, online databases and knowledge repositories are rarely capable of coping with badly phrased questions. In these and other ways, vernacular knowledge sharing benefits from some sort of help—intermediary, kibitzer, mentor.

Technology does mitigate the third weakness of vernacular knowledge, its tendency to move slowly and only to adjacent areas. It's not enough to create a rich, nurturing environment where people can share. Xerox has lots of those. There's an online "Knowledge Universe" where best practices are catalogued and communities of practice can set up chat rooms; a company Yellow Pages; a section of the public Web site, called Knowledge Street, devoted to promoting the virtues of knowledge sharing (and promoting Xerox products and services). Three years running, Xerox has been named one of the world's top ten knowledge-sharing companies by Teleos, a UK-based research group.

Environments are essential; but life, we're told, emerged only when the primordial glop was repeatedly struck by lightning. One good little idea offered up for sharing at Teamwork Day was an application that would save sales reps time and paperwork by collecting approval signatures digitally. A good bigger idea would have questioned why they need to get three to five signatures in the first place.

Quality at Xerox has to be "fast and focused," COO Anne Mulcahy says. That's where the urgent, energizing demands of leadership—lightning bolts—come in. Without them, ideas won't travel far enough or fast enough.

PLANNED SERENDIPITY: VIANT'S DESIGN FOR SHARING

Knowledge sharing doesn't happen without help. I was discussing this proposition with Chris Newell, as hoary a veteran of knowledge management as there is. He said: "Come up and visit us. We've designed the whole company around knowledge sharing." So I did.

"Up" is Boston and "the whole company" is Viant, headquartered near South Station in what used to be the leather district, which now sports the usual downtown-revival mix of wine bars, lofts, funk, and tech. Viant is a consulting company, public since January 1999, that specializes in helping clients build e-commerce businesses. Newell is its chief knowledge officer.

It's an almost-true truism that the greatest number of innovative management ideas come from start-ups and from companies in trouble. Viant is a bit of each. It was, gasp, almost immediately profitable—partly because it was helping Internet start-ups spend money. Among its clients are WIT Capital and CMGI, born with a silver @ in their mouths; the company also works for old-line businesses like Schering-Plough and Sears, which sought its advice about getting onto the Web. When the dot-com bubble deflated, both kinds of clients cut back e-commerce investments as they sifted through the lessons of the past months' turbulence. As a result, Viant's stock got hammered in the last two quarters of 2000, when the company posted losses.

At this writing, it's hard to tell how viable Viant will prove to be. Whatever its future, however, it has developed a truly impressive, emulatable set of knowledge-sharing ideas. Some highlights:

Initiation. It's astounding how many companies flub the opportunities orientation provides to give newcomers knowledge of the company, some firm-specific skills, and the beginnings of the most important element of knowledge sharing, a network of friends. Not Viant. Every new employee, wherever from or wherever bound, begins his Viant career with a three-week QuickStart class in Boston. A group of sixty—the thirty-fifth Quick-Start class—was finishing the Friday I visited. On Monday morning the thirty-sixth cohort would arrive. That day they'd get laptops, fully loaded with off-the-shelf and proprietary software; that week they'd learn team skills and get a cram course in Viant's strategy and methods; then for two weeks they'd toggle between classroom work and teams, doing a mock consulting engagement. They'd bond, meet all the officers, party with CEO Bob Gett, and quaff Flying Fish Beer, a microbrew that Newell says is Viant's "official tacit knowledge accelerant." Then they'll disperse. In the Army or not, basic training works. New hire Reginald Foxworth told me, "I'll go back to Dallas knowing someone in every office in the company." That's no small thing.

Location. Layout works, too. Adele Pascale, Viant's space maven, talks about "a leaky knowledge environment." It's not just the open-plan offices, but also subtler arrangements to encourage what Pascale calls "knowledge accidents"—where you fly down the street on the chance that you will meet, and you meet not really by chance, but because a snack area happens to stand where four project teams' work areas intersect. At the top level, all the "CXOs"—Gett, Newell, CFO Dwayne Nesmith, COO Ben Levitan, chief marketing officer Tara Knowles, chief people officer Di Hall, and others—share one room.

Balancing openness and privacy is tricky. "Something there is that doesn't love a wall" and "Good fences make good neighbors" are points on a continuum, not points of contrast. Long corridors of identical offices with closed doors are obviously unconducive to collegiality; at the same time, aggressively open space destroys the intimacy on which collaboration often depends. Says Tim Andrews, Viant's chief technology officer: "People underestimate how much private offices are used for meetings." Moreover, dormitory-style living scales only up to a point. In an unpublished essay, John Seely Brown and Paul Duguid describe how Fairchild Semiconductor's Robert Noyce, Gordon Moore, Jean Hoerni, Gene Kleiner, and Jay Last worked in overlapping pairs to solve the problems of making the first semiconductors, marveling at the group's "shared knowledge, inherent coordination, and collective understanding." They add: "Were these, by contrast, tasks performed by five different labs within a corporation, the challenge would be quite different." But you can retain lots of that simplicity and directness. The brass at Cisco Systems have offices—glass-walled, but offices nevertheless—but every Friday a lunch cart is wheeled onto the executive floor, and parked by some comfortable chairs, a shelf of books, and other amenities, to lure whoever wants to schmooze.

Colocation. Consultants and clients learn together, traditionally on the client's premises. Viant reverses that: Clients work chez Viant more than 80 percent of the time. That not only alleviates a big consulting-industry beef—long absences that attenuate home life—but also promotes knowledge sharing. As we stopped beside a team from a major bank, Andrews said: "We're not brain-surgeon consultants—'You lie there, we'll operate.' When the client is here, we get better cross-pollination."

The more dispersed a work group, the more important it is to meet face-to-face. Notes Peter Fuchs, a strategy consultant at Accenture: "Network relationships are very transactional, not very social. All kinds of people work together who have never laid eyes on one another. A certain remoteness comes out of that." While it is easy to stay in touch electronically, it is not easy to get warm. The managerial skills that become most important when employees work free of close supervision—skills such as mentoring, aligning staff around a vision, nurturing relationships—require human contact. Bill Raduchel, now the chief technology officer of AOL Time Warner, says, "You can't have a virtual conversation unless you also have real conversations. The indispensable complementary technology to the Net is the Boeing 747."

Rotation. At any given time, Viant's leadership team consists of a score of *ex officio* members and about an equal number of rotating "fellows" nominated by their peers in the field. Consultants have no fixed relationship to a boss; instead, senior people act as "advocates" for a handful of "advocados." Conventional reporting relationships don't work where people rotate in and out of assignments. Performance reviews emphasize the growth in the employee's own skill level, while stock options recognize knowledge shared—"replication of our DNA," in the firm's lingo.

Documentation. The forms are simple but inescapable: Before every project, consultants must complete a "quicksheet" that describes the knowledge they'll need, what can be leveraged (i.e., picked up from previous projects), and what they'll need to create, along with lessons they hope to learn that can be shared. A longer report, a sunset review, is produced at a team meeting to document what did and didn't work well. "File and forget" is the common fate of reports like these. At Viant forgetting's harder. First, almost every Viant document ends up on its internal Web site, hotlinked every which way; the files are, in effect, alive. Second, sunset reviews are done with a facilitator who wasn't on the team, which helps make them honest documents, rather than sanitized and therefore less than believable. Third, every few weeks Newell's knowledge-management group picks a report or two that's particularly valuable, annotates it, and posts it to everyone's e-mail.

Agitation. Viant has created an unusual, particularly valuable role, that of outside agitator. "Project catalysts" are picked from the top consultants in the company, are pulled off client work for several months and assigned to watch twenty or so other projects. They don't supervise, nor are they passive "resource people"—they meddle. What are you doing? How can I help? Looks like you need an example of a business plan to adapt for your client—let me get one. Don't you think you should set up your logistics before promising worldwide delivery? And so on. Says Mavis Chin, the first "P-Cat": "This is in-your-face, not just call-me-if-you-need-help."

Viant's example points up important principles of knowledge sharing. The first: *Knowledge sharing yields to many initiatives, not just one*. It's a messy process. In a previous chapter we discussed two different metaphors for innovation, the machine and the magic garden. There is a place for knowledge-sharing machinery, as we'll see—especially to do it on a large scale. But cultivating magic gardens is the more important means of knowledge sharing. Where knowledge is tacit, even its possessor might not know he has it until someone asks a question. Says Lance Devlin, marketing vice president of Tacit Knowledge Systems: "You can't force people to share knowledge. What you can do is design a system that makes it impossible for people who *do* want to share to miss each other." Viant, builder of Web pages, rightly emphasizes low-tech systems such as colocation, traveling knowledge salesmen, networks of friends, and beer.

Second, it is, indeed, natural for people to share their thinking, but *the companies that are best at sharing knowledge all have some kind of forcing mechanism*, something that oils the jaw of the corporate Tin Woodsman, something that lends urgency to the task. At General Electric, it was a hectoring and indefatigable CEO, supported by an almost bottomless number of opportunities for people to get together. At Viant, it's the P-Cat's job, supported by sophisticated knowledge-sharing technologies and obligatory routines like sunset reviews.

Leaders have many ways to bring to a magic garden the fertilizer, the water, and the hot sun they need above all:

Set an example. Great bosses love teaching; great teachers produce great students. Once, interviewing AlliedSignal CEO Larry Bossidy, I confessed to having "forgotten" (i.e., not knowing) what working capital is. Bossidy positively lit up, grabbed a sheet of paper, scooted around the table, and taught me; his pleasure in teaching turned an interview into a sharing of minds.

Nudge. Nothing gets the troops to use knowledge-sharing technology faster than a leader who asks a staff meeting, "I'd like to hear everyone's thoughts about Kay's posting about the situation in Germany. Bill, what do you think we should do?"

Create incentives. No, not T-shirts that say "I shared knowledge today."

What would happen if, from this day forth, you based promotions and bonuses chiefly on how well people shared and borrowed ideas?

Benchmark. Make sure Phoenix knows it has twice as much bad debt as Dayton, and knows that you expect the gap to close.

Give credit where it's due. If Dayton sends five people to Phoenix to share its collection process, what does it get back? Warm, fuzzy feelings don't count.

Make it fun. When digital cameras were new and exotic, a group at Monsanto made knowledge sharing fun by loaning them out to people who went on trips to customers or conventions; when they returned, they brought their laptops to the next staff meeting and showed the pictures— sharing what they'd seen and learned.

Walk the talk. When you return from a convention, which do you write up first, your expense account or your trip report? Which is read more attentively? Which contains more creative thinking? Why's that, do you think?

Take advantage of your organization's culture. If teamwork is a reality (not just a lip-serviced ideal) at your company, use teams to share knowledge. By contrast, companies that have a star system can use it as a vehicle for knowledge sharing. One macho Wall Street firm rewarded its brokers every year with an expensive, none-too-sober celebration at a resort; by tradition, the top brokers got up in front of their colleagues and told how they'd done what they had—knowledge sharing in the guise of bragging.

Tell stories. The fundamental act of leadership is to embody a vision in a story. Everything a leader does becomes part of the stories people tell about the company; one of the most important things a leader can do, then, is to tell stories himself. Pick one or two about knowledge sharing, and tell them. People will respond by telling you more stories about knowledge sharing, which you can add to your repertoire.

THE SHARING MACHINE:
FORD'S INDUSTRIAL-STRENGTH PROCESS

Dale McKeehan, Ford Motor Company's VP of manufacturing until he retired in 1998, was the kind of manufacturing guy who could pick over a factory like a school nurse hunting head lice. In 1995, as part of Ford's effort to manufacture a "world car," he toured company plants in Europe. There he saw that the factories had some ideas Americans could use, and vice versa. Back home, he summoned his vehicle operations people—the heads of body construction, painting, and final assembly—and said: "Figure out a way to share best practices. And I don't want you to travel to do it." Says Stan Kwiecien, then head of a group working on plant productivity: "We were told to figure it out. So we figured it out. We're engineers."

About the same time, in another part of the forest, Dar Wolford was at work in a Ford staff group charged with reengineering the company's business processes. A nontechnologist surrounded by IT types, she was adapting General Electric's Work-Out program into something she called RAPID—Rapid Actions for Process Improvement Deployment—a quick, nothing-fancy workshop to get rid of small irritants and inefficiencies. One day McKeehan said to her: "When you do these RAPIDs you find the same problems in Hermasillo and in Kansas City. Can't you replicate the solutions so you don't have to invent them twice?"

Early in 1996, Kwiecien and Wolford found each other. The resulting confluence—a Huron of proven best practices and an Erie of new ideas from RAPID workshops—has become known as Ford's Best Practices Replication Process. In four and a half years, more than 2,800 proven superior practices have been shared, some more than once, across Ford's manufacturing operations. The process has been licensed to Royal Dutch/ Shell and Nabisco; portions of it have been patented. The documented actual value of the shared knowledge: $850 million. Another $400 million stands to be won from work in process; that's $1.25 billion. (If you're keeping score at home, in 1999 only eighty-six U.S. corporations made a profit greater than $1.25 billion.)

Kwiecien's work proved the adage that fancy tools aren't necessary—or even a good idea—when a new process begins. Travel, though, is a necessity, McKeehan's admonition to the contrary notwithstanding. Plant managers from Saarlouis in Germany and Kansas City in the United States, together with a few production engineers, exchanged visits in late 1995 and early 1996. From a walk around Saarlouis, the Americans saw fifteen of what Kwiecien, in a happy phrase, called "golly-gee-I-didn't-know-you-could-do-it-that-way-type things." On the reciprocal visit, the Germans found sixteen comparable instances of Yankee ingenuity. They snapped photographs, took the film to Arbor Drugs near Kwiecien's Dearborn office, glued 4-by-6 prints to sheets of paper, and wrote a quick description of each golly-gee-type thing, what it cost, what it saved, and whom to call to learn more.

These "picture sheets" were a marvelous invention. Pictures convey tacit knowledge. Experienced engineers can look at a snapshot of, say, a robot arm installing a windshield wiper, and see instinctively and immediately what's different and, often, why it's better. At the same time the picture sheets documented explicit knowledge—the who, what, where, when, how, and why of daily journalism.

The thirty-one picture sheets that resulted from the Saarlouis–Kansas City visit were passed out at the next North American plant managers' meeting. Plant managers are proud people; immediately the other managers bragged that they, too, had stuff they did better than anybody. How to bolt on a bumper 20/100ths of a minute faster. How to apply paint 1/1,000th of a mil thinner. The process snowballed. More photos; more trips to Arbor Drugs; more picture sheets. But low tech has its limits, and Kweicien struggled to stay ahead. Then someone said to Kweicien: "You ought to show this to PL"—Process Leadership, Wolford's group. She recalls: "Stan wheeled over three boxes of info, one hundred thirty different practices, and said, 'I can't keep doing this manually.' We were already using the intranet for RAPIDs. All we did was blend the two—we Webified Stan's process."

Well, not all. Wolford and Kwiecien bonded like Krazy Glue. They made three quick decisions. First, there'd be a system that would be managed. There are, I've suggested, questions of scale in knowledge sharing. Simple organisms don't need a central nervous system; complex ones can't live without them. Says Wolford: "You need a process with distinct roles and responsibilities." Second, no practice would get into the system unless it was proven—"stuff that's working, not stuff we think might work." Third, the system would belong to operations, not finance or anyone else. From that came an important implication: Every improvement would be documented in the language used by the work group involved: time, head count, gallons, whatever. It would not be the responsibility of engineers to say how much money they saved—that translation would be done later, by Wolford, Kwiecien, et al. That way Mexicans and Frenchmen could compare *manzanas* to *pommes*, not pesos to francs.

The work groups—which Ford calls communities of practice, though that stretches the term a bit—are natural ones, given how vehicles are

KEY ROLES IN THE KNOWLEDGE-SHARING PROCESS

A knowledge-sharing process works best when certain roles are filled, regardless of how tightly or loosely managed the process is. These are the most important ones:

The champion: This is an executive with authority, budget, and the power to enforce rules and compel behaviors. When sharing is done right, ideas cross organizational boundaries, which makes people defensive. Champions can put a stop to that. At GE, Jack Welch is the champion; at Ford, the director of manufacturing, who appoints community administrators, plays the role.

Knowledge-asset owners: Someone must be responsible for content, affirming that it is important and that it is correct. Asset owners are practice leaders, and might be functional: the head of cardiology, the expert on hedging. Ford's community administrators, who are usually engineers, have that role. At Xerox, a team of people validate tips that are submitted to the Eureka database.

The local focal point: The term is Ford's, and it's a good one and an important role—someone who is explicitly charged with the job of being a conduit for shared best practices, and who takes it upon him- or herself to look for them, too.

The itinerant knowledge peddler and meddler: This is the informal organization's counterpart to the focal point. These are the "Rudis" I described in *Intellectual Capital* (p. 99). They were named by Patricia Seeman, then at Hoffman-LaRoche (now at Zurich Group), who, while working on a knowledge-management project, found several people—the first was named Rudi—who said, "I sort of help people out" by pointing out the whereabouts of essential knowledge. Seeman said: "The Rudis are the gray mice, whom senior management never notices—people who not only know something, but take the time to share and are very good storytellers." Viant's P-Cats are a variation on the idea, only, being cats rather than gray mice, they're predators, not scavengers.

The standard-setters: Managers, administrators, librarians, makers of templates—and the SWAT team that helps communities set themselves up—these are the visible manifestations of the knowledge-sharing process. Their business cards are likely to say something about it. Wolford and Kwiecien fill this role at Ford, as does Newell at Viant.

Communicators: Editors, writers, journalists who work to prepare knowledge assets. It's hard for busy people to take the time to describe what they know. Sunset reviews, summaries of lessons learned, and other after-the-fact documentation gets done more assiduously if it's someone's job to nag for information and then put it into readable form. Communicators might work for standard-setters or for asset owners.

Wise man/guru: Rudi with nerve, experience, and maybe a bit of madness. This is knowledge sharing's chief ideologist. He will disagree with the champion and argue with people who put security ahead of sharing.

---

made: central engineering, body assembly, final area assembly, paint, materials planning and logistics, and so on. Each has a company-wide "community administrator," picked by the director of manufacturing, thus giving executive sponsorship to the process. The administrator role takes half a day a week. He—say, in paint—goes to the paint community in every plant and gets its people to choose a "focal point." This role, usually held by a process engineer but in a few cases by an hourly, takes one or two hours a week. No one's paid extra.

The detailed best-practice-replication process has forty-two steps, but the outline's simple. The focal point looks for a neat new practice (or its inventors come to him). He makes up a picture sheet. Its format is like Kwiecien's old ones, only these days it's a Web page. Fill-in-the-blank templates prompt him to quantify benefits (time, materials, etc.); pictures are scanned in. When the page is done, the focal point e-mails it to the community administrator, who looks it over, compares it to what he knows about other plants, and, if it passes muster, designates it a gem.

Immediately—immediately—the picture sheet is posted on the intranet and e-mailed to all the focal points in that community. Their job is to show it to local management and engineers as quickly as possible. Once it's reviewed, local plant management must—that's a key word—announce a decision: to adopt or adapt it (and say when); to investigate it; or to reject it (and explain why). Wolford keeps—and the Web displays to all—a scorecard by community and by plant. In August 2000, for example, out of sixty-one gems in painting, the St. Louis plant had adopted or agreed to do forty-three, was investigating two, had rejected seven as inapplicable and nine as not economically feasible (in this budget cycle, at least), and had originated two. If a plant or a community isn't adding or adopting its share of ideas, it's obvious.

Plant managers love the process. Every year Ford headquarters hands down a "task" to managers—a 5 percent, 6 percent, 7 percent gain in costs, throughput, energy use, and so on. The best-practices database is the first place they go after getting their task. Importantly, the process fosters knowledge sharing below the plant-manager level. Says Jeff Wood, who runs the Michigan Truck Plant: "I can walk into a plant managers' meeting with thirty ideas, but there are twenty of us there and only so much time; how much can we get done? This allows us to get all the engineers in various departments to get at things." And there's pride. Wood's plant has thirty-five patents pending, from new and old ideas no one had realized were unique and valuable, the work of gearheads with callused hands, not pantywaist Ph.D.s in lab coats. Says Wood: "What's in it for us? No monetary reward, except for the corporation. But there's pride of ownership. The whole world comes to Michigan Truck to watch us work."

Given Ford's proven ability to share knowledge, it's a tragic irony that a catastrophic failure of knowledge sharing seems to have lain at the root of the scandal that embroiled Ford and Firestone in 2000. The two companies suffered a death of a thousand cuts, in part because knowledge that might have alerted the companies to the calamitous mismatch of Ford Explorers and Firestone tires was scattered in different places in both companies, each item innocuous in isolation.

Why, given the billion-dollar benefit of Ford's Best Practices Replication Process, did it not help in this case? Two reasons. First, knowledge is best shared within communities. People with something in common talk more than strangers do. Neither Ford's nor Firestone's social network is rich enough to support the kind of extramural communication that might have uncovered the problem. In other words, Ford's focus on natural work communities is both a strength and a weakness. By creating communities that cross hierarchical and geographical boundaries, Ford produces a lot of knowledge sharing that wouldn't otherwise happen, connecting grassroots groups that otherwise would have no reason to know about each other. But communities have their own language and culture: What painters know tends to stay in the paint shops. Clearly Ford is better at moving ideas horizontally than at surfacing problems like those found in the Firestone/Explorer disaster.

Second, the more widely dispersed knowledge is, the more powerful the force required to share it. Such a force supports Ford's Best Practices Replication Process in manufacturing—a tight, compelling link to Ford's business model. The "task" does that at Ford. It sends plant managers off looking for a source of money. Like a magnet, the task draws knowledge from its hiding places. Likewise, the process's use of e-mail, its rules (focal points must report a decision about every gem), and its scorecard all give it energy.

Lamentably, there seems not to have been a link between safety data—especially far-flung, scattered safety data—and Ford's business model. There was no routine, built-into-the-work reason for people to go looking for information that might have saved lives—not to mention millions upon millions of dollars.

There's an important lesson here for knowledge-management types: If your baby isn't tied into the realities of the business, it won't do squat.

We end, thus, as we began at the beginning of these chapters on knowledge processes, with a story about knowledge that might have been shared but wasn't. If anything in these chapters makes it appear that managing knowledge processes is easy, let's be clear: It's not. But success and failure tell one identical story: The value of identifying, developing, and managing knowledge processes is enormous, as is the cost of failure to do so.

CHAPTER 11

A NEW CULTURE:
DEVELOPING A
KNOWLEDGE PERSPECTIVE

I would like to be the air that inhabits you for a moment only. I would like to be that unnoticed and that necessary.

MARGARET ATWOOD

The knowledge economy rests on three pillars: knowledge's growing role, and that of information, as factors of production, which are bought, employed, and sold; the increasing value of intellectual capital; and the development of vocabularies, tools, and strategies to manage knowledge and intellectual capital. A knowledge company is more than the sum of these parts, however, just as to know is more than to have a headful of facts. A true knowledge company is one in her bones. Says Elizabeth Lank, currently of TFPL, a knowledge-management consulting and research firm in London: "It isn't enough to have a CKO and a team supporting him—it has to be how the company thinks." A knowledge company looks at its world, its problems, its opportunities, its people, and its risks in the belief that its triumphs and troubles will lie in the domain of knowledge.

Culture may be intangible, but there's nothing unreal about it. Doug West, head of human resources for Toyota Motor Sales in the United States, defines culture as "how we do what we do." When a knowledge perspective becomes part of the "how" and the "what," the effect on performance can be powerful. We'll look at four areas in which this is particularly so: problem solving, risk management, leadership development, and building trust.

WHAT'S YOUR PROBLEM?

I worked in book publishing for nearly two decades. In the end, the business of publishing comes down to successfully answering three questions: Which books shall we publish? How much should we pay to acquire them? How many should we print? If you can get those right most of the time, it's a pretty healthy business. Few can.

Take the last question, which ought to be the simplest—how many should we print? To accommodate booksellers in the Great Depression, publishers agreed to let them return unsold copies. Returns became a trap from which publishers have been unable to extricate themselves for two-thirds of a century. An adage in the business says that a book's last printing (which might also be its first) comes back as returns. Today more than 35 percent of hardcover books come back, like bread cast upon the waters and found again after many days. That doesn't count the books that never leave the warehouse at all. At the same time, books are invariably in the wrong place: While stacks of books in Chicago don't move, Cleveland is sold out and the increasingly peevish author has your private line, unwisely given in happier times. It's an absurdly expensive problem.

We editors thought it was a sales problem: The reps or the stores were to blame for not putting out enough copies, or the benighted public didn't know what it was missing. Sales reps, for their part, said it was a marketing problem: The stores took too few because the house wasn't really behind it, there wasn't enough of a marketing campaign, the first printing was too small (curious that we had too many books as a result of printing too few, but . . .). Marketing and publicity, in turn, blamed the editors, who were naive or out of touch with real people or snookered by fads or agents, except that the editors knew that publicity hadn't done enough with reviewers and the bozos in marketing were functionally illiterate. Round and round it went: sales problem, marketing problem, editorial problem. After the fact, of course, everyone could see the things other people should have seen before the fact.

Twenty/twenty hindsight is the tip-off: This was, and is, a knowledge problem. Inventory problems almost always are. What do we know? Is what we know the same as what we believe? When do we know it? How can we know more, earlier? How can we better share our knowledge? With whom? How can we react more quickly to news? How can we take, that is, a knowledge perspective? If information were instantaneous and perfect (it never is, but it can always be faster and better), production and distribution could be precisely calibrated to match supply to demand. Seen through that lens, undistorted by misinformation (to get books into stores, publishers lie to bookstores about how many they intend to print) or politics (it must be someone's fault, and I know it's not mine), inventory becomes a problem that can be mitigated by knowledge management.

All kinds of afflictions are actually knowledge problems, things that repeatedly go wrong because of inadequate intellectual capital, poor knowledge management, or a misconceived reading of the market. Like Lyme disease, knowledge problems have symptoms that mimic other problems. Each item on the following list, adapted from the work of David Smith, who pioneered knowledge management at Unilever, is a symptom that suggests a failure to take a knowledge perspective on business problems. They mean people aren't finding the knowledge they need, aren't moving it around, aren't keeping it refreshed and up-to-date, aren't sharing it, aren't using it.

You repeat mistakes. "Your best teacher is your last mistake," says Ralph Nader, who made a career out of pouncing on companies that dozed off in class. Many people and companies are so busy trying to hide boners (from the boss, from stock analysts, from customers and competitors) that they tuck away the learning with the evidence. Fear is the number-one reason: fear of being embarrassed, chewed out, or canned. In America, add fear of lawyers. Yet negligence lawyers don't wear Gucci loafers because companies make mistakes; they wear them because companies make the same mistake twice.

You don't, obviously, want to encourage goofs just to learn from them. But the best way to avoid repeated errors is to take a knowledge perspective: Celebrate learning, not just success. The history of medicine shows that you can learn as much from autopsies as you can from cures.

You duplicate work. "Reinventing the wheel" is the inevitable phrase, and most companies are so good at it you'd think they were suppliers to Schwinn. A classic example: You inspect the goods before you ship them, and your customer inspects them again after they arrive. Worse, you do the same in-house. Some people duplicate work because they have what one might call an overdeveloped engineer's mind: Bob already did this, but I can do it better, or my case is different. Other times, they fail to copy success for the same reasons that they succeed in copying mistakes: They're afraid or embarrassed to ask. They don't know where to look or there is no accessible store for corporate memory or looking takes too much time.

You have poor customer relations. If you do, it's probably for one of three reasons, all knowledge problems. First, miscommunication at the point of sale: Either he didn't understand what you were selling or you didn't understand what she was buying. Second, service: If service is a problem, perhaps your design and manufacturing people aren't hearing about the problems your people encounter, or service people aren't learning from each other. The third reason is subtler and more interesting. Knowledge work tends to be custom work, or at least customized work, and that changes the nature of the sale. You don't sell janitorial services the same way you sell Top Job and mops. Too often, salespeople are in a hurry to hear "yes" so can they write up the order. (Too often, their incentives encourage that practice.) Result: You made the sale, but not the deal.

Good ideas don't transfer between departments, units, countries, etc. Knowledge sharing—or its failure—may be the single most common knowledge problem, underlying many on this list. (See Chapter 11.) Certain kinds of office politics fall under this heading, too—the battles that arise when people can't agree on a common set of facts, for example.

You know the phrase "Not invented here"? You invented it. 'Nuff said.

You're competing on price. If you can win a sale only by dropping your price, the problem is almost always knowledge, or the lack of it. You can usually avoid the price game if you increase the knowledge intensity of products and services, or if you and your customer ride a learning curve together. Everything you learn about a customer—his future plans, how he likes pallets stacked, his secretary's daughter's birthday—is an opportunity to make it harder for competitors to keep up or horn in.

You can't compete with market leaders. Don't blame your problems on scale until you have explored this question: What do they know that we don't know? Toyota, Wal-Mart, and Southwest Airlines are just three examples of formerly small companies that outwitted bigger competitors.

You're dependent on key individuals. Nothing's more dangerous than depending on a few key people. They might leave. They might be wrong. Usually this signals too little teamwork or a too-controlling leadership style. Note, though: The fault doesn't always lie in your stars. When decisions are made too high in the organization, take it as a sign that people lack knowledge that would allow them to think for themselves, or permission to act on what they do know.

You're slow. Diagnosing this knowledge problem can be tricky; as with cases of referred pain, the source may be far from the symptom. Among other things, it could be a weak lab, a sludge-slowed commercialization process, budgetary bureaucracy, or a failure of competitor and market intelligence. Until it hits a wall, knowledge moves at 186,000 miles per second.

You don't know how to price for service. Do you bury the cost of service in your price so your customer can't see it? Sell a service contract? Bill by the hour, the day, the job? Let someone else in the distribution channel handle it? Can you explain why you do what you do, or are you just following industry practice? If you do not know how to price for service or why to charge one way vs. another, it's a sign that you don't fully understand the knowledge content of whatever it is you are selling—you haven't looked at your offerings as knowledge products.

Each of these knowledge problems represents a way to examine business problems from a knowledge perspective. Companies need to test every business activity, as well, to see whether it meets the demands of a knowledge-based century: Do we understand the disciplines of a knowledge business? Are old skills able to deal with new business realities?

WHAT'S AT RISK?

Risk management—usually a function of the treasury department—is a superb instance where a knowledge perspective can add value. Treasurers and CFOs know a lot about currency risks, environmental and legal risk, political risk in developing countries, or risks such as fire, hurricanes, strikes, and product liability; but the field of intellectual risk management basically doesn't exist—and needs to, since intellectual risk is the real threat twenty-first-century companies face. Like the drunk in the old joke who looks for his lost keys under the streetlamp because the light is better, risk management is dealing with visible classes of risk while greater, unmanaged dangers accumulate in the dark.

Risk—let's get this straight up front—is good. The point of risk management isn't to eliminate it; that would eliminate reward. The point is to manage it—that is, to choose where to place bets, where to hedge bets or lay them off, and where to avoid betting altogether. Though most risk-management tools—insurance, hedging, diversification, and so on—have to do with reducing loss, the goal is to safeguard the gains from the risks you take. The familiar, under-the-streetlamp risks—hazards, fraud, currency fluctuation, politics, war—are known company-killers, by no means trivial. The 1984 plant disaster at Bhopal, in India, which left more than 6,000 dead, claimed a final casualty fifteen years later when a much smaller, much-altered Union Carbide agreed to merge with Dow Chemical Company. Shareholders of Cendant are still not whole from fraud at the former CUC Corporation, but at least their company exists—more than can be said for Barings Bank. Anyone who has done business in Asia or Russia knows all too well how dangerous currency and political risks can be. These are palpable risks to tangible things: buildings, bankrolls, inventories. Says Donald Lessard, deputy dean of the Sloan School at MIT and a risk management expert: "Much of risk management is focused on which objects are at risk. The emphasis is on the physical or financial object, not on the source of risk."

That shortcoming leaves the most important risks unmanaged. It also immures risk management in a corner of the finance department. Managing intellectual risks ought to be a core activity of a knowledge company, and the skills of risk managers need to be brought widely to bear.

British philosopher Alfred North Whitehead described what he called "the fallacy of misplaced concreteness"—the mistake of confusing the manifestation of something with the thing itself: "By emphasizing objectively valid elements of the world whose properties we can validate in subject-neutral fashion [the fallacy of misplaced concreteness] hides elements that are not fully objective. . . . Concrete and objective things are believed to exist; less-concrete things such as leadership, empathy, etc., are not." For example, a fever is not a disease—it's a manifestation of a disease, and it is important to manage the disease, not just the fever. Similarly, a baseball player doesn't hit .325; he swings the bat, and if he does so very well, a .325 batting average might be the expression of it.

Misplaced concreteness is a major reason companies fail to manage intellectual risks. A warehouse full of valuable goods waiting to be shipped is a risk you might want to manage, by insuring it and its contents. But the risk is really lost revenue. It could take other forms. You might eliminate the warehouse by developing a highly sophisticated build-to-order manufacturing system. In that case the risk still exists, but it is differently bodied-forth—the risk of your computers crashing or problems with suppliers or labor unrest in the factory. Don't confuse the physical form of the risk with the risk itself.

Just as intellectual assets have come to dominate tangible assets, so risks to intellectual assets and processes now dwarf traditional sources of risk. Often, these risks never take objective form. Lessard explains: "Think of the difference between the e-world and the physical world. Today if you were to value a shopping center you'd go out and count the visitors; before, you'd look at the buildings."

What are these disembodied risks?

Your reputation or brand. When a bad batch of carbon dioxide in Coca-Cola sickened some Belgian children in the summer of 1999, Coke's European operating income fell about $205 million and Coca-Cola Enterprises, the bottler, incurred $103 million in costs. What about the cost to brand equity? One highly imperfect proxy for the hit: Coke's market capitalization fell $34 billion between June 30 and September 30 that year. The hit to Coke's intangible assets was 113 times greater than the operational cost. Worse, the company responded to the crisis by, it seemed, paying more attention to operations than to intangibles, though the latter risk was far greater—the company seemed more interested in (irrelevantly) refuting charges of poor practices than in presenting an image of concern and openness. Ironically, the cause of the schoolchildren's illness might have been intangible, as well: The illnesses were psychosomatic, according to a Belgian psychiatrist who studied 150 children who reported being sickened. A funny-smelling batch of Coke combined with anxiety over food safety and exam-period jitters to produce real symptoms—just as damage to an intangible asset caused real, severe financial loss.

Your business model. Asset-free, knowledge-intensive competition is to entrenched business models what the Panzer was to the Maginot Line. Napster and Gnutella, whatever their eventual fate in court, have changed the music business more fundamentally than anything since radio. E*TRADE, eighteen years old, forced Merrill Lynch, 180, to change its way of doing business. Yet the new guys' very nimbleness creates its own risks, which traditional risk management can't help. You can protect the hard assets of a brick-and-mortar mall. Click-and-order stores are much more exposed: Cash flow is just about all they've got. A company that carries assets runs the risk that three kids in a dorm room are about to make them obsolete; companies without them face the risks of volatility in stock price, reputation, and so on.

Your intellectual property. Many risks to intellectual property—theft, for example—can be dealt with in obvious, if sometimes onerous, ways. Fine old laws forbid disclosing trade secrets, but other obstacles have disappeared or become less formidable, making inhibitions against spilling company beans almost entirely voluntary. Consider how hard Daniel Ellsberg worked to copy the Pentagon Papers, a seven-thousand-page secret archive of documents about the war in Vietnam. Every night for weeks, he left his office with his briefcase stuffed with pages, bound for an advertising agency whose owner let him and a friend use her photocopying machine. Before the job was done, Ellsberg got cold feet. Months later he resumed, finally finishing a year after he began. Eventually he proposed to loan the copy for a weekend to Neil Sheehan of *The New York Times,* who understood that this was an invitation to make a copy himself. In March 1971, Sheehan flew to Boston, where Ellsberg was. Two copy shops (machines at the first shop broke down under the load) worked all weekend to make a copy at a cost of $1,500. An Ellsberg today could publish an equally large archive in minutes by dragging and dropping it onto the Net. His chances of doing it anonymously are less than they were a couple of years ago, but still greater than Ellsberg's were, and for what Sheehan spent—about $6,200 in today's dollars—he could buy a lot of anonymity and have enough money left for an airline ticket to pretty much any destination he chose.

Given this situation, is risk to intellectual property best managed by policing or by making sure your company behaves ethically and develops human resources policies that reward loyalty?

Your network. No company is an island, entire of itself; odds are your business is embedded in a network you do not control. It's not just that AOL might crash and cost you a few days' sales; your whole business may depend on tangible and intangible assets that belong to outsourcing partners, franchisees, sugar daddies, or standard-setters. For example, hundreds of companies and all of e-commerce depend on the World Wide Web Consortium to keep standards like XML from becoming an incomprehensible muckup of dialects.

Your human capital. The obvious human capital risk is flight—a famous example being the death of Shockley Transistor Corporation after the 1957 departures of Gordon Moore, Robert Noyce, and six others, who set up Fairchild Semiconductor. Ex–Fairchild employees in turn started more than three dozen companies, including Moore's and Noyce's second brainchild, Intel, which today is worth 140 times more than Fairchild. Flight is only part of a larger, subtler problem. When the CEO intones, "People are our most important asset," he's wrong, even if he's sincere. As we will see in the next chapter, people are your most important *investors.* Your flow of human capital matters at least as much as your stock of it. Turbulence—and is there anything but turbulence these days?—can disrupt the flow, damaging your ability to attract human capital or people's desire to share it. Says Thomas Davenport, a partner at the Towers Perrin firm, which specializes in human-resources issues: "Uncertainty is a real enemy of human capital. People rebalance their ROI by cutting back the investment." When uncertainty causes people to withhold tacit knowledge, business suffers. Therefore change management becomes a vital part of risk management. When was the last time anyone from risk management talked to anyone from HR?

A second category of human-capital risk is "empowerment risk," so called by James DeLoach, the head of Andersen's Business Risk Management Competency Development Center. This is the risk that managers and employees may be poorly led, not know what to do, exceed their authority, or be wrongly motivated—for example, if salesmen receive bonuses based on quantities sold at a time when the company's strategy is to improve gross margins. Outsourcing has increased empowerment risk.

Notice a couple of patterns in this list of intellectual risks. First, an ever-greater portion of risk comes from sources a company can't own— people, partners, environments. Second, volatility isn't just a currency or stock-market risk anymore. Labor markets, technologies, even business models oscillate at higher frequencies—their behavior more and more resembling that of financial markets.

In those patterns are hints of how to manage risk from a knowledge perspective.

The first step in managing intellectual risks is naming them, which isn't always easy. Says MIT's Donald Lessard, "With intangibles, what is at risk is likely to be the cash flow from a value proposition, as opposed to the cash flow from a physical or financial asset." Selling customized chemicals is a value proposition. What assets lie behind it, and what is their structure? As we saw in Chapter 1, the intangible assets might be human capital (skilled chemists), structural capital (the company's patents, manuals, databases, and systems), or customer capital (its relationship to customers). Each has a different risk profile. Brand, for example, is a mixture of structural and customer capital. One way it is at risk is in product quality. Where is that risk incurred and where should it be managed? Procurement, inspection, production, relationships with distributors—all are potential hot spots. If product quality is a significant risk and you reward procurement people only for keeping costs down, your risks and rewards are out of alignment. To protect the cash flow from a people-based asset, you might diversify its ownership by emphasizing teamwork, guard against obsolescence by developing learning programs, improve your attractiveness to new employees, and shackle key people in golden handcuffs. These are not the usual subjects of talk in treasurers' offices, where risk management usually resides—yet these "soft" risks cry out for treasury's hard mathematical and actuarial skills.

Consider the analogy between managing risks and planning strategy. Says Art DeTore, senior vice president for strategy at Lincoln Re, one of the largest reinsurers in the United States: "Our strategic planning process works like asset allocation for a portfolio." Existing lines of business, like bonds, provide a steady cash flow with a high degree of certainty; Lincoln Re evaluates them using discounted cash flow analysis. New opportunities are less predictable and best evaluated as if they were stocks. Untried ideas are start-ups, and evaluated using real-option pricing models (see Chapter 14), which allow you to set a fair price for an asset today even though its ultimate worth might vary across a wide range.

This kind of thinking works for risk management as well as for strategy.

It's not difficult to put a value on a patent for a drug that is already being sold; it is all but impossible to value a single research project at an early stage. However, such intellectual risks can be securitized—at least metaphorically—and managed as parts of a portfolio, with bets periodically reweighted as each project's value becomes clearer.

All-or-nothing bets, such as insurance, have limited use in protecting cash flows from intangibles whose value is hard to pinpoint. Says Anjana Bhattacharee, director of Aporia Ltd., a British start-up developing tools to manage intellectual risks: "Risk transfer"—insurance—"becomes based on such inaccurate models that the premiums shoot up in order to account for the margin of error." Hedging also has problems, says Bjarni Ármannsson, head of the Icelandic Investment Bank in Reykjavík: "It's difficult to find a counterparty for intellectual risks."

General managers instinctively want to reduce risk by planning; portfolio managers exploit it via markets. Thus Ármannsson makes equity investments in companies whose main asset is intellectual capital, but won't give them loans. He says: "These companies are volatile. If you lend to 100 companies and just one or two go bankrupt, you lose all your profit. If you have equity, you might need just one or two winners to get an excellent return."

The risk to intellectual assets is magnified by "network effects." Just as the value and usefulness of a network grow exponentially as more nodes join it, so does its vulnerability: A network amplifies the cost and reach of catastrophe. Says Hewlett-Packard's CEO, Carly Fiorina: "To strategic vision—which looks foward—leaders have to add peripheral vision." To planning, in other words, add agility.

The usual risks—profit and loss, strategy, hazard and currency, and value at risk—are challenging enough. Add risks to intangible assets—and the catastrophic, by-definition-unpredictable risk of terrorism—and risk seems both discontinuously large and beyond the scope of planning. Welcome to the developing world, says Khalid Aliraza, chairman of Xenel/Saudi Cable Company: "In the developed world, risks are measurable or hedgeable, or there are safety nets." Absent those conditions, he says, companies need to be "smaller, more agile, more opportunistic." They should constantly reassess business strategy and make lots of short-term moves rather than depend on big, slow-to-develop approaches.

That's not to propose the strategic plan of the jellyfish, to float any which way, eat what passes by, and hope the tide doesn't leave you high, dry, and dead. Instead, it means making sure that Murphy (whose law says that whatever can go wrong, will) sits in on your planning process. Stephen Sprinkle, a partner at Deloitte Consulting, says: "One of the worst things you can do is an excellent job of executing a strategy based on only one view of the future—because then you have in effect bet the enterprise."

Nothing's more flexible than markets; nothing reallocates resources better. One way to increase agility, and hence protect intellectual risks, is to create internal markets—for example, for talent. Enron, which developed some innovative management ideas that don't deserve to die (and innovative accounting ideas that do), created flexible internal labor markets. Common compensation structures meant no one lost money by changing jobs. Titles went with the person, not the position; once a VP, always a VP, whatever the post. Equity was a substantial piece of pay, giving people an incentive to want to avoid sinecures and move to work where the company was (or in Enron's case, seemed to be) making the most money. And performance appraisals were made by committees of twenty-four people, not just supervisors. That way a person's evaluation came from the organization, not the boss, which made mobility less risky.

Markets, of course, are full of risk; but they're less risky the more you know—and a lot less risky than rigidity. Intellectual assets and operations obey no one's command and are subject to discontinuous—that is, quantum—change. Before, says Jim Highsmith of the Cutter Consortium, a technology consulting firm, "management viewed change as incremental and periodic. In that environment, predicting and controlling practices worked pretty well." When risks are not cast in stone but floated as ideas, and when change is rapid and profound, its calculus changes:

Respectable people tend to ignore this. We believe in rationality: we believe it all has to be worked out in advance, and the numbers have got to work. The risk takers and the visionaries work completely differently. . . . It is not what they know that makes them successful, it is their desire to know. . . . Creating the knowledge inventory or knowledge reservoir is therefore not enough: to be truly knowledge based, we need . . . space for entrepreneurs, visionaries, mavericks, risk-takers and explorers within jobs, teams and projects. . . . Managers need risk much as doctors need sickness—without it, they had better find something else to do.

There are four ways to respond to a risk: avoid it; reduce it; transfer it; or accept it. The one thing you can't do, if it's intellectual risk, is tie it up and subdue it.

WHO'S THE BOSS?

"You Must Know Everything" is the title of a story by the Russian writer Isaak Babel. Sometimes it seems like the phrase ought to be inscribed over business school entrance gates as a challenge to entering students. Tomorrow's captains of industry must be e-commerce-adept and tried-and-true-commerce-tested; must have powerful analytical skills together with superb instincts, including perfect pitch when it comes to hiring people; must know EPS, TCP-IP, ROE, HTTP, EVA, and WAP; must be innovators, visionaries, and change agents; must know the difference between a thin client, lean manufacturing, and gross margins; must be coaches and team players; must have spent several years working on another continent; must know least squares and be, if not hip, at least not square; must be able to work harder, longer, than most people, while keeping their personal lives in balance; must be youthful but seasoned enough to make consistently mature judgments; and must have good teeth and look great in a suit and, on Friday, in chinos and a sweater.

What's an ordinary schlumpf supposed to do?

Behind that is a serious question: How important is a knowledge perspective in the development of leaders, and talent generally? Some intriguing answers are in a 1999 study from Andersen Consulting—now Accenture—called "The Evolving Role of Executive Leadership." Led by Andersen partners Cathy Walt Greenberg and Alastair Robertson, with help from leadership experts Warren Bennis, John O'Neil, and others, the study team interviewed dozens of current CEOs from around the world, together with hundreds of younger people whom Andersen consultants had tagged as candidates for leadership roles in the future. Their purpose: to create a "profile of the global leader of the future."

Greenberg and Robertson defined fourteen dimensions of leadership. The perfect leader, if she existed, would be someone who thinks globally, anticipates opportunity, creates a shared vision, develops and empowers people, appreciates cultural diversity, builds teamwork and partnerships, embraces change, shows technological savvy, encourages constructive challenge, ensures customer satisfaction, achieves a competitive advantage, demonstrates personal mastery, shares leadership, and lives the values. It's a terrific list of attributes; I'd add only "possesses physical and mental stamina."

The leaders and leaders-to-be were asked to rate the importance of these traits on a scale of 1 to 10, with 10 tops, for leaders of the past, present, and future. The "past" and "future" were just five years ago and ahead, which says something about the attention spans of businesspeople—as Henry Ford said, "History is bunk"—and about career spans, for half a decade is about the average tenure for a CEO.

First interesting finding: The respondents said that every one of the fourteen traits is getting significantly more important. "Embraces change," for example, rates a 5.88 for the past, a 7.99 today, and 8.59 for the future. "Thinks globally" jumps from 4.13 to 7.10 and 8.78. Not one leadership dimension ranked above 6.6 in importance in the respondents' view of the past; not one will rank below 8.2 in their view of the future. The average leadership trait ranked 5.86 on a scale of 10 back in 1994, ranks 7.79 today, and will rank 8.64 in 2004.

That's just silly. Ratings of 5.95, 8.24, and 8.83 say nothing about the importance of ensuring customer satisfaction, which was every bit as vital five years back as it is today and will be tomorrow.

What's behind this perception that leadership is getting ever more demanding in absolute terms? The consultants took it at face value, partly because consultants always say the world's getting harder (which implies you need more consulting help). But there's evidence, notably shareholders' increasing willingness to dispose of a chief executive who disappoints them, that we expect more from leaders. Surely globalization, deregulation, and information technology have complicated leaders' lives, turning strategy into a three-dimensional game of chess, in which threats and opportunities can come not just from traditional rivals but from formerly noncompeting companies and from anywhere in the world.

Nevertheless, we can doubt that standards for leaders are absolutely higher now than they were in Alexander's day, let alone five years ago. Business lives on the idea of progress. Sales go up; stock prices rise; productivity improves; research produces inventions; performance reviews "raise the bar" every year. "New and improved!" have always been the most powerful words on Madison Avenue. Note the paradox: "New and improved!" have *always* been powerful. It's a dead giveaway. We're in the presence of knee-jerk optimism and its corollary: Every day in every way we're getting better and better.

Greenberg and Robertson recognized this problem of inflated expectations and probed deeper. The leaders and future leaders rated not only fourteen leadership dimensions but an additional eighty-two subsidiary characteristics—like the ability to identify priorities, or genuinely listen to others, or demonstrate self-confidence. Instead of looking at their absolute rating of importance, Greenberg and Robertson examined their relative standing. When you see which characteristics ranked in the top ten for the past, present, and future, a revealing pattern emerges.

Back in the mists of prehistory, 1994-ish, the leader's most important challenges were to demonstrate self-confidence, create and communicate a clear vision, and strive for personal excellence; after that, he should expect high standards from others, be a role model for values, identify priorities. This leader was a hero, a general, a tribal chieftain leading a band of warriors, who got his job because he was braver, brawnier, and better than you.

Nowadays, self-confidence, vision, and personal excellence remain the top three attributes of a leader. Setting priorities moves up from number six to number four, followed by increasing shareholder value (which was number ten before). Several new attributes emerge: The leader views business from the customer's perspective and ensures that commitments to customers are met; he creates effective teams, genuinely listens, and inspires people to commit to the organization's vision. This guy's a boss: Tough, challenging, caring, a touch paternalistic, he got the corner office because he sees and plans better than you.

And tomorrow? Vision, values, and setting priorities are one, two, and three. Next come having a customer perspective, team building, and listening. Then come four traits not listed before: building alliances with other organizations, making decisions that reflect global considerations, building partnerships across the company, and treating people with respect and dignity. This is an image of the leader as partner, deal maker, social director, and broker—*primus inter pares,* first among equals. Getting results—that is, making money—doesn't figure in the top ten attributes. Nor do personal excellence and self-confidence. What does figure is getting the process right—making sure the right people are talking to each other about the right things and have the right tools to do what they decide needs doing. That could be the kind of touchy-feely nonsense that often dominates management talk deep into a boom, only to disappear when profits shrink. But I think not.

Rather, I think the leaders and future leaders are describing an agenda for a knowledge-based economy. The leader of the past, they're saying, was a doer; of the present, a planner and coordinator; of the future, a teacher. Her job is to develop capabilities: not to plan the company's actions, but to increase its capacity to act, its responsiveness, its repertoire; it's to build and nurture intellectual capital rather than amass or deploy other assets. This kind of leader doesn't need to know everything; on the contrary, she'll be most comfortable surrounded by people who know a whole lot more but trust her to weigh competing claims.

Knowledge-conscious leadership—that's what we want. The best leaders are learners and teachers. As Howard Gardner reminds us, "The arena in which leadership necessarily occurs [is] the *human mind,*" including the minds of followers. There are lots of ways to instill learning and teaching in the process of developing talent.

Stretch. Do you hire people for what they know or for what they can know? The question came up at a meeting of chief knowledge officers sponsored by TFPL. These were the attributes they valued the most: ability to learn, self-initiation, collaborativeness, humility—and confidence, the ability to connect thinking to action and vice versa—and what they called "intellectual linking," the ability to connect an idea or experience picked up in one place to an opportunity or a problem somewhere else. All are fostered by making sure leaders and future leaders have "stretch" assignments to build learning into the job. P&L responsibility and autonomy are the most important elements of stretch. "Make development a fundamental part of organizational design," the McKinsey consulting firm urges. "Don't choose the best-qualified person. . . . The best-qualified person may not be the one who can learn most" from the assignment.

Teach and learn all the time. I'd been six days in a "stretch" job when my new boss, Pat Knopf, who I been warned had a volcanic temper, appeared at the door of my office and declared: "Stewart, you've been here just long enough to start making mistakes." Not till my heart stopped pounding did I realize that was the first sign that he would become the best boss I'd ever had. U.S. companies spend somewhere between $30 billion and $50 billion a year on formal training, but an estimated 70 percent of all workplace learning is informal. Executives say that informal coaching and feedback are second only to the job itself in importance to their development. Among manufacturing workers, 80 percent say that on-the-job training from peers provides important information about how to do their jobs well; only 29 percent credit their managers with providing similarly important information. Says a software programmer, Dave Long: "I visited a radiology department recently, and was reminded of how much real offices run on informal annotations: sticky notes with settings or warnings, taped signs of the latest deltas [changes] for procedures, pencil and paper as tools for efficient workflow rather than instruments for bureaucratic tortures, etc. As users of software, however, we lose the ability to help our colleagues (or our future forgetful selves) via simple immediate annotations." *Simple, immediate annotations:* That's a perfect description of talent and leadership development at a company that has a knowledge perspective. This is not to dismiss formal assessment. On the contrary, plenty of evidence suggests that assiduously managed performance evaluation and leadership development processes feed informal learning. Performance reviews are too often perfunctory, go-through-the-motions exercises in anticipation of the "real" performance review—your raise.

Learn to lead in an "informated" environment. It's not a pretty term, "informated," but Shoshana Zuboff's coinage aptly describes a workplace where smart machines perform much of the daily grind of the management noncommissioned officer, adding spreadsheets and analyzing sales, work that paid off many a mortgage in Levittown. Software is reshaping the art of managing. It's possible to buy commercial, off-the-shelf software that purports to manage virtually every business function. You can find HR-in-a-box, financials-in-a-box, manufacturing-in-a-box, supply-chain-in-a-box, sales-and-service-in-a-box. Even outfits like Accenture, which churns out more code than Wisconsin does butter, increasingly turn to off-the-shelf software, or to what at Lotus Development they call "consultantware"—semifinished products that consultants then tailor to their clients' needs. It's not as simple as its vendors want you to think, of course, but software has become competent to do real managerial work—not grand strategy but day-to-day work—and that creates a chance to rethink what to manage and what to leave to others. "Technology is just a tool," people pooh-pooh; but these tools, powerful already and getting stronger fast, have minds. SAP even has a "management cockpit" that puts all the key indicators you need on one screen, live. Says one SAP executive: "In effect you'll be running a simulation of the company in the computer, and when the numbers diverge from the model, that signals here's something to look into." As for you: Take the rest of the day off. Play a little golf. Everything's in good hands.

This stuff changes the content of management changes—that is, what managers do all day. Let one example stand for many. Primus, a company in Seattle, makes software for customer-support centers. The next time you call Microsoft, wailing and gnashing your teeth, the nice person on the phone will use Primus software, which will check the words you say (ignoring the blue ones) against a database of known problems and solutions till it finds a match—the way a physician matches your symptoms against her mental disease database. If your problem has been solved before, the software pulls it up; no more getting a different wrong answer from a different rep every time you call.* If it's a new problem and the rep solves it, he's supposed to write it up and stick it in the system for the next caller. The system also keeps track of how often a problem crops up, information that's used to improve the product.

Look at how that changes the job of managing a call center. Without software, management was a brute-force effort. First it involved finding who knew—and who didn't know—the solution to a problem; then it required preparing manuals; training, training, and training everyone; monitoring their work "for quality purposes"; and managing turnover in a high-stress job. Now, says Primus's CEO, Michael Brochu: "Mostly you manage the quality of the information in the system. You're managing less, basically. That's the ROI." In theory managers can spend more time teaching skills like teamwork, problem solving, and communication. In practice, many spend less time managing people altogether, and devote themselves to managing software upgrades.

---

* All these systems are imperfect, of course, but that doesn't make them bad. (See pp. 114–15.)

Informated environments are new, and it's uncertain what their strengths and dangers are. Does the locus of competitive advantage change, and if so, in the direction of software or what geeks call wetware—the stuff between your ears? What's the best use of the time freed up? Managing knowledge workers calls on new attitudes and sets of skills;* a learning organization in which much of the learning happens in silicon will make still more demands on leadership.

WHOM ARE YOU GOING TO BELIEVE?

In April 1994, Marc Andreessen filed the papers incorporating Netscape, the company that made the World Wide Web navigable. *Fortune* was doing a story about how e-mail and other tools of electronic networking were beginning to affect companies, and I wanted to talk about it with Warren Bennis, professor at the University of Southern California, expert on both the style and substance of leadership. We met for breakfast at Shutters, a hotel in Santa Monica—in *Casablanca,* everybody goes to Rick's, and in management, everybody has breakfast at Shutters with Warren.

Here's what he said: Networks, by definition, connect everyone to everyone. Hierarchical organizations, by definition, don't do that: They create formal channels of communication, and you're expected to follow them. A hierarchy, Bennis went on, acts as a "prosthesis for trust." Organization charts—showing who reports to whom, who owes fealty to whom—define more than reporting relationships. They are the trellises on which trust's fragile vine twines and blooms. Indeed, bureaucratic rules and procedures came into being in part as safeguards against untrustworthy behavior like nepotism, favoritism, and corruption. Bennis said: "That organizational armature reinforces or replaces interpersonal trust."

Reinforcement and replacement: Both are important. Personal trustworthiness might need reinforcement by organizational strictures; if the rules are clear enough and the hierarchy strong enough, personal trustworthiness might not even be an issue. In *The Organization Man,* William

---

* See *Intellectual Capital,* especially pp. 48–50 and 79–106.

H. Whyte showed how in large, hierarchical corporations, the Protestant Ethic, with its notion of individual responsibility for one's actions, mutated into an organizational ethos. In that regime, real interpersonal trust is unnecessary: Its doppelgänger will do. You can count on me because you're my boss; I can count on you for the same reason; together we can count on others because the boss of bosses has told us what he wants. Everyone has his place, and everyone else knows what that place is. Position substitutes for persuasion. In theological terms, it's a rule of law, not grace—and it works.

In knowledge companies, networks become the main means by which information is conveyed and work gets done, and those hierarchical crutches are knocked away. Networked organizations have few promotions to give out. Rank is unclear and not the same as prestige. Colleagues might be thousands of miles away. Rewards may go to teams, not individuals. Those teams may be interdepartmental—so that hierarchical power isn't around to guarantee that work gets done. More and more often these teams are temporary—like floating crap games, Bennis said—which disband when the project is done; today's team leader is tomorrow's underling. Networks encourage people to operate informally, outside the rule of law. Relationships therefore depend much more on cooperation than on control. Cooperation, in turn, depends on trust. This is true not just intramurally but also in interactions between businesses. To what extent are strategic partners on the same team?

Flattened hierarchies change the sources and uses of power—a subject about which there's a fair amount of scholarship. Power mystifies few businesspeople. Yes, bosses can't throw their weight around as they did, but power is easy to recognize, and when the boss says, "Jump!" the reply is still "How high?" more often than it's "Make me."

Networks also change the sources and uses of trust. That's a subject far less studied. A visit to Amazon.com and a simple search on the word *power* turns up 28,003 possible titles, vs. just 1,819 for *trust*. These are mostly self-help books, but the fifteen-to-one ratio feels about right for studies of organizations, too. Yet trust is more important. Bennis's book *Douglas McGregor, Revisited* (written with Gary Heil and Deborah C. Stephens) says: "Gathering information, and above all developing trust, have become the key source of sustainable competitive advantage." Trust is certainly essential to managing a company from a knowledge perspective. Work done by IBM's Laurence Prusak with companies like Eli Lilly and Capital One shows that trust is the most important variable in knowledge sharing. Says Prusak, "Without it, nothing happens. It's more salient than reciprocity or power."

Trust, unlike power, baffles people. How do we create a climate of trust in the company? How do I know if we can trust our suppliers? How can I guarantee people will do what they promise, when they don't report to me? How do I know you won't use what I told you to go after my customer or my job? How can we reconcile openness with the need to protect confidential information?

These questions are hard. Without pretending to answer them, we can examine some of the sources and uses of trust in a postmodern corporation. One note in this regard: There's a difference between deep, interpersonal trust and what one might call functional or good-enough trust. Real trust is hard even between people who have chosen to be together and have years to work on it, like spouses. It's harder still where they have little or no say in selecting their colleagues and where time is short. Impossible where an organization is large. Certainly there are and should be limits to the trust between colleagues or between boss and subordinate or between buyer and seller. Trust at work is functional, rooted in ethics and pragmatism and self-interest. It therefore needs support—forces that create incentives for trustworthy behavior. In the absence of hierarchy, what organizational strictures will keep someone in line?

Competence. This is trust's first truss: I can trust you if I believe you're good at what you do, and cannot trust you if I doubt your skill. We trust competence all the time, with automobile mechanics, physicians, computer technicians, chefs. Hierarchies were a way of vouching for competence. Traditionally industrial tasks were handed from one department to another—from research to development to design to manufacturing to distribution, sales, and service. Each department head was responsible for the competence of his staff. Indeed, the boss became boss because he was the best—at least, that was the agreed-upon fiction. One day in an earlier life, when I was working for a large company, the chairman walked by while I was typing something. He poked his head into my office and asked, "How fast can you type?"

"About fifty words per minute," I answered, looking up from the manual machine I ostentatiously preferred.

He said: "If you ever want to be the head of a *Fortune* 500 company, you have to be able to do everything better than everyone else. I type sixty." (No doubt this explains why I am writing this book rather than having my assistant summarize it for me.) Leaving his arrogance aside, not to mention the fact that few CEOs could type at all in those days, what's interesting about his quip is the assumption that the boss has to be best at everything, a notion almost as quaint as typewriters.

"Smarter Than My Boss," says a button I keep in my office. I won't say whether that's true in fact (power being something recognizable), but it's true in theory. The boss today isn't the most talented specialist in a functional department; she is Peter Drucker's conductor-CEO, a coordinator of specialists. She knows the score best, but the trumpeter knows how to blow his own horn. When musicians have trouble with a passage, conductors say, "Take it to your teacher"—not the boss. The boss expects specialists to work more or less unsupervised.

She trusts in their competence—but can she judge it? In the functional organization, she could. The chief engineer hired, trained, evaluated, and promoted other engineers. He assigned people to jobs he could do himself, on the basis of his expert knowledge of their ability—he chose to delegate, rather than to entrust. The leader of a team consisting of a butcher, a baker, and a candlestick maker has less ability to evaluate and no choice but to entrust. "I leave it in your hands," he tells the butcher, because he's all thumbs.

So trust needs a second crutch.

Community. Networked organizations naturally spawn informal groups of like-minded souls. When these communities emerge around a common discipline or problem—a work-related subject like graphic design or the behavior of derivative financial instruments—they become "communities of practice," a term coined in 1987 by Etienne Wenger and Jean Lave of the Institute for Research on Learning in Palo Alto, California. These communities are where work and (particularly) learning occur. I elsewhere described them as "the shop floor of human capital, the place where the stuff gets made."

Communities of practice support trust because they create and validate competence, a role hierarchies performed. The boss may not know which butcher's best, but the other butchers do. And when butchers get together, they teach one another, and coalesce around unsolved problems.

General Electric demonstrates the role of informal communities in creating trust, or at least something that substitutes for it. General Electric's core competence is leadership; leadership development, therefore, is its most important business process. Over the years I've spoken with dozens of GE executives, who uniformly say they spend between a quarter and half of their time on it. With 340,000 employees, a highly competitive culture, and wildly varying lines of business, GE might easily be an impersonal, difficult-to-navigate company. Instead, largely because the place is riddled with communities of practice, the company is remarkably informal, so successful at creating topflight executives that it consistently produces more than it needs and exports its "trade surplus" in talent to companies around the world, and so networked that everybody at GE, it seems, knows people in every other GE business everywhere.

Communities play a key role in leadership development at GE. The company has elaborate formal leadership programs. There's training—not only at Crotonville but in many other locations, and every candidate for a leadership position in the company undergoes extensive training in Six Sigma quality methodologies as well as in traditional subjects. To evaluate talent, GE uses a forced ranking of employees into "A, B, and C players," a second ranking in which every manager rates his direct reports on a strict bell curve regardless of letter grade, and, most important, an annual staffing review, called Session C, for which all GE professional employees submit self-assessments and career-development plans and during which they are evaluated by squads of senior managers.

The formal processes depend, however, on GE's many communities of practice. The literally hundreds of interdisciplinary and interbusiness affinity groups spawn the networks of friendships young GE leaders will use during the rest of their careers. They're expected to bring ideas to share at these meetings, where their friends and equals debate them, improve them, and take them home to implement in their own businesses. It is here that they get noticed, and it is from these communities that managers learn who's *really* good, who's *really* up-and-coming (and whom they want to poach). Communities will unmask someone who is a gossip or a cowbird who steals other's ideas. Good "grades" in reviews and accomplishments in training, however searching the tests or superb the school, cannot create, show, or anneal leadership talent—and cannot produce trust—the way communities of practice can.

Commitment, a third source of and support for trustworthiness, is an adjunct to both competence and community, neither of which necessarily implies loyalty to the organization. Indeed, communities of practice create a rival allegiance, where the interests of a community (for example, advanced research in cardiology) might conflict with the goals of an employer (such as a managed-care company).

Trust obviously depends on the degree to which people are willing to support the organization's purposes. This is not a question of motivation. As Douglas McGregor argues, people are intrinsically motivated—but to do what? Kim Philby and Aldrich Ames were highly motivated men. As companies become more entrepreneurial, as they flatten hierarchies so that bosses supervise fifteen or twenty people instead of six or eight, as they empower people, commitment to the same mission and values becomes vital. Moreover, in a knowledge economy, where unthinking jobs have been automated, companies are asking all workers—and especially managers and knowledge workers—to make decisions. Their inner gyroscope must be aligned with the corporate compass.

That can't happen unless people know what they are committing to. Statements of vision and mission are notoriously vacuous, and breed cynicism, not trust. George Bailey of PricewaterhouseCoopers once printed up half a dozen companies' vision statements, then challenged their CEOs to identify which one was theirs. Half failed. And who wouldn't? Most companies could get better mission statements if they used Mad-Libs, or tried the Dilbert Web site (http://www.dilbert.com/comics/dilbert/career/html/questions.html), which will generate both mission statements and performance reviews by randomly combining buzzwords and bromides. It just gave me "Our mission is to completely negotiate enterprise-wide materials while continuing to proactively leverage existing error-free solutions to exceed customer expectations." I couldn't agree more—or care less.

Vision is a clear understanding of what makes the difference between success and failure, and how that translates into behavior and decisions. No more hiding the business model behind high-sounding nonsense. One company makes money by being the low-cost producer: We drive hard bargains, are a no-nonsense kind of place, are fussy about expense reports and impatient with slow learners, and if that makes you uncomfortable, don't work here. Another makes money by being the leader in innovation: We'd rather see half-baked ideas than fully cooked ones, and if you haven't failed around here, you haven't tried. A third makes money by coddling customers, so it cherishes empathy and attentiveness. It's crucial to link the mission to the business model; crucial, too, that personal success—career advancement—comes to people who commit to the behavior you ask of them. The company that asks for innovation and rewards punctiliousness should not be surprised if its creative people seem alienated.

Beyond competence, community, and commitment, trust of course depends on communication, which can be its best friend or its worst enemy. That morning in Santa Monica, Bennis said that communication "will take a hell of a lot more time than it used to. And it will take a lot of emotional labor on the part of the leader." He understated the case. Hierarchies can lie, and get away with it pretty well. Naked emperors go unchallenged. Incoming CEOs rewrite history with an avidity Orwell would recognize, and for reasons he would understand. Their newest trick is to take a big restructuring charge as quickly as possible after taking office, thereby reducing current earnings so that, a year later, they can boast the improved results while polishing their résumés in preparation for their next gig.

A revolutionary way to build trust: Tell the truth. A few years ago the corporate communications head at AlliedSignal asked me: "What news travels faster than any other news through a factory?" He answered himself: news that a competitor won a contract the company was bidding for. "And what news," he went on, "is never, never, never even mentioned in any plant newspaper?" It was a struggle, he said, to get the editors of those newspapers to understand that credibility mattered.

"If you can't say something nice, don't say anything at all" might be good etiquette, but it's bad management, certainly in the age of networks. Rick Levine, Christopher Locke, Doc Searls, and David Weinberger, the authors of *The Cluetrain Manifesto,* a rabble-rousing, best-selling credo of the posthierarchical age, exaggerate only slightly when they say: "There are no secrets. The networked market knows more than companies do about their own products. And whether the news is good or bad, they tell everyone. . . . As with networked markets, people are also talking to each other directly inside the company—and not just about rules and regulations, boardroom directives, bottom lines. . . . We are immune to advertising. Just forget it." In a 1964 essay, Bennis asked, "Is Democracy Inevitable?" He was writing about geopolitics, but his answer—it is—was also correct when it comes to the management of organizations.

Compensation. If trust is a source of competitive advantage, it should pay. Failure always breeds mistrust—backbiting, toxic politics. "I get the willies when I see closed doors," says Bob Slocum, the protagonist of Joseph Heller's novel *Something Happened:*

> In the office in which I work there are five people of whom I am afraid. Each of these five people is afraid of four people (excluding overlaps), for a total of twenty, and each of these twenty people is afraid of six people, making a total of one hundred and twenty people who are feared by at least one person. . . . In the normal course of a business day, I fear Green and Green fears me. I am afraid of Jack Green because my department is part of his department and Jack Green is my boss; Green is afraid of me because most of the work in my department is done for the Sales Department, which is more important than his department, and I am much closer to Andy Kagle and the other people in the Sales Department than he is.

Trust needs to be seen to be good business. Bosses should display it in stormy times as well as in balmy, palmy ones. If, when the going gets tough, managers dust off their old command-and-control hats, they destroy the comity that's their best chance of getting out of the mess.

Business begins with trust. It begins with a deal: If you pay me X, I will give you Y. *Bureaucratic* means "enforce it," and it's good business: The Republic of Singapore is a good example, where bureaucracy created an island of almost obsessive punctiliousness and impressive prosperity. These mechanisms break down in knowledge companies, which get the greatest value from their knowledge assets and materials by being fast, collaborative, and informal. To lead a knowledge company, managers need to use the tools of trust as deftly as they do the tools of power.

PART III

THE PERFORMANCE OF A KNOWLEDGE BUSINESS

They are ill discoverers that think there is no land, when they can see nothing but sea.

FRANCIS BACON

CHAPTER 12

THE HUMAN CAPITALIST

During the act of knowledge itelf, the objective and subjective are so instantly united, that we cannot determine to which of the two the priority belongs.

SAMUEL TAYLOR COLERIDGE

The modern corporation, like modern art, is over. The postmodern corporation is different. Companies may look the same from outside—same brushed aluminum logos on the wall by the door, same flowers on the receptionist's desk—but behind the façade, everything is different. You can't operate them by pulling on the same old levers and turning the same old dials: They're no longer connected to the boiler.

Our purpose is to find the new levers and dials, so as to learn how to create the most value in knowledge-based companies. All the activities of knowledge-based organizations—strategizing, producing, managing—need to be put into a context of reward and measurement. Mae West reportedly explained that she had a mirror on the ceiling of her bedroom "so I can see how I'm doin'." Companies, too, must be able to hold a mirror up to their performance. The first requirement is to know who's doing what and with which and to whom. Says Robert Reich, secretary of labor in the Clinton administration: "Corporate boundaries are going to be defined in the future almost entirely by two questions. First, who has the property rights to certain forms of intellectual capital that emerge? Second, who is entitled to what cash flows? There will obviously be a big overlap between those two questions."

WHOSE COMPANY IS IT, ANYWAY?

Shareholders are kings, and the duty of a company's directors and officers is to make them rich. That's the hard-boiled view of how corporations should run. Things go wrong, from this perspective, if managers feather their own nests and forget who owns the coop. This is the "principal-agent problem" that dominates lawyers' and economists' thinking about companies. Good governance occurs when managers—the agents—are persuaded, by sugar cubes or the lash, to serve only the shareholder. It is an article of free-market faith that society at large will be served if managers devote themselves solely to the interests of capital. Overwhelming evidence both proves and disproves this belief.

A cuddlier view, symbolized by the word *stakeholders,* holds that a company is obliged to a host of parties in addition to shareholders—employees, communities, the planet, etc. Here, too, is an amply arguable article of faith: If stakeholders are served, shareholders will do just dandy. In its credo, Johnson & Johnson says, "When we operate according to these principles"—caring for doctors and nurses, babies and mothers and fathers, employees and communities—"the stockholders should realize a fair return." The stakeholder view, put forth by über-guru Charles Handy among others, has more support in both law and economics than many Divine-Right-of-Shareholders types realize. In parts of Europe it is enshrined in law and institutions such as union representation on corporate boards.

Neither view fits the facts of the knowledge economy. Implicit in the shareholder notion is the idea that employees are innocents—passive passengers on titanic ships of enterprise, along for the ride, not responsible if it strikes an iceberg. An old labor-union argument says workers shouldn't suffer because of decisions they have no part in making. (Nice try, guys.)

The stakeholder argument is subtler, since stakeholders think of themselves as having influence: We are not alienated but participating; we have a stake in the company, not a knife at its throat. The employee is an asset, "our most important asset."

There is a whiff of charity in this appeal. Notice that stakeholder talk rises and falls with corporate profits: Evidently noblesse is more obliging at the top of the business cycle. The employee-asset, like the environmentalist on the board or the gadfly who's good for comic relief at the annual meeting, has a sham legitimacy—she sits at the table but below the salt. Marshall Hickok canters off on his Appaloosa, Buckshot, while stakeholder Jingles, aslosh in the saddle, calls, "Hey, Wild Bill, wait for me!"

The hard-boiled shareholders-only argument, on the other hand, is plain loony in every real-world context, which in this case excludes courts of law. The industrial worker might have shown up at 8 A.M. with nothing but a lunch bucket and pair of hands, clocked in, and worked all day with a set of company-provided tools. Not the knowledge worker. In knowledge-intensive companies most of the value is produced by talent. Philip Harris, the CEO of PJM Interconnection, which manages the electric-power grid for the Middle Atlantic states, puts it this way: "As business changes, the individual is the one who brings the tools to the company. I can't overstate the importance of this." There's a noisome, phony egalitarianism in the corporate newspeak that calls employees "associates," but however silly it sounds, the impulse behind it is dead-on. Says GE's Jack Welch, "Getting a company to be informal is a huge deal, and no one ever talks about it." Few still defend the finger-in-your-eye CEO, like "Chainsaw" Al Dunlap, who wrote a book called *Mean Business*—and meant it—and who, after sending thousands of people from Scott Paper and Sunbeam to the unemployment lines, posed for a *People* magazine photograph plushly robed and lounging in bed with his wife, reading the business section of the paper while offering a bone to their German shepherd.

Sure, companies strive to increase shareholder value, and many say that's all they strive to do, but the day-to-day working out of that effort always involves trade-offs on behalf of stakeholders, particularly employees. (Often this is disguised by being called "building shareholder value *over the long term*.") Stockholders come and stockholders go. Says Bill Gates, chairman of the Evil Empire: "Take away our twenty most important people, and I tell you we would become an unimportant company."

In the knowledge economy, people are neither employees nor "assets." Head count is no way to tally human capital. In fact, we should not confuse human beings with human capital at all. Surely people are not assets in the same way that desks and trucks and factories are. A school of "human capital accounting" foundered some time back partly because it seemed inappropriate—and in any event impossible—to put a dollar value on people.

It's more accurate—and more useful—to think of employees in a new way: not as assets but as investors. Shareholders invest money in our companies; employees invest time, energy, and intelligence. Shareholders pay an opportunity cost: The money they put into Sara Lee cannot be put into Solectron. Employees, likewise, when they hitch their wagon to one star, forgo the ride with another. "I've given the best years of my life to the XYZ Company," people say, usually after XYZ has treated them shabbily. That statement shows an instinctive grasp of this view of employees: not wage slaves, not assets, but investors. What they invest is capital—their personal human capital, the sum of all they know, all they can do, all they might become.

For this investment, they expect a return. "Work is a two-way exchange of value, not a one-way exploitation of an asset by its owner"—the idea not only rings true, it sets off whole carillons of thinking. It fuzzes up, if it does not obliterate, old distinctions between labor and capital. When a low-level employee at, say, Cisco Systems receives more compensation from the appreciation of his stock than from his salary, is he a worker or a capitalist? It has controversial implications for training and development. It provokes new thinking about pay, particularly incentive pay. It opens a rich vein of thought about the difference between an individual's human capital and that of a company—and, especially, how companies can enrich both themselves and their investors.

THE PROFESSIONALIZATION OF WORK

Job tenure has decreased. (See table.) Labor markets evolve slowly; even a deep downswing in job tenure would become visible only gradually. Year-to-year numbers rise and fall with business cycles. They also vary with sex. The trend is nevertheless clear: People change employers more often than they used to.

JOB TENURE

Median Years with the Same Employer

Age Group	1983	1987	1991	1996
25–34	3.0	2.9	2.9	2.8
35–44	5.2	5.5	5.4	5.3
45–54	9.5	8.8	8.9	8.3
55–64	12.2	11.6	11.1	10.2

Source: Bureau of Labor Statistics, "Employee Tenure in the Mid-1990s," news release, January 30, 1997, p. 6, cited in Thomas O. Davenport, *Human Capital* (San Francisco: Jossey-Bass, 1999), p. 12.

But they change occupation less often. The data are sketchy, and again vary by sex, but John Bishop, chairman of the human resources studies department at Cornell University, has discerned the trend. People are beginning to have more different employers (no surprise) but fewer different occupations. In the old dispensation, IBM might have hired you as a salesperson, then over the years moved you into marketing, manufacturing, finance: one company, four occupations. Still dominant, that pattern is starting to evolve toward one in which you stay in marketing but move from IBM to Procter & Gamble to Verizon to Wells Fargo.

This pattern—mobility across employers, stability across profession—is one reason learning has taken on such psychic importance for human-capital-investing employees. Schooling, or at least credentials, partly replaces promotions, which flat organizations can't offer. Quasi-professional certification exams are showing up in all kinds of general management areas, such as project management, management consulting, and human resources management. The newly lean HR department may no longer have benefits managers and senior benefits managers, but you can take a test (offered by the Human Resources Certification Institute) and become a "professional of human resources," then take a harder test and become a "senior professional of human resources." In the 1990s the number of people who sat for the HR exams dectupled, to more than 9,000. When asked why they came, the number-one reason they offered was "I did it for personal growth." And gain: The sheepskin helps you get work and raises.

Mobility and the eagerness for credentials square perfectly with the notion of people-as-investors. Schooling and experience build a person's

HOW TO TRAIN MORE EFFECTIVELY

Emphasize action learning. Classroom training has its place: a small one. It's inefficient: Half the people in the room are secretly working on their "real" jobs, and half are so relieved not to be doing their real jobs they've turned their minds entirely off, and half already know half the stuff being taught; half will never need to know more than half of it—and that not until after they've forgotten half of what they do need.

Action learning—learning by doing—has several advantages. First, it works. Second, while people are learning, they're doing real work for the company—so the company gets an immediate return on its investment. Third, and possibly most important, action learning builds social networks. The more friends you have at work, the less susceptible you are to the seductive blandishments of strangers. Ask any GE person about the value of attending courses at Crotonville, its fabled leadership development institute. The answer is always, as it is with any great school: "The people I met were more important than the courses I took."

Action is the key to action learning, says consultant Ram Charan, who helped design the practice at GE: Teams of people solve real business problems—doing market research for medical systems in Eastern Europe, for example, with a bit of classroom instruction thrown in. Top engineers get into the "technical leadership program," a tough, two-year gig that involves three eight-month projects interwoven with classroom work in project management, process-improvement methods, and so on. The projects must be real ones, not Tinkertoys; and the company must actively and visibly support learning by implementing teams' recommendation, rather than leaving them on a shelf next to long-forgotten strategic plans. Taking action creates a fourth benefit: It calls top management's attention to rising stars.

Build informal learning into the work. As with action learning, there's evidence that people learn more from informal training than from formal or classroom instruction. Make it easy—and culturally acceptable—to ask for help. Informal learning is just-in-time learning; the return on investment is immediate for both employer and employee; it boosts morale and aids retention.

Train for today's job, not tomorrow's, and train to increase the overall flex-

ibility of the workforce. Cinergy, the big energy-services company in Cincinnati, has come to recognize that individuals must be the prime investors in and beneficiaries of what it now calls "talent development." Says Elizabeth Lanier, a self-described "recovering lawyer" who is chief of staff: "The premise is that we want to have the smartest people in every layer in every job. If it's a janitor in a power plant, I want him smarter than any other janitor." If you recruit and train only high-potential leaders for the organization, says Lanier, you not only run the very high risk that your best talent will take your investment to the competition but "you get a high piss-off factor. You tick off all existing employees. Our business is changing fast. Our ability to respond to opportunities is not a function of how well we recruit MBAs but of how many smart people we have that we can lateral to and say run with it."

Focus on key skills and knowledge workers. A company's training should emphasize what differentiates it from its competitors. Ordinary skills and ordinary employees don't. Insofar as generic training is worth doing—and it is—buy it off the shelf from trade associations, community colleges, or outside providers. Focus your efforts on what makes your company unique.

In a survey of six thousand executives, Helen Handfield-Jones of McKinsey found that the factors they most often rated "very important" or "absolutely essential" to their development were the way their jobs were structured—how the work itself stretched them and taught them—and the informal coaching and feedback they received. Formal feedback and role models came next. Traditional training trailed far behind.

---

stock of human capital; the more he can invest, the more he can expect to get back. But this plays havoc with systems for employee development and training. Says Peter Cappelli of the Wharton School: "Increased mobility across companies means that investments in skills pay off relatively more for individuals and relatively less for companies." That is, the more mobile employees are, the less incentive companies have to train them. At the same time, however, employees who want to increase their stock of human capital avoid companies that don't train them; they value it enough that evidence shows that training reduces turnover.

Companies are—or should be—desperate to keep and develop good employees, especially those who will become its future leaders. The McKinsey consulting firm has documented that throughout the developed world there is a coming, inevitable, and inexorable shortage of people in their prime working years. This is baked into the demographic pie. Japan's population is already shrinking. Barring changes in immigration laws, the European Union's population will decline by 25 percent in the next forty or fifty years. The United States is aging. There will be too few workers, particularly the most desirable, technical workers—that is, the prime consumers of training. The value of employee retention is already huge—one of the big five professional services firms saves $25 million for every 1 percent drop in the rate at which people leave—and can only grow as trained people become scarcer. In addition, as companies have stripped layer after layer from their hierarchies, they have removed on-the-job training opportunities for future top executives.

Ultimately, employers and employees must learn to adjust to the notion that people are bearers of human capital, who choose where to invest it for an immediate reward—that is, pay—but also for a longer-term one—that is, their continued growth. Companies must woo human capital as they woo Wall Street. Knowledge companies don't talk about retirement gold watches for employees. They say: "If you stay with us for one more year, you will be more marketable than you are today." One year. The trick is to make it true every year.

THE CAPITALIZATION OF PAY

Zurich Financial Services Group had a problem. The U.S. subsidiary of one of Europe's biggest and richest financial services companies was struggling to compete for talent with its American competitors. Annual turnover was just 10 percent of the employees, but 40 percent of it came from among the best people—the so-called A players. With 6,000 U.S. employees and some $260 billion in assets under management in the United States, Zurich Group had lots to offer; but it couldn't offer stock options. They're uncommon in Europe, and any grant of options to U.S. employees that resembled the lavish ones American rivals issued would cause all kinds of intramural problems.

The solution found by Dinos Iordanou, CEO of Zurich Group, was simple, fair, and successful. He began by calculating the U.S. company's return on equity. When that number is above 10 percent—not a particularly challenging number—a bonus pool starts to fill. Above a 10 percent ROE, 85 percent of profits stays in the company or is returned to shareholders; 15 percent flows into the bonus pool. Of that amount, half goes to the top third, the A players; 35 percent to the middle third; and 15 percent to the rest. The bonuses are paid in company stock—real stock, bought at the market price, not options. Zurich adopted this bonus program in 1998; it replaced one where bonuses were paid in cash, based on a percentage of profits, regardless of management's judgment of the value of the individual's contribution. In the years since, the employee turnover rate has stayed about the same, 10 percent, but its profile has changed dramatically. Now only 20 percent of those who leave come from the A players, while 45 percent come from the least effective C players.

Iordanou's experience highlights one of the most nettlesome—yet potentially salubrious—issues arising from the fact that workers are investors: how to reward employees. Companies today have two principal classes of equity investors: public shareholders, who contribute financial capital, and employees, who put up human capital. It's all too easy to design systems that reward the wrong investors, or that don't align the interests of the two classes.

When the key capital is human, trouble comes if employees do not square their interests with that of the business. Some knowledge workers are takers rather than contributors. For them, this job is "good training" or "a learning experience" or "just a job." Another kind of misalignment comes when the company can't use the talent, or not all of it. The colorist genius of the poet Wallace Stevens was of limited value in the gray-suited environs of Hartford Accident & Indemnity Co., of which he was vice president. The misalignment can work the other way, rewarding shareholders inappropriately for what really was achieved by human capital— top performers of Zurich Group were acting on that belief when they left the company.

The traditional garb of corporate governance fits knowledge companies about as well as medieval armor suits a hurdler. Those coats of mail are based on the notion that management owes its first and only allegiance to the people who put up the money. They're ill-suited to reward employees with equity. Yet should capital gains go only to people who put up financial capital, when human capital investments are equally or more important?

Traditional companies go through all kinds of contortions to reward employees with equity while maintaining the legal fiction that they are run solely for the benefit of outside shareholders. In the worst of the schemes, they shower employees with stock options, like stage-door Johnnies presenting nosegays to the girls in the chorus.* Stock options give the recipient the right to buy a certain number of company shares at a set price (usually the market price on the date the options are granted) after a vesting period (usually one to three years) and before the grant expires (usually after 10 years). Stock options began in the 1950s, as a response to the old "principal-agent" problem. In the mid–twentieth century day-to-day management of companies slipped from the hands of founder-owners to a new class of hired executives, who, like any stewards, might tailor the outfit to suit themselves rather than the owners. An executive with stock options, the argument goes, has a powerful motive to drive the stock price up so that the options become worth something; thus entrepreneurial incentives trump bureaucratic urges, and management "thinks like an owner."

Stock options aren't a bad way to solve the principal-agent problem in the old economy. There the goal was to motivate a handful of top executives to keep costs down and profits up. But options are a lousy answer to the governance problem at the heart of the new economy, which is how to compensate people who invest human capital. If everyone's a knowledge worker, then doesn't everyone deserve options? That question assumes its own, false answer. The right question is: Do people who invest human capital deserve a return in the form of equity, and if so, what's the best way to provide it?

To that question, options aren't the answer—particularly not options fecklessly lavished, which has become the order of the day. In 1999 alone, America's 200 biggest public companies gave out options equivalent to 2.1 percent of all their outstanding shares. In total, unexercised options for

---

* Yeah, yeah, I realize that not even the Knight of the Woeful Countenance would be so quixotic as to think he can stop stock options. Nevertheless they are, as I hope you'll see, the wrong solution to a nifty problem, and perhaps this discussion will inspire someone to come up with a right approach. (I should further note, for the benefit of management at AOL Time Warner, that this argument against stock options does not imply that I have anything against them personally.)

those companies amount to a remarkable 13.7 percent of their shares. When employees exercise their options, new shares are issued to them—so the "overhang" represents the potential dilution of the value of currently outstanding shares. This overhang more than doubled in the last decade. Big companies aren't the big offenders. Start-ups, particularly in technology, have handed out options with the generosity of a punk who got his hands on your credit card and decided to throw a party for a few hundred of his new best friends. For companies in *USA Today*'s index of 100 Internet stocks, the average potential dilution is an astounding 24 percent.

Says Eric D. Roiter, general counsel at Fidelity Investments: "Option plans are redistributing corporate ownership"—but without the beneficiaries having to pay for it, since they get options at no cost and exercise them only if they will make a profit.* This is ersatz, risk-free capitalism and basically a way of slipping equity to employees under the table, because the arcane accounting rules for stock options mean that their cost does not show on financial statements. (The potential dilution from stock options is reported to investors, and the theoretical cost is announced, if *announced* is the word, in footnotes in annual reports.) Diluting ownership via options is like looking the other way when employees walk out the door with staples and paper and pens—only in this case they're walking off with maybe 20 percent of the joint.

Legitimacy must be legitimate. If human capitalists want as much right to equity as financial capitalists, then they shouldn't get a significantly better deal on stock. That means no stock options. None. Zero. Zip. Zilch. Options do put the recipient in the same boat with investors, but the optionee gets a first-class cabin, doesn't pay for it, and assumes no risk—

---

* It's even worse in practice than it is in theory: When options are "underwater," companies tend to find ways to make up the "loss" to employees. Sometimes they lower the strike price on previously granted options. Sometimes they simply issue lots of new options at today's lower price. Sometimes they replace options with cash. At the end of 2000, with Microsoft stock trading at 43⅜ vs. 116⁹⁄₁₆ at the beginning of the year, many Microsoft options, granted when the stock was higher, were worthless. The company's response: raise wages—boring old wages—at the same time that it was trying to cut costs because of weakness in its earnings. Had Microsoft's staff been paid for an honest day's profits in real, honest-to-God stock—real shares, not options—they'd have seen their wealth diminish as the stock dropped, yes, and would have been unhappy. But they'd have had half a loaf. Instead they had none—so the company gave them raises. But did it give shareholders dividends? Of course not.

nice work if you can get it, but it's charity, not capitalism. Real capitalists put up real money—green stuff printed with pictures of dead presidents.

If stock options are a bad solution, they respond to a real problem. Says Margaret Blair, a senior fellow of the Brookings Institution who is studying the role of human capital in corporate governance: "When you understand that a corporation is more complex than a bundle of assets owned by shareholders, that it involves lots of investments by lots of participants, it changes everything."

The first thing it should change is the duty of directors. It's their responsibility to maximize investors' rewards. But which investors, what rewards? That's a question for the board. Says corporate-governance expert Ira Millstein, a senior partner in the law firm Weil Gotshal & Manges: "Human capital is really important, and boards should be thinking about it as an assignment, just as monitoring the CEO should be an assignment." That is, it should decide how to apportion risks and rewards between people who invest money and people who invest themselves. Blair and a colleague, Georgetown University law professor Lynn Stout, argue that solving this "team production problem"—how to divide the loot where a mixed bag of inputs results in an inseparable output—is why companies come into being. The board becomes "a mediator of team rents."

The board—on behalf of both human capitalists and financial investors—also needs to decide how to pay the proceeds. Boards already decide how to structure the financial capitalization of a company—so much debt, so much equity. They also allocate the return on investment along a spectrum of risk, from interest on bonds, dividends on stock, stock repurchases, to reinvestment in the business in the expectation of capital gains. They should give similar thought to returns to human capital. Millstein proposes that today's compensation committee, which exists to figure out new ways to overpay CEOs, should be replaced with a "remuneration committee" responsible for the entire reward system. Obviously boards shouldn't approve every raise. Instead, they should set a mix of different kinds of compensation that's appropriate given the nature of employees' human-capital investment. Boards can analyze, by line of business, the relative importance of human vs. financial capital, and their level of risk. The cost of (financial) capital can be ascertained, and the board, on behalf of those investors, can levy an assessment for it. Then a fair price can be determined for the services corporations provide—the community-building, warranty, a brand-equity-building,

and financial services discussed in the previous chapter. From these elements, it ought to be possible to infer approximately what the earned and
legitimate reward of human capital is.

For example, people who put up financial capital for a company like
Alcoa shoulder a fair amount of risk. Their money goes into building large,
illiquid, ungeneric factories to smelt and shape aluminum; also, it's a cycli-
cal industry. Relatively speaking, Alcoa's public shareholders have assumed
more risk than people who have invested in, say, an office buidling, whose
space can be occupied by many different tenants. It's appropriate, then,
that Alcoa's shareholders receive relatively more of its profits, employees
relatively less. (Wages are another matter.) By contrast, Macquarie Bank,
Australia's premier investment bank, is closer in style to a professional firm.
Macquarie, which went public in 1996, believes its human capital should
"wear the volatility." The bank therefore divides profits according to a
formula whereby, as return on equity rises, the staff takes an ever higher
percentage of the pot. All of the first 10 percent of ROE goes to shareholders—that is, there are no bonuses. But as profits rise, human capital takes
progressively more, until it is getting the lion's share. At U.S. investment
banks, according to Macquarie, remuneration as a percentage of equity
tends to hold steady (and high), while return on equity bounces up and
down; the Down Under bank turns that upside down.

Most companies fall somewhere between these two instances. The guid-
ing principle is this: The investors who bear the most risk should get a shot
at the greatest rewards. The more important human capital is to a business,
the more those investors should stand to gain—or lose—and the greater
voice they should have in governing it. The more human capital an individual employee puts at risk, the more she should be rewarded with equity.

You can think of pay as falling across a spectrum just like the returns
offered financial investors: Wages are analogous to the interest paid to
bondholders; bonuses are like dividends; stock is riskier still, and offers
employees a chance to share in the company's growth. Just as investors
diversify their portfolios with stocks, bonds, and other instruments,
employees/investors need some ability to decide how much risk they want
in their pay packets, and to vary it from year to year. Obviously, low-paid
employees usually can't afford anything other than wages—they need current cash. But the ability to invest human capital in one's employer is not
a function of status. Dana Corp., for example, has used an enthusiastically

managed suggestion system to harvest millions of dollars' worth of ideas, mostly from blue-collar workers. Wherever employees make specific human-capital investments—working on special projects, offering suggestions—they deserve gainsharing returns, preferably in the form of equity.

Why gainsharing? Because it works. Typical gainsharing plans are established in organizational units of a moderate size—perhaps a thousand employees—and reward improvements in areas over which the employees can have an impact. Thus factory workers might be rewarded for conserving energy or reducing scrap, and clerks for reducing the cost of sending out invoices or reducing outstanding payables. When performance improves, some percentage, often half, goes to the workforce that made it happen. Gainsharing comes in lots of varieties, and all programs need tweaking to keep them effective over time. But every study of gainsharing plans shows that they improve performance, not just momentarily but over a period of several years.

Why stock? First, it's fairer. Time was, employees who risked brainpower got a pretty good promise of lifetime employment; for that security, they gave up the potential rewards of securities. With lifetime employment kaput, equity provides the knowledge investor with a way to keep a portion of the returns even if he loses his job. Second, good governance suggests it makes sense to remunerate human capital and financial capital in the same way. The voting power of employee investors and public investors offers each the means to protect their investments. If employees legitimately earn equity, then they're legitimately entitled to the power that goes with it. If that means control, so be it—provided the equity has been honestly earned. That's not a radical notion. During the heyday of defined-benefit pension plans, those heavily funded piles of assets—a holding pond for company-specific human capital, to be paid out to its investors when they retired—sometimes became big enough that they were used as vehicles for taking over the company, as Carl Icahn did with TWA.

DIFFERENT STAKES FOR DIFFERENT FLAKES

Retaining human capital means rewarding it for what it creates. The locus of invention isn't the boardroom or the corner office; it's the team. Says Philip Harris, CEO of PJM Interconnection, the electricity-grid manager,

"The traditional way [of getting into a new business or service], with massive studies and internal hurdle rates, no longer works. What seems to be working is that a group of individuals get together to meet a need." A skunk works, rapid prototyping, rapid piloting, and rapid ramp-up, and bingo! a new business. "This," Harris continues, "allows the individual to put their tools, their equity, at risk." Says Gary Hamel:

> Even the largest companies are going to have to look, in the future, more like kind of mega incubators than organizations with fairly impermeable boundaries where the goal is simply to build the biggest possible legal entity. The essential principle is: If you have people who want to do something new, create a place, create an incubator. Create a climate in which they innovate. And offer at least a share in the wealth that's being created there.

Companies are creating all kinds of hybrid forms of governance—equity carve-outs, spin-offs, alliances, joint ventures, tracking stocks—all of which are part of a redefinition of the very nature of the corporation and caused, in particular, by the changing ratio between physical and financial capital and intellectual capital. The old governance structures too often reward the wrong investors. In the knowledge economy, intellectual investments come first; physical and financial capital form around it. Like whorehouses around a harbor, they are a consequence, not a cause.

That's theory, and it fits the facts. The old structures, in which the corporation is defined by the physical capital it controls, lead companies into "the innovator's dilemma." That phrase, the title of a book by Harvard Business School professor Clayton Christiansen, argues, essentially, that success hog-ties innovation. Companies with a leading technology in a market usually do a good job of improving what they have, but rarely develop a new technology that displaces the old. Too many (in)vested interests (money, talent, assets, mind-set) are tied to the existing product. Moreover, a new technology almost always starts out less capable (and less profitable) than a dominant old one. If you own a goose that lays golden eggs, it seems irrational to give its food to a quail that lays silver ones. Christiansen doesn't make a point of it, but there's a third reason dominant companies innovate badly: Big companies have a problem making other-than-big bets. If it's not worth a few hundred million, you can't get the CEO's attention. When a company has poured enough concrete, its thinking hardens, too; it confuses the building with the business, the reef with the coral.

Teradyne Corp. found a way out of the innovator's dilemma. The Boston company is big (1998 sales: $1.49 billion) and dominates its market. It makes automated testing equipment used by electronics and telecom companies to test semiconductor chips, circuit boards, telephone networks, and software—complex machines that cost as much as $2 million each. In 1998 Teradyne introduced a tester, called Integra, based on a new, low-cost technology; it's not yet good enough for high-end applications (like testing microprocessors), but in a few years will be able to do so—at perhaps one-quarter the cost of the old technology. The product was profitable within eighteen months, after which about 250 Integra systems had been sold—that's a big number, generating sales at an annualized $150 million, the fastest ramp-up in company history.

What's important for the purpose of this discussion, however, is that they did it by tinkering with the governance model. Alex d'Arbeloff, Teradyne's founder (1960), chairman, and CEO until 1997, never lost the entrepreneurial itch: He's been an active venture capitalist, serving on the boards of a dozen start-ups over the years. That might be why he conceived of a novel way to start Integra: not as a project sponsored by a business unit, not as a line item in the budget, but as an ersatz start-up, whose head reported not to a boss but to a board of directors. "We'd never done this before," d'Arbeloff recalled. "I just thought it was a good idea to set it up as a venture—it was a good argument for recruiting talent, a way to give the team a feeling of independence."

This wasn't wildly radical. The board was an internal board, its members all top Teradyne executives, including d'Arbeloff and George Chamillard, the CEO; and Integra wasn't given any phantom stock or out-of-the-ordinary compensation scheme. But it was enough to change the environment in which Integra operated. Integra's general manager, Marc Levine, had a business plan, not a budget. He explained: "The idea was to think of this as a business from the start, not an R&D project. The board setup allows more of a coaching attitude. A boss has to deal with the heat he gets about budget, goals, metrics, and so on."

Using an internal board benefited both Levine and Teradyne's leadership. The structure allowed senior management to be highly involved—

without tying up their time or binding Levine's hands. In the words of Edward Rogas, a Teradyne VP: "Being on the board let us jump up out of the daily crap, which is the toughest thing for a division manager to do and which can easily fill up thirty hours in a twenty-four-hour day." Levine got independence—"It's not in the nature of a hierarchy to give people independence," d'Arbeloff observed—that he used, first, to recruit aggressively both inside the company and out. Said Chamillard: "We could have given the project to a division, told them to spend $10 million a year on it, but they would never have put their best people on it." Autonomy also allowed Levine to take more technology risk—purchasing software outside rather than developing it in-house as Teradyne usually does, for example. Integra's strategy—to produce a low-cost product for the low end of the market—was fundamentally different from that of the rest of the company, and couldn't have been executed within existing structures. Above all, the board gave Integra enough remove from Teradyne's day-to-day business that Levine could focus on getting his product right without worrying that every hour, every dollar, and every technological advance was time, money, and progress taken from elsewhere. Said Rogas: "A division is always pressed to do the next logical thing—and make it compatible with the existing line. We told Marc: Be aggressive on the technology. Do something no one else has done. Because we had no revenue at stake, we could push the risk."

Three years after it began, Integra became a "normal" division of Teradyne. Levine got his budget through the same planning process as everyone else; he had customers to serve, improvements to make—the daily crap. A different kind of venture, or a venture in another company, might have resulted in a spin-off or some permanent form of semi-independence.

E PLURIBUS UNUM

As business increases in both speed and knowledge intensity, structures have to adapt, too. This is not an argument for the atomization of corporations, an "every-tub-on-its-own-bottom" approach. That way lies a kind of corporate Articles of Confederation, an uncoordinated creature that's as unlikely to make progress as a squid whose tentacles have minds of their own.

After all, people choose to invest their human capital in an organization in the belief that it will be better rewarded that way than left to its own devices. Our personal investments create something collective. That's the *company's* human capital—two heads that are better than one, better even than one + one—and it's not the same as yours or mine. The corporate stock of human capital is created when the employee's investment, plus the investments of other employees, plus the company's other intangible assets (such as processes, intellectual property, and customers), plus the financial capital provided by shareholders, combine.

Think of corporate human capital as having three elements:

Collective skills. You have talents your colleagues lack, and vice versa. You can call on each other's abilities, provided the place is run in such a way that like-minded but heterogeneously talented people can collaborate.

Communities of practice. Everybody always knew that companies are and contain communities—all social organizations do—but a decade ago it was unusual and a little wiggy to propose that this was important for getting work done. Now we know that "knowledge production favors the organization over the market." The nature of knowledge work required companies to foster communities where there's a high level of candor, where corporate-speak has no place. These communities of practice have become a recognized part of the business life.* They are where knowledge creation happens.

Social capital. The word *colleague* comes from the Latin *colligare,* "to bind together." Social capital makes workers into colleagues; it is "the stock of active connections among people, the trust, mutual understanding, and shared values and behaviors that . . . make cooperative action possible." The importance of social capital was proved beyond question in the horrific aftermath of the attacks on the World Trade Center in New York in 2001. Leaders and employees alike instantly and instinctively reached out to affirm and renew their social bonds, knowing that no business could be done otherwise. There's no room for social capital in hard-boiled shareholders-only corporate theory, but it's a considerable portion of the real capital structure of any enterprise.

---

* For an extended discussion of communities of practice, see *Intellectual Capital,* pp. 93–100.

It's a quick step from questions of reward to questions of accounting and measurement—issues that are vital to the management of a knowledge enterprise. People will work for many kinds of reward. Money is just one, and often the least, of their motives. In business particularly, though, money is the most visible symbol that one's work is valued and has been rewarded. Equity—in the sense of fairness—is an important part of the reward structure of a corporation. Equity—in the sense of ownership—is the essential mechanism by which to deliver it in the knowledge economy. Reward cannot be meted out in the absence of accurate, effective tools to account for the performance of a business.

CHAPTER 13

GENERALLY UNACCEPTABLE ACCOUNTING PRINCIPLES

This parrot is no more. It has ceased to be. It's expired and gone to meet its maker. This is a late parrot. It's a stiff. Bereft of life, it rests in peace. If you hadn't nailed it to the perch, it would be pushing up the daisies. It's rung down the curtain and joined the choir invisible. This is an ex-parrot.

MONTY PYTHON

Accounting, long dead, is not yet buried, and the situation stinks. Okay, that overstates the case, but not a lot. In the last several years, the inadequacies of industrial-age accounting have been proved again and again. Both financial accounting, which appears in annual reports, and management accounting, the data that land on your desk, go wrong in specific ways, and with demonstrable consequences. Investors have been systematically misled. The cost to them is incalculable—meaning not that the cost is enormous, though it surely is, but that it is literally incalculable: No one knows how to figure out how much. Insiders—that is, managers—have profited from information that ordinary investors cannot see. At the same time, accounting distorts their own planning. They cannot allocate resources wisely when much of the information they collect, publish, and audit is irrelevant or worse. A friend, taking the accounting course required of first-year MBA students at one of America's top business schools, told me what his professor said the first day: that in this class "we'll be talking about the assets on financial statements. They are not the only assets and probably not the most important ones, but they are the only ones we will be discussing here." How pointless is that—that students should strain to understand gnats and be left to figure out the camel for themselves?

SOMETHING'S ROTTEN

In their much-praised *Relevance Lost: The Rise and Fall of Management Accounting,* H. Thomas Johnson and Robert S. Kaplan wrote: "Corporate management accounting systems are inadequate for today's environment." They cited technological change, globalization, and expanding information processing as three reasons old charts of account aren't useful. Yet that lament was written in 1987, when men were men and P/Es were 10. Since then, the Internet has grown from minnow to leviathan; the Berlin Wall has fallen and in greater or lesser degree opened all but a handful of small nations to the global market; and computing speeds and volumes have risen exponentially. It has only become clearer that today's most important assets and activities—intellectual capital and knowledge work—aren't measured or reported adequately. Generally accepted accounting principles generally do an unacceptable job of accounting for the principal activities of knowledge companies.

In December 1999 Alan Greenspan, chairman of the Federal Reserve Board, complained that accounting wasn't tracking investments in intellectual assets, and that technological change has "muddied" the "crucially important" distinction between capital assets and ordinary expenses:

Twenty, thirty years ago when you built a steel plant, it was perfectly obvious what it was and it was capitalized. And when you consumed coke or ore, it was expensed. But in today's world it has become very much more difficult to figure out whether a particular outlay is expensed . . . or whether it is capitalized. . . . A major shift in the process of how one evaluates what we're producing is occurring. . . . The stock

market—not its levels, but its difference from company to company—
is telling us that . . . certain outlays are indeed capital expenditures irre-
spective of what the accountants call them.

Software was an obvious manifestation of the first problem: Accounting
rules used to specify that computers were assets but software, homegrown
or bought off the shelf, an expense. That didn't make sense—often the
software was longer-lived than the computer, and anyone could see that
software is a kind of machine, not a kind of raw material. The rule has
been changed, but the question persists. Should the skill and flexibility of
a workforce be considered an asset, and training a capital expenditure? Is
brand equity an asset, and advertising an investment? Are patents capital,
and is R&D capital spending? Rajat Gupta, the head of the McKinsey
consulting firm, says our accounting systems "do a lousy job" of distinguishing between ordinary business expenses and investments in intangible assets. It's not an issue if, say, a manufacturer pays $500,000 for a
piece of machinery, then trains 100 workers to use it at a cost of $50 per
worker; the machine is booked as an asset and depreciated over its useful
life, and the $50,000 training bill is an expense. But is it really accurate to
omit the patent portfolio from the asset base of a biotech company, or to
say that the training given to professionals like lawyers and accountants is
not an investment that adds to the value of the firm for which they work?
In an economy now dominated by knowledge-based companies, accounting's failure to document intellectual assets becomes important. If the situation isn't cleared up, said Greenspan, "there are going to be a lot of
problems in the future."

Actually, problems are here now. Then-SEC Chairman Arthur Leavitt
told the Economic Club of New York: "We have long had a good idea of
how to value manufacturing inventory or assess what a factory is worth.
But today, the value of R&D invested in a software program, or the value
of a user base of an Internet shopping site, is a lot harder to quantify. As
intangible assets continue to grow in both size and scope, more and more
people are questioning whether the true value—and the drivers of that
value—is being reflected in a timely manner in publicly available disclosure." The issue is transparency, the ability to see far enough and clearly
enough into a company's financial statements to judge accurately what it

is worth and how well it is doing. Among many ways of creating financial opacity—managed earnings, one-time charges, and so on—the failure to account for intangible assets is probably the greatest, in dollar terms. When something is booked as an asset, it's there for investors to see. The company has to tell investors what its assets cost, and every year it has to report what they are now worth. Expenses, by contrast, disappear: Like the Diet Coke I drank with lunch today, they are presumed to have no residual value. And if they do? Shareholders never are told.

The Financial Accounting Standards Board, the profession's vestal virgins, says that accounting's fundamental purpose is to "provide information that is useful . . . in making rational investment, credit, and similar decisions." That is not happening. If the books were telling a story investors found useful, then a company's market value should roughly correlate with the value accountants ascribe to it. But it doesn't: Arthur Andersen consultants Richard Boulton, Barry Libert, and Steve Samek compared market value with book value for 3,500 U.S. companies over a period of two decades. At the beginning, in 1978, the two were pretty well matched: Book value was 95 percent of market value. Now they've gone astray, every one to his own way. They shouldn't match precisely, because financial reports tell what has happened and stock prices anticipate what will come. But the past *is* prologue, and there should be some correspondence between what accountants count and what investors value. Moreover, there's an inverse relationship between asset intensity (fixed assets divided by sales) and total return to shareholders. Assets are supposed to work for you to produce returns, but the assets accountants count seem to be liabilities, or at least drags.

Not even earnings and cash-flow numbers seem to help investors make decisions. Says Baruch Lev, a professor of accounting at the Stern School of Business at New York University: "If a message is informative, people will act on it." But they don't. Lev discovered that changes in earnings and cash flow have trivially weak relationships to changes in market capitalization. (For the mathematically inclined: regressing changes in earnings and cash flow vs. market cap produces an R^2 of 3.75 percent and 3.99 percent respectively.) In other words, those pieces of information do not motivate investors to act. In other cases, they're motivated to act incorrectly.

INTANGIBLE ASSETS, TANGIBLE HARM

Make no mistake: Accounting's failure to disclose intellectual capital is not just a theoretical problem. It costs investors money—perhaps you, dear reader, among them. At the very least it reduces prosperity by distorting flows of investment capital, which should go to where it can be most productively employed.* According to Gregory Wurzburg of the Organization for Economic Cooperation and Development:

> Valuing [intangible assets] at zero (as is presently the case) leads to distortions in the allocation of resources. Because accounting systems influence how performance is rewarded, they affect economic behavior of managers within firms, and investors on the outside.

We're not talking fraud, except in a few cases—we're talking irrelevance, with the result that investors are kept in the dark and managers are operating by guess and by gosh.

As the century turned, investors and executives were preoccupied by Internet hype, stories of 30-year-old billionaires, dot-coms that would destroy brick-and-mortar companies quick as Bob's your uncle, and the like. There was reality behind the hype, since the Internet *is* an extraordinary, world-altering technology. There was also surreality in the claims (and stock prices) of some Internet companies. Sooner or later, reality bites. Now it has, and business faces anew the age-old challenge: Show me the money. In 1998, at Berkshire Hathaway's annual meeting, Warren Buffett was asked, as he had been before, about investing in technology stocks, and he answered, as he had before, "Technology is just something

---

* It also distorts public policy, sometimes in surprising ways. Among other things, by treating investments in intellectual capital as expenses, accounting gives them a tax subsidy. If Merck spends $100 million on new laboratory buildings and machinery— a capital investment—and uses twenty-year straight-line depreciation, the company deducts $10 million from its income every year for a decade. If Merck spends $100 million on training—costs treated as expenses—it deducts the full cost in the year in which it is incurred. There's nothing wrong with tax preferences openly debated and arrived at; for example, Congress has said that it approves of subsidies for some intellectual-capital investments—it allows R&D costs to get a tax credit, not just a tax deduction. But public policy should be made in public.

we don't understand, so we don't invest in it." Usually memorable, Buffett was unusually memorable when he went on to discuss Internet stocks. He said: "If I taught a class, on my final exam I would take an Internet company and ask [my students], 'How much is this company worth?' Anyone who would answer, I would flunk."

With the dot-coms having returned to Earth (in some cases, six feet under the earth), it's worth reexamining Buffett's comment. Is the challenge of putting a value on a company different when the company has few if any tangible assets, its future depends on its ability to make and leverage investments in research and development and other knowledge, and its market environment is changing rapidly? If the value can't be known by ordinary means, can it be known at all? These are partly investment questions. They are also—profoundly—management questions. Because creating value is what managers are supposed to do, they need to know if they have done it.

The answers are yes, it's different, and yes, it's knowable, and one can prove both propositions with an almost Pythagorean certainty. Mind you, there are those who deride as bunkum the whole notion of a new economy based on intellectual capital. One magazine editor denounced it as the construct of a cadre of "business Bolsheviks," including Peter Drucker and your humble & ob't servant, whose presumably sinister aim is the "justification of irrationally overvalued companies." Why we Bolshies want the market to be high, I don't know. Pocket-watch-wearing, boot-on-the-neck-of-the-people capitalists have known for years that smart money invests in intangible assets. Notice, for example, that Buffett said he doesn't understand technology—but said nothing about intellectual capital, which he buys all the time. He got interested in Coca-Cola, one of Berkshire Hathaway's core holdings, about when legendary CEO Roberto Goizueta decided to hive off a lot of tangible assets, putting them on the balance sheets of Coke's bottlers in order to become, as Chief Financial Officer James Chestnut said, a company whose market capitalization is the sum of the values of its brand and its management systems—that is, a vat of intellectual capital. As for Internet and other technology companies, the market, in its collective wisdom—this is a given, comrades, that the market is wise, *da?*—puts a value on them every day, not just during exam period.

Of course, Buffett doesn't want to be as wise as the market. He looks for occasions when he is wiser; he wants to know what he calls "intrinsic value," which is why he's happy when stocks are cheap and he can buy them for less than he knows they're worth. And intrinsic value is much harder to determine for companies with high intangibles, high R&D, and changing markets than it is for companies like Exxon Mobil or International Paper—particularly when the companies are young.

That's the conclusion of an elegant study by Baruch Lev and Paul Zarowin, Lev's colleague at the Stern School of Business at NYU. The question they sought to answer: Does financial reporting convey information that investors find useful? They looked at three foundation pieces of reported financial information—earnings, cash flow, and book value—for the thousands of companies in the Compustat database; then they correlated the information with changes in the companies' stock prices. This allowed them to determine, for example, how much value investors ascribed to a dollar's worth of reported earnings, cash flow, or equity. Their conclusion: "The association between key financial statement variables and both stock returns and prices has been declining over the last 20 years."

Because their sample was big—as many as 6,800 companies, 1,300 of which have remained in the database for two decades—Lev and Zarowin were able to dig deeper to find out why the numbers reveal less than they did. The conjoined twin villains: change and innovation. Where companies are young, where they change a lot (measured by changes in relative book or market value), or where they significantly increase or reduce the amount they invest in innovation (measured by R&D intensity), accounting information is much less useful than it is for mature companies. If a Merck or a Pfizer increases R&D by 15 percent, the market knows from experience what kind of a return those companies get on those investments. Put the same R&D increase into the budget of a start-up in a fast-changing industry, and the market's response is much less predictable, because investors don't know if these guys are onto something or pissing money away.

What's true of research and development seems also to be true of investment in human capital. A slowly growing body of knowledge demonstrates that top-of-the-line HR practices have bottom-line benefits. The so-called high-performance work system—a gallimaufry of practices including superior recruitment policies, incentive compensation, training,

INVESTMENT IN HUMAN CAPITAL PRODUCES WEALTH

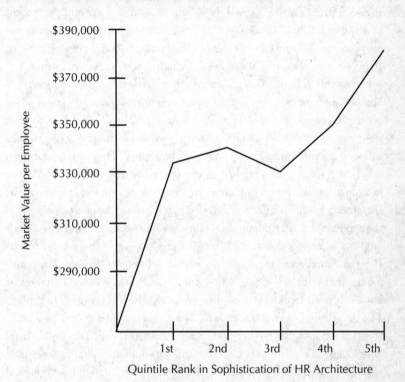

Source: Mark A. Huselid and Brian E. Becker, "The Strategic Impact of High Performance Work Systems," 1995

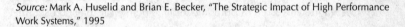

performance appraisal, and employee involvement—pays off for shareholders. For example, a study by Mark A. Huselid of Rutgers University and Brian E. Becker of the State University of New York at Buffalo ranked companies according to the sophistication of their HR practices, then examined the market value per employee. Companies in the top groups in HR made their investors much wealthier than the others did.

In the absence of consistent, reliable, and reported information about investments in human capital, however, investors don't know what to make of this information. Wall Street (i.e., you, since you probably own stocks either directly or through retirement programs) is suckered into thinking that human capital is a euphemism for spendthrift mush-headedness. When "Chainsaw" Al Dunlap became CEO of Sunbeam, the stock jumped. By the time he was pushed out, the company was in ruins. Dunlap's an easy target these days (though it took braver men than I to prophesy his failure), but the fact is that markets (and therefore managers) systematically undervalue investments in human capital. Two scholars, Theresa Welbourne and Alice Andrews, made a study of the HR practices in companies making initial public offerings, to see if they influenced the companies' odds of surviving. They examined 136 nonfinancial companies, mostly in the United States, but a few overseas, in industries ranging from biotech to food-service retailing. Here is what the study found: Companies that discussed human resources policies in their published IPO documents (such as prospectuses) and cited their employees as a competitive advantage were 20 percent more likely to survive than companies that made no mention of people. Furthermore, companies that put their money where their mouth was by giving employees equity through stock or stock options were nearly twice as likely to survive. The tough guys on Wall Street didn't see it that way, however: Those IPOs were priced lower when they first came to market. That is, the equity markets looked at investments in and rewards to human capital as a negative when the stocks first went public. And with reason, though not with good reason: Given what's in financial statements, there's no way for investors to know if money invested in human capital is being put to good use; furthermore, there is considerable evidence that some HR practices are wasteful and even destructive, and the absence of reporting protects them from sunlight's disinfecting power.

The evidence from R&D and human capital is matched by evidence of the value of brands. One of the best-known measures of brand equity is done by a London firm, Interbrand. Interbrand calculates a brand's value by comparing the operating earnings of branded products to what could be earned by generic, commodity versions of the same goods, multiplying this figure by a measure of the brand's strength as reflected in such factors as its market dominance, global reach, and longevity. (The detailed method is described at www.interbrand.com.) Out of it comes a number—the Coca-Cola brand, the world's most valuable, was worth $72.5 billion in

2000, Interbrand says. Brand equity is an intangible asset, of course; as such, it's largely ignored in accounting. When a brand is homegrown, the rules do not allow its value to be shown on its books. If a company acquires a brand and pays more than the value of the tangible assets associated with it (as it usually does), the difference is booked as "goodwill," which must be depreciated, even if the value of the brand is growing. Unreported brand equity may be; but it turns out to correlate very strongly with what you'll pay for "real" equity if you buy the stock. A highly statistical study by a quartet of academics at Stanford—Mary Barth, Michael Clement, George Foster, and Ron Kasznik—examined the relationship between stock market prices and brand equity as valued by Interbrand, concluding: "We find consistent evidence that brand values are significantly associated with equity market values."

Look at the evidence: R&D (which produces structural capital), high-performance work systems (which produce human capital), and brand equity (a measure of customer capital) all produce significant gains in the value of companies. Investors and managers ought to know about them, but accounting rules mandate that much of the information remain hidden. That, naturally, encourages gumshoes to investigate it. Two of the Stanford scholars, Barth and Kasznik, made a trio with Maureen F. McNichols in another study. The less useful financial statements are, they hypothesized, the more useful analysts' coverage is likely to be. Since the value of intangibles is rarely disclosed, Barth, Kasznik, and McNichols figured, analysts would want to ferret out the information, because "the net benefits to covering these firms [should] exceed those for firms whose values are well-captured by recognized assets." That is, you're better off devoting an analyst's time to biotechnology stocks than to ExxonMobil, whose stock price and intrinsic value are probably in sync. Sure enough: After controlling for factors like company size, the Stanford trio found that the more companies invest in R&D and advertising (two proxies for intellectual capital), the more research Wall Street does.

Not that the coverage satisfies investors' appetites. In 1998, Shelley Taylor & Associates, a management consulting firm based in Palo Alto and London, asked twenty-five of the world's largest institutional investors—ten in the United States, ten in the United Kingdom, and five in Switzerland, which together managed nearly $3 trillion—to rate the value of the information they received from companies and to discuss the information they wished they could get. According to Taylor, "Investors have moved the issue of intellectual capital to their front burners with 72 percent considering the issue 'very important,'" while less than 10 percent of U.S. and British companies addressed it. Economist Joseph Stiglitz explains the reason straightforwardly: "If we are going to know what are the high-return activities and we want our resources to be allocated toward high-return activities, we have to have accurate ways of measuring what those returns are."

Venture capitalists and bankers who work with knowledge-intensive companies have learned that the key to making good investments isn't knowing the numbers or even the technology, but knowing the management. Banker Susan Smith says: "We form an extraordinary level of intimacy with management. We have to. The quality of the management team that the technology is able to attract tells us a lot about the quality of the technology—more than anything else." The true value of intangible-intensive companies seems inherently unknowable and therefore volatile, at least until they become old and wise, like Coca-Cola. "You can know the value of these companies, just not for long," Smith says. With few tangible assets, they have few flywheels, few anchors, and little safety. Microsoft keeps a ten-figure wad of cash—that's why Bill Gates's house is big, to have enough mattresses in which to stuff it—out of fear that the company might need to be reinvented overnight. Others live in mortal dread that Microsoft will wipe out their worth simply by shifting in its chair.

NYU's Lev and Zarowin say that accounting rules are partly responsible for the difficulty in evaluation and (because ignorance produces uncertainty) some of the volatility. Investments in intangibles—R&D, training, brand building, training, some software, and so on—are treated as expenses. Unlike investments in tangibles—such as trucks, computers, and buildings—their estimated value is never disclosed. As Lev and David Aboody (of UCLA) say: "This accounting treatment, amounting to an assumption of a 100 percent amortization rate for intangible capital, denies investors timely and vital information on the success of the projects under development." You can't even know their full costs (except for R&D, which is reported), because they're lumped in with many other expenses. Training expenses, for example, are scattered among so many departmental ledgers that it would be impossible for many companies to find the numbers to add up. Once I asked GE—which counts damn near everything—for an estimate of its annual training expenses, and got back a figure that, I was told, was "accurate plus or minus $100 million." According to a Brookings Institution study of accounting's problems in today's economy:

> Managers need to know what levers to pull, which activities to encourage, what kinds of investments to make, and what kinds to avoid to improve the overall performance of the company. . . . Poor understanding of the role of intangibles makes it harder for them to judge the performance of individual employees or teams within the firm, as well as the true costs and benefits of a large share of their business activity.

But managers know generally what's happening and whether it's working, as banker Susan Smith says. An ingenious study by Aboody and Lev proves it like a smoking gun. They studied stock trades and option exercises by insiders at nearly 2,900 companies, as reported to the SEC. They divided the companies into quintiles according to what percentage of sales they invested in intangibles, using R&D spending as the only available proxy. They then compared insiders' gains to those of public investors, across the quintiles. These are legal "insider" trades—reported purchases and sales of stock by company officers. In general, as one would expect, executives' intimate knowledge of corporate performance makes them smarter than the public when it comes to buying and selling their own company's stock. What Lev and Aboody found was that the insiders' advantage grew with R&D intensity. As companies invest more in intellectual capital, insiders do better and better and better than the public. The market didn't know the value, but management did.

Bingo: It's possible to know the value of intangibles—managers' behavior proves they know it and that they know they know it. But no one—perhaps not even the managers—can tell you how they know it. And that's a problem. Managers, as a class, are not smarter than Warren Buffett. If he's stumped and they're not, financial reporting isn't fulfilling its first responsibility.

THREE BLIND MICE

"The basic financial documents give lousy information for digital-age companies," says Robert A. Howell, visiting professor of management and accounting at the Tuck School of Business at Dartmouth. To Howell, one of the world's foremost authorities on the changing role of finance and accounting, the "big three" financial statements—the income statement, balance sheet, and statement of cash flow—are about as useful as an eighty-year-old Los Angeles road map.

Their very logic is outmoded, Howell argues.* The income statement, boiled to its bones, looks like this:

	Revenues
–	Cost of Goods Sold
	Gross Margin
–	Operating Expenses
	Earnings before Interest and Taxes
–	Interest, Taxes
	Profit

It was set up that way to highlight the most important cost—the cost of goods. Where raw materials and direct labor made up most of the cost of a product, that was a number managers and investors had to know. Today, forget it. For Microsoft, the cost of goods ("cost of revenue," they say) is just 14 percent of sales, giving an 86 percent margin. Coca-Cola's gross margin is 70 percent. For Revlon, it's 66 percent. When gross margin is about as meaningful as your ex's promise of eternal love, why bring it up? Further, the income statement has long since ceased to be a decent measure of profit or loss—"profit" having become a subjective number that depends on when revenues and expenses are recognized. Many companies manage earnings better than they manage anything else.

Therefore, Howell argues, forget about profit and focus on cash. Call it an "operating statement" rather than an income statement. Add back all

---

* The innumerate among you might be intimidated because the next several pages include what looks like arithmetic. Please don't be. It's actually very easy stuff—I know, being largely innumerate myself—and, besides, it's written with such verve and wit that you'll enjoy the trip even if you don't remember any of it.

the noncash items—which analysts take out anyway. Format it like this (again, a bare-bones view, leaving out taxes, interest, and so on):

	Revenue
–	Cost to serve customers
–	Cost to produce products/services
–	Cost to develop products/services
–	Administrative costs
	Earnings before interest and taxes
–	Taxes
+/–	Noncash adjustments
	Cash Earnings

That change would give readers a decent idea of where a company spends money, without spilling proprietary beans. It replaces manipulable Gumby "profit" with gen-yew-wine cash money. It doesn't waste a lot of time counting raw material but focuses on the real work of twenty-first-century corporations: taking care of customers (sales and marketing, shipping, service), producing things to sell (manufacturing or providing services, materials, equipment), and producing future offerings (research and development, knowledge creation). It draws a tight box around administrative expense and serves as a goad to greater efficiency. Today's commonly used "sales, general, and administrative cost" is anachronistic. It assumes selling costs are trivial and something to be minimized—which is true for old-line manufacturers but often not so for knowledge companies. For many service companies, the cost of selling and the cost of producing are pretty much the same thing. Linda Loman, Willy's wife, was right: Attention must be paid. Also, aggregated "SG&A" can and does hide a multitude of sins. Does Bristol-Myers Squibb run a tight ship? It's impossible to see, because the company lumps administration with marketing and sales, a category that totals about 24 percent of costs.

Howell would also rewrite balance sheets to partially account for intellectual assets and bring them in line with high-speed, real-time business. Balance sheets are snapshots—frozen-in-time pictures of what resources (assets) a company controls, and where it got them (whether from investors of equity or by borrowing). The old balance sheet—which took its present form in 1868—did a reasonable job of portraying old realities. As Howell says: "To support a dollar's worth of sales, old-line companies might have had to put fifteen to twenty cents' worth of earnings back on the balance sheet in the form of working capital"—inventories and receivables. Another big tranche of earnings would be turned into fixed assets to make up for depreciation and to support growth, which depended on adding new fixed assets like ships, factories, lines of track, and stores.

That's a lot less meaningful for companies like Dell and Amazon.com, which have negative working capital. Thanks to electronic data interchange and now Internet-based e-commerce, even traditional manufacturers need much less working capital than they did: As we saw in Chapter 1, durable-goods makers would be carrying an extra $115 billion in inventory—about a third more than they do—if they operated by the ratios that prevailed in 1988. Today's companies need less in the way of physical assets, too.

The fundamental balance-sheet equation is, of course,

$$\text{Assets} = \text{Liabilities} + \text{Equity}$$

Howell would change it to

$$\text{Investments} = \text{Financings}$$

The money invested in a business has to equal the money raised for it. (If it doesn't, look for your missing CFO on Grand Cayman.) On the investment side go the three usual suspects—working capital (receivables and inventory), fixed assets (but at market value, not cost), and investments (at market value), plus cash. Howell would put a set of intangibles with them, also real investments for Information Age companies: R&D, brand equity, and people.

How should these intangibles be valued? Various tested ways of valuing R&D are around. A transaction-based evaluation, most compatible with traditional accounting, would book the cost and amortize it over average product lifetimes. Alternatively, you can value R&D using "real options" methods or put an asset value on intellectual property using a net-present-value calculation. Likewise there are established ways to say what a brand is worth (as we've discussed). Where brand equity is not an appropriate measure, one could substitute a capitalized value for customer loyalty. It's done all the time in mergers and aquisitions work. As for people, says Howell: "At a minimum, I would book as assets such costs as recruitment and training and development, and amortize them over some sort of employ-ment life. Why aren't they as much an asset as some piece of machinery?"

The counterargument is that by definition an asset is something that can be owned, and you can't own people. Yesss . . . that's the definition, but what of it? The whole point is that the definition is inadequate to the realities of a knowledge economy. Some might protest that adding recruitment and train-ing, R&D, and brand equity to the balance sheet would dramatically lower returns on equity, but them's the breaks; people would quickly adjust to a world where 10 percent was a fabulous return on equity.* Debt-to-equity ratios would also go down, which is a plus. More to the point: This balance sheet, like Howell's proposed operating statement, tells a story that managers and investors should know: What are you doing with the money you raise?†

---

* When I started at *Fortune* in 1989, 20 percent was a stellar return on equity. Of the industry groups on the 1988 *Fortune* 500, only drug and beverage companies man-aged to hit it. (Note that both are intangible-intensive.) Now eight manufacturing industry groups are above 20 percent; pharmas are 36 percent, soaps and cosmetics are 29 percent—in 1999 even motor vehicles hit 18 percent. Are they really that much more profitable? Or are we just not seeing the assets? I'd argue the latter. One piece of evidence: The 500's profit as a percentage of sales isn't all that different—it's actually down a bit, to 5 percent from 5.5 percent.

† There is a serious case against putting intellectual assets on balance sheets. Insofar as measurements of intangibles are subjective, for example, they might further muddy an already grimy picture. However, what Howell proposes is not at all subjective, and (as we'll see) the objectivity of supposedly "hard" numbers is open to question.

I'd like to see audited accounting for human, organizational, and customer capi-tal, but I am not convinced these apples belong with financial oranges on a single bal-ance sheet. My problem with combining them is with the right side of the page, the financings bit. Current and long-term liabilities and debt are easy enough—you'd have to add the value of employee contracts and other liabilities, but that's no prob-lem. What's not debt is equity—but whose equity? That's more difficult. In a knowl-edge business, not all the assets belong to shareholders; some are really "employees' equity" and "customers' equity," and much is jointly owned. There's human capital and company-specific human capital, and it's hard to say which is which—or even when company-specific human capital is company property. (For a discussion of com-pany-specific human capital, see Paul A. Strassmann, "The Value of Knowledge Cap-ital," *American Programmer,* March 1998, or www.strassmann.com; also see Margaret M. Blair, *Ownership and Control: Rethinking Corporate Governance for the Twenty-First Century* (Washington, D.C: Brookings Institution, 1995).) Likewise with cus-tomers: In the knowledge economy, C. K. Prahalad says, "customers cocreate value with sellers, becoming investors in their suppliers." On whose balance sheet should this

Last but not least, Howell would revise the Statement of Cash Flows—"an abomination" in its present form. Now it looks like this:

$$+/-\quad \text{Operating cash flows}$$
$$+/-\quad \text{Investing cash flows}$$
$$\underline{+/-\quad \text{Financing cash flows}}$$
$$\text{Change in cash}$$

The purpose of the cash-flow statement is to illuminate a company's liquidity and show how management uses financial resources. The new operating statement that we've already discussed would do a better job of the latter. As for revealing liquidity, the candlepower of the cash-flow statement is low. The story it tells—is the cash account up or down at the end of the year?—is trivial, says Howell: "It's useless to a manager." What managers (and investors) need to know is how much cash a business produces over and above what's needed to operate it—free cash flow, that is. To get that, the cash-flow statement ought to look like this:

$$\text{Cash earnings}^*$$
$$\underline{-\quad \text{Investing activities}^\dagger}$$
$$\text{Free Cash Flows}$$

Free cash flows have to equal financing flows—a company either invests the money it makes or has to raise more—thus tying all three financial statements together.

This architecture, which Howell calls a digital-age accounting framework, makes sense for lots of reasons: It tells a clear story, makes flimflam

---

intangible equity be put? Structural capital is less ambiguous—patents, documents, databases, methods, trade secrets, and processes are company property; insofar as some structrural intangibles might be shared with an alliance partner, there's usually a contract describing who owns what. If you mingle human and customer capital with financial and fixed assets on one balance sheet, you're creating a balance sheet for an extended enterprise, not a corporation. That's meaningful in an anagogic sense, and useful for managers, but both they and investors should get something tighter.

* From operating statement.

† Plus or minus working capital and minus investments in fixed and other assets.

hard to hide, and—most important of all—it focuses on the real concerns of business: producing cash and creating value.

From a historical perspective, a lot of the old setup came into being to account for the long lag between investment and return: If a Genoese merchant sent out a ship laden with cargo to trade, it might be years before he knew whether the venture was profitable. Double-entry book-keeping, which matches up debits and credits, began in Venice more than 500 years ago as a way to put a value on such businesses, particularly when the merchant might have several ships, some out at sea, some profitably (or unprofitably) home, others God knew where.

Today, with credit cards and e-commerce and the Dell business model and the like, these sorts of long-term arrangements are less important. "Buy now, pay later" is becoming "buy now, pay cash now." In goods industries, including manufacturing and wholesale and retail trade, inventories, lead times, and capital intensity are all shrinking. The economy is service-dominated, and many services—electricity, phone calls, restaurant meals—are produced and sold simultaneously, or nearly so. Everywhere flexible networks have replaced integrated value chains, and a company's ability to create wealth is better explained by its intangible assets than by its tangibles. It's about time investors got statements that focused on real—that is, intellectual—assets and showed how they produce real cash.

TIME AND TIDE

Calls to revamp accounting, lonely cries in the forest just a few years ago, have become full-voiced howls within sight of the campfire. Among the petitioners are executives like Ray Lane, former COO of Oracle and now a partner at venture capital firm Kleiner Perkins Caufield & Byers, who complained to the *Financial Times:* "We don't have a place in the balance sheet for intelligence or knowledge and that is becoming a much more important factor than the physical assets. We don't have a way to classify the intellectual capital or knowledge." Acting to do something about it, thousands of companies have adopted the Balanced Scorecard, a management accounting method developed by Robert S. Kaplan and David P. Norton that shows how to put nonfinancial indicators of performance on the management dashboard with the usual financial measures. In

Chicago, the Center for Advanced Valuation Studies is pulling together extensive academic work on the subject, preparing a syllabus for public distribution. Adding their voices are accounting professionals like Robert Herz, a partner at PricewaterhouseCoopers, who vows, "One of these days there will be standards for the reporting of intellectual capital." The major professional services firms smell both a need and a potentially huge new line of business. What's the use of all those green eyeshades if, as KPMG chairman Stephen Butler says, "people who are investing in [new economy] companies are not using traditional financial statments" that give no information about know-how, human capital, and other knowledge assets? The firms have undertaken big projects to explore new valuation methods and models. Andersen gave $10 million to MIT to set up a New Economy Value Research Lab; Ernst & Young holds annual conferences on the subject; they publish books.

What holds them up? Fear, basically—the dread of something after GAAP, the undiscovered counting. One argument is that measures of intangibles are imprecise and subjective. "Balderdash" is the polite response. There's plenty of hooey in supposedly objective valuations of fixed assets. Humanity, which includes accountants, lives and lives well with numbers that are wrong or meaninglessly vague. Take this description of semiconductor manufacturing: "Intel's space-suited workers etch more than seven million [transistors], in lines one four-hundredth the thickness of a human hair, on each of its thumbnail-sized Pentium II chips. . . ."

How thick *is* human hair? I've run my fingers through a few headfuls of the stuff and it's obvious, even to the blunt insensitive digital instruments with which I was born, that it varies quite a lot. According to Kao Corp., the average Japanese person's hair is 50 percent thicker than the average Caucasian's. Does that mean Japanese-made transistors are 50 percent bigger than those made in, say, Holland? According to Procter & Gamble, the diameter of a shaft of a human hair can be anywhere from fifty-seven micrometers (millionths of a meter) to 120 micrometers. That's a 111 percent difference. In other words, if semiconductor manufacturing were as imprecise as the language used to describe its precision, Intel would be bankrupt.

We're surrounded, in business and outside it, by measurements that pretend to be precise but aren't. We say, "Close doesn't count except in horseshoes," but we count fuzzy things all the time. Football games are often decided on the basis of ersatz accuracy, for instance. The offense is close to a first down, the chain gang comes in from the sidelines, and we see precisely—to within fractions of an inch—whether it's first-and-ten or punt-and-pray. Yet that precision rests on approximation: a ref's spotting the ball from the previous play and a chain gang's eyeballing a line that might be perpendicular to the sideline. Both the ref and the chain gang probably are accurate within an inch or two, and therefore together might be inaccurate by four inches or so.

Businesspeople like accuracy. If the Financial Accounting Standards Board suggests that the value of stock options ought to be charged against earnings, CEOs squawk that it's misleading because the future value of an option can only be estimated, not calculated. Similar criticism—"inaccurate, subjective, imprecise"—is leveled against putting brand equity onto balance sheets, treating R&D as a capital investment, or in other ways accounting for the intellectual assets upon which a knowledge economy depends.

Precision's a virtue; I wouldn't go to a barber—let alone a brain surgeon—whose margin of error was, in percentage terms, as large as the variation in the thickness of human hair. But consider whether the measurements accounting principles generally accept are precise. In the 1990s, telephone companies began doing their books according to a different accounting standard—one for unregulated industries, not regulated ones. Presto-chango, overnight their telephone poles became less valuable, because they depreciated over a fifteen-year period rather than thirty-five years. In 1999, General Motors told the Securities and Exchange Commission that it would take a $2 billion to $3 billion charge against earnings. The reason for the monster charge: "asset impairment." It seems GM decided that some tangible assets carried on its books at cost minus depreciation had become "impaired" and should be valued lower. The new value was an estimate—necessarily imprecise—of fair market value. The difference between the precise-but-supposedly-wrong historical cost and the imprecise-but-supposedly-right market value was enormous, about 4 percent of the total value of GM's property, plant, and equipment—so big that one might describe it as, well, splitting hairs.

In the next chapter, we'll look at several of the most promising ways to measure intellectual assets. None is perfect—all involve estimates and all are experimental. The valuation of intangibles is getting better all the time. Is it as good as GAAP numbers? Almost certainly not. Is that a reason not to do it? Certainly not. Surely it's better to be approximately right than precisely wrong.

Various other objections can be lodged against scuppering GAAP, or at least hauling it into dry dock for a major refitting. Fear of lawsuits if information turns out to be unreliable is one, especially in the litigious United States. It can be met. The SEC, FASB, or regulatory bodies elsewhere could create open-to-scrutiny pilot projects and Congress can create legal "safe harbors" so that companies can release data about intangibles without fear of inciting piranhas in the plaintiffs' bar. Another is fear of disclosing information that might reveal confidential information. That's more plausible on its face, until you look at the face that's saying it. Historically companies have resisted releasing any data beyond name, rank, and serial number. In the 1930s, when the SEC first established that the top line of the income statement should be the "Sales" number, not the "Gross Profit" number (which was widely used then), companies fiercely objected that they were being forced to reveal proprietary information. Worse, they'd have to reveal their cost of sales, the other component of gross profit. In droves companies filed requests with the SEC, asking that the requirement be waived in their case; all were turned down. Secrets bared, capitalism nevertheless survived—in fact, capitalism thrived precisely because it became more honest. Sure, there are trade secrets, but these turn out to be remarkably few. Anything that helps investors and managers put capital to work more efficiently is good for the system in the long run.

Last there's the conservative argument, the excellent point that one shouldn't lightly discard a system that has, for all its faults, served business and the public well, like an octogenarian butler. It is no small thing that GAAP makes fraud difficult and, in its absence, produces reliable numbers—even if they are not always useful ones. In an information economy, says Steven M. H. Wallman, a former commissioner of the SEC who cochaired the Brookings Institution task force that studied the need to measure and disclose intangible sources of value: "Some of the most useful information is not necessarily the most reliable, and some of the most reliable is not necessarily the most useful." He's right—financial reporting is too important to be imprudently cast aside, and the dot-com bubble reminds us that novel accounting is often touted by fools and charlatans. At the same time (as Wallman agrees) there's increasing evidence that the faithful servant isn't just misplacing a spoon here or there, but has lost track of the most valuable jewelry in the house and, from having paid no attention to the furnace and the water heater, put the place at risk. Whatever your company reports to the public, certainly internally you can't look at traditional balance-sheet numbers and be confident that you are getting an accurate portrait of your resources. Certainly internally you want to add back R&D and consider it a capital expenditure. The National Science Foundation estimates that 35 percent of all patents are orphaned. You wouldn't allow 35 percent of your factory space to lie idle— so certainly internally you want to put in place the measures and controls that will allow you to manage R&D as well as you do plant and equipment. Certainly internally you want to capitalize some portion of what you spend on recruiting, training, and developing your workforce, so that you can get some idea of what it would cost to replace—and what it is worth to retain—your most valuable people.

Apologists for accounting are like people who pooh-pooh global warming. The evidence that something is happening builds up and up and up, yet it's still possible, always possible, to say that maybe there's another explanation. Take the dot-com boom and meltdown of 2000–2001. Memories are short, and people don't recall what Warren Buffett said in 1998, when the party was first getting out of hand. Remember: He said that anyone who tried to put a value on an Internet stock should get a failing grade *no matter what the answer was.* That shouldn't be. There should be room for differences of opinion—without them there would be no markets— but no one as astute as Buffett should have to throw up his hands and say, "It's anyone's guess." Former SEC chairman Arthur Leavitt has suggested that the dot-com debacle might partly have resulted from accounting system weaknesses. Maybe the meltdown, like the shrinking polar ice caps and the vanishing snows of Kilimanjaro, is early evidence of real harm— billions of dollars of harm—caused by the failure of accounting to acknowledge intellectual capital. Or maybe not. Maybe there's another explanation. Maybe it was just one of those things, like tulip bulbs.

CHAPTER 14

MANAGEMENT ACCOUNTING FOR THE INFORMATION AGE

We are the mimics. Clouds are pedagogues.

WALLACE STEVENS

Cultural revolutions are tricky. For every hundred flowers that bloom, there sprout, it seems, a million noxious weeds. The Internet, a wag said, proves that an infinitude of monkeys typing incessantly will not write even one of the books in the British Library. But hundreds of people are monkeying with how we account for corporate performance and producing genuinely useful, perhaps revolutionary results. A decade back, thinking about how to track intellectual capital, Harvard Business School professor Robert S. Kaplan told me: "We don't even have a nonfinancial number to measure enhanced ability." Now we do—and we have financial measures as well. In the last handful of years, people in North America, Europe, and Japan, in consulting and accounting firms, in universities, governments, even in advertising agencies, have floated a raft of ideas to evaluate intellectual capital and measure how productively companies use knowledge—and to do these things with useful precision. In some cases the measures are financial. Other measurements are nonfinancial, but nevertheless quantitative and rigorous.

Before looking at some of them, it's important to discuss their importance and their limitations. "You cannot manage what you cannot measure" is one of the oldest clichés in management, and it's either false or meaningless. It's false in that companies have always managed things—people, morale, strategy, etc.—that are essentially unmeasured. It's meaningless in the sense that everything in business—including people, morale, strategy, etc.—eventually shows up in someone's ledger of costs or revenues. Twenty minutes I spend in idle chat with an officemate will show up as reduced productivity; twenty minutes I spend brainstorming with a colleague will show up as increased innovation. The problem, as this example suggests, is that the connection between an activity and its consequences is often hard to find and not directly measured.

Measurements matter because people use them to make sense of what they see. They describe—is it big, fast, good, strong, healthy? They diagnose—is it damaged, overheated, underused? And they evaluate—is it fixed, stronger, better? Without them managers would be like physicians in centuries past who knew a patient was sick but not why, and could not say whether he was cured by the prayers, the country air, or the leeches. Measurements also matter because they pervert. An orthopedist, knowing everything about bone, may be hard pressed to diagnose the pain in your shoulder if its origin is in soft tissues; an engineer may have difficulty understanding that his work group's productivity problem comes from morale rather than machinery.

Measurement, in other words, is a worldview, not just a scorecard. It is a means of thinking and acting, as well as measuring. Unless you measure knowledge assets and activities, your ability to change will be hindered. In a battle between change advocacy and the measurement system, the measurement system will win. Kaplan, coinventor of the Balanced Scorecard, advises companies to use measurements "not for measurement's sake but as the basis for a continuous organizing framework." Knowledge measurements—analyses of intellectual capital and the effectiveness and productivity of knowledge work—should be made so that businesspeople judge their acts and improve their decisions.

There can be no single gauge of a company's intellectual capital or its performance as a knowledge business. There is no single measurement of financial performance, either. There is an ultimate long-term-performance number—return on invested capital—but all kinds of data, such as free cash flow, return on equity, earnings before interest, taxes, and depreciation, are revealing, and under some circumstances crucial. There is an ultimate long-term measure of a stock—total return to shareholders—but P/E, dividend yield, growth in earnings per share, and the like, are part of the picture. There is an ultimate long-term measure of operations—productivity growth*—but innovation, growth, cost containment, and many other factors contribute to it in essential ways. In *Intellectual Capital* (pp. 222–246), I described a set of tools for measuring intellectual capital. They are not bad, if I say so myself—the only reason not to repeat them here is that you can find them there. There are many additional, exciting approaches, a few of which I describe below.

There is no generally accepted intellectual capital accounting. The field is too young and too much is unknown; you must roll your own. I believe every company should develop at least one measurement that describes the aggregate value of its intellectual capital. (At least two of the items that follow, Bates Gruppen's CompanyIQ and Baruch Lev's knowledge capital, do that.) Beyond that, they should pick and arrange

---

* Productivity is output divided by input: How much X can you produce per unit of Y? Measuring productivity is more difficult than it would seem to be at first blush. First, what's X? It's easy to measure the output of widgets, but much harder in knowledge-intensive service businesses. How do you measure the output of a schoolteacher? Number of students per class? Total SAT scores of former students? Number of former students who say, "He changed my life"? Do you measure a lawyer's productivity by the length of her briefs or by their brevity? By the number of cases she argues or the number she wins?

Second, what's Y? The down-and-dirty way to measure productivity is output per unit of labor, but that's meaningless for companies that use very little labor, such as phone or chemical companies: You could double labor productivity and improve operations negligibly. Or you could spend $2 a year on machinery and power to save $1 a year in labor, and end up performing less well, though your labor productivity rose. The better measure is total factor productivity. Total factor productivity is output divided by all costs—labor, raw materials, and capital equipment. (When I refer to productivity I mean total factor productivity unless I say otherwise.) That's far and away the better measure, but even the U.S. government mostly relies on labor productivity numbers, because they're more readily available.

indicators and measurements that relate to important aspects of their own performance. The key point is to *select ways to measure intellectual capital and knowledge management that illuminate* your *strategy and* your *financial performance*. The pages that follow offer, in effect, patches of cloth. It's your quilt.

I've organized this discussion according to the four-step process for managing intellectual capital described in Chapter 4: (1) Identify and evaluate the role of knowledge in your business—as input, process, and output; (2) analyze the knowledge assets that produce those revenues; (3) develop a strategy for investing in and exploiting your intellectual assets; (4) improve the efficiency of knowledge work and knowledge workers. Unless you have a much better memory than I do, you'll probably want to review the various sections of that chapter as we proceed.* I will conclude with a discussion of financial accounting for knowledge capital.

MEASURING THE ROLE OF KNOWLEDGE

The first step in measuring the performance of a knowledge business is to identify the role knowledge plays in it, as an input, a means of production, and an output. (See pp. 58–66.)

Rating Knowledge Intensity

In jargon: How important is knowledge as a driver of your business? The more important, the more rewarding it can be to manage it. Conversely, if a business is not particularly knowledge-intensive, you might get more bang for your buck by improving your management of physical or financial assets.

We've seen several ways of measuring knowledge intensity:

- Research and development spending as a percentage of revenues
- Other innovation measures, such as percentage of sales from new products, patents pending and awarded, and patents cited

---

* And if you didn't read Chapter 4 or any of the early parts of this book and turned directly to this chapter, looking for plug-and-play formulae, fie and shame! "Think for yourself" is the one unbreakable rule of managing intellectual capital.

- Percentage of knowledge workers ("professionals, senior management and technical, engineering and scientific staff; in other words, the people in the organization who are paid to 'think'")

Each of these gives a general picture of the knowledge intensity of an industry or a company. The measure of R&D intensity, for example, shows that pharmaceuticals are more knowledge intensive than chemicals; it can also, since R&D is a published number, be used to compare the knowledge intensity of individual companies, Merck vs. Schering-Plough vs. Eli Lilly, and so on.

Three Revelatory Ratios

Value added per dollar of employee costs. Professor Ante Pulic of the University of Graz in Austria has developed a measure of knowledge-capital efficiency, which he calls VAIC, Value Added Intellectual Coefficient. The first part of his method uses a measure of labor value added that can be used to gauge knowledge intensity. Pulic's premise is that the role of labor is entirely changed in modern companies from what it was in industrial companies. He explains: "Depending on their capabilities the same quantity of labor may now achieve completely different business results, in contrast to prior times when a given amount of routine work produced more or less the same quantities of a product." That is, for industrial companies, labor was a commodity whose value depended on other factors, such as what machinery was used; time—number of hours worked—was a pretty good proxy for labor's output. (That is one reason to pay laborers by the hour.) But a knowledge worker's output cannot be inferred from hours worked. It has to be inferred from value added. Therefore Pulic calculates as follows: From all outputs (i.e., all revenues from goods and services sold) he subtracts all non-employee inputs (i.e., all purchased expenses, excluding expenses for payroll and benefits). That produces a measure of value added. He then divides the result by the payroll and benefit costs, which he uses as a proxy for human capital. Thus

$$\frac{\text{Value Added}}{\text{Human capital}} =$$

how much value added has been created by one money unit invested in the employees. This is what Pulic calls the Value Added Human Capital Coefficient.

A major benefit of this number is that it can be calculated from published company reports. Like Pulic, analysts of human-resources effectiveness widely accept value added per dollar of labor cost as a measure of return on investment in human capital. I'm reluctant to give it that much meaning. Some percentage of pay isn't an investment in human capital; it's just plain old labor cost, an expense like electricity or work gloves or printer paper. (To get a divisor that more accurately represents investment in human capital, you need to refine the pay-and-benefits number by calculating how much of employees' work is devoted to current-year tasks and how much to seeding the future, in activities such as training, planning, and business development. A method for doing this is described in *Intellectual Capital,* pp. 232–234.) In addition, pay and benefits costs vary dramatically from country to country and industry to industry, though they should be roughly the same within an industry. If big differences in labor cost are an issue, calculate value added per full-time employee.

The proxy is imperfect as a measure of human capital or investment in it, but we're not using it for that. It's a perfectly acceptable way to characterize the knowledge intensity of a business, to compare one kind of business with another, or to compare one company with another. The greater the result—that is, the higher the value added per unit of labor cost—the greater the knowledge intensity.

Market value/book value and Tobin's q. The market-to-book ratio divides a company's market value by the book value of its assets (physical, financial, and goodwill). Tobin's *q,* a statistic invented by Nobel Prize–winning economist James Tobin, is the ratio of a company's market value to the replacement value of its assets, found by adding depreciation back into book value; as *q* moves above 1, the market seems to be placing increasing value on a company's intangibles. (See *Intellectual Capital,* pp. 224–226.)

It's tempting to say that the difference between market value and book value *is* the value of a company's intangibles, but it's a dangerous little-bit-of-knowledge sort of temptation. There are several reasons why these numbers are not truly measures of intellectual assets. First, book value is a historical-cost number, whereas market value includes the stock market's valuation of future earnings. Second, and most egregious: Stock-market-based, these ratios rise and fall with market exuberance, however sane. Thus they assume that tangible assets have a fixed underlying value, regardless of moves in the market, but intangibles do not; one's real, the other's whimsical, a random walk—yet trying to find a real value for intangibles is precisely the point of the exercise.

That being said, both market-to-book and Tobin's q are perfectly useful indications of knowledge *intensity,* and it would be reasonable to use them to compare industries and companies within an industry.

Knowledge Intensity + Profitability

Any of these numbers—R&D intensity, patents, Tobin's q—will reveal more if it is compared to a measure of financial returns, such as economic value added. (See Chapter 4, p. 62.) Note, also, that it is possible—difficult, but possible—to calculate knowledge-intensity figures for business units as well as for entire companies. In all likelihood outsiders do not have access to figures that would allow them to know the payroll or impute a notional market value for, say, GE Appliances, so that it could be compared to that for Whirlpool; but management can do this work intramurally. When comparing one company to another or one business unit to

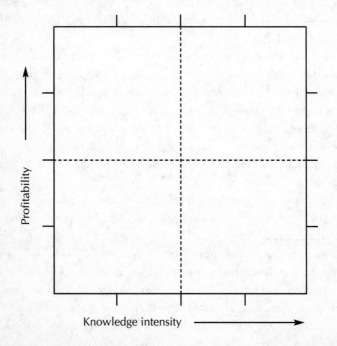

another, locate them on a grid like the one on page 296, which you may recall from Chapter 4. It allows you to compare financial results to knowledge intensity. A highly knowledge-intensive company with mediocre profitability merits investigation.

Measuring Knowledge Spending

One way to discover the role of knowledge in your business is to keep track of what you spend on it. Simply adding up all the money you spend to purchase knowledge and pay for knowledge work would, in most companies, be a revelation, just as it would shock most families to discover how much they spend on snacks. A more revealing calculation would entail tracking spending on knowledge and on physical inputs along the duration of a business process, such as new-product development or the order-to-fulfillment process. This is, essentially, a process-mapping exercise. Make a chart like the one below. Mark the horizontal axis with major decision points or stage gates, as you would any process map. Costs are incurred as the process runs its course, and are marked on the vertical

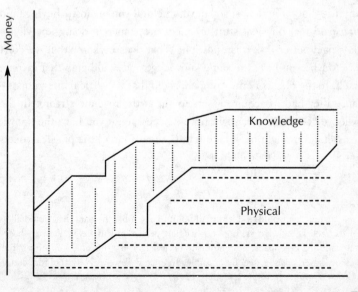

axis. Some of the spending is for knowledge—research, analysis, software, marketing. Some is for physical processes—equipment, raw materials. Labor costs should be allocated according to the nature of the labor: Clerical work and direct manufacturing work are physical costs; training and planning are knowledge costs.*

A chart like this serves multiple purposes. First, it's a vivid picture of knowledge intensity. Second, it's a neat way to see and manage costs. The entire area under the lines is working capital—money tied up in materials, knowledge, and payroll. There are two ways to reduce it. One is to lower the lines on the vertical axis—i.e., cut spending. The other is to shorten the horizontal axis—i.e., cut time, since time is money. Where knowledge is concerned, the latter is likely to be particularly powerful, because knowledge-intensive products and services tend to incur their highest costs up front. Manufacturing processes, by contrast, tend to have lower up-front costs and higher late costs. This is because the marginal cost of producing and delivering knowledge is usually very low—sometimes zero.

A chart like this can be extended beyond the boundaries of your business, to track the entire knowledge-value chain for a product or a process. Then it becomes not only a way to measure knowledge spending, but also a map that shows the richest soil in your field. If you're mostly buying (and getting paid for) physical stuff, chances are someone doing knowledge work is paid better. Ask this question: What does he know that we don't know? Maybe you have the same knowledge and could grab that income yourself. In the old economy, companies did that via vertical integration—because they had to acquire assets to get at the revenue stream. In the knowledge economy, that might not be necessary; if you have the knowledge assets, you might be able to rent (i.e., outsource) the physical assets required.

---

* Some companies would find it very difficult to assemble the data that would allow them to track knowledge vs. nonknowledge expenses in this detail. Activity-based cost accounting is probably a prerequisite for a ledger like this one. For information on activity-based costing, see, for example, Terence P. Paré, "A New Tool for Managing Costs," *Fortune*, June 14, 1993, pp. 124ff.

TAKING STOCK OF KNOWLEDGE ASSETS

The second step in the intellectual-capital-management process is to match your knowledge revenues with the knowledge assets that produce them.

CompanyIQ

An ingenious way to identify and analyze knowledge assets (and compare them with other companies) has been developed by an advertising agency: Bates Gruppen, the Norwegian arm of Bates Worldwide, part of giant Cordiant Communications Group. Ad agencies are in the business of creating intangible assets—brand equity in particular—which partly explains why Bates, Norway's biggest agency, undertook to measure them.

Bates Gruppen's CompanyIQ is a numerical but nonfinancial measurement. The method has three steps. The first, which was sketched in Chapter 4, is to identify what a company produces that gives it an advantage: why people come to you rather than a competitor. Says Bastian Lie-Nielsen, a strategy consultant at Bates Gruppen: "These are not core skills; we're trying to find unique aspects in what you deliver"—things like rapid response, reliability, and design. In a day-long workshop, management debates and selects eight, ten, a dozen attributes that it thinks are both unique and valuable. The list then goes to employees and to customers in the form of a questionnaire. They rate each attribute twice— once for uniqueness and again for value to customers—in each case using a 1-to-7 scale. Management, it turns out, usually thinks more highly of itself than employees and customers; the last are particularly likely to deflate claims of uniqueness. When the results come back and are tabulated, parcel out the attributes into the four quadrants of a two-by-two. The two, three, or four items that make it into the upper-right quadrant are what management, employees, and customers agree are highly valuable, unique capabilities of a company—manifestations of its intellectual capital. "That by itself is an eye-opener," Lie-Nielsen says.

Step two is to find the intellectual capital that produces the advantages you've just uncovered. Bates follows the standard scheme, that intellectual capital has three components, human capital (talent), structural cap-

FINDING INTELLECTUAL ASSETS

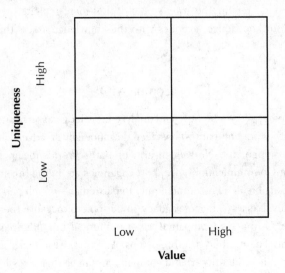

ital (intellectual property, methodologies, software, documents, and other knowledge artifacts), and customer or relationship capital (client relationships). Every company has all three, but, as we discussed, some rely more on one or two than the others.

What you want is a list. Knowledge assets, remember, transform raw material into something more valuable. The ability to write software code transforms Java and caffeine into innovativeness, for example. Superior market intelligence adds to speed and flexibility. World-class R&D in laser technology produces new products. A database of lessons learned improves quality and lowers costs. That is, assets produce the attributes and the cash flows you identified above. To list them, management returns to a workshop; working from and adding to a long list Bates has developed, it compiles a set of about a hundred measurable knowledge assets, divided about equally among human, structural, and customer capital. For example, human capital measures might include training costs and results, the company's degree of dependence on a few key employees, and customers' perceptions of the excellence of the management team or the company's innovativeness. Structural capital measurements might include administrative costs in relation to sales, IT investment, response time, and customers' ratings of your efficiency. Possible customer capital measurements are the percentage of loyal customers, the company's winning percentage when it pitches new accounts, and customers' opinion of its quality in absolute terms and compared to its rivals.

There are three rules for these measures. First, the hundred or so items chosen, whether tailor-made or from the list, should relate strongly to the core advantages that were uncovered earlier: If response time is one of your advantages, you want to measure attributes having to do with speed. If you are a follower, not an innovator, measures of innovation should take a back seat. Second, everything must be measurable, either in absolute terms (such as training expense) or on a scale of 1 to 5 (e.g., for a customer's rating of your efficiency). Third, and vital, at least 60 percent of the items must be comparable, apples to apples, with data from reputable benchmarking studies or the PIMS Database.

For years intellectual-capital savants have been looking for objective, multicompany sources of data about knowledge assets, not thinking that, like Poe's purloined letter, one was lying in plain view. PIMS (the acronym stands for Profit Impact of Market Strategy) began at General Electric in the 1960s when GE was studying how to manage a portfolio of different businesses; it was taken over by Harvard, then in 1975 went private, as it were, in the Strategic Planning Institute, a consultancy in Cambridge, Massachusetts, which owns it. PIMS Europe, headquartered in London, is Bates's partner in CompanyIQ. For a third of a century PIMS has been collecting data on market share, quality, pricing, innovation, advertising, R&D spending, and so on from thousands of companies. Data are collected at the business unit level and kept anonymous; when a client uses the PIMS database, he gets back information about "businesses like us"—businesses in comparable industries whose size and other characteristics roughly match yours. PIMS didn't set out to gather information on human, structural, and customer capital, of course. But much of what's in the database can be sorted into those categories—and it's from PIMS data that Bates developed its list.

Now the notion of IQ comes in. Back come the answers to the hundred or so questions. "We turn them into PIMS numbers—usually dollars or ratios," says Doug McConchie of PIMS Europe, then compare them to all companies with a similar profile (size, industry, etc.) in the database as a whole. How do your training expenses compare to your peers? How does your quality stack up? As with IQ, Bates and PIMS peg the median company at 100. If you're above the median, you'll get a CompanyIQ of, say, 112. That's the score Bates got when it tested one of its divisions, Bates Allen Design.

Once you have your score, you can look inside it, analyze it, and do something about it: This is the third step in the CompanyIQ process. Bates Allen's IQ was strongest in human capital, weakest in structural capital. "We were very dependent on a few stars," says Lie-Nielsen; "also, we discovered our prices were lower than they needed to be." That led to various decisions—most important, to increase structural capital by working with the star performers to see what parts of their talent could be distilled into processes others could emulate.

As this is written CompanyIQ is being beta-tested, so to speak, by a consortium of eight Norwegian companies. Its virtues seem evident. Its methodology requires top management participation. It isn't overly complex or time-consuming. It uses customized data that illuminate a company's unique intellectual capital and strategy, yet produces results that can be compared with reliable numbers from a broad range of companies. And it provides a clear link to follow-up actions and investments by management—that is, a chance to build the strengths and shore up the weaknesses the process uncovers. That, of course, is the third step in the process of managing intellectual capital, which we will examine after looking at a couple of other ways to analyze and evaluate knowledge assets.

IC Rating

A Swedish group, Intellectual Capital Sweden AB (IC AB), has developed a useful way to take the pulse of a company's intellectual capital. Bates Gruppen's CompanyIQ, like a complete physical exam, probes deep to discover and evaluate what it is that makes you tick, and to offer specific suggestions about how to improve. The results of the IC Rating are, while quantifiable, more subjective because they do not involve comparisons to a public database like PIMS.

The IC Rating examines intangibles in five aspects: an overall intellectual capital rating, plus separate ratings for human capital, structural capital, relational (customer) capital, and "business recipe"; this last is "the company's business idea and strategy in combination with the conditions in the chosen business environment." One indication of its strength is how well a company differentiates itself from competitors. To rate each of these areas, IC AB designs a set of questions for managers, employees, customers, and suppliers that grade each of these areas from three different perspectives:

Efficiency. How good it is now? Does the company have top people, well-developed and efficient processes, strong intellectual property, rewarding customers, top brands? An A means extremely good potential for becoming or remaining successful; a B, good potential; a C, limited potential; a D, no potential.

Renewal. How strong are the company's efforts to rejuvenate and grow its assets? Is it hiring great youngsters and developing them well? Is it creating new products or milking aging cash cows? Are its brands robust or undernourished? Letter grades from A to D rate whether the company is or is not making good efforts in the right direction.

Risk. How great is the danger that the company's intellectual assets will lose value? Is a killer competitor moving into its market? Do new technologies threaten to make the company's patents obsolete? Risks are graded –, R, RR, and RRR, depending on whether they are negligible, moderate, high, or very high.

A university-conducted study in 2000 showed a strong correlation between a high IC Rating and growth in revenues and employees. It's a good lens through which to view intellectual capital, with two significant weaknesses. First, the method does not by itself force a company to connect its revenues and expenses with specific knowledge—which technologies, which processes, which set of customers. A lazy company (surely not yours) might simply praise its people as team players without bothering to demonstrate that teamwork mattered. Second, as I've suggested, its lack of an objective correlative, such as benchmarking data, means it is only as good as the questions people are asked and the respondents' willingness to remove rose-colored glasses and answer frankly and fearlessly. On the other hand, it's easy to apply at the business unit level, and it delivers a clear, easy-to-interpret message that carries with it strong implications for follow-up action. It's especially smart to address questions of renewal and risk, for rating your ability to protect your knowledge assets is a key part of analyzing them.

Core-Competence Valuation

A group of analysts in the Netherlands-based Knowledge Advisory Services group at KPMG have developed a formula for valuing core competences, which are roughly synonymous with knowledge assets. To be a core competence, a skill or talent must be intangible, of added value, and of strategic importance; it's always described in a phrase beginning "the ability to . . ." For *Fortune*, the abilities to select, report, write, and edit stories are core competences; for magazines that use mostly freelance writers, reporting and writing cease to become core competences, but the ability to attract writers joins selection and editing. Core competences can be technologies or softer skills. 3M, for example, clearly has a core competence in inventing new products and bringing them to market, but the company's thirty-some "technology platforms"—adhesives, fluorocarbons, microreplication, etc. are core competences, too.

On its simplest level, the value of a core competence is the product of five factors: its added value (what it's worth to customers) x competitiveness (how it compares to your competitors' skill in the same area) x potential (how much demand for this ability is growing) x sustainability (how difficult it is to duplicate) x robustness (how much at risk it is). You can put numbers on all of them. The most delicate part of the job is to determine how much added value to ascribe to each knowledge asset that contributes to a product or service. The KMPG team does this as follows: First, it calculates the gross profits of a product or service; second, it rates each ability's contribution on a 0-to-3 scale, depending on whether its role was nonexistent, supporting, substantial, or essential; then each competence's score is added up and the profits distributed among them in proportion to their total scores. If you were obsessive-compulsive, you could reckon what portion of profits should go to a particular competence by methods similar to those used to calculate the value of a brand. To go whole hog, as the KMPG team does, you can calculate the net present value of a core competence by means of this formula:

$$Vcc = \left[\sum_{t=1}^{s} \frac{GP \times (1 + P)^t}{(1 + i)^t} \right] \times R$$

That values a core competence by taking its life cycle into account (from $t = 1$, i.e., today, until S, its sustainable life), where GP is the share of gross profit attributable to the competence, P is potential for the future (expressed as a percentage growth rate), R is robustness (again a percentage), and i is the cost of capital. Don't ask me how it works.

Done right, this could be a calculation of incalculable value, because it allows you to compare the relative contributions of different knowledge assets, as well as to gauge the degree to which they are at risk because of declining potential or inadequate robustness. That information, in turn, produces an agenda for investment—a subject that brings us to the third step in the intellectual-capital-management process.

RATING INTELLECTUAL-CAPITAL STRATEGIES

The third step in the process of managing intellectual capital is to establish plans to exploit your knowledge assets and to invest in them to increase their value. Doing this demands discovering the mechanisms by which assets produce money. If there's no connection between investing in a knowledge asset and improving performance, don't do it. There's no reason to teach calculus to Jennifer Lopez: No one cares if she can calculate precisely the area under a curve.

A Knowledge Value Tree

Years ago, in a presentation at Skandia, the Swedish insurance company where Leif Edvinsson did pioneering work in intellectual capital, I suggested that the company turn its own skills—tools that help it estimate life expectancy, evaluate property, and so on—to the valuation of intangible assets. Eight years and a quarter of the globe away, two executives have done that at Indiana-based Lincoln Re, the big reinsurance subsidiary of Lincoln National Corp (1999 revenues: $6 billion). For Lincoln Re, Arthur DeTore (VP and director of strategic planning and knowledge management) and Mark Clare (assistant VP for ditto) developed a ploddingly—no, exhilaratingly—thorough approach to analyzing investments in knowledge and knowledge assets.

The details are in their book, *Knowledge Assets.* Their essence is what they call a "knowledge tree"—a logically laid-out schematic that shows you how knowledge creates value and allows you to calculate how much. There are three ways knowledge can create value, DeTore and Clare argue: in the form of a product (adding "smarts" to a product or service, or selling knowledge itself); as intellectual property; or through knowledge work. Different factors create value for each strategy:

- Knowledge products, a technology strategy, can create value through features, enhancements, new offerings, or increasing returns.
- Intellectual property, a legal strategy, can create value through licensing, commercialization, blocking, or positioning.
- Knowledge work, an alignment strategy, can create value by means of transformational learning, maintenance learning, reducing transaction costs, creating positive feedback, or producing network effects.

Every investment in knowledge, DeTore and Clare argue, ought to be one of these kinds and produce one or more of these benefits. Thus a corporate Yellow Pages is a knowledge work strategy designed to reduce internal transaction costs (by making it easier to find in-house experts and reducing duplicate work) and produce network effects—that is, increasing returns (by helping like-minded people find each other).

How to evaluate it? The insurers' matter-of-fact doggedness reappears. Value can be measured in discounted cash flow or real options value. The former shows up in six, and only six, places: greater revenue, higher margins, lower costs, reduced capital requirements, lower cost of capital, and lower taxes. All of these are quantifiable—indeed, a lot of what you need to know to quantify them is in your notebooks from your first year in business school. Net-present-value calculations work best in relatively stable environments: If you know the size of the headache-remedy market and can reasonably forecast what nostrums are available, you can measure the value of investing in brand equity for Tylenol by calculating the net present value of increased sales resulting from your ad campaign.

If the world's unpredictable, it may be better to think in terms of options. Options give you the right but not the obligation to do something.

A patent gives you the right to produce products using that patent, but you don't have to. How much is flexibility worth? If you wait, will it be worth more or less? If you buy time to make better decisions, what price should you pay? What's it worth to keep your options open? For knowledge investments, Clare and DeTore say, look for four kinds of real-option value: increased potential return, increased investment duration, lowered cost of learning, and lowered market-share depletion.

In general, the value of real options is affected by six factors. One is the time until the option expires. For a stock-market option, that's a specific date; comparable real-option expiries are the term of a license or patent, the life cycle of a product or technology, or the amount of time until a competitor is likely to appear. Second is the uncertainty of expected cash flows; just as some stocks are more unpredictable than others, so real-world bets vary in risk. Third comes the present value of expected cash flows. For an option you might buy on the stock market, that would be the price of the stock today; for a real option, it's what you figure the opportunity is worth now—the bird in the hand vs. the possible pair in the bush. The fourth factor in an option's value is the value lost over its duration. The equivalent of forgone dividends on a stock-market option, this is what it costs you to keep the option in force—for example, fees to maintain a patent—or the danger that someone else will catch fire while you fiddle. Fifth is the risk-free interest rate; by not acting, you are keeping your powder dry at no risk, so you should credit yourself with a return equal to that of investing in Treasuries. Last is the present value of fixed costs, a calculation of the fixed costs that await you if and when you exercise the option—the equivalent of the strike price on a stock-market option. Options produce interesting math. For one thing, greater uncertainty increases their value—a counterintuitive idea for most managers.

How does it work? To analyze a knowledge strategy or a particular investment, construct a knowledge tree like the one on page 308. Then fill in the boxes. If you invest in R&D, you might increase revenues via new products—how much? You might increase margins because you will have patent protection—how much? In the real options area, your knowledge investments might increase your potential return by getting you into a hot new technology—what's that worth? Your patent might buy time by allowing you to block a competitor—worth what? Not every investment produces every kind of return, of course. But every investment can be looked

SOURCES OF VALUE

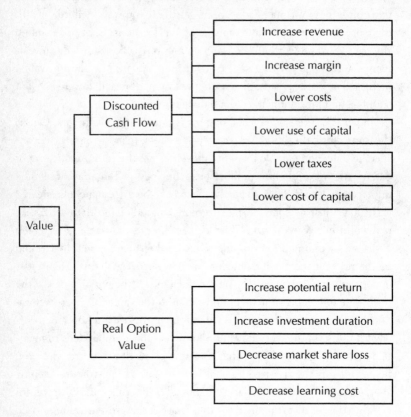

Source: Adapted from Mark Clare and Arthur W. DeTore, *Knowledge Assets.*

at on this tree. Take some human capital investments. Training might increase revenue by increasing labor productivity; it might also lower your need for capital and reduce transaction costs. Investments in recruiting—more aggressiveness, higher entry pay—might get you smarter employees, which could lower the cost of learning and increase potential revenues. The Lincoln Re knowledge tree is a way for management to judge the worth of ideas and projects—no small thing—and to understand the levers by which knowledge investments produce value—which is a very big thing.

Measuring Human Capital

Ray Marcy, CEO of Spherion, Inc., has presided over tremendous growth in the Fort Lauderdale–based company, which provides staffing and search services, particularly in accounting, banking, finance, and technology. Today Spherion employs about 600,000 full- and part-timers, making it America's fifth-largest private employer. No wonder Marcy says: "Here's what I want to know: What is our talent level? What is our talent level compared to the competition? What is our talent utilization—how efficient are we? And can you report these to me on a quarterly basis?"

Those seemingly reasonable questions are in fact unanswerable. "I'm glad he didn't ask me that," says Jac Fitz-enz, founder of the Saratoga Institute. "Doctor Jac" is the pasha of performance measurements for HR departments—and the Saratoga Institute is a Spherion subsidiary. Fitz-enz's own work at the Saratoga Institute has produced many ways to measure the efficiency of human-resources departments and the effectiveness of a company's human capital.*

A couple of recent studies have begun to chart the routes by which human capital is created and turned into shareholder value. Well-known work at Sears demonstrated a cause-and-effect relationship from employee satisfaction to customer satisfaction to shareholder value. Work done by Laurie Bassi for the American Society for Training and Development has shown that training produces positive effects on stock prices. It is crucial to understand these levers, since people are the greatest source of cost and value for most companies. Among lots of interesting human-capital studies, two add rigor to what's long been a slack bunch of figures.

The Watson-Wyatt Human Capital Index

One of the big human-resources consulting firms, Watson-Wyatt has a vested interest in showing that its work is worth paying for. The firm's Human Capital Index attempts to correlate economic value with a set of

---

* You can read about them in his *The ROI of Human Capital: Measuring the Economic Value of Employee Performance* (New York: AMACOM [American Management Association], 2000). The Saratoga Institute (http://www.saratogainstitute.com) publishes an annual *Human Resources Financial Report* that includes extensive survey data that can be used for benchmarking.

human-resources practices. Says Ira Kay, head of the firm's human-capital practice: "High-performing companies have different human-capital practices from low-performing companies. That is indisputable." Correlation isn't causation, yadda yadda yadda; but you're not likely to be wrong if you infer that raising your score on the Human Capital Index would add to the jingle in your shareholders' pockets. Most likely good financial results and superior human-resources practices feed each other in a virtuous circle.

Here's how the Human Capital Index works. Watson-Wyatt got 405 North American companies, publicly traded and with revenues or market caps over $100 million, to fill out a detailed questionnaire about their HR practices. In it, respondents ranked themselves on a 1-to-5 scale concerning employee eligibility for stock ownership, flexible work arrangements, significant differentiation in pay for top vs. average employees, shared knowledge about business plans and results, and so on—each of which has been widely considered a good thing, that is, something that helps companies make money. There were fifty factors in all, grouped in five areas: recruiting excellence; clear rewards and accountability; collegial, flexible workplace; communications integrity; and prudent use of resources.

The scores—self-scores, which is a weakness, and measured on a relative scale rather than absolutely, another weakness—were then matched against the companies' financial performance, as reflected in market capitalization, total return to shareholders, and Tobin's q. Thirty of the fifty factors had correlations with the financial measures. (Twenty didn't, and were tossed.) Watson-Wyatt weighted the factors to create an index, with 100 representing ideal, and 1 stinky, of human capital management. The results in a nutshell: The higher a company's Human Capital Index, the higher its financial performance. Over five years, the top third in human capital gave shareholders a 103 percent total return, vs. just 53 percent for the bottom third. The top group's Tobin's q averaged 3.04, vs. 1.28 for the low scorers.

Things get really interesting inside the numbers. Hiring well matters big: In the "recruiting excellence" category, every point on the 5-point scale suggests a 10.1 percent difference in market cap. That is, after controlling for other factors, companies that score 5s on recruiting had market caps 10.1 percent higher than companies that scored 4s; the 4s had values 10.1 percent higher than the 3s, and so on. The obvious but important-to-reiterate lesson: Better raw material makes better human capital—indeed, it's the single most important factor. Other factors mattered strongly, too:

Clear rewards and accountability have a 9.2 percent impact on market cap; a collegial and flexible workplace a 7.8 percent effect; "communications integrity" a 4 percent relationship. Curiously, the factors the firm grouped under the heading "prudent use of resources" (which included 360-degree evaluations, training, and profit sharing based on business unit success) were negatively linked with financial results. That doesn't necessarily mean they're bad; perhaps they are badly implemented. For whatever reason, says Watson-Wyatt, "companies that create a lot of shareholder value do less of these practices" than the other companies do.

The Watson-Wyatt Human Capital Index was launched in 1999; it needs to be tested over time—this is happening—and in daylight. That is, the firm should expand its survey enough to publish (not just for clients) mean or median scores by industry. If—these are made-up numbers—a retailer knew that his company's HCI was 56 vs. an industry median of 65, he could target investments in human capital to close the gap, or open one on the upside. The firm should also find a way to vet companies' self-assessment for self-delusion. Its value is that it provides plausible cause-and-effect hypotheses to help managers know which investments in human capital are most likely to increase the value of their companies.

Human Capital Effectiveness

Nick Bontis, a professor at McMaster University in Hamilton, Ontario, is one of the first people to earn a Ph.D. for studies of intellectual capital. Working with the Saratoga Institute and Accenture, Bontis has been examining what one might call human capital formation: What affects what and to what degree? Does employee satisfaction create employee motivation, or vice versa? Does knowledge sharing reduce human capital depletion, and if so, how much?

Bontis's study relied on Accenture's legwork and access and money, Saratoga's frame of reference for measuring HR effectiveness, and his own cleverness in constructing ways to test ideas. Twenty-six organizations, most big and mostly in financial services, took part. They included Allstate Insurance, ABN AMRO North America, three Blue Cross companies, the International Monetary Fund, Merrill Lynch, and Northwestern Mutual Life. Executives at each company offered up a lot of standard Saratoga Institute data in areas like human capital effectiveness (e.g., revenue, profit, and expenses divided by head count), valuation (payroll divided by revenue, expenses, and head count), investment (training numbers and costs), and depletion (rates of voluntary and involuntary separations).

Each executive—there were about three from each company—then picked three areas of concern from a list of fifteen. (The top choices were management leadership, business performance, and retention of key people; others included process execution, employee commitment, employee satisfaction, knowledge integration, etc.) Within those areas, respondents registered, on a scale of 1 to 7, how much they disagreed or agreed with several perceptual statements. One in the retention area, for example, was "our organization is more successful than the competition in retaining its most important employees"; it scored 4.83 among survey takers.

Bontis stuck all this data into a top hat and began stirring, muttering incantatory phrases taught in statistics classes at Hogwarts: "Cronbach alpha measure . . . partial least squares . . . structural equation modeling . . . Likert-type scales . . . significant Pearson correlations . . ." Some interesting doves flew out, among them:

Leadership matters enormously. You can explain nearly 70 percent of the variation in companies' ability to retain key people through just two factors, leadership and employee commitment, with the former most important. Leadership affects retention directly—people want to work for leaders they admire—and also indirectly: Good leaders bring people to share values, and people who share values share knowledge, and (as we will see) people who share knowledge tend to stay together.

Human capital makes money, but not by itself. The two biggest contributors to human capital, Bontis found, are education (good raw material) and employee satisfaction. For human capital to make a difference, though, it needs to be mediated through customer capital. That is, your smart, satisfied people have to be engaged in work that suppliers and customers see and value. Thus education + satisfaction —> human capital, which, funneled through customer capital, —> increased income per employee.

Employee sentiment is a big deal. Bontis turned up a couple of powerful causal links. First, employee satisfaction produces employee commitment, which is a highly important factor in knowledge generation (new ideas, products, and services). Second, satisfaction and commitment together produce employee motivation, a powerful determinant of knowledge sharing; and knowledge sharing, in turn, reduces human capital depletion—that is, when knowledge sharing is low or absent, people leave. Together employee commitment, knowledge generation, and human capital depletion explain 44 percent of the difference in companies' business performance.

These are nifty numbers. Bontis's charts, with arrows showing which factors influence other factors by how much, look like Rube Goldberg machines, and make your fingers itch to try the same kind of play: Pull the "employee commitment" lever and one set of things happens; pull the string on "process execution" and get another response; pull them both and—whirr! clank!—knowledge sharing.

MEASURING THE EFFICIENCY OF KNOWLEDGE WORK AND KNOWLEDGE WORKERS

The fourth step in managing intellectual capital is to increase the productivity of knowledge assets and knowledge workers. The number of ways to measure the efficiency of knowledge-management tools and projects is remarkably high, particularly given the depth of our ignorance of how to measure the productivity for many knowledge-work activities. On the next page is a list, culled from various sources, of possible ways to measure how efficiently you use human, structural, and customer capital. What should you make of this list? No one of these measures is as valuable as a collection of them can be. As I said, these are patches: It's your quilt. Remember that there are three basic families of knowledge-based strategies—knowledge-intensity strategies, knowledge-asset strategies, and knowledge-management strategies. Pick and choose a few indicators that, in your judgment, best show how you are doing. If reusing knowledge is valuable, measure how many times people download stuff from the best-practices database; if originality is what you're selling, measuring reuse will only discourage it. Do not use too many measurements: He who tracks everything knows nothing.

Assessing Knowledge-Management Infrastructure

To improve knowledge work, Peter Drucker points out, two questions must be asked: What is the job? What is the knowledge base required to

HUMAN CAPITAL	STRUCTURAL CAPITAL	CONSUMER CAPITAL[†]
Avg. years of service	Administrative expense/sales	Market share
Avg. education level	Knowledge reuse: hits on intranet sites, best practices replicated, etc.	Customer loyalty
% with advanced degrees		Avg. duration of customer relationship
Hiring cost		Customer satisfaction
IT literacy	Quality measures: errors, rework, etc.	Ratio of sales contacts to sales closed
Hours of training/ employee	Productivity gain attributable to new equipment vs. new ideas	Gross margin
Employee satisfaction		Age of receivables
Success of employee-suggestion programs		Growth of collaborative arrangements like electronic data interchange and automatic stock replenishment
Employee turnover (separations)	IT investment	
Value-added/employee	Cycle and process times	
Various measures of innovation:[*] sales from new products, gross margin from new products, R&D intensity, R&D efficiency (profits from new products/ R&D spending)	Patents cited by others	
	Inventory/sales	Customer acquisition cost
New colleague-to-colleague relation-ships spawned		

* Innovation is human capital's output, but when it produces intellectual property, it becomes structural capital. Some analysts therefore put measures of innovation in the structural capital category. If you are trying to measure *stocks* of intellectual capital—how much you have—then intellectual property is structural capital. If you are measuring the *flows*—where it comes from and how efficiently you produce it—it belongs with human capital. It's your call.

† Customer capital looks both upstream and downstream—after all, I am a customer to my suppliers. Many customer capital measures (such as loyalty) will work, or

do the job? Chief knowledge officers and other knowledge-management practitioners have staked their careers and billions of shareholder dollars on building the knowledge base (and the tools to get at it).

Here's a way to evaluate these and their cousins, which I adapted from work by Wouter deVries of Unilever. DeVries lists a dozen factors critical to the success of a knowledge-management project or initiative:

1. Knowledge vision: Do we know what knowledge we need for this project or in this line of business?
2. A clear connection to performance: Will this save money? Grow sales? And so on.
3. A knowledge-friendly structure: e.g., teams vs. functional silos.
4. A knowledge-friendly culture: Do people share or hoard?
5. Adequacy of resources.
6. Technical infrastructure: How good are our knowledge-management tools?
7. Knowledge structure: Have we established a vocabulary and taxonomy for the knowledge we are using?
8. Motivation: Are the right incentives in place?
9. Clarity of purpose and goals.
10. Is there a common terminology about knowledge management itself?
11. Top management support.
12. Power: How great is our ability to break through any organizational barriers we encounter?

---

should, left to right or right to left. (Looked at another way: If your company is acquired, the buyer will probably pay something for your book of orders—i.e., your customer relationships. Will he also pay something for your relationships with your suppliers, or pay less if they are broken? If so, then it's part of your intangible assets.) To evaluate supplier relationships, some of these measurements have to be rethought. A seller can calculate the net present value of future sales from a customer; you'd have to do a different calculation of the value of a supplier relationship. A company's most valuable suppliers are often those that supply high-value components and collaborate in product development; in those relationships, the supplier often holds intellectual and fixed assets that, in less intimate relationships, the customer would otherwise have to own. An interesting measure of supplier capital, therefore, would be the value of fixed and intangible assets that do not burden your balance sheet.

To appraise a knowledge-management effort, ask its participants, leaders, users, and other interested parties to rate it on some sort of scale (I picked 1 to 7 because I wear a size-7 hat), then average and plot the results on a scale like the one on page 317. It's a subjective measure, of course, but well-designed questions asked of enough people will give reliable results. I like it for three reasons. First, it's simple to do, read, and understand. Second, it's easy to spot problems: These guys have problems with structure and purpose. Third, comparisons among assessments of five or six knowledge-management initiatives within the same company are almost certain to turn up important information, such as frequent problems with top management support or inadequate resources.

Measuring Organizational Vitality

General Electric, with its passion for leadership development and determination to measure everything, has developed a powerful system for measuring the talent level of a workforce. Organizational Vitality, as they call it, is very GE: It's unapologetically tough, sharply differentiates between top performers and everyone else, and is designed to help a big company exploit the advantages size should, but too often does not, provide. There's nothing egalitarian about GE's HR philosophy. It finds the best and culls the rest—period. For years, GE has divided salaried employees into A, B, and C players, with pay and promotions disproportionately given to A players, and C players left back. Now, as part of GE's unending Session C leadership development process, every GE manager, at the beginning of a year, ranks the people who work for him on a bell curve. As it was originally designed, Organizational Vitality required every manager to rank his staff—even if they're all A players—into a Top 10, a Next 15, a Productive 50, a Caution 15, and a Least Effective 10. That was too tough even for GE, and now there are just three divisions, a top 20 percent, productive 70 percent, and a bottom 10 percent. By itself, the ranking forces managers to begin thinking about how to improve the level of talent of the people working for them. The bottom 10 aren't necessarily destined for the showers—there could be extenuating circumstances, or they might be superb players on an unusually good team—but their future's doubtful.

The vitality measurement gets really revelatory when numbers from many managers in a business are combined and ranked again. At this point

ASSESSING KNOWLEDGE MANAGEMENT

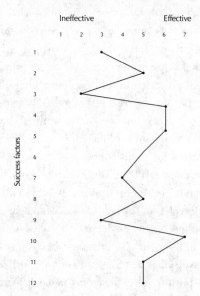

they start giving you hard data about the relative quality of your staff vis-à-vis other departments or businesses. How many of your top 10 percent make it into the top 10 percent for the division or business unit? How many of the 1998 Yankees made the All-Star team? You can measure the gap between the number you "should" provide and the number you do. Or you can measure by position: You might find that salespeople and engineers are plentiful in the ranks of the best in the whole business, but that HR and marketing people are barely represented at all—signs that a whole function needs upgrading. Organizational Vitality is an internal measure—GE's data don't say anything about how it compares to Siemens or ABB. It does provide a rigorous intramural scorecard, however, and could easily be adapted to other corporate circumstances.

CALCULATING A DOLLAR VALUE
FOR INTELLECTUAL CAPITAL

In *Intellectual Capital*, I described something called "Calculated Intangible Value," a means of putting a dollar value on intangible assets by means of a return-on-assets calculation. You do this essentially in the same way that brand equity is calculated, by trying to identify what portion of a company's profits it earns over and above what can be explained by its "generic" activities. Calculated Intangible Value (which is approved "to determine the fair market value of the intangible assets of a business" by the U.S. Internal Revenue Service in its Revenue Ruling 68-609) has a number of limitations. Because it requires calculating "excess" or "premium" returns, it doesn't work for companies without profits, and—worse—won't work if a company's profits are below the average for whatever peer group is used for comparison.

Since then, a far more powerful and versatile means of calculating the value of intellectual capital has been devised. It is the work of NYU's Baruch Lev. Lev got interested in the subject a decade ago, when he was augmenting his salary as a professor at Berkeley by consulting about valuation issues that arose in the course of litigation. Lev is a radical insider: an indefatigable, controversial critic of his profession whose own methodology, first described in print in *CFO* magazine, is a ballsy attempt to put a dollar value on intellectual capital in a way that can be tested in the market and also can be useful to managers.

Balance-sheet numbers for tangible assets are produced by adding up transactions—all the money spent on property, plant, and equipment, minus depreciation, plus the market value of financial assets. Accountants like Bob Howell (see Chapter 13) urge companies to do the same, as best they can, for knowledge assets. Lev argues that you can't get a comprehensive enough number that way, because often knowledge assets are homegrown, so no transaction takes place. It's hard to mark them to market; there may be no market in which they can be sold, except mergers and acquisitions.

Lev therefore takes an approach similar to the CIV method: He seeks to infer the value of intangible assets from the returns they produce, a "watch what we do, not what we say" method. But rather than compare a company to a peer group and get at the value of its intangibles by seeing how much it outperforms the group, he looks at the company itself, and metes out its profits among various classes of revenue-producing assets, till he arrives at a portion that must be attributed to knowledge capital.

Step one is to ascertain what Lev calls "normalized earnings" for a company. Working with Marc Bothwell, a vice president of Credit Suisse

Asset Management, he does this by taking three years of past reported earnings and adding three years of analysts' consensus forecasted earnings, as reported by I/B/E/S International, which collects these forecasts for 18,000 companies. Because the market gives extra weight to anticipated earnings, so does Lev: He gives the consensus estimates double the weight of past earnings—"a judgment call," he admits—then averages the numbers to produce a "normalized" year's earnings.

Next question: What assets produce those earnings? If a company owns a billion dollars of cash and cash equivalents, and if the average after-tax return for such assets is 4.5 percent—that's about right—then you can attribute $45 million of earnings to the financial assets. It's also possible to calculate an expected return on physical assets. The number Lev plugs in, 7 percent, is the average after-tax profit for all companies with physical assets in databases such as Compustat for the last twenty years. A company with $5 billion in property, plant, and equipment would, therefore, expect to earn $350 million from them.

That 7 percent number isn't perfect. First, companies with tangible assets also have financial and intellectual capital, so it's muddied. Second, it seems obvious that some physical assets produce more than others: One ought to expect a greater rate of return from a supercomputer than from a humble hammer, for instance. (Arguably the difference is attributable to the greater intelligence of the computer; in other words, physical assets that produce above-average returns do so because intellectual capital, in the form of capability, flexibility, and so on, has been instilled into them, making them half muscle, half mind. I grant you, however, that sometimes a computer acts so stupidly that I get half a mind to pick up a hammer to teach it a good lesson.) An individual company, or buyers and sellers of capital goods to an industry, could refine the 7 percent number by calculating ROIs for their own physical capital. For a broad, multi-industry calculation, however, Lev asserts that a 7 percent proxy is close enough.

Subtract the earnings attributable to financial and physical assets from the total earnings. Whatever's left must have come from other, unaccounted-for assets—hence Lev calls the remainder "knowledge-capital earnings" (KCE).

The final step is to infer the knowledge capital from the earnings it produces. That means taking the knowledge-capital earnings and dividing them by an expected rate of return on knowledge assets:

$$\text{Knowledge capital} = \frac{\text{Knowledge earnings}}{\text{Knowledge capital discount rate}}$$

The divisor, the discount rate, is another proxy. Lev derives it from the average after-tax profits of two industries that depend on knowledge assets almost to the exclusion of any others: software and biotechnology. Recent Value Line numbers show that Microsoft's market-to-book ratio is 8.8 to 1 (leave out the company's $20+ billion cash stash and it would be double that); Amgen's ratio is 16 to 1. Alcoa and DuPont, by contrast, have market-to-book ratios of 2.6 to 1 and 3.5 to 1. Put another way, the market-to-book ratios of both software and biotech would look a lot more like metals and chemicals if copyrights and patents were booked as capital assets.

The average after-tax return in software and biotech—10.5 percent—thus becomes Lev's proxy discount rate for intangible assets. By inserting it into the formula, it's possible to put a dollar figure on a company's knowledge capital. Imagine a company with $10 billion in earnings, of which half can be explained by its physical and financial assets. The remainder, $5 billion, comes from intellectual assets. At 10.5 percent, to produce $5 billion in profits you'd need $47.6 billion in knowledge assets. (The math is actually a bit more complicated. Returns on knowledge capital wane over time as competition tries to commoditize them. After five years, Lev assumes, the return begins to decline until, after ten years, it reaches 3 percent, which is the growth rate of the economy as a whole. The discount rate therefore is lower for older knowledge assets.)

QED—sort of. Lev's expected returns from physical assets and the expected return from intellectual assets might be said to have been plucked from the air, except for one stunning thing: The market validates Lev's formulations. Working with Feng Gu of Boston University, Lev looked at whether cash flow, traditional earnings, or knowledge earnings most correlates with total return from the stock. The results: They found just a 0.11 correlation between stock returns and cash flows, a 0.29 correlation with earnings, and a strong 0.53 correlation with knowledge earnings.

Lev's work has lots of implications. By themselves the three after-tax rates of return—4.5 percent for financial, 7 percent for physical, and 10.5 percent for intellectual assets, however imprecise—ought to tell managers something about where to invest. Lev did a study for the chemical industry that dramatically confirms the value of investing in knowledge: Looking at eighty-three companies over a span of twenty-five years, he found that their R&D investments returned 25.9 percent pretax, whereas their capital spending earned just 15 percent The latter is about 10 percent after tax, approximately the cost of capital, meaning that the money they poured into property, plant, and equipment didn't do much more than maintain the status quo. Says Lev: "The ability to leverage physical and financial assets is limited and getting more so. The ability to leverage knowledge capital is unlimited and getting less so. An airplane can fly on just one route. A reservation system is limited only by the number of people in the world."

Lev's figures have stock-market implications, which he has been investigating with Bothwell. Among other insights, they say that calculating

AVERAGE AFTER-TAX RETURNS ON FINANCIAL, PHYSICAL, AND INTELLECTUAL ASSETS

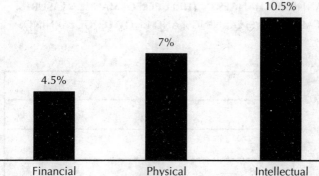

Financial	Physical	Intellectual
4.5%	7%	10.5%
10-year average return on U.S. Treasury bonds	Average ROE for all companies with physical assets and inventories, Compustat, 1995–97; also studies by Nadiri and Kim, 1996, and Poterba	Average expected return— Ibbotson & Associates' cost of equity—for the computer software and biotechnology industries

Source: Baruch Lev, New York University

knowledge capital can change your opinion about whether a stock belongs in the growth category or the value camp. Today a company is put in one category or the other mostly on the basis of its market-to-book ratio. "That is ridiculous," Lev maintains. He'd add the knowledge value to the book value, call the sum "comprehensive value," and see how that compares to the market value. In case after case, Lev and Bothwell find that stock-market returns tend to move in the direction suggested by the comprehensive value, not the book value. For example, on August 31, 2000, Costco and Target had almost identical market-to-book ratios (3.3:1 and 3.5:1), but Costco had a considerably higher market-to-comprehensive value ratio (1.52:1 vs. 0.98:1), indicating that Target was the better value. In the six months that followed, through February 28, 2001, Target returned 68 percent to shareholders, Costco 21 percent. In the same period, an investor looking just at the market-to-book ratios for Verizon and WorldCom would have thought that Verizon, with a 3.5:1 ratio, was more richly priced than WorldCom, at 1.9:1. Comprehensive value told a dif-

CORRELATION BETWEEN STOCK RETURNS AND ANNUAL CHANGES IN THREE PERFORMANCE MEASURES: CASH FLOWS, EARNINGS, AND KNOWLEDGE EARNINGS

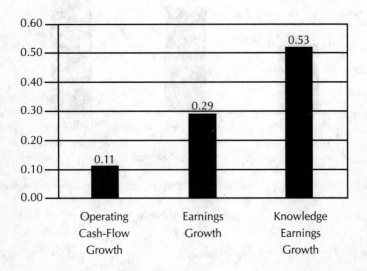

ferent story, however: Verizon's market-to-comprehensive ratio was 0.80:1, vs. 1.35:1 for WorldCom. The stock market performance? Verizon up 15 percent, WorldCom down 54 percent.

Lev's measure needs testing over time—especially given the wild valuations of dot-coms in 1999 and 2000. (In the spring of 2000 Lev himself spoke with what hindsight shows to have been undue enthusiasm about the valuation of some Internet stocks. He was by no means alone, of course.) The proxies need testing; and it would be good if the proxy for knowledge capital returns were expanded to include returns for pure-knowledge service companies, such as advertising agencies or publicly traded professional firms. In addition, Lev hasn't yet figured out how to apply his method of the results of banks and insurance companies; the financial assets they manage act like lead aprons, preventing him from X-raying their operations. Also, knowledge capital, as Lev calculates it, isn't comparable to book value, as GAAP calculates it. The former is oranges inferred from revenues; the latter is tangerines, derived from transactions—that is, actual spending on plant and equipment. Their sum—Lev's "comprehensive value"—is a financial tangelo whose validity needs to be tested. It would also be fascinating to test historical-cost transaction data for tangibles and intangibles (as Howell, for example, would book them) against Lev's data.

Yeats said that the intellect is forced to choose perfection of the life or of the work. Without in any way claiming perfection of the work, I've chosen a sensible limitation on its length, and therefore have left out a great many worthwhile approaches to valuing intellectual capital. In particular, I regret having omitted Karl-Erik Sveiby's intangible-assets monitor, an excellent scorecard described on his Web site (http://www.sveiby.com.au/) and employed in the annual report of Celemi (http://www.celemi.se); various useful techniques (especially for measuring intellectual property) in Patrick Sullivan's *Profiting from Intellectual Capital: Extracting Value from Innovation*; Paul Strassmann's methods for calculating knowledge capital (http://www.strassmann.com); and the Skandia navigator developed by Leif Edvinsson (http://www.skandia.com). All of these are well worth examining.

The work of measuring intellectual capital will never be perfected.

Nothing human ever is, and business is nothing if not human. Nor must it be perfected. Constant experimentation, continuous improvement, and an unending passion to get it right are what we can hope for—and what we need. Companies need to be able to track, reliably, their progress in managing the most important resources they have, and to demonstrate their progress to the investors—the employees, the shareholders, and the customers—who entrusted those resources to them.

. . . AND YET SO FAR

What is the city but the people?

WILLIAM SHAKESPEARE

In the spring of 2001, Deutsche Bank took out a big ad in the *Wall Street Journal*. Its headline: "Ideas Are Capital. The Rest Is Just Money." The same year, J. P. Morgan Chase, created when J. Pierpont Morgan's famous old bank was acquired by Chase, the descendant of a bank begun by Aaron Burr, presented its debut annual report. In bold type, it proclaimed: "The power of intellectual capital is the ability to breed ideas that ignite value." At 23 Wall Street stands a building that was once J. P. Morgan's headquarters. In it—it's a bank building, after all—is a vault. No money is stored there. It's a breakout room for the bank's training center. There—in the knowledge and skills of its people, as manifested in intellectual capital—is where the real wealth of J. P. Morgan Chase, or any company, can be found.

We've come a long way, baby. As I said in the Foreword, my 1991 story, "Brainpower" was, I'm 99 percent sure, the first time the business press wrote about intellectual capital. It's hard for me to recall the blank looks that greeted the phrase a decade ago, the puzzled "You mean like patents?" queries, or the flippant "Smart's nice, but I like money" superciliousnesses.

That story gave a push to something that has become big. Anniversaries are a good excuse for taking stock. In ten years, what's been won? Laurence Prusak, director of the Knowledge Management Institute at IBM, raised that question; what follows is my take on it, which owes something to his. (All of us concerned with intellectual capital owe Larry.) Four accomplishments stand out. The biggest is the simple fact that any board of directors today will listen if you bring up the subject. The idea that know-how is a competitive advantage wasn't exactly shocking back in those Precambrian times. My father, who was general counsel for Hartmarx, the clothing company, says that the hardest part of outsourcing manufacturing wasn't the contract or the royalty arrangements, but figuring out what know-how needed to be transferred, how best to do it, and which intellectual assets should and should not be shared.

For the most part, however, companies then didn't think about knowledge as a resource or about what their knowledge assets were. You heard "core business" but not "core competence," for example. The latter phrase entered the business lexicon about the same time "intellectual capital" did, in a 1990 article by Gary Hamel and C. K. Prahalad. Criticism of accounting—that it looked backward, that it ignored important nonfinancial numbers and information—didn't translate into interest in intangible assets. Today the Balanced Scorecard—which provides a method for selecting and measuring these performance indicators—seems like a big "duh, of course"; but Robert Kaplan and David Norton proposed it only in 1992. Today the discussion of knowledge as a resource has become extraordinarily rich. Managers as well as business thinkers are aware of what knowledge resources are overabundant (i.e., information overload) and what is scarce (notably attention, about which Thomas H. Davenport has written).

The first time I met Jack Welch, just after that 1991 story, he said excitedly, "Intellectual capital is what it's all about. Releasing the ideas of your people is what we're trying to do, what we've got to do if we're going to win." That puffed me up, though the air came out of my vanity when I learned that Welch is *always* excited. But he meant it. In the past year or so, GE has added a new item to its values: "Prize global intellectual capital and the people that provide it . . . build diverse teams to maximize it."

With fame come fads, however. Before intellectual capital became a GE value, it made it to the *Dilbert* Web site; it's used in Dilbert's random mission statement generator (http://www.dilbert.com/comics/dilbert/career/bin/ms2.cgi), which just offered me this uplifting aim: "Our mission is to continue to assertively customize cost-effective content as well as to continually revolutionize market-driven intellectual capital." You betcha!

Surviving fad-dom is not a trivial accomplishment. I bet that so far more money has been wasted than made in knowledge management. At one point Forrester Research estimated that six out of seven knowledge-management projects were undertaken with no promised return on investment, and I'm sure they delivered handsomely on that commitment. A few companies—Coca-Cola, Morgan Stanley—have appointed chief knowledge officers and then let them go.

Eppur si muove, "and yet it moves," Galileo purportedly said on his way from the Inquisition's chambers: My files bulge with stories, many of which I have told in the pages of this book, about organizations that have improved performance by managing knowledge more effectively. When the effort goes wrong, it's usually because it's done for faddish reasons— "Get us some of that, Culligan!"—without thought for the ends to which it might be the means. More and more I see companies looking first to discover their knowledge business, their knowledge value proposition—what they know that they can sell, and how to sell it profitably—and then figuring out how to manage knowledge. That approach—the approach I've argued for in this book—works.

Third, the concept of a "community of practice" has assumed what looks like a permanent, high place in management thinking. Companies' informal organizations became a matter of practical urgency as well as academic interest after 1987, when Etienne Wenger and Jean Lave identified these special groups. Communities of practice are groups that emerge around a discipline or problem—a work-related subject like graphic design or the behavior of derivative financial instruments. They have no agenda; they are defined by the subject that engages them, not by project, rank, department, or even corporate affiliation. They are where learning and innovation occur—the shop floor of human capital.

Learning is social, we have learned. Managers who focus on communities and teams can improve performance and grow social capital (about which Prusak and Don Cohen write in their book, *In Good Company*). The mere fact that management cares about learning at all is an accomplishment. My wife once got chewed out by her boss for reading the newspaper "on company time," though she worked in a publishing business where news, reviews, and features were a prime source of information. As for the social nature of learning: Bosses used to try to break up the gang by the water cooler and send everybody back to work. Now they support them with Web sites and off-sites (and foosball tables, which is going too far).

Fourth, most companies seem to have changed from a smug, knowledge-hoarding mentality to one of knowledge sharing. Benchmarking got started in the 1980s under the aegis of the quality movement and was spurred by the Malcolm Baldrige awards; every company in America, it seemed, trekked to Freeport, Maine, to see how L. L. Bean handled shipping. GE, a bellwether in this too, started systematically sharing best practices with other companies in 1988. The International Benchmarking Clearinghouse of the American Productivity and Quality Center in Houston was established in 1991 and led the group into knowledge management. Best-practices sharing, along with intellectual-capital theory and two key collaborative information technologies, Lotus Notes and HTML (the software protocol behind the Web), made knowledge management happen.

Departments or companies that once scorned anything "not invented here" now boast of good ideas "probably found elsewhere" in the company or around the world. Information hoarding, which began with Adam's cover-up, will persist as long as ambition, vainglory, and politics do—that is, till the last of his descendants turns up his toes. But the ethos of sharing, like the realization that learning is social, seems stronger than ever.

That's four; there's more. It's no small deal that there's a mostly agreed-upon vocabulary for describing intellectual capital. Without terms like *human, structural,* and *customer capital, tacit* and *explicit knowledge,* it would be impossible to create a management discipline. Learning about storytelling as a management tool—one narrative is worth a thousand PowerPoint slides—is another big win for a decade's work.

But there is also a great deal more to learn. The body of knowledge about intellectual capital is a half-grown, funny-looking thing. What knowledge-management projects are surefire moneymakers? How reliably can intellectual capital be measured? Why is knowledge leaky and flowing in some environments, sticky and parochial in others? What are the best links between training and improved performance? What technologies are most cost-effective? The list is as endless as art is long.

A WORD ABOUT THE WORLD

Sometimes I hear that intellectual capital is relevant only in advanced economies. That notion is as wrong as the idea that it matters only in high tech—indeed, it's dangerously wrong. The millennial St. Vitus's dance of world markets—starting with the Asian financial crisis of 1997 and including the dot-com meltdown three years later—was in fact a manifestation of the importance of the Knowledge Economy.

The Asian crisis underscored the danger of what I call "the commodity trap." There are any number of ways to hang a tale on it. We might begin ours on a hot night in the Amazon jungle. In 1839 Charles Goodyear discovered how to vulcanize rubber, a process that turned it from a curiosity into a useful material. In the years that followed, thanks especially to cars, great fortunes were made in rubber—and great calamities caused by it, especially in Africa, where Europeans hideously mistreated inhabitants of the Congo basin in their pursuit of rubber. Ground zero of the rubber boom, though, was the Brazilian city of Manaus, smack in the middle of the Amazon rain forest, halfway between the great river's source and its mouth. A century ago, Manaus stank of money. It was the second city in Latin America to be electrified, and had an electric tramway before Boston did. The city's famous opera house, its marble and bronzes and chandeliers imported from Europe, its auditorium ringed with busts of great European composers and playwrights, was the venue for performances to delight the rubber barons and their wives, whose mansions stud the city and its surrounding jungle, like cloves in ham fat. The boom went bust. In the 1870s an Englishman named Henry Wyckham eluded Brazilian inspectors and smuggled rubber-tree seeds out of the country. These seeds—germ plasm, filled with information—were planted at Kew Gardens outside London. From there, seeds were sent to tropical British colonies in Malaya and Ceylon, and rubber plantations created. When they became productive, in the years just before the First World War, the price of rubber plunged and Manaus's prosperity with it.

You'll hear the story time and again if you visit Manaus, and always with the wrong moral. One version emphasizes the perfidy of Albion and foreign capital generally. Another argues that unmanaged, unsustainable harvesting from the rain forest is doomed to failure. The version I heard from a jungle guide says that Big Money vowed never again to let the people of the forest prosper from the wealth it contains. After the rubber boom ended, he said, "they" hatched a long conspiracy to block the development and exploitation of a periodic tableful of gold, niobium, and on and on in the Amazon basin. "They" have, most recently, concocted environmental scare stories to keep the Amazon off-limits to development, because, if the wealth of the Amazon found its way to market, prices would plunge and banks would fail. I didn't ask, but "they" no doubt are history's usual cabal—Jews, Freemasons, bankers, and corrupt politicians—up to their usual sinister conspiracies.

A circle of light in a dark forest is a perfect place for far-fetched paranoia, surrounded as one is by inexplicable sounds, crocodiles with glowing eyes, hordes of insects, and Lord knows what else. (By the same token, a house in a first-world suburb is a perfect setting from which to oversimplify the struggles of people living in developing countries.) It almost seems possible that city slickers in air-conditioned rooms could maintain, for decades, a global plot to keep valuable resources off the market, even though the interests of most of the conspirators would be better served by developing them.

But the really dangerous fantasy, because it has condemned hundreds of millions to poverty, is mundane: the all-too-common dream that wealth can be found in material goods.

Money doesn't grow on trees, and never did, not even in the rubber boom. The money made by Dunlop and Michelin and Goodyear dwarfs what the world's rubber growers made. Gold, black gold, black earth, doesn't matter: Every commodity is a mug's game, because over time all commodities decline in price. They always have; they always will. To build your economic house on commodities is to build it on an inexorably sinking foundation. The world contains the same number of atoms as it did when it began, give or take a few billion delivered by meteorite. In atomic terms, its value is unchanging. Indeed, entropy makes it decline.

People keep getting this wrong, too. They multiply Malthusian logic by the law of diminishing returns. Then, like economists, they leave out knowledge and innovation. They come to the conclusion that led Paul Ehrlich, author of *The Population Bomb*, to make his celebrated losing wager with the late Julian Simon, a professor of business at the University of Maryland. Simon bet that a basket of five metals chosen by Ehrlich— he picked copper, chrome, nickel, tin, and tungsten—would be cheaper in 1990 than in 1980. To Simon, it was the surest thing since Citation. He wrote later: "The costs of raw materials have fallen sharply over the period of recorded history, no matter which reasonable measure of cost one chooses to use." The International Monetary Fund calculates that real commodity prices have declined on average 0.6 percent a year since the turn of the century.

Yet nations rich in natural resources still fall into the commodity trap, the belief that their mines are the key to their prosperity, rather than their minds. Little do they understand that a wealth of natural resources will be exploited by people with a wealth of knowledge; that value of natural resources is *extracted from* a place, not *created in* a place. Not that gold in the ground is worthless: All else being equal, I'd rather have it than not— but the "all else" is what matters. Notice that Asia's most successful postwar economies, and the ones that hung toughest in the financial crisis of 1997, were Taiwan, Hong Kong, and Singapore—which boast nary a smidgen of natural "wealth." By contrast, Russia and Indonesia are rolling in resources, and in the gutter.

The same is true wherever you look. "Forty years ago," writes economist Joseph Stiglitz in the introduction of the World Bank's 1998 Development Report, "Ghana and the Republic of Korea had virtually the same income per capita. By the early 1990s, Korea's income per capita was six times higher than Ghana's. Some reckon that half the difference is due to Korea's greater success in acquiring and using knowledge." In the Middle East, oil has made a few sheikhs and princes fabulously wealthy. But the region's old apothegm—"My grandfather rode a camel; my father drove a pickup truck; I ride in a Mercedes; my son will ride a camel"—will prove true, in the absence of investments in intellectual capital. Today a development called Internet City in Dubai, a little princedom on the Persian Gulf, has attracted regional headquarters for Oracle, Microsoft, IBM, and 200 other technology firms, drawn by low taxes, good governance, and an understanding of the importance of knowledge assets. *The New York*

Times's Thomas L. Friedman explained—and note the verb he chose: "Many of the smaller Arab states were not cursed with large amounts of oil, so they have had to live more by their wits and by learning to trade with the rest of the world. 'We diversified out of oil early, because we had to,' said Bahrain's innovative Crown Prince Salman. 'We really concentrated on developing our human capital.'"

BLOWING BUBBLES

In the spring of 2000, three out of four senior executives believed "the Internet will completely transform every aspect of business in the fore-seeable future." More than half said it was time to put away "enduring wisdom" about how companies should operate. A scant plurality—38 percent to 32 percent—felt that established companies would prevail over dot-newcomers, with the rest uncertain. Only a minority, three out of ten, felt that the Net is "not really that different."

Those numbers come from a survey designed by Harvard Business School professor Rosabeth Moss Kanter. Its 785 replies, from a self-selected group skewed in favor of technologically literate companies, were gathered between mid-January and mid-May 2000. By happy chance, that period perfectly brackets the Nasdaq composite index's high, 5048.62, reached March 10, 2000. Thus Kanter's survey represents a high-water mark of sorts. "*Completely* transform *every* aspect of business"—it seems as long ago and far away as "one pill makes you larger, one pill makes you small . . ."

Eighteen months and 3000 points on the Nasdaq later, as I write these words, we're deep in the second phase of Schumpeterian economics—the "destruction" that comes after "creative." Tim DeMello, former CEO of Streamline.com, a Boston company that, like Webvan, sold groceries and other household goods over the Net and turned up its toes late in 2000, said: "Business went through a period of accelerated experimentation—a lot of money spent to learn a lot." As one who owns shares in Internet Capital Group, I know it was expensive. But was it an education?

I was brooding on this when we had a problem with the company firewall. I'd gotten to work early with tons to do. I fired up my e-mail, and . . . Nothing. Tried the alternative, getting at the e-mail via the Web . . .

Nada. Tried another e-mail account . . . Zilch. I said, "phooey," or words to that effect. It was 8:15. The techies wouldn't be in the office for three-quarters of an hour, nor compos mentis for at least an hour after that. How, I tried to remember, did we put out a magazine six years ago? It was noon before anyone could get to the Net. Colleagues' faces wore the expression you see in airport lounges after a storm while people wait for service to get back to normal, whatever that is these days.

When I finally got my e-mail, it included a newsletter from Financial Institutions Consulting, a New York outfit that works with financial services companies. The subject was e-commerce. "Are you an emperor or a unabomber?" it asked. Emperors—the famous naked ones—overeagerly overinvested in online banking. Now, embarrassed, they had become afraid to venture outside again. Unabombers, proud of having been neutral during the Internet revolution, are smug ignoramuses with quill pens. Ironically, while the unabombers are unaware of their ignorance, the emperors are unaware of their knowledge.

The fact is, the Net is changing banking in all kinds of ways—just not the ways its more foolhardy proponents claimed. It won't do away with branches, for example, any more than ATMs did. Studies by Gigi Wang and Ian Rubin of the research firm IDC show that since 1967 the number of bank branches in the United States has doubled (to about 75,000) even as the number of banks has declined due to consolidation and even as ATMs, call centers, and the Internet have provided other distribution channels.

However, Internet banking is not just *It's a Wonderful Life* with a modem. Online customers behave differently. Those who sign up for electronic bill paying, for instance, become fabulous assets. At Bank of America, which has more online customers than any other U.S. bank, "bill-pay customers" change banks 60 to 70 percent less often, keep checking account balances 20 to 30 percent higher, and park 30 to 40 percent more total assets with the bank, compared to others in similar demographic groups. According to John Rosenfeld, head of consumer e-commerce for the bank: "The real value in a bill-pay customer isn't cost savings, it's the stickiness of the relationship."

What's the point? It's wrong to say that the Net changes everything. But it's equally wrong to say that its changes are merely incremental and incidental. What the Net changes, it changes to the bone. We journalists don't work the way we did a decade ago. Those bankers have a whole new kind of opportunity. And every manager and leader has a second chance. We've been to an expensive school; whether we got a valuable education is up to us. Halsey Minor, CEO of 12 Entrepreneuring, remembers how terrified old-line CEOs were a couple of years ago, when "to amazon" was a verb. He imagined each one of them kneeling at his bedside to pray, "Dear Lord, give me another chance. I promise I won't screw up the Internet this time. . . ." Now, he says, it's the humbled dot-com CEO on his knees, saying, "Dear Lord, give me another chance. I promise I won't screw it up this time. . . ."

The Nasdaq bubble did terrible harm to the knowledge-business business, because people believed that the two are the same. When the bubble burst, you heard a chorus of second-guesses: There never was a new economy, it's all the same. In a controversial article, Rosabeth Moss Kanter's Harvard colleague Michael Porter set forth the proposition that the Information Age is business as usual, that the Net is no big deal, and that competitive advantage is the same as it always was: "The 'new economy' appears less like a new economy than like an old economy that has access to a new technology . . . the fundamentals of competition remain unchanged."

In a word, no. In three words, yes and no.

The new economy was never about the market's irrational exuberance, though some of its boosters and bashers linked the two. Nor is it about the Web and high tech—though, again, the Internet bubble clothed itself in new-economy rhetoric. The dot-com companies and stocks were the froth on the wave of change; that foam has been blown away—but the change is here. Just as consulting firms, addicted to the revenues from reengineering and enterprise-resource-planning software, seized on knowledge management as the next thing to offer their customers and keep their staffs of programmers and systems integrators busy, so Wall Street analysts and venture capitalists, seeing tremendous opportunity, heralded dot-com stocks as a new breed of company, immune from gravity, that would wipe the economic floor with the old.

This bubble burst. All bubbles do. "Dinosaur" old-economy companies turned out to possess assets—mostly intellectual assets, such as brands and relationships—that allowed them to adapt and to bring the weight of their balance sheets and income statements to bear on their attackers.

They, like all companies, compete for strategic advantage—Porter's familiar ground. But more and more often that advantage is found in knowledge assets—new weapons—and exploited using new tactics. As I showed in Chapter 3, electronic commerce is here to stay; speed, as we saw in Chapter 5, is here to stay; the increased power of customers, discussed in Chapter 9, is here to stay; and the redrawing of corporate boundaries along lines defined by knowledge assets, which we analyzed in Chapter 2, is here to stay. Above all, the value of knowledge in creating and delivering competitive advantage is here to stay. Wall Street and venture capitalists made money in the dot-com boom the way convenience stores make money in the hours before a hurricane, playing on hurry and hysteria. But the storm is real, and its winds have begun to reshape the business landscape.

In the twenty-first century, companies will need connectivity—emotional and intellectual connections as well as electronic. They will need speed—not recklessness, but the ability to decide quickly, deploy resources quickly, advance and retreat quickly. They will need to be able to act as fast as they think—"business at the speed of thought," as Bill Gates put it. (But not faster, please.) They will need a richer understanding of their customers than they can even imagine now, so that they scarcely know where they leave off and their customer begins. They will, overlying and underlying all, need to understand what they are capable of. They will need to know their intellectual assets (what valuable things they know) and their intellectual aptitude (what valuable things they can come to know).

Knowledge companies will, in short, have to learn to think of themselves almost in biological terms, rather than in mechanical ones. For nearly two centuries we have conceived of work in industrial terms, in factory imagery. William Blake wrote of "dark Satanic mills"; Charles Dickens, in *Hard Times* and other novels, described smoke-fouled land- and cityscapes and made us hear the loud clank of machinery; in our century, painter Fernand Léger, photographer Margaret Bourke-White, and filmmaker Charlie Chaplin gave us images of man as machine, machine as man.

It's no wonder that we thought of organizations, too, as mechanical things, with pistons and valves, parts that wore out or broke down; no wonder we thought that corporations should be "restructured" or "rationalized" or "streamlined" or "reengineered"; no wonder we thought that duplication was the enemy of efficiency, redundancy the antonym of productivity.

It's time we learned anew. Organizations are complex human systems. They can adapt, grow, and improve the way human beings do—without having to be taken apart, their parts spread out over the garage floor by a consulting mechanic. Organizations are not so much collections of parts as they are connections of brain cells, nerves, and sinews. To discover this is to discover the power of knowledge set free and of technology made human. It is to discover that it's possible to improve not only a company's performance today, but its responsiveness, its repertoire of skills, and its capacity to deal with the future.

NOTES

FOREWORD

p. ix "We exported God knows how": Interview with Joseph M. Juran, November 3, 1998.

p. xii "An idea is not necessarily a biotech idea": John F. Welch, interview at the Fortune 500 Forum, Charleston, S.C., October 1991.

p. xiv "The intellectual capital": Morris Kronfeld and Arthur Rock, "Some Considerations of the Infinite," *The Analysts Journal,* November 1958, p. 6.

p. xv Knowledge assets, they proposed: Karl Erik Sveiby and Tom Lloyd, *Managing Knowhow: Add Value . . . By Valuing Creativity* (London: Bloomsbury, 1987).

p. xv In Japan, meanwhile: See Ikujiro Nonaka and Hirotaka Takeuchi, "The Knowledge-Creating Company," *Harvard Business Review,* November–December 1991. Nonaka and Takeuchi later expanded their ideas into the superb book *The Knowledge-Creating Company* (Oxford University Press, 1994).

p. xv In 1991 I wrote: Thomas A. Stewart, "Brainpower: How Intellectual Capital Is Becoming America's Most Important Asset," *Fortune,* June 3, 1991, pp. 44ff.

CHAPTER 1
THE PILLARS OF THE KNOWLEDGE ECONOMY

p. 4 The oldest known key: History of keys from *The New Encyclopaedia Britannica,* vol. 7, Micropaedia, pp. 433–434.

p. 6 "is about shifting": David Kiley, "Ford Plans Challenge to GM OnStar," *USA Today,* August 1, 2000, p. 3B, and Tim Burt, "Alliances in the Scramble for Smarter Cars," *Financial Times,* 3 Oct 2000, p. 13.

p. 7 Today's jetliner: Andrew Pollack, "Chips Are Hidden in Washing Machines, Microwaves and Even Reservoirs," *The New York Times,* January 4, 1999, p. C17.

p. 7 Airlines' spending: Andy Pasztor, "Virgin to Offer Web Access on All Flights," *The Wall Street Journal,* March 26, 2001, p. B6.

p. 7 Inventories held by manufacturers: Secretariat on Electronic Commerce, U.S. Department of Commerce, *Digital Economy 2000* (Washington, U.S. Department of Commerce, 2000; http://www.ecommerce.gov), p. 64. A more detailed discussion about how information substitutes for inventory can be found in my previous book, *Intellectual Capital: The New Wealth of Organizations* (New York: Doubleday, 1997), pp. 24–29.

p. 7 Manufacturing companies are creating: John Griffiths, "Ford's 'Virtual' Assembly Lines to Save $200m," *Financial Times,* April 14, 1997, p. 1.

p. 8 We produce an extraordinary: Peter Lyman, Hal R. Varian, et al., *How Much Information* (Berkeley, California: School of Information Management and Systems, 2000; http://www.sims.berkeley.edu/how-much-info).

p. 8 In 1999, knowledge: Bernard Wysocki, Jr., "In U.S. Trade Arsenal, Brains Outgun Brawn," *The Wall Street Journal,* April 10, 2000, p. A1. Canadian exports: Brenda E. Blum and Cindy M. Gordon, "Use of Emergent Theory to Explore Perspectives on Knowledge Management," unpublished paper, 1997 citing B. Eiley, "Who's Doing What in KBI Lending?" *Canadian Banker,* pp. 19–20.

p. 8 "The most important": Robert J. Shapiro, introduction to U.S. Department of Commerce, *Digital Economy 2000* (Washington, D.C.: U.S. Department of Commerce, June 2000; http://www.ecommerce.gov), p. xiv.

p. 8 Product service revenues: GE company reports.

p. 8 Corporate capital spending: U.S. Census Bureau, *Annual Capital Expenditures,* cited in U.S. Census Bureau, *Statistical Abstract of the United States* (Washington, D.C.: U.S. Department of Commerce, 1998), table 900, p. 568.

p. 9 Nearly half of that: Secretariat on Electronic Commerce, U.S. Department of Commerce, *Digital Economy 2000* (Washington, U.S. Department of Commerce, 2000; http://www.ecommerce.gov), p. 28.

p. 9 Add $144 billion: National Science Foundation, cited in U.S. Census Bureau, *Statistical Abstract of the United States: 1999* (Washington, D.C.: U.S. Department of Commerce, 1999), table 988, p. 617. Investment in training: Julia Kirby, ed., *Perspectives on Business Innovation* (Cambridge, Mass.: Ernst & Young Center for Business Innovation, n.d.), p. 20.

p. 9 Even for old economy stalwarts: Lucent, Pfizer, Genentech, and Procter and Gamble data: company reports.

p. 9 The cost to U.S. corporations: Dan T. Swartwood and Richard J. Heffernan, *Trends in Intellectual Property Loss, Special Report* (Alexandria, VA: American Society for Industrial Security International, 1998), p. 7.

p. 10 Every job: Kent Greenes, presentation to Knowledge Management &

Organisational Learning Conference, Linkage International, London, April 19–22, 1999. College-educated craft workers: Bureau of Labor Statistics, as reported in Robert D. Hershey Jr., "The Rise of the Working Class: Blue-Collar Jobs Gain, but the Work Changes in Tone," *The New York Times,* September 3, 1997, p. D1.

p. 10 "The profession has gone . . . :" Edwin McDowell, "Lasers and Laptops Join Hard Hats at Construction Sites," *The New York Times,* November 19, 2000, section 11, pp. 1, 8.

p. 10 A business's highest-cost processes: Thomas H. Davenport, presentation to IHRIM, Nashville, TN, May 20, 1998.

p. 10 So rapidly has the demand: Elizabeth G. Chambers, Mark Foulon, et al., "The War for Talent," *The McKinsey Quarterly* 1998, number 3, pp. 44–57.

p. 10 The squeeze is worst: Thomas A. Stewart, "In Search of Elusive Tech Workers," *Fortune,* February 16, 1998, vol. 137, no. 3, p. 171.

p. 10 To get a sense: Nuala Beck and Joseph Connolly, "CMA's Guide to the New Economy," *CMA Magazine,* vol. 70, no. 1, pp. 11ff. High-tech Texans: Allen R. Myerson, "A New Breed of Wildcatter for the 90's," *The New York Times,* November 30, 1997, section 3, p. 1.

p. 11 "By 2006": David Henry, Patricia Buckley, et al., *The Emerging Digital Economy II* (Washington, D.C.: Secretariat on Electronic Commerce, U.S. Department of Commerce, 1999; http://www.ecommerce.gov), p. 6.

p. 12 "This means that . . .": Lowell L. Bryan, "Stocks Overvalued? Not in the New Economy," *The Wall Street Journal,* November 3, 1997, p. A22.

p. 12 The "factory" where Yahoo!: Geoffrey Colvin, "How to Be a Great E-CEO," *Fortune,* May 24, 1999, vol. 139, no. 10, pp. 104ff.

p. 14 "The energy": Diana B. Henriques, "Sewing a Label on a Decade," *The New York Times,* January 4, 2000, p. C3.

p. 14 But it can be done: Kevin Maney, "Citicorp's Billion-Customer Plan Relies on High Tech," *USA Today,* April 16, 1998, p. 4B.

p. 14 In 1997, Sara Lee Corp.: James P. Iller, "Sara Lee Plans 'Fundamental Reshaping,'" *The Wall Street Journal,* September 16, 1997, p. A3.

p. 15 The knowledge-intensive: Company reports and Allen R. Myerson, "A New Breed of Wildcatter for the 90's," *The New York Times,* November 30, 1997, section 3, p. 10.

p. 16 The idea, says Welch: Interviews conducted by Thomas A. Stewart, "See Jack Run. See Jack Run Europe," *Fortune,* September 27, 1999, vol. 140, no. 6, pp. 124ff, and company reports.

p. 16 Cemex: See Adrian J. Slywotsky and David J. Morrison with Karl Weber, *How Digital Is Your Business?* (New York: Crown Business, 2000), pp. 80–103.

p. 17 For every $1: See Erik Brynjolfsson and Shinkju Yang, "The Intangible Costs and Benefits of Computer Investments: Evidence from the Financial Markets," MIT Sloan School of Management, December 1999 revised draft; related papers by Brynjolfsson and coauthors Yang, Timothy F. Breshahan, and Lorin Hitt can be found at http://css.mit.edu/erik.

p. 17 More than half: U.S. Department of Commerce, *Digital Economy 2000* (Washington, D.C., June 2000; http://www.ecommerce.gov), pp. vi and 1, 35–36.

p. 18 Finally: Robert Shapiro et al., *Digital Economy 2000* (Washington, D.C.: Secretariat on Electronic Commerce, U.S. Department of Commerce, 2000; http://www.ecommerce.gov), p. xiv.

p. 18 Other sources of competitive advantage: For a discussion of the issues, see Thomas A. Stewart, "Welcome to the Revolution," *Fortune*, December 13, 1993, pp. 66ff.

p. 18 "Work on the productivity": Peter F. Drucker, *Management Challenges for the 21st Century* (New York: Harper Business, 1999), pp. 136, 142.

p. 19 "The basic problem": Neil Munro, "Byte-Size Taxes," *National Journal*, November 13, 1999.

CHAPTER 2
WHAT COMPANIES DO AND WHY THEY EXIST

p. 22 Not surprisingly: Kenneth Warren, *The American Steel Industry 1850–1970: A Geographical Interpretation* (Oxford: Clarendon Press, 1973), esp. chapters 1–3, 6.

p. 22 All of this . . . "an underlying assumption . . .": Margaret M. Blair, "Firm-Specific Human Capital and Theories of the Firm," in Margaret M. Blair and Mark J. Roe, eds., *Employees and Corporate Governance* (Washington, D.C.: Brookings Institution, 1999), pp. 58–59.

pp. 22–23 "You only exist": Interview with Gerhard Schulmeyer, March 1998.

p. 23 At the dawn of the twentieth: See, *inter alia*, Jean Strouse's biography, *Morgan: American Financier* (New York: Random House, 1999), especially chapters 13 and 16.

p. 24 For the last two decades: Florian Budde, Brian R. Elliott, et al., "The Chemistry of Knowledge," *McKinsey Quarterly* 2000, number 4, pp. 99–107. For a discussion of Dow's Intellectual Asset Management Process, see Thomas A. Stewart, *Intellectual Capital: The New Wealth of Organizations* (New York: Doubleday, 1997), pp. 62–63.

p. 24 Dow Chemical managed to cut: Thomas A. Stewart, "Marakon Runners," *Fortune,* September 28, 1998, vol. 138, no. 6, pp. 153ff.

p. 24 "Customers' power": Quoted in Thomas A. Stewart, "Customer Learning Is a Two-Way Street," *Fortune*, May 10, 1999, vol. 139, no. 9, p. 158.

p. 24 Forward-thinking companies: See DuPont's 1999 annual report; for

Dow, see Stewart, *Intellectual Capital*, pp. 62–63; for Buckman, see, *inter alia*, Harvard Business School case N9-899-175, by William Fulmer, September 17, 1999 (http://www.knowledgenurture.com/web/bulabsty.nsf/pages/buckman+story? opendocument).

p. 25 The best companies in every industry: "This is all about moving intellectual capital—taking ideas and moving them around faster and faster and faster," he told me on June 4, 1999. See also Thomas A. Stewart, "See Jack. See Jack Run Europe," *Fortune*, September 27, 1999, vol. 140, no. 6, p. 124.

p. 25 In the opinion: Jeanne Terrile, "A New GE," Merrill Lynch Global Research Highlights, December 15, 1998, pp. 10–11.

p. 25 The other sources of competitive advantage: David J. Teece, *Managing Intellectual Capital: Organizational, Strategic, and Policy Dimensions* (New York: Oxford University Press, 2000), pp. 4–6, 29–30.

p. 26 "The essence of the firm . . .": Teece, op. cit., p. 29.

p. 26 "The necessity of adding . . .": Riel Miller: quoted in Don Tapscott, "Strategy in the New Economy," *Strategy & Leadership*, November/December 1997, p. 10.

p. 26 Indeed, given the primacy of knowledge: Jonathan Dan and Jim Wendler, "The New Economics of Organization," *McKinsey Quarterly*, 1998, no.1, p. 15; also see AnnaLee Saxenian, *Regional Advantage: Culture and Competition in Silicon Valley and Route 128* (Cambridge, MA: Harvard University Press, 1994).

p. 26 One way to see: A good discussion of these is in Peter Cappelli, *The New Deal at Work: Managing the Market-Driven Workforce* (Boston: Harvard Business School Press, 1999), pp. 75–112. For a discussion of the effects of lower transaction costs on organizational size, see Stewart, *Intellectual Capital*, pp. 192–95, and Erik Brynjolfsson, *Information Technology and the Re-Organization of Work: Theory and Evidence*, CCS TR 3144, Sloan School WP #3574-94 (Cambridge: Massachusetts Institute of Technology, Sloan School of Management, May 1993), pp. 82–100.

p. 26 Utilities: U.S. Census Bureau, *Statistical Abstract of the United States* (Washington, D.C.: U.S. Department of Commerce, 1998), p. 428.

p. 27 "One consequence . . .": Peter Cappelli, *The New Deal at Work: Managing the Market-Driven Workforce* (Boston: Harvard Business School Press, 1999), p. 95.

p. 27 The share of the American workforce: David Leonhardt, "Entrepreneurs' 'Golden Age' Is Fading in Economic Boom," *The New York Times*, December 1, 2000, p. A1. Antihype to the contrary notwithstanding, it's unquestionably true that the ties that bind people to companies are looser: More people temp (but show up not on the lists of the self-employed but on payrolls of companies like Manpower and Spherion), we change jobs more often, new-business formation is at record highs, and pensions and insurance are more portable.

p. 27 What, then, ties us: For more on these forces, see Thomas A. Stewart,

"Gray Flannel Suit? Moi?" *Fortune*, March 16, 1998, vol. 137, no. 5, pp. 76ff. Quotes from Snow, Waterman, Amabile, Germain, Witte, Stevenson, Hall, and Dudley are from interviews conducted for this article.

p. 28 A study conducted: Dave Stum, Ray Seghers, et al., *Employee Loyalty in America* (Ann Arbor, MI: Aon Consulting, 1997), p. 39.

p. 29 In the knowledge economy: See Stewart, *Intellectual Capital*, pp. 191–92.

p. 31 "When I designed . . .": Bharat Sastri, presentation to the Knowledge Forum, Haas School of Business, University of California at Berkeley, September 28, 2000.

p. 32 "Web sites are much cheaper": Viant Innovation Center, "Traffic Visualization: A tool for making group behavioral patterns visible" (Boston, MA: Viant Corporation, 2000), p. 3.

p. 32 *Ba* is a mental space: Ikujiro Nonaka, "The Boundary and Roles of a Firm in the New Economy: A Firm as a Tacit Knowledge-Creating Ba," presentation to 4th Annual Knowledge Workshop and Forum, Haas School of Business, Berkeley, CA, September 28, 2000.

CHAPTER 3
THE E-CORPORATION

p. 34 Early in 2000, Greg Lapidus: Bethany McLean, "The Internet Is a Lemon," *Fortune,* November 27, 2000, p. 146.

p. 34 In December 1999, Michael Jackson: AutoNation, PR Newswire, "Internet Christmas Includes Cars; AutoNation Hits $1 Billion Sales Mark," December 23, 1999 (http://www.prnewswire.com/cgi-bin/micro_stories.pl?ACCT=750525&TICK=ARII&STORY=/www/story/12-23-1999/0001103363&EDATE=Dec+23,+1999).

p. 34 "Dealers are sitting ducks": Philip Evans and Thomas S. Wurster, *Blown to Bits: How the New Economics of Information Transforms Strategy* (Boston: Harvard Business School Press, 1999), p. 56.

p. 35 The problems and opportunities: I am not making the argument Michael Porter makes in his controversial *Harvard Business Review* article "Strategy and the Internet" (March 2001, pp. 62ff.). Porter called the Net "just another technology" comparable to railroads and telephony. Certainly he's right to put business fundamentals (the horse) ahead of technology (the cart). Porter, however, fails to recognize that business fundamentals have changed as knowledge has become the most valuable factor of production. That is what made computing, the Internet, and the Web worth developing. It doesn't eliminate the need to make a profit or define and protect a source of competitive advantage. But it does mean that the most value—and therefore the greatest potential profit and advantage—is found in knowledge, and that technologies that produce, store, and distribute knowledge are of supreme economic importance.

p. 35 In 1999, *Purchasing* magazine: quoted in Economics and Statistics Administration, Office of Policy Development, *Digital Economy 2000* (Washington, D.C., U. S. Department of Commerce, 2000, p. 16; http://www.ecommerce.gov).

p. 36 Same goes for "B2C": Forrester Research, cited in Michael S. Katz and Jeffrey Rothfeder, "Crossing the Digital Divide," *Strategy and Business,* issue 18, first quarter 2000, p. 40.

p. 36 In September, 1999: Cutter Consortium Research Brief, September 28, 1999.

p. 36 None is omnipotent: I owe some of these ideas to a presentation by Andrea Cuomo, STMicroelectronics, at a seminar, *Creare Valore d'Impres attraverso la gestione della Conoscenze e del Capitale Intellettuale* ("Creating Business Value by Managing Knowledge and Intellectual Capital") sponsored by TESI Consulting, September 20, 1999, Milan, Italy.

p. 37 "Every one of these": Interview with Gary Hamel, July 19, 2000.

p. 37 "The key to success": Interview with John F. Welch, June 4, 1999.

p. 38 "The information system": Ian Angell, "Beyond Good and E-ville," presentation to Global Excellence in Operations Conference, sponsored by *Fortune* and A. T. Kearny, New York, May 19, 2000.

p. 39 Up for grabs: Interview with James Duffy, August 10, 1998.

p. 39 Sales forces: Boston Consulting Group: "Strategy and the New Economics of Information," 1997, pp. 4–5; the "if" is mine.

p. 40 "When information is power": Stewart, *Intellectual Capital*.

p. 40 "The basic process": Interview with Robert Wayland, quoted in Thomas A. Stewart, "Customer Learning Is a Two-Way Street," *Fortune,* May 10, 1999, vol. 139, no. 9, p. 158.

p. 41 By March 2000: "Seller Beware," *The Economist,* March 4, 2000, pp. 61–62. By summer, the shakeout: Nate Lentz, Steven Wolin, Tim Byrne, "Beyond the Exchange," *Business 2.0,* June 1, 2000 (http:www.business2.com/content/insights /opinion/2000/06/01/12974).

p. 41 Setting up EDC is expensive: Boston Consulting Group, "The Business-to-Business E-Commerce Market," *BCG Research Bulletin,* December 1999.

p. 41 New software models . . . "next-generation Web": John Markoff, "Fast-Changing Genie Alters the World," *The New York Times,* December 11, 2000, pp. C1, C4.

p. 42 He therefore required . . . "offer not only": Shawn Tully, "Going, Going, Gone! The B2B Tool That Really Is Changing the World," *Fortune,* March 20, 2000, vol. 141, no. 6, p. 132.

p. 44 In telecommunications . . . the battle for wireless telephone subscribers: Wayne Arnold, "Singapore Delays License Sale for New Cellular Networks," *The New York Times,* January 4, 2001, p. W1.

p. 45 "The originality of the Champagne fairs": Fernand Braudel, *Civilization & Capitalism, 15th–18th Century*, vol. III. *The Perspective of the World* (Berkeley and Los Angeles: University of California Press, 1992), p. 112.

p. 48 Sixth most effective: 20 percent creates a nearly unassailable strongpoint of strategic control for an incumbent. An insurgent might need even more in order to dislodge rivals: "At the start of their breakouts, McDonald's, Midas, Nucor, Home Depot, and Southwest Airlines all had 30-to-45-percent unit cost advantages over competitors," according to Charles E. Lucier and Janet D. Torsilieri ("The Trillion-Dollar Race to 'E,'" *Strategy and Business* [Booz Allen & Hamilton]) issue 18, first quarter 2000, p. 7.

p. 49 "I heard Warren Buffett": Fred Andrews, "Rock-Solid Values at Reinvention's Core," *The New York Times*, April 30, 2000, section 7.

CHAPTER 4
AN INTELLECTUAL CAPITAL STRATEGY: THE FOUR-STEP PROCESS

p. 53 By 1999: Cited in *Knowledge* in July 1999 issue.

pp. 53–54 Executives all too easily confuse: I owe this distinction (between an organization and a business) to Stan Davis, who I first heard make it during a presentation to The Knowledge Advantage III, a conference held in San Diego, California, December 11, 1996.

p. 54 "Can you think": Information about 12 Entrepreneuring: Interviews with John Hagel, Halsey Minor, Ken Jones, Eric Greenburg, and Scott Durchslag, New York and San Francisco, August 24 and September 6, 2000, and May 15, 2001.

p. 55 John Hagel: John Hagel III and Arthur G. Armstrong, *Net Gain: Expanding Markets Through Virtual Communities* (Boston: Harvard Business School Press, 1997). John Hagel III and Marc Singer, *Net Worth: Shaping Markets When Customers Make the Rules* (Boston: Harvard Business School Press, 1999).

p. 55 The trend is biggest: "Contract Manufacturers Winning Orders on Cost, Speed," Bloomberg, January 4, 2000.

p. 61 Dell is much like Medco: The Merck/Medco story is told in detail in Stewart, *Intellectual Capital*, pp. 145–49.

p. 62 In business: Nuala Beck and Joseph Connolly, "CMA's Guide to the New Economy," *CMA Magazine*, vol. 70, no. 1, pp. 11ff. High-tech Texans: Allen R. Myerson, "A New Breed of Wildcatter for the 90's," *The New York Times*, November 30, 1997, section 3, p. 1.

p. 63 An excellent: Paul Strassmann, former chief technology officer of Xerox, defines management as "every information activity that is not directly engaged in the generation of revenues. . . . General orientation and indoctrinating meetings . . . the work of an executive secretary . . . training, consultations, giving advice, accounting, administration, interviewing, or correcting quality defects are by this definition all managerial functions, since if they were fully accounted for, they would be charged to 'overhead' and not to direct costs of sales." Strassmann uses the figure to calculate "management value-added," which is the surplus created after suppliers, labor, taxes, and shareholders have all been paid. See http://www.strassmann.com.

p. 66 "If our operating margins": Jonathan D. Day and James C. Wendler, "Best Practice and Beyond: Knowledge Strategies," *The McKinsey Quarterly*, 1998, no. 1, pp. 23ff.

p. 68 In 1985, Harvard Business School professor: Michael Porter, *Competitive Advantage: Creating and Sustaining Superior Performance* (New York: The Free Press, 1985).

p. 69 To apply it to services: Charles B. Stabell and Øystein D. Fjeldstad, "On Value Chains and Other Value Configurations," Working Paper 1995/20 (Sandvika, Norway: Norwegian School of Management, 1995).

p. 71 No companies better exemplify: The GE and IBM stories are best told through successful chairman's letters in the annual reports for the two companies during the 1990s. See also, for GE, Thomas A. Stewart, "See Jack. See Jack Run Europe. The Globalization of General Electric May Be the Greatest Legacy of Jack Welch's 19 Years as CEO," *Fortune*, September 27, 1999, pp. 124ff.

p. 72 Buckman's secret: The Buckman story is told, briefly, in Stewart, *Intellectual Capital*. For a longer discussion, see "Buckman Laboratories (A)," Harvard Business School case N9-899-175, rev. September 17, 1999, which can be found at http://www.buckmanlabs.com.

p. 73 Chevron is a case in point: Greta Lydecker, "Knowledge Management as a Key Component of a Learning Organization," presentation, December 2, 1997; Kenneth T. Derr, "Managing Knowledge the Chevron Way," remarks prepared for the Knowledge Management World Summit, San Francisco, California, January 11, 1999.

p. 73 According to Brookings Institution: Steve Liesman, "Productivity Gains Extend Beyond Technology Area," *The Wall Street Journal,* January 8, 2001, p. A3.

p. 73 Today the cost of shipping: James Surowiecki, "The Box That Launched a Thousand Ships," *The New Yorker,* December 11, 2000, p. 46.

p. 74 Though the company appears: Thomas A. Stewart, "3M Fights Back," *Fortune,* February 5, 1996, vol. 133, no. 2, pp. 94ff.

p. 74 Accenture's focus: See Morten T. Hansen, Niten Nohria, and Thomas Tierney, "What's Your Strategy for Managing Knowledge," *Harvard Business Review,* March-April 1999, pp. 106–16.

p. 74 The ten biggest pharmaceutical companies: Alberto Torres, "Unlocking the Value of Intellectual Assets," *The McKinsey Quarterly,* 1999, no. 4, p. 32.

p. 75 Indeed, of the total: Philips company reports and Jelto W. Smits, "Opening Up the R&D Value Chain," presentation at conference sponsored by Yet2.com, Amsterdam, September 25, 2000.

p. 76 Among the questions to ask: This series of questions is adapted from Michael H. Zack, "Developing a Knowledge Strategy," unpublished paper, College of Business Administration, Northeastern University, September 1998.

p. 76 Economic evidence: Steve Liesman, "Productivity Gains Extend Beyond Technology Area," *The Wall Street Journal,* January 8, 2001, p. A3.

p. 76 Still, raising productivity: "Leading Lights: Management Theorist Peter Drucker," interview in *Knowledge Inc: The Executive Report on Knowledge, Technology & Performance,* February 1997, vol. 2, no. 2, p. 8.

pp. 76–77 Says management demigod: Peter F. Drucker, "The New Productivity Challenge," *Harvard Business Review,* November-December 1991, pp. 69–79.

p. 77 A decade ago, engineers at Bell: Robert Kelley and Janet Caplan, "How Bell Labs Creates Star Performers," *Harvard Business Review,* July-August 1993, p. 130.

p. 78 "Efficiency-driven knowledge management": "Knowledge Management: A Secret Engine of Corporate Growth," *Executive Agenda,* vol. II, no. 2, fourth quarter 1999.

CHAPTER 5
INVESTING IN INTELLECTUAL CAPITAL: WORKING KNOWLEDGE HARDER, SMARTER, AND FASTER

p. 80 "Now that we have realized": Stephen Denning, *The Springboard: How Storytelling Ignites Action in Knowledge-Era Organizations* (Boston: Butterworth-Heinemann, 2000), p. 166.

p. 80 "We need to invest": quoted on Stephen Denning's Web site, www.steve-denning.com.

p. 81 For each domain: See Thomas A. Stewart, "Is This Job Really Necessary?," *Fortune,* January 12, 1998, vol. 137, no. 1, pp. 154ff; also presentation by Stephen Denning to conference "Measuring and Valuing Intellectual Capital," Garden City, N.Y., November 4, 1998; and Stephen Denning, *The Springboard: How Storytelling Ignites Action in Knowledge-Era Organizations* (Boston: Butterworth-Heinemann, 2000), p. 166.

p. 81 *If Only We:* Carla O'Dell and C. Jackson Grayson Jr., with Nilly Essaies, *If Only We Knew What We Know: The Transfer of Internal Knowledge and Best Practice* (New York: The Free Press, 1998).

p. 84 "You have to": Interview with Elizabeth Lank, October 1998.

p. 84 "Don't manage all": quoted in Nuala Moran, "Knowledge Is the Key, Whatever Your Sector," *Financial Times,* Business Solutions Series, April 28, 1999, special section: Financial Times Survey Knowledge Management, p. I. See also Elizabeth Lank, "Putting Management Focus on Intangible Assets," in Stuart Rock, ed., *Knowledge Management: A Real Business Guide* (London: Caspian Publishing Ltd., n.d.[1999]), pp. 32–37.

p. 84 Call it a knowledge audit: One description of what a knowledge audit entails can be found in Larry Stevens, "Knowing What Your Company Knows," *Knowledge Management*, vol. 3, no. 12, December 2000, pp. 38–42.

p. 92 "Coordinating the flow of data": Amy Kover, "Why Brandwise Was Brand Foolish," *Fortune*, vol. 142, no. 11, November 13, 2000, p. 208.

p. 92 Factories become smaller: A terrific example of the future of manufacturing is Pyramid Operating Systems (www.pyracomp.com), which can set up a factory in three days and manage it remotely in real time over the Net. See Frank Gibney, "The Revolution in a Box: Manufacturing Meets the Internet in a New Technology That Could Make Factories Obsolete," *Time*, vol. 156, no. 5, July 31, 2000, pp. 30ff. And Gene Bylinsky, "Heroes of U.S. Manufacturing," *Fortune* (Industrial Management and Technology edition), vol. 141, no. 6, March 20, 2000, pp. 192ff.; Barnaby J. Feder, "New Economy," *The New York Times*, August 21, 2000, p. C3.

p. 92 Clothing makers: Interview with Jeff Streader of Fasturn, November 17, 2000.

p. 92 "We fly an airplane": Interview with Philip Harris, February 25, 2000.

p. 93 "More and more companies": Comments by Gerhard Schulmeyer, panel discussion, "Leading the Knowledge Organization," World Economic Forum annual meeting in Davos, February 1, 2000.

p. 93 "Amex just pissed me off": E-mail to author from G—— B——, January 15, 2000.

p. 94 "Companies aren't just": Interview with Richard Schroate, February 28, 2000.

p. 95 "This requires audit": Interview with Saj-nicole Joni, February 11, 2000.

p. 95 "There's a real advantage": Bob Tedeschi, "E-commerce Report: A Nobel Prize-Winning Idea, conceived in the 30's, Is a guide for Net business," *The New York Times*, October 2, 2000, p. C12.

p. 95 The value chain: Stephan H. Haeckel, *Adaptive Enterprise: Creating and Leading Sense-and-Respond Organizations* (Boston: Harvard Business School Press, 1999), pp. 60–62; interview with Stephan H. Haeckel, February 11, 2000.

p. 96 "The marketplace of the future": Interview with Glenn Ballman, March 15, 2000.

p. 96 GE Power Systems: Jennifer Reingold and Marcia Stepanek, "Why the Productivity Revolution Will Spread," *Business Week*, February 14, 2000, pp. 112ff.

p. 97 In real time: Interview with Christopher Locke, March 2000.

p. 97 That requires unprecedented openness: Speech by Jacques Nasser, February 3, 2000. Story and Real Player file at http://www.ford.com/default.asp?pageid=106&storyid=674.

p. 98 In 1999, Alcoa: Information about Alcoa from interviews with Keith Turnbull, Alain Belda, and Rick Kelson, April 6, 2000.

p. 99 Credit goes to: An excellent description of the Toyota Production System, the basis of Alcoa's, is in Steven Spear, "Decoding the DNA of the Toyota Production System," *Harvard Business Review,* September-October 1999, pp. 97–106.

p. 99 Wasteful drawdowns and buildups of stock: This is the Beer Game, described in Peter Senge, *The Fifth Discipline: The Art and Practice of the Learning Organization* (New York: Doubleday/Currency, 1990).

p. 101 "The location": Interview with Keith Turnbull, April 6, 2000.

p. 102 Most of a continent away: Information about Cisco from interviews with Larry Carter and Randy Pond, April 14, 2000.

p. 103 Cisco made several mistakes: Stephanie Mehta, "Cisco Fractures Its Own Fairy Tale," *Fortune,* May 14, 2001, vol. 143, no. 10, pp. 104ff.

p. 105 "Real-time understanding": quoted in Knowledge Capital Group, *Real Time Business,* at http://128.121.112.159/required/kcg1.pdf.

p. 106 Paul Hindes: Interview, May 4, 2000.

CHAPTER 6
THE CASE AGAINST KNOWLEDGE MANAGEMENT

p. 109 Circulating correspondence was: My wife worked for a larger company that also had circulating correspondence; given the company's size, however, the circulating was kept within her department. The practice ended after a merger, when the new department head, who came from the other half of the merged company, announced that she didn't like it because it embodied the "clubbiness" of the other half. I can think of no more powerful endorsement of a practice than someone's wish to abolish it precisely because it reinforces the identity, culture, and work habits of a group.

p. 109 Reasons for the lost money: Gerry Murray, *Knowledge Management Factbook,* IDC, September 1999 (http: //www.nua.ie/surveys/?f=VS&art_id=905355362 &rel=true).

p. 109 "If the subject of intellectual capital": Stewart, *Intellectual Capital,* p. 111.

p. 110 a search of the World Wide Web: using Google, www.google.com, January 23, 2001.

p. 110 By IDC's estimate: IDC press release, September 15, 1999 (http://www.idc.com/Services/press/PR/SV052300PR.stm).

p. 110 A 1998 survey: cited in the Centre for Strategic Business Studies, *The Antidote* (Winchester, Hampshire, UK), issue 11, "Managing Knowledge and Intellectual Capital," p. 14.

p. 110 Forrester Research estimated: Ron Shevlin, "Measuring and Justifying Knowledge Management Efforts," presentation to the Annual Knowledge Management World Summit, sponsored by Braintrust International, San Francisco, January 13, 1999.

p. 110 Beleaguered HR: I was among the beleaguerrillas; see "Taking on the Last Bureaucracy" and "The Last Bureaucracy Strikes Back," *Fortune,* January 15, 1996, vol. 133, no. 1, pp. 105ff, and May 13, 1996, vol.133, no. 9, pp. 175ff.

p. 111 Yet, Braudel suggests: See, for example, Paul Strassmann's trenchant critique, *The Business Value of Computers* (New Canaan, CT: The Information Economics Press, 1990).

p. 111 "Can it have been": Fernand Braudel, *Civilization and Capitalism 15th–18th Century,* vol. 1; *The Structures of Everyday Life: The Limits of the Possible,* Berkeley, CA: University of California Press, 1992, p. 323.

p. 112 HR is so marginalized: These data from a survey published by the Conference Board in "Managing Knowledge: The HR Role," *HR Executive Review,* vol. 6, no. 4, 1999, pp. 5–6.

p. 112 Knowledge management is: I took this definition from the 4r Group, a consulting firm in Annapolis, Maryland.

p. 113 At Cigna Corp.: Thomas A. Stewart, "Getting Real About Brainpower," *Fortune,* November 27, 1995, vol. 132, no. 11, pp. 201ff.

p. 113 The Holy Grail of CRM: The Galahad of one-to-one marketing is Don Peppers, author (with Martha Rogers) of *The One to One Future* (New York: Doubleday, 1993) and *Enterprise One to One* (New York: Doubleday, 1997); they're worth reading.

p. 117 Knowledge-management activities: I took this list from a presentation by Brook Manville, "What's the 'Management' in 'Knowledge Management'?" The Knowledge Management Conference, Boston, June 22, 1998.

p. 118 "Most of my memory": Adam L. Beberg, "Grilled Over RATS," FoRKarchive, September 13, 2000, www.xent.com/FoRKarchive/sept00/0185.html.

p. 118 "We should be finding out what it is": Interview with David Snowden, "Creating Task Forces for the Future," *Knowledge Management* (UK), June 1998.

p. 119 In either case: Treading the path from information to knowledge: These are sins 4 and 6 in Liam Fahey and Laurence Prusak, "The Eleven Deadliest Sins of Knowledge Management," *California Management Review,* vol. 40, no. 3, spring 1998, pp. 268–69.

p. 120 "Design, development, and deployment": Amrit Tiwana, "Implementing KM: Two Points of Failure," *The Cutter Edge,* an electronic newsletter published by the Cutter Consortium, Arlington, Mass. (http://www.cutter.com/consortium/), January 18, 2000.

p. 120 Are you a standardizer: Morton T. Hansen, Nitin Nohria, and Thomas Tierney, "What's Your Strategy for Managing Knowledge," *Harvard Business Review,* March-April 1999, p. 115.

p. 120 "Moore's Law solutions": John Seely Brown and Paul Duguid, *The Social Life of Information* (Boston: Harvard Business School Press, 2000), pp. 14–15. The disapprobatory quote "embrace dumb power" is from Kevin Kelly, *New Rules for a*

New Economy: 10 Radical Strategies for a Connected World (New York: Viking, 1998).

p. 121 "It seems that technology": Jeffrey Kaz, "Happy Fifty Birthday," Dec. 25, FoRK archive (www.xent.com/FoRKarchive/sept00/0185.html).

p. 123 "Technology helps collect, store, transfer": Amrit Tiwana, "Implementing KM: Two Points of Failure," *The Cutter Edge* (an electronic newsletter published by the Cutter Consortium, Arlington, MA; (http://www.cutter.com/consortium/), January 18, 2000.

p. 125 People are trained: Some of the items listed in this and the preceding paragraph come from Brook Manville's presentation, "What's the 'Management' in 'Knowledge Management'?"

p. 125 Most knowledge management: Ikujiro Nonaka and Hirotaka Takeuchi, *The Knowledge-Creating Company: How Japanese Companies Create the Dynamics of Innovation* (New York: Oxford University Press, 1995).

p. 126 "Sharing tacit knowledge": David Snowden, "Thresholds of Acceptable Uncertainty," *Knowledge Management,* vol. 1, no. 5, April-May 1998, p. 1. (He is Welsh and a bit mad, Snowden.)

p. 126 In 1998, Nippon Roche: Hiroaki Shigeta, "SST Super Skill Transfer 1998–1999," presentation to the Knowledge Forum, Haas School of Business, University of California at Berkeley, September 28, 2000; also Ikujiro Nonaka et al., "Transferring and Developing High Quality Tacit Knowledge: Japan Roche's Challenge Through the 'Super Skill Transfer' Project," unpublished draft paper, September 2000.

p. 127 "The excellent MR": Quoted in Nonaka et al., "Transferring and Developing . . ." p. 5; I have edited slightly to improve the English translation of Mr. Shigeta's words.

p. 128 Some very interesting: Tacit Knowledge Systems, 990 Commercial Street, Palo Alto, CA 94303 (www.tacit.com); the reader should know that the company sponsored three meetings about intellectual capital and knowledge management at which I was a paid speaker.

p. 129 "KM has hit a wall": Interview with Andy Michuda, January 2001.

CHAPTER 7
A NEW OFFERING: SELLING KNOWLEDGE PRODUCTS

p. 131 He got his payment: Information about SeaFax/Gofish from interviews with Neal Workman, June 1998; company reports; E. Young, "The Payment Factor," *The Industry Standard,* July 24, 2000, pp. 92–93; and Bob Metcalfe, "The Story of the Rebirth of a Company, Gofish.com, a B2B Exchange for . . . Fish," *Info World,* February 7, 2000.

p. 136 Those are but two of many: The others were collected by Debra Amidon of Entovation Associates; they and still more examples can be found at http://www.entovation.com/info/cccknow.htm.

p. 137 Between 1992 and 1998: "Compaq Goes After the Leaders Where It Hurts—Profits," Bloomberg wire story, February 4, 2000.

p. 138 "The marketplace is increasingly": IBM fourth-quarter 2000 earnings statement (http://www:investors.ibm.com/4q00/4q00earnings.phtml).

pp. 138–39 Merrill Lynch analyst Thomas Kraemer: "Global Research Highlights," Merrill Lynch, September 29, 2000, p. 12.

p. 139 There are two basic ways: Interview with Stan Davis, September 1998. *Blur*, by the way, is worth reading, as is everything Stan has written: Stanley M. Davis and Christopher Meyer: *Blur: The Speed of Change in the Connected Economy* (Reading, MA: Addison-Wesley, 1998).

p. 139 "These are cases": Interview with Michael Zack, September 1998.

pp. 140–41 Lincoln Re: Information from company reports, interviews with Art DeTore and Marc Clare, September 1998, and from Mark Clare and Arthur W. DeTore, *Knowledge Assets* (San Diego: Harcourt Professional Publishing, 2000).

p. 141 "They allow customized, intelligent solutions": Presentation by Art DeTore, Conference Board 1998 Conference on Knowledge Management, April 1998.

p. 143 "Creating knowledge products": C. K. Prahalad, presentation to Global Excellence in Operations Conference, New York, sponsored by *Fortune* magazine and A. T. Kearney, May 18, 2000.

p. 144 GE's competitor in medical systems, Siemens AG: Dr. Richard Hausmann, presentation to Global Excellence in Operations Conference, New York, May 19, 2000, sponsored by *Fortune* and AT Kearney.

p. 144 Another example: London-based Thomas Miller: Presentation by Mark Holford, TFPL tenth anniversary celebration, London, October 7, 1997.

p. 148 *Risk*: Thanks to Dan Holtshouse of Xerox for some of this thinking.

p. 149 At Helsinki University: Interview with Antti Koivula; see also Antti Koivula, *Knowledge Commercialization—A Case Study of the Process of Creation of the Team Coach Plus Knowledge Product,* dissertation for the degree of Doctor of Technology presented October 17, 1998, Helsinki University of Technology, Department of Industrial Management, Report No. 8.

p. 150 One of the most innovative companies: Information from KRDL's application for the Singapore Innovation Award, 2001. Art Buchwald story: Personal communication from Judith Martin.

p. 152 Ross Dawson, CEO: Ross Dawson, *Developing Knowledge-Based Client Relationships: The Future of Professional Services* (Boston: Butterworth Heinemann, 2000), pp. 8–10, 189. This is a very smart book.

p. 153 David Smith, chief knowledge officer: Presentation by David Smith to

Strategic Management of Knowledge and Organisational Learning, consortium sponsored by The Performance Group, Amsterdam, February 24, 1997.

p. 153 "Creating this new company": Procter & Gamble press release, Los Gatos, CA, January 23, 2001 (http://www.ProjectEMM.com).

p. 154 "Price corridor of the mass": Chan Kim and Renée Mauborgne, "Knowing a Winning Business Idea When You See One," *Harvard Business Review,* 2000.

p. 155 A more interesting example: Cisco Systems 1999 Annual Report, pp. 5–19, CA.

p. 155 John Chambers . . . "an emerging 'internet ecosystem' ": Cisco Systems 1999 Annual Report, pp. 5–19, San Jose, CA.

CHAPTER 8
A NEW AGENDA: MANAGING KNOWLEDGE PROJECTS

p. 158 "Manual workers as well as highly skilled": Quoted in Thomas A. Stewart, "Gray Flannel Suit? Moi?" *Fortune,* March 16, 1998, vol. 137, no. 5, pp. 76ff.

p. 158 "We would almost": Frederick Lewis Allen, *The Big Change: America Transforms Itself 1900–1950* (New York: Harper & Brothers, 1952), p. 237.

p. 159 "If we introduce?": Quoted in Thomas A. Stewart, "Gray Flannel Suit? Moi?" *Fortune,* March 16, 1998, vol. 137, no. 5, pp. 76ff.

p. 159 As many as 19 million Americans . . . "creativity should": Winston Wood, "Work Week," *The Wall Street Journal,* February 6, 2001, p. A1.

p. 161 Other kinds of projects: An excellent discussion of knowledge projects, to which this chapter is indebted more implicitly than explicitly—but deeply indebted nevertheless—can be found in Thomas H. Davenport and Laurence Prusak, *Working Knowledge: How Organizations Manage What They Know* (Boston: Harvard Business School Press, 1998), especially pp. 144–61.

p. 161 "Every organization has a unique": Microsoft, "Practicing Knowledge Management: Turning Experience and Information into Results," Digital Nervous System Business Strategy White Paper, 1999, p. 5 (http://www.microsoft.com/dns).

p. 161 "Just as every economic activity": Charles Goldfinger, "Financial Markets as Information Markets: Preliminary Exploration," paper prepared for the ENSSIB Conference "Economie de l'information," Lyon, France, May 20, 1995, p. 7.

p. 161 "Here is our advice": The Performance Group, *Value from Knowledge: Managing from the Knowledge Perspective, Developing the Knowledge Agenda* (Oslo: The Performance Group, 1998), p. 60.

p. 162 Among companies: The percentages are the sum of current and planned projects, according to a 1997 survey of 431 organizations conducted by the Ernst & Young Center for Business Innovation and reported in Rudy Ruggles, "The State of the Notion: Knowledge Management in Practice," *California Management Review*, vol. 40, no. 3, spring 1998, pp. 80ff.

p. 163 "We did this five years ago": Quotes from Greenes and material on BP Amoco from interview with Kent Greenes, April 21, 1999, from his presentation to Knowledge Management and Organisational Learning conference, London, April 20, 1999; from Amber Payne Currie, "Video Tools and Supporting Philosophy Make Knowledge Management 'Lively' at BP," *Knowledge Management in Practice*, issue 11, 1998, published by the American Productivity and Quality Center (Houston); and from "Sharing Knowledge at BP," *The Antidote* (published by the Centre for Strategic Business Studies, Winchester, UK), issue 11, 1998, pp. 38–40.

p. 168 "We pinched the BP Amoco connect system": Discussion with Elizabeth Lank at TFPL meeting in Dublin, Ireland, October 9–10, 2000.

p. 168 Xerox's late Webmaster Bill MacLain: Interview with Dan Holtshouse, Xerox Corp., March 1999; see Thomas A. Stewart, "Customer Learning Is a Two-Way Street," *Fortune*, May 10, 1999, vol. 139, no. 9, pp. 158ff.

p. 171 Every year: *Quality Matters,* an internal publication of Philips Electronics, September 2000, no. 101, pp. 7–9.

p. 171 Unilever, the world's: Information from Wouter de Vries, "Knowledge Management Practice in Unilever," presentation to European Executive Symposium on Knowledge Management, Zurich, March 2, 1999; Georg von Krogh, Ikujiro Nonaka, and Manfred Aben, "Steps to a Knowledge Strategy," unpublished article submitted to *Sloan Management Review*, 2000; interviews with Georg von Krogh and Manfred Aben, autumn 1999. The first quote is from the presentation, the second from the article.

p. 172 IBM Global Services: David J. Snowden, "Intellectual Capital Deployment—A New Perspective: A Case Study in Combining Knowledge Management and Organisational Change," working paper, 2000; various inverviews with David Snowden.

p. 175 There are many . . . "see more visibility in text books": Robert G. Cooper, Scott J. Edgett, and Elko J. Kleinschmidt, "New Product Portfolio Management: Practices and Performance," *The Journal of Product Innovation Management,* vol. 16, no. 4, July 1, 1999, p. 335.

p. 175 Far more successful "business strategy decides": Robert G. Cooper, Scott J. Edgett, and Elko J. Kleinschmidt, "New Product Portfolio Management: Practices and Performance," *The Journal of Product Innovation Management,* vol. 16, no. 4, July 1, 1999, p. 335.

p. 175 Businesses are living . . . "is not something that can simply be taken": Ad Huijser, quoted in *Quality Matters,* an internal publication of Philips Electronics, September 2000, no. 101, p. 3.

p. 176 By themselves: On the multitasking nature of knowledge projects, see Thomas H. Davenport, David W. De Long, and Michael C. Beers, "Building Successful Knowledge Management Projects," Ernst & Young Center for Business Innovation Working Paper, January 1997, from which comes also the quote "Very few contribute . . ."

p. 176 "When knowledge gained somewhere": Jac Fitz-enz, presentation at the Saratoga Conference, New Orleans, Louisiana, October 18, 2000.

CHAPTER 9
A NEW DESIGN: SUPPORTING KNOWLEDGE PROCESSES 1: PROCESSES THAT CREATE

p. 177 "is divided into a number of branches": Adam Smith, *An Inquiry into the Nature and Causes of the Wealth of Nations,* ed. Edwin Cannan (London: Methuen, 1961), p. 7.

p. 179 Sewing a pair of trousers: Frederick H. Abernathy, John T. Dunlop, Janice H. Hammond, and David Weil, *A Stitch in Time: Lean Retailing and the Transformation of Manufacturing—Lessons from the Apparel and Textile Industries* (New York: Oxford University Press, 1999), p. 167.

For other material on the progressive bundle system and team sewing, see John T. Dunlop and David Weil, "Diffusion and Performance of Modular Production in the U.S. Apparel Industry," *Industrial Relations,* vol. 35, no. 3, July 1996, pp. 334–356. For Levi's bad experience, see Ralph T. King, Jr., "Levi's Factory Workers Are Assigned to Teams, And Morale Takes a Hit," *The Wall Street Journal,* May 20, 1998, p. A1; Charles Gilbert, "Did Modules Fail Levi's or Did Levi's Fail Modules," *Apparel Industry Magazine,* September 1998, pp. 88–92; Evelyn Dunagan, "Another perspective on modular manufacturing: Levi's was right," *Apparel Industry Magazine,* January 1999, pp. 96, 98. Also see Mike Fralix, "Team Sewing: The Results Are In—and, for Many, They Look Favorable," *Apparel Industry Magazine,* February 1999, pp. 72–73, and Lila Moore, "K-Products Walks Fine Line of Modular Production, *Apparel Industry Magazine,* January 1995, pp. 64–70.

p. 179 "Instead of breaking sewing and assembly": Abernathy, Dunlop, et al., op. cit., p. 168.

p. 179 "lean production" systems: The best book on this subject in the auto industry, and one of the best books on manufacturing ever, is James P. Womack, Daniel T. Jones, and Daniel Roos, *The Machine That Changed the World* (New York: Rawson Associates, 1990).

p. 179 Overall, it cuts costs: A good discussion of team sewing is in Eileen Appelbaum and Thomas Dailey, eds., *Manufacturing Advantage: Why High-Performance Work Systems Pay Off* (Ithaca, New York: Cornell University Press, 2000).

p. 179 "a landmark in labor relations": John T. Dunlop and David Weil, op. cit., p. 351.

p. 180 "You can see a high-performance": William Buehler, quoted in Thomas A. Stewart, "The Search for the Organization of Tomorrow," *Fortune,* May 18, 1992, pp. 92ff.

p. 180 Jeffrey Pfeffer: Jeffrey Pfeffer and Robert I. Sutton, *The Knowing-Doing Gap: How Smart Companies Turn Knowledge into Action* (Boston: Harvard Business School Press, 2000).

p. 181 "How do we realize the potential": David Norton, presentation to the Third Intangibles Conference: Knowledge: Management, Measurement and Organization, May 19, 2000, sponsored by the Vincent C. Ross Institute of Accounting Research and the Intangibles Research Project at the Stern School of Business at New York University.

p. 181 Many companies even changed: See Frank Ostroff, *The Horizontal Organization* (New York: Oxford University Press, 1999), and Michael Hammer, *Beyond Reengineering: How the Process-Centered Organization Is Changing Our Work and Our Lives* (New York: HarperBusiness, 1996).

p. 181 "Rather than thinking of what group": Private communication from Gregory Alan Bolcer, June 5, 1999.

p. 181 Knowledge . . . "is generated in practice": John Seely Brown and Paul Duguid, "Practice vs. Process: The Tension That Won't Go Away," *Knowledge Directions: The Journal of the Institute for Knowledge Management,* vol. 2, no. 1, spring 2000, p. 87.

p. 181 Does your customer-service process: See Thomas H. Davenport and Michael C. Beers, "Managing Information About Processes," *Journal of Management Information Systems,* vol. 12, no. 1, summer 1995, pp. 57–80.

p. 182 Does HR's planning process: Thomas H. Davenport, presentation to the International Human Resources Information Management conference, Nashville, TN, May 20, 1998.

p. 182 Some, like R&D: I owe this list (creating, discovering, packaging, applying, and reusing) to Thomas H. Davenport, Sirkka L. Jarvenpaa, and Michael C. Beers, "Improving Knowledge Work Processes," *Sloan Management Review,* vol. 37, no. 4, summer 1996, p. 57.

p. 182 To boil it down further: The Performance Group, *Value from Knowledge: Managing from the Knowledge Perspective—Developing the Knowledge Agenda,* p. 24.

p. 184 Consequently, "knowledge creation": "'Knowledge Management' Gaining Ground," *Newsline* (published by AACSB—the International Association for Management Education), vol. 28, no. 1, fall 1997, St. Louis, MO.

p. 185 In the late 1990s: Interviews with Simon Spencer, BorgWarner Automotive, December 4, 2000, and David Sutherland, Business Innovation Consortium, November 29, 2000.

p. 185 "We'd give speeches": Interview with George Bailey, July 11, 2000.

p. 189 The result is "generating creative options": Dorothy Leonard and Walter

Swap, "Generating Creative Options," *Knowledge Directions: The Journal of the Institute for Knowledge Management,* vol. 1, fall 1999, pp. 34–45. See also—read, mark, and inwardly digest also—Prof. Leonard's book: Dorothy Leonard, *Well-springs of Knowledge: Building and Sustaining the Sources of Innovation* (Boston: Harvard Business School Press, 1995).

pp. 189 "The questions asked by management": Presentation by Chad Halliday to the World Economic Forum, Davos, Switzerland, February 1, 1999.

p. 190 "While the traditional supply chain": "DuPont: A Case Study," supplement to *Innovative Leaders in Globalization* (Geneva and New York: World Economic Forum and Deloitte Touch Tohmatsu, 1999), pp. 3–4. My italics.

p. 191 A group of scholars: Presentation by Mark Rice to Managing Technology in the eCommerce World, conference sponsored by Yet2.com, Amsterdam, The Netherlands, Sept. 25, 2000; see also Richard Leifer, Christopher M. McDermott, Gina Colarelli O'Connor, Lois S. Peters, Mark Rich, and Robert W. Veryzer, Jr., *Radical Innovation: How Mature Companies Can Outsmart Upstarts* (Boston: Harvard Business School Press, 2000).

p. 192 3M, for example: Thomas A. Stewart, "3M Fights Back," *Fortune,* February 5, 1996, vol. 133, no. 2, pp. 94ff.

p. 192 They collect it, buy it: See, among many other articles, Susan Stellin, "Dot-Com Liquidations Put Consumer Data in Limbo," *The New York Times,* December 4, 2000, and John C. Hagel III and Jeffrey F. Rayport, "The Coming Battle for Customer Information," *The McKinsey Quarterly,* 1997, no. 3, pp. 64–76.

p. 193 An intercontinental study: Presentation to Fortune Global Excellence in Operations Conference, New York, May 19, 2000.

p. 193 Says Bontis: "You're": Presentation by Nick Bontis to Saratoga Institute forum, New Orleans, October 17, 2000.

p. 193 "They knew these things were failing": Interview with J. M. Juran, November 3, 1998.

p. 194 Consumers still buy: C. K. Prahalad, Venkatram Ramaswamy, and M. S. Krishnan, "Customer Centricity," *Information Week,* April 10, 2000, p. 74.

p. 194 "The basic process by which customers learn": See Thomas A. Stewart, "Customer Learning Is a Two-Way Street," *Fortune,* May 10, 1999, vol. 139, no. 9, pp. 158ff.

p. 194 "Most CRM strategies view": C. K. Prahalad, Venkatram Ramaswamy, and M. S. Krishnan, "Customer Centricity," *Information Week,* April 10, 2000, p. 74.

p. 194 CRM is a $4 billion: Jane Carmichael and Peter Orlay, "A Smarter Way to Build Profitable Relationships," *Executive Agenda* (published by A. T. Kearney), vol. 3, no. 2, fourth quarter, 2000, pp. 37–38.

p. 194 Microsoft, it's estimated, got $500: This and the Cisco example from C. K. Prahalad and Venkatram Ramaswamy, "Co-opting Customer Competence," *Harvard Business Review,* January-February 2000, pp. 79ff. For Lotus, see Stewart, *Intellectual Capital,* p. 156.

p. 195 "We know more now": This and Amazon statistics from Alec Apelbaum, "Amazon's Juggling Act," *Money,* vol. 30., no. 3, March 2001, p. 36.

p. 195 "Before companies wanted": Ephraim Schwartz, "Controlling the Clients," *InfoWorld,* August 28, 2000 (http://www.infoworld.com/articles/hn/xml /00/8/28/000828hnclient.xml).

p. 196 In the late 1990s . . . "the most discerning and demanding": Thomas A. Stewart, "A Satisfied Customer Isn't Enough," *Fortune,* July 21, 1997, vol. 136, no. 2, pp. 112ff.

CHAPTER 10
A NEW DESIGN: SUPPORTING KNOWLEDGE PROCESSES 2:
PROCESSES THAT SHARE

p. 200 There's lots more: Carla O'Dell and C. Jackson Grayson Jr., *If Only We Knew What We Know* (New York: The Free Press, 1998), p. 8.

p. 202 That makes it easy to change jobs: Lew Platt, presentation at the World Economic Forum, Davos, Switzerland, January 31, 1999.

p. 202 "The pace of economic evolution": Interview with Gary Hamel, July 19, 2000.

p. 203 The paucity: Korn/Ferry International in conjunction with the Center for Effective Organizations, Marshall School of Business, University of Southern California, *Strategies for the Knowledge Economy: From Rhetoric to Reality,* 2000, pp. 9, 34.

p. 204 This is the famous: See John Seely Brown, "Research That Reinvents the Corporation," *Harvard Business Review,* January-February 1991, pp. 102–11; John Seely Brown and Paul Duguid, "Organizational Learning and Communities-of-Practice," *Organizational Science,* vol. 2, no. 1, February 1991, pp. 40–57; John Seely Brown and Estee Solomon Gray, "The People Are the Company," *Fast Company,* premier issue (autumn 1995), pp. 78–82.

p. 205 Says Allen: Thomas J. Allen, *Managing the Flow of Technology: Technology Transfer and the Dissemination of Technological Information Within the R&D Organization* (Cambridge, MA: MIT Press, 1977), p. 236.

p. 206 For example: Subramanian Rangan, "Search and Deliberation in International Exchange: Microfoundations to Some Macro Patterns," *Journal of International Business Studies,* vol. 31, no. 2, second quarter 2000, p. 206.

p. 206 "Absolutely not": Phone conversation with Larry Prusak, February 15, 2001.

p. 206 We had four teams: E-mail from a communications company executive who requested anonymity, July 25, 2000.

p. 206 In studies of informal technology-swapping: Eric von Hippel, "Cooperation Between Rivals: Informal Know-How Trading," *Research Policy,* 16:6 (December 1987), pp. 291–302.

p. 207 Bernard Avishai, director of intellectual: Presentation to seminars sponsored by Tacit Knowledge Systems, Boston, New York, and Rosemont, Illinois, spring 2000.

p. 210 Notes Peter Fuchs: Fuchs and Raduchel (who was then at Sun Microsystems) are quoted in Thomas A. Stewart, "Managing in a Wired World," *Fortune,* July 11, 1994, pp. 44ff.

p. 212 Says Lance Devlin: "You can't force people . . .": Lance Devlin, presentation to seminar sponsored by Tacit Knowledge Systems, June 6, 2000.

p. 213 One macho Wall Street firm: private communication, anonymity requested.

p. 213 The fundamental act of leadership: Howard Gardner in collaboration with Emma Laskin, *Leading Minds: An Anatomy of Leadership* (New York: Basic Books, 1995), passim, but especially Chapter 1.

p. 214 "We were told to figure it out.": This discussion is based on interviews with Dar Wolford and Stan Kwiecien, August 2, 2000.

p. 216 These are the most important ones: This list partly grows out of a discussion at a gathering of chief knowledge officers sponsored by TFPL, Ltd., held in Dublin, October 9–10, 2000.

CHAPTER 11
A NEW CULTURE: DEVELOPING A KNOWLEDGE PERSPECTIVE

p. 220 "It isn't enough": Comments by Elizabeth Lank at CKO Summit, sponsored by TFPL, Dublin, Ireland, October 10, 2000.

p. 221 Doug West . . . "how we do what we do": Doug West, presentation to *Fortune* HR Forum, San Francisco, California, November 19, 1998.

p. 221 An adage in the business: Alfred Knopf said: "Gone today, here tomorrow."

p. 224 Risk management—usually a function: I am grateful to Anjana Bhattacharee for opening my eyes to this topic and being my first guide to it.

p. 225 "Much of risk management": interview with Donald Lessard, December 16, 2000.

p. 225 "By emphasizing objectively valid": Alfred North Whitehead, *Science and the Modern Mind* (1925), p. 51. Also see A. Chaudhury, D. N. Mallick, H. R. Rao, "Knowledge and Skill," paper presented to Association for Information Systems Americas Conference 1996 Phoenix, AZ, August 17, 1996, http://hsb.baylor.edu /ramsower/ais.ac.96/papers/KNOW_SKI.htm.

p. 226 When a bad batch of carbon dioxide: Patricia Sellers, "Crunch Time for Coke," *Fortune*, July 19, 1999, vol. 140, no. 2, pp. 72ff, "What Really Happened at Coke," *Fortune,* January 10, 2000, vol. 141, no. 1, pp. 114ff.

p. 226 The illnesses were psychosomatic: Lili H. Li, "Origin of Coke Crisis in Europe Is Termed Psychosomatic," *The Wall Street Journal,* April 3, 2000, p. A21.

p. 227 Consider how hard Daniel Ellsberg: David Rudenstine, *The Day the Presses Stopped: A History of the Pentagon Papers Case* (Berkeley, CA: University of California Press, 1996), pp. 42–53.

p. 228 "Uncertainty is a real enemy": Interview with Thomas H. Davenport, December 17, 2000.

p. 228 Therefore change management: Interview with Arthur DeTore of Lincoln Re, quoted in Thomas A. Stewart, "Taking Risk to the Marketplace," *Fortune,* March 6, 2000, vol. 141, no. 5, p. 424.

p. 228 A second category of human-capital risk: James W. DeLoach, *Enterprisewide Risk Management: Strategies for Linking Risk and Opportunity* (London: Financial Times/Prentice Hall [Pearson Education Limited], in association with Arthur Andersen, 2000), pp. 255–56.

p. 229 If product quality: Mark Davies, "Enterprise Risk Management," presentation at *Power in Professionalism*, Canadian Association of Management Consultants, Toronto, April 7, 2000.

p. 230 "Risk transfer": Interview with Anjana Bhattacharee, April 19, 1999.

p. 230 "It's difficult to find a counterparty": Interview with Bjarni Ármannsson, May 11, 1999.

p. 230 Says Hewlett-Packard's CEO: This comment and the two following were made during a panel discussion of risk at the World Economic Forum annual meeting in New York, January 2002.

pp. 231–32 "Respectable people": Patrick Lambe, "The New Landscape of Risk," *The Business Times* (Singapore), February 2, 2000, and April 18, 2000.

p. 232 Some intriguing answers: Cathy Walt, Alastair Robertson, et al., *The Evolving Role of Executive Leadership,* the Andersen Consulting Institute for Strategic Change, 1999.

p. 235 As Howard Gardner . . . "the arena in which leadership": Howard Gardner in collaboration with Emma Laskin, *Leading Minds: An Anatomy of Leadership* (New York: Basic Books, 1995), p. 15.

p. 235 The question came up at a meeting: Knowledge Strategies in Action, TFPL's Third International CKO Summit, Dublin, Ireland 8–10, 2000. Hubert Saint-Onge and Elizabeth Lank were the chief contributors to the list of attributes.

p. 235 "Make development a fundamental part": Helen Handfield-Jones, "How Executives Grow," *The McKinsey Quarterly,* 2000, no. 1, pp. 120–22.

p. 236 U.S. companies spend somewhere: Center for Workforce Development, *The Teaching Firm: Where Productive Work and Learning Converge* (Newton, MA: Education Development Center, Inc., 1998), p. 9. Most numbers about learning aren't even soft—they're gassy. Fewer than half of all companies attempt to measure the value of training, and most of them do not put the measurement in financial terms. Training is very important for leadership development, say 92 percent of companies, but only 18 percent measure the return on their investment; for management development, the corresponding numbers are 32 percent and 4 percent. (Brian Hackett, *The Value of Training in the Era of Intellectual Capital,* Report Number 1199-97-RR [New York: The Conference Board, 1997], pp. 7–8.)

p. 236 Executives say that informal coaching: Helen Handfield-Jones, "How Executives Grow," *The McKinsey Quarterly,* 2000, no. 1, p. 118.

p. 236 Among manufacturing workers: Center for Workforce Development, *The Teaching Firm: Where Productive Work and Learning Converge* (Newton, Mass.: Education Development Center, Inc., 1998), p. 84.

p. 236 "I visited a radiology department": Dave Long, e-mail, "Informal Annotation," http://www.xent.com/FoRK-archive/sept00/0820.html, September 26, 2000.

p. 236 It's not a pretty term: Shoshana Zuboff, *In the Age of the Smart Machine: The Future of Work and Power* (New York: Basic Books, 1988).

p. 237 "In effect you'll be running": Interview with Kevin McKay, COO and CFO of SAP America, July 23, 1998.

p. 237 "Mostly you manage": Interview with Michael Brochu, October 21, 1998.

p. 238 Whom are you going to believe?: This discussion of trust was originally presented at a Festschrift in honor of Warren Bennis, held in Marina Del Rey, California, May 6, 2000; a version of it is published in Warren Bennis, Gretchen M. Spreitzer, and Thomas G. Cummings, eds., *The Future of Leadership: Today's Top Leadership Thinkers Speak to Tomorrow's Leaders* (San Francisco: Jossey-Bass, 2001), pp. 67ff.

pp. 238–39 In *The Organization Man*: William H. Whyte, Jr., *The Organization Man* (New York: Touchstone, 1956), pp. 14ff.

p. 239 In knowledge companies: I owe this insight to Charles Green of Trusted Advisor Associates, www.trustedadvisor.com.

p. 239 "Gathering information": Gary Heil, Warren Bennis, and Deborah C. Stephens, *Douglas McGregor, Revisited: Managing the Human Side of the Enterprise* (New York: John Wiley & Sons, Inc., 2000), p. 6.

p. 240 "Without it": Laurence Prusak, presentation to the Knowledge Forum, Haas School of Business, Berkeley, CA, September 28, 2000. Trust is a theme woven all through *In Good Company: How Social Capital Makes Organizations Work,* by Prusak and Don Cohen (Boston: Harvard Business School Press, 2001).

p. 242 I elsewhere described them: *Intellectual Capital,* pp. 93–100. Wenger's own book, *Communities of Practice: Learning, Meaning, and Identity* (Cambridge, U.K.): Cambridge University Press, 1998), is excellent.

p. 243 As Douglas McGregor argues: Douglas McGregor, *The Human Side of Enterprise* (New York: McGraw-Hill, 1960), pp. 35ff.

p. 245 "In the office": Joseph Heller, *Something Happened* (New York: Alfred A. Knopf, Inc., 1974), pp. 3, 13, 16.

CHAPTER 12
THE HUMAN CAPITALIST

p. 250 "Corporate boundaries": Robert Reich, "The Reich Stuff," interview in *Context* magazine (published by Diamond Technology Partners, Chicago), August-September 2000, p. 40.

p. 251 "As business changes": Interview with Philip Harris, February 25, 2000.

p. 251 "Getting a company to be informal": Interview with John F. Welch, June 4, 1999, quoted in Thomas A. Stewart, "See Jack. See Jack Run Europe," *Fortune,* September 27, 1999, vol. 140, no. 6., p. 124.

p. 251 Sure, companies strive to: Jonathan D. Day and James C Wendler, "Industrial Venture Capitalists: Sharing Ownership to Create Value," *McKinsey Quarterly,* 1998, no. 2, pp. 26ff.

p. 252 It's more accurate: So far as I know, I was the first to broach the notion that people should be considered investors of human capital, briefly in *Intellectual Capital,* pp. 224–246; I then developed the metaphor/argument more explicitly and began to consider issues of return on investment and the mechanisms of *corporate* human capital formation in two articles in *Fortune:* "A New Way to Think About Employees," vol. 137, no. 7, April 13, 1998, p. 169, and "Will the Real Capitalist Please Stand Up?" vol. 137, no. 9, May 11, 1998, p. 189. The idea has begun to gain wide currency. Thomas O. Davenport's *Human Capital: What It Is and Why People Invest It* (San Francisco: Jossey-Bass) appeared in 1999; Don Tapscott, David Ticoll, and Alex Lowy refer to the concept in *Digital Capital: Harnessing the Power of Business Webs* (Boston: Harvard Business School Press), pp. 180–81; a Siemens AG videotape, produced in 2000, is titled "The Future of Work: From Employees to Investors of Human Capital."

p. 252 "Work is a two-way": Thomas O. Davenport, *Human Capital* (San Francisco: Jossey-Bass, 1999), p. 15.

p. 252 They also vary with sex: See data in John Bishop, "Expertise and Excellence," working paper #95-13 Center on the Educational Quality of the Workforce and Cornell's Program on Youth and Work and Center for Advanced Human Resource Studies, Cornell University, April 28, 1995, pp. 32–33.

p. 253 The data are sketchy: Cited in Thomas A. Stewart, "Gray Flannel Suit? Moi?" *Fortune,* March 16, 1998, vol. 137, no. 5, pp. 76ff.

p. 254 Action is the key: Interview with Ram Charan, December 22, 2000.

p. 254 As with action learning: See, *inter alia,* Center for Workforce Development, *The Teaching Firm: Where Productive Work and Learning Converge* (Newton, MA: Education Development Center, Inc., 1998).

p. 255 In a survey of six thousand executives: Helen Handfield-Jones, "How Executives Grow," *McKinsey Quarterly,* 2000, no. 1, p. 118.

p. 255 "Increased mobility across companies": Interview with Peter Cappelli,

January 1998. Cappelli writes extensively about training and development in *The New Deal at Work: Managing the Market-Driven Workforce* (Boston: Harvard Business School Press, 1999).

p. 255 At the same time: Cappelli, op. cit., pp. 47–48, 152–153.

p. 256 The McKinsey consulting firm: Elizabeth G. Chambers, Mark Foulon, et al., "The War for Talents," *McKinsey Quarterly,* 1998, no. 3, pp. 47–57.

p. 256 The value of employee retention: Not-for-attribution interview with human resources executive, 1999.

p. 256 At Enron, they don't: Interview with Jeff Skilling, January 21, 2000.

p. 256 Zurich Financial Services Group had a problem: Dinos Iordanou, talks at Commitment to America conferences sponsored by Fortune and the Organization for Foreign Investment, Charleston, S.C., 1998, and Philadelphia, Penn., 1999.

p. 258 In the mid-twentieth century: This argument was first and famously put forth in Adolf A. Berle and Gardiner C. Means, *The Modern Corporation and Private Property* (New York: Macmillan, 1933); it got a postwar refurbishment in John Kenneth Galbraith's *The New Industrial State* (Boston: Houghton-Mifflin Company, 1967).

p. 258 In 1999 alone: "Whose Company Is This Anyway?" Pearl Meyer & Partners, June 20, 2000.

p. 259 This overhang: Watson Wyatt Worldwide, *Stock Option Overhang: Shareholder Boon? Or Shareholder Burden?* (Bethesda, MD: Watson-Wyatt Worldwide, 1998), p. 5.

p. 259 For companies in *USA Today*'s: Matt Krantz, "Online Workers' Windfall Could Flatten Investors," *USA Today,* October 26, 1999, pp. 1B–2B.

p. 259 The company's response: See Floyd Norris, "The Fed's Challenge: How to Cope with a Burst Bubble," *The New York Times,* December 22, 2000, p. D1.

p. 260 "When you understand": Interview with Margaret Blair, quoted in Thomas A. Stewart, " Will the Real Capitalist Please Stand Up?," *Fortune,* May 11, 1998, vol. 137, no. 9, p. 189.

p. 260 "Human capital is really important": Interview with Ira Millstein, March 27, 1998.

p. 260 Blair and a colleague: See Margaret M. Blair, "Human Capital and Theories of the Firm," in Margaret M. Blair and Mark J. Roe, eds., *Employees and Corporate Governance* (Washington, D.C.: Brookings Institution, 1999), pp. 58–90; Margaret M. Blair and Lynn A. Stout, "A Team Production Theory of Corporate Law," *Virginia Law Review,* vol. 85, no. 2, March 1999, pp. 247ff.; for a nontechnical summary of the argument, see Linda Keslar, "Team Ownership," *The Daily Deal,* http://www.thedailydeal.com/features/todaysfeature/A27311-2000Aug17.html.

p. 261 By contrast, Macquarie Bank: Interviews at Macquarie, Sydney, March 4, 1998.

p. 262 Typical gain-sharing plans: Edward E. Lawler III, *Rewarding Excellence:*

Pay Strategies for the New Economy (San Francisco: Jossey-Bass, 2000), pp. 220–45.

p. 262 If that means control: For a survey of reasons offered to explain why worker-managed companies are relatively rare, see Gregory Dow and Louis Putterman's "Why Capital (Usually) Hires Labor: An Assessment of Proposed Explanations," in Margaret M. Blair and Mark J. Roe, ed., *Employees and Corporate Governance* (Washington: Brookings Institution, 1999), pp. 17ff. Such companies may be more common than people think. About one out of nine workers is self-employed; another large number work for law and accounting firms and other partnerships; many temporary and contingent workers might be said to be, and might describe themselves, as free agents and thus their own employers.

p. 263 "The traditional way": Interview with Philip Harris, February 25, 2000.

p. 263 "Even the largest companies": Interview with Gary Hamel, July 19, 2000.

p. 263 That phrase, the title: Clayton M. Christensen, *The Innovator's Dilemma: When New Technologies Cause Great Firms to Fail* (Boston: Harvard Business School Press, 1997).

p. 266 Everybody always knew: See, for example, Thomas A. Stewart, "Can Your Company Save Your Soul?" *Fortune,* January 14, 1991.

p. 266 Now we . . . "knowledge production": John Seely Brown and Paul Duguid, "Organizing Knowledge," draft paper, September 18, 1997, p. 11.

p. 266 Social capital . . . "the stock of active connections": Don Cohen and Laurence Prusak, *In Good Company: How Social Capital Makes Organizations Work* (Boston: Harvard Business School Press, 2001), p. 4.

CHAPTER 13
GENERALLY UNACCEPTABLE ACCOUNTING PRINCIPLES

p. 269 "Corporate management accounting systems": H. Thomas Johnson and Robert S. Kaplan, *Relevance Lost: The Rise and Fall of Management Accounting* (Boston: Harvard Business School Press, 1987), p. xi.

p. 269 In December 1999: Alan Greenspan, "Remarks by Alan Greenspan, Chair, Federal Reserve Board," in "GDP: One of the Great Inventions of the 20th Century," *Survey of Current Business* (Washington: U.S. Department of Commerce, January 2000), p.12.

p. 270 Software was an obvious manifestation: Walter Wriston, former chairman of Citicorp, was urging that software be capitalized at least as far back as 1991.

p. 270 Rajat Gupta: "Embracing Strategic Freedom," presentation to the World Economic Forum annual meeting, Davos, Switzerland, February 2, 1998.

p. 270 "We have long had a good idea": Arthur Leavitt, "Quality Information: The Lifeblood of Our Markets," speech to the Economic Club of New York, New York City, October 18, 1999.

p. 271 Among many ways of creating: For discussions of the other ways, see Carol J. Loomis, "Lies, Damned Lies, and Managed Earnings," *Fortune*, August 2, 1999, vol. 140, no. 3, pp. 74ff.

p. 271 Moreover, there is an inverse: Richard E. S. Boulton, Barry D. Libert, Steve M. Samek, *Cracking the Value Code: How Successful Businesses Are Creating Wealth in the New Economy* (New York: HarperBusiness, 2000), p. 16.

p. 271 "If a message is informative": Interview with Baruch Lev, September 13, 1999. No one has done more to make the case against current accounting and for measuring intellectual capital than Prof. Lev. His book *Intangibles: Management, Measurement and Reporting*, published by the Brookings Institution (Washington, D.C.) in 2001, sets it forth vigorously and in doubt-crushing detail.

p. 272 "Valuing [intangible assets] at zero": Gregory Wurzburg, "Towards More Systematic Human Resource Reporting," in Julia Kirby, ed., *Enterprise Value in the Knowledge Economy* (Cambridge: Ernst & Young Center for Business Innovation and Organization for Economic Cooperation and Development, 1997), p. 41.

p. 273 "If I taught a class": Warren Buffett, comments to Berkshire Hathaway shareholders meeting, May 4, 1998, quoted, among other places, http://news.cnet.com/news/0,10000,0-1003-200-328988,00.html.

p. 273 One magazine editor . . . "business Bolsheviks": Jason Pontin, "What Business Revolution?" *Red Herring*, January 1, 1998.

p. 273 He got interested: "The Real Thing?" interview with James Chestnut, *CFO*, vol. 14, no. 5, May 1998, p. 38.

p. 274 That's the conclusion of an elegant: Baruch Lev and Paul Zarowin, "The Boundaries of Financial Reporting and How to Extend Them," *Journal of Accounting Research*, Autumn 1999.

p. 275 For example, a study by Mark A. Huselid: Mark A. Huselid and Brian E. Becker, "The Strategic Impact of High Performance Work Systems," paper presented at the Academy of Management annual meetings, Vancouver, B.C., 1995.

p. 276 Two scholars: Alice O. Andrews (with Theresa Welbourne), "Predicting the Performance of Initial Public Offering Firms: Should HRM Be in the Equation?" *Academy of Management Journal*, no. 39, 1996, pp. 891–919.

p. 276 considerable evidence that some HR practices: See, among many, Thomas A. Stewart, "Taking on the Last Bureaucracy," *Fortune*, January 15, 1996, vol. 133, no. 1, pp. 105ff, and "Human Resources Bites Back," May 13, 1996, vol. 133, no. 9, pp. 175ff.

p. 277 A highly statistical study: Mary E. Barth, Michael Clement, George Foster, and Ron Kasznik, "Brand Values and Capital Market Valuation," working paper, Gaduate School of Business, Stanford University, January 1998.

p. 277 Two of the Stanford scholars: Mary E. Barth, Ron Kasznik, and Maureen F. McNichols, "Analyst Coverage and Intangible Assets," Stanford Graduate School of Business Research Paper 1475 R3 1999, http://gobi.stanford.edu/researchpapers/detail1.asp?Paper_No=1475, April 1998.

p. 278 "Investors have moved the issue": Shelley Taylor & Associates, *Full Disclosure 1998: An International Study of Disclosure Practices and Investor Information Needs* (Palo Alto, CA, and London: Shelley Taylor & Associates, 1998), p. 24 (http://www.infofarm.com).

p. 278 "If we are going to know": Quoted in Carolyn Kay Brancato, "Communicating Corporate Performance: A Delicate Balance," The Conference Board, Special Report 97-1, 1997, p. 12.

p. 278 "This accounting treatment": David Aboody and Baruch Lev, "Information Asymmetry and Insider Gains: The Case of R&D-Intensive Companies," *Journal of Accounting Research*, 1998.

p. 279 "Managers need to know": Margaret M. Blair, Steven M. H. Wallman, et al., *Unseen Wealth: Report of the Brookings Task Force on Understanding Intangible Sources of Value* (Washington, D.C.: Brookings Institution, 2000).

p. 282 Where brand equity is not an appropriate: For measures of customer loyalty, see my *Intellectual Capital*, pp. 241–43, and Frederick R. Reichheld, *The Loyalty Effect: Growth, Profits, and Lasting Value* (Boston: Harvard Business School Press, 1996).

p. 285 "We don't have a place": Paul Taylor, "In Search of New Structures," *Financial Times*, May 5, 1999, p. 11.

p. 285 the Balanced Scorecard: see Robert S. Kaplan and David P. Norton: *The Balanced Scorecard: Translating Strategy into Action* (Boston: Harvard Business School Press, 1996).

p. 286 "One of these days . . .": private communication.

p. 286 What's the use . . . "people who are investing": Michael Peel, "New Vision Emerges from Victorian Values," *Financial Times*, Financial Times Survey: Shareholder Communication, p. I, June 30, 2000.

p. 286 they publish books: From Arthur Andersen: Richard E. S. Boulton, Barry D. Libert, Steve M. Samek, *Cracking the Value Code: How Successful Businesses Are Creating Wealth in the New Economy* (New York: HarperBusiness, 2000). From PricewaterhouseCoopers: Robert G. Eccles, Robert H. Herz, E. Mary Keegan, and David M. H. Phillips, *The Value Reporting Revolution: Moving Beyond the Earnings Game* (New York: John Wiley & Sons, 2001). From KPMG: Daniel Andriessen and René Tissen, *Weightless Wealth: Find Your Real Value in a Future of Intangible Assets* (London: Financial Times Prentice Hall, an imprint of Pearson Education, 2000).

p. 286 "Intel's space-suited workers": Walter Isaacson, "Man of the Year," *Time*, December 29, 1997–January 5, 1998, vol. 150, no. 27, pp. 46ff.

p. 286 Does that mean Japanese-made: If this were so, it would be an example of companies acting on the basis of the Fallacy of Misplaced Concreteness.

p. 287 In the 1990s, telephone companies: Thomas A. Stewart, "A New 500 for a New Economy," *Fortune*, May 15, 1995, vol. 131, no. 9, pp. 166ff.

p. 288 In the 1930s, when the SEC: Private communication from Gary John

Previts, professor of accountancy, Weatherhead School of Management, Case Western Reserve University, April 25, 2001.

p. 288 "Some of the most useful": Steven M. H. Wallman, "Measuring and Valuing Intellectual Capital: Why, How, and the Next Steps," presentation to World Trade Conferences, "Measuring and Valuing Intellectual Capital," Garden City, N.Y., November 4, 1998.

CHAPTER 14
MANAGEMENT ACCOUNTING FOR THE INFORMATION AGE

p. 290 "We don't even have a nonfinancial": Interview with Robert Kaplan, quoted in Thomas A. Stewart, "Brainpower," *Fortune*, June 3, 1991, pp. 44ff.

p. 291 Kaplan, co-inventor: Robert S. Kaplan, "Balanced Scorecard Progress Report: The Secrets of Successful Strategy-focused Organizations," presentation to Balanced Scorecard 2000: The 2nd Annual Balanced Scorecard Summer, October 13, 1995, San Francisco.

p. 294 "professional, senior management": Nuala Beck and Joseph Connolly, "CMA's Guide to the New Economy," *CMA Magazine*, vol. 70, no. 1, pp. 11ff.

p. 294 Professor Ante Pulic: For a full discussion of Prof. Pulic's methods, see http://www.measuring-ip.at/Papers/ham99txt.htm.

p. 294 "Depending on their capabilities": Ante Pulic, "VAIC™—An Accounting Tool for IC Management," unpublished paper, 1999, p. 2.

p. 295 Like Pulic: See, for example, Jac Fitz-enz, *The ROI of Human Capital: Measuring the Economic Value of Employee Performance* (New York: AMACOM [American Management Association], 2000), pp. 36–37. Fitz-enz points out that certain unproductive HR costs, such as absence and turnover costs, should be subtracted from pay and benefits, because they are clearly not investments.

p. 296 In all likelihood: For how, see James M. McTaggert, Peter W. Kontes, and Michael C. Mankins, *The Value Imperative: Managing for Superior Shareholder Returns* (New York: The Free Press, 1994).

p. 297 Make a chart like this: I got the idea for this chart from one shown to me in 1998 by Carl Arendt of Westinghouse, where it was used as part of the company's Total Quality Management process. So far as I know, Westinghouse did not, however, try to sort the costs into categories.

p. 299 Bates Gruppen: The discussion that follows is based on interviews with Jan Blichfeldt, Bastian Lie-Nielsen, Hein Espen Hattestad, Sally Dickerson, in Oslo, October 29, 1998, and London, July 23, 1999.

p. 299 When the results come back and are tabulated: Bates based this 2 x 2 on one proposed for tracking human capital on pages 88–93 of *Intellectual Capital*. I, in turn, developed it based on conversations with Leif Edvinsson when he worked at Skandia Corp.

p. 302 A Swedish group, Intellectual Capital Sweden AB: For more about IC AB, see http://www.intellectualcapital.se. TurnIT, a Swedish information technology services company, has applied the method and describes it in detail in its annual reports (available online at http://www.turnit.se).

p. 304 A group of analysts: The KPMG methodology is described in Andriessen and Tissen, op. cit. For a discussion of the idea of core competence, see Gary Hamel and C. K. Prahalad, *Competing for the Future* (Boston: Harvard Business School Press, 1994) and their article, "The Core Competence of the Corporation," *Harvard Business Review,* May-June 1990, pp. 79–91,

p. 306 The details are: Mark Clare and Arthur W. DeTore, *Knowledge Assets Professional's Guide to Valuation and Financial Management* (San Diego: Harcourt Professional Publishing, 2000).

p. 307 In general, the value of real options: Keith J. Leslie and Max P. Michael, "The Real Value of Real Options," *McKinsey Quarterly,* 1997, no. 5, esp. pp. 8–10. The McKinsey firm has done lots of work on real options. Two other articles in the *McKinsey Quarterly,* both by Thomas E. Copeland and Philip T. Keenan, are worth reading: "How Much Is Flexibility Worth?" (1998, no. 2, pp. 38–49) and "Making Real Options Real" (1998, no. 3., pp. 128–41). Another good discussion of options for those, such as I, who are not much mathematically bent, focuses on financial options: Gary Stix, "A Calculus of Risk," *Scientific American,* May 1989, vol. 278, no. 5, pp. 92–97.

p. 309 "Here's what I want to know": Ray Marcy, speech to the Saratoga Conference, New Orleans, October 18, 2000.

p. 309 Well-known work at Sears: Anthony J. Rucci, Steven P. Kirn, and Richard T. Quinn, "The Employee-Customer-Profit Chain at Sears," *Harvard Business Review*, January-February 1998, pp. 82ff.

p. 311 Bontis's study relied on: As this is written, Bontis's study is not yet published. Information about it can be found at www.bontis.com.

p. 313 One the next page: I picked and chose from the appendix in my *Intellectual Capital* and a compilation (and some new measurements) in Jay Liebowitz and Ching Y. Suen, "Developing Knowledge Management Metrics for Measuring Intellectual Capital," *Journal of Intellectual Capital,* issue 1, vol. 1, 2000 (available online at http://www.emerald-library.com). Liebowitz and Suen, in turn, listed measurements found in the following places: ICM Group, Inc., "What Are Companies Currently Measuring," http://www.icmgroup.com/presentpub/LES_MEASUREMENT; J. Roos, G. Roos, N. Dragonetti, and L. Edvinsson: *Intellectual Capital: Navigating in the New Business Landscape* (New York: New York University Press, 1998); Canadian Management Accountants, "Focus Group Draft: Measuring Knowledge Assets," April 16, 1999.

p. 315 Here's a way to evaluate these: Wouter de Vries, "Knowledge Management Practice in Unilever," presentation to European Executive Symposium on Knowledge Management, Zürich, March 2, 1999.

p. 318 It is the work of NYU's Baruch Lev: More information about Lev and his work can (and should) be explored at http://www.baruch-lev.com.

p. 318 First described in print: S. L. Mittz, "Seeing Is Believeing," *CFO*, vol. 15, no. 2, February 1999, pp. 29–37.

p. 322 For example, on August 31: e-mail from Baruch Lev, March 11, 2001.

AFTERWORD

p. 326 As I said: Thomas A. Stewart, "Brainpower: How Intellectual Capital Is Becoming America's Most Important Asset," *Fortune,* June 3, 1991, pp. 44ff.

p. 326 The latter phrase: Gary Hamel and C. K. Prahalad, "The Core Competence of the Corporation," *Harvard Business Review,* May-June 1990, pp. 79–91.

p. 326 Managers as well as business thinkers: For attention, see Thomas H. Davenport, *The Attention Economy.*

p. 327 Companies' informal organizations: See Etienne Wenger, *Communities of Practice: Learning, Meaning, and Identity* (Cambridge, U.K., and New York: Cambridge University Press, 1998).

p. 329 In the years: See Adam Hochschild, *King Leopold's Ghost: A Story of Green, Terror, and Heroism in Colonial Africa* (Boston: Houghton-Mifflin, 1998).

p. 331 "Forty years ago, Ghana": Joseph Stiglitz, "Knowledge Is Like Light."

p. 332 Thomas L. Friedman, "The Fast Eat the Slow," *The New York Times,* February 2, 2001, p. A19.

p. 332 In the spring of 2000: The survey is described in Rosabeth Moss Kanter, *Evolve! Succeeding in the Digital Culture of Tomorrow* (Boston: Harvard Business School Press, 2001).

p. 334 In a controversial: Michael E. Porter, "Strategy and the Internet," *Harvard Business Review,* March 2001.

INDEX

Page numbers of illustrations and charts appear in italics.

ABOUT THE AUTHOR

THOMAS A. STEWART is the editor of the *Harvard Business Review*. Formerly a member of the Board of Editors of *Fortune* magazine and Editorial Director of *Business 2.0*, he is a fellow of the World Economic Forum. He is also the author of the bestselling *Intellectual Capital* (Currency), which was named one of the most important business books of 1987 by the *Financial Times* and has been translated into seventeen languages. Stewart divides his time between Boston and New York City.